PIANO · VOCAL · GUITAR

THE GRAND IRISH SONGBOOK

MW00785532

ISBN-13: 978-1-4234-1135-2
ISBN-10: 1-4234-1135-8

HAL•LEONARD®
CORPORATION
7777 W. Bluemound Rd. P.O. Box 13819 Milwaukee, WI 53213

In Australia Contact:
Hal Leonard Australia Pty. Ltd.
4 Lentara Court
Cheltenham, Victoria, 3192 Australia
Email: ausadmin@halleonard.com

For all works contained herein:
Unauthorized copying, arranging, adapting, recording or public performance is an infringement of copyright.
Infringers are liable under the law.

Visit Hal Leonard Online at
www.halleonard.com

4 Arthur McBride
10 Avondale
7 The Banks of Claudy
12 The Banks of My Own Lovely Lee
16 Banna Strand
24 The Bard of Armagh
26 Believe Me, If All Those Endearing Young Charms
19 Black Velvet Band
28 Bold Fenian Men
31 The Bold Tenant Farmer
34 The Bonny Boy
40 Boston Burglar
37 Botany Bay
42 Boulavogue
46 The Boys from the County Armagh
45 The Boys of Fairhill
50 Brennan on the Moor
52 A Bunch of Thyme
54 Butcher Boy
56 Carrickfergus
62 Castle of Dromore
59 Cliffs of Doneen
64 Cockles and Mussels (Molly Malone)
66 Come Back to Erin
72 Come to the Bower
74 The Croppy Boy
76 The Curragh of Kildare
78 Danny Boy
80 Dicey Reilly
82 Do You Want Your Old Lobby
86 Down by the Salley Gardens
69 Easy and Slow
88 The Enniskillen Dragoon
90 Fiddler's Green
93 Finnegan's Wake
96 The Foggy Dew
98 Follow Me up to Carlow
104 The Galway Races
101 The Galway Shawl
106 Green Grow the Rashes-O
108 Henry My Son
110 High Germany
112 Highland Paddy
117 The Hills of Kerry
120 The Holy Ground
124 The Humour Is on Me Now
126 I Know My Love
123 I Know Where I'm Goin'
128 I Never Will Marry
130 I Once Loved a Lass
132 I'll Take You Home Again, Kathleen
138 I'll Tell Me Ma
140 I'm a Rover and Seldom Sober
142 The Irish Rover
135 Isn't It Grand, Boys?
144 James Connolly
146 Johnny I Hardly Knew Ye
148 Johnson's Motor Car
150 The Jolly Beggarman
156 Jug of Punch
158 The Juice of the Barley
153 Kelly of Killane
160 The Kerry Recruit

162 Lanigan's Ball
166 The Lark in the Clear Air
168 Lark in the Morning
172 Leaving of Liverpool
174 The Little Beggarman
182 Love Is Teasing
186 Lowlands Low
188 MacNamara's Band
190 The Meeting of the Waters
192 The Mermaid
177 The Merry Ploughboy
196 Minstrel Boy
204 Mrs. McGrath
198 The Mountains of Mourne
206 Muirsheen Durkin
201 My Singing Bird
210 My Wild Irish Rose
213 A Nation Once Again
216 The Nightingale
222 O'Donnell Aboo
224 Oft in the Stilly Night
226 Old Maid in the Garret
228 The Old Orange Flute
230 The Old Woman from Wexford
232 Paddy Works on the Railway
219 Paddy's Green Shamrock Shore
234 The Parting Glass
236 The Patriot Game
244 The Queen of Connemara
246 The Raggle-Taggle Gypsy
239 Red Is the Rose
248 The Rising of the Moon
251 The Rocks of Bawn
254 The Rocky Road to Dublin
258 Roddy McCorley
260 The Rose of Allendale
264 The Rose of Mooncoin
267 The Rose of Tralee
270 Rosin the Bow
277 Sally Brown
278 Sam Hall
280 Skibbereen
274 Slievenamon
282 The Snowy-Breasted Pearl
284 Spancil Hill
286 The Spanish Lady
288 Star of County Down
290 Sweet Carnlough Bay
170 'Tis the Last Rose of Summer
292 Three Score and Ten
298 Too-Ra-Loo-Ra-Loo-Ral (That's an Irish Lullaby)
295 The Town of Ballybay
300 The Wearing of the Green
302 Weile Walia
304 The West's Awake
306 When Irish Eyes Are Smiling
310 Whiskey in the Jar
313 The Wild Colonial Boy
318 Wild Rover
316 The Zoological Gardens

ARTHUR McBRIDE

Traditional Irish Folk Song

Moderately
mf
G D A7
D
I had a first cous - in called
He says, "My young fel - lows, if
G D G
Ar - thur Mc - Bride. He and I took a
you will en - list, a guin - ea you
D G A7
stroll down by the sea - side, a -
quick - ly shall have in your fist. Be -

Copyright © 2006 by HAL LEONARD CORPORATION
International Copyright Secured All Rights Reserved

D
Bm
G
seek - ing good for - tune and what might be -
sides a crown for to kick up the
D
F♯m
tide, 'twas just as the day was a -
dust, and drink the king's health in the
G
A7
D
dawn - ing. Then af - ter
morn - ing." Had we been such
G
D
rest - ing we both took a tramp, we
fools as to take the ad - vance, the

G D G
met Ser - geant Har - per and Cor - po - ral
wee bit - ter morn - ing we had run to
A7 D Bm
Cramp, be - sides the wee drum - mer who
chance, for you'd think it no scru - ple to
G D
beat up for camp, with his row - dy - dow -
send us to France, where we would be
A7 D
1 2
dow in the morn - ing.
killed in the morn - ing.

THE BANKS OF CLAUDY

Traditional Irish Folk Song

Moderately fast
G
F
mf
G
F
G
1. 'Twas
on a pleas - ant morn - ing all
2. bold - ly stepped up to her, I
3. on the way to Clau - dy's banks, if
4.-6. (See additional lyrics)
F
C
G
in the month of May, down
took her by sur - prise. I
you will please to show. Take

Copyright © 2006 by HAL LEONARD CORPORATION
International Copyright Secured All Rights Reserved

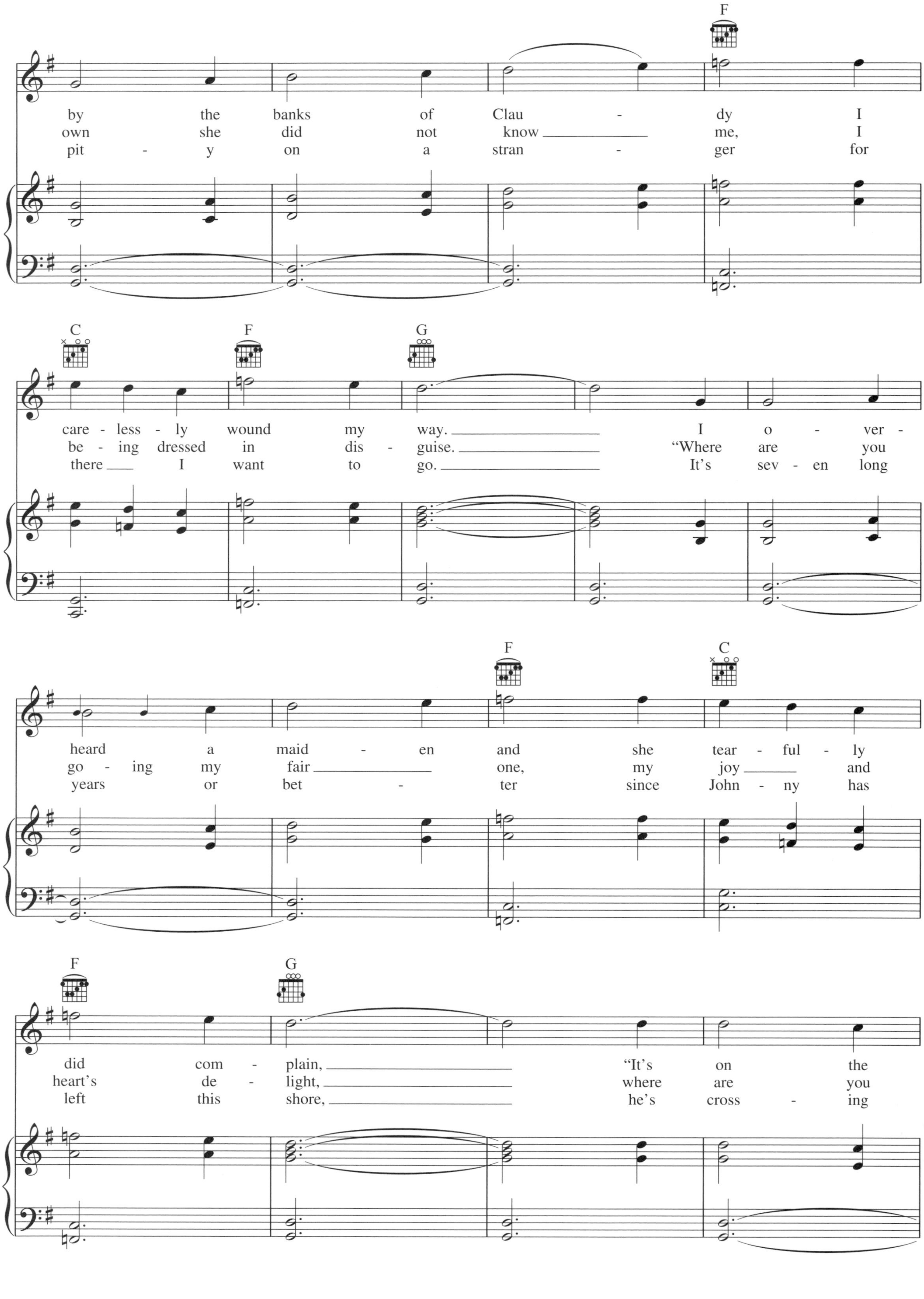
F
by the banks of Clau - dy I
own she did not know me, I
pit - y on a stran - ger for
C F G
care - less - ly wound my way. I o - ver -
be - ing dressed in dis - guise. "Where are you
there I want to go. It's sev - en long
F C
heard a maid - en and she tear - ful - ly
go - ing my fair one, my joy and
years or bet - ter since John - ny has
F G
did com - plain, "It's on the
heart's de - light, where are you
left this shore, he's cross - ing

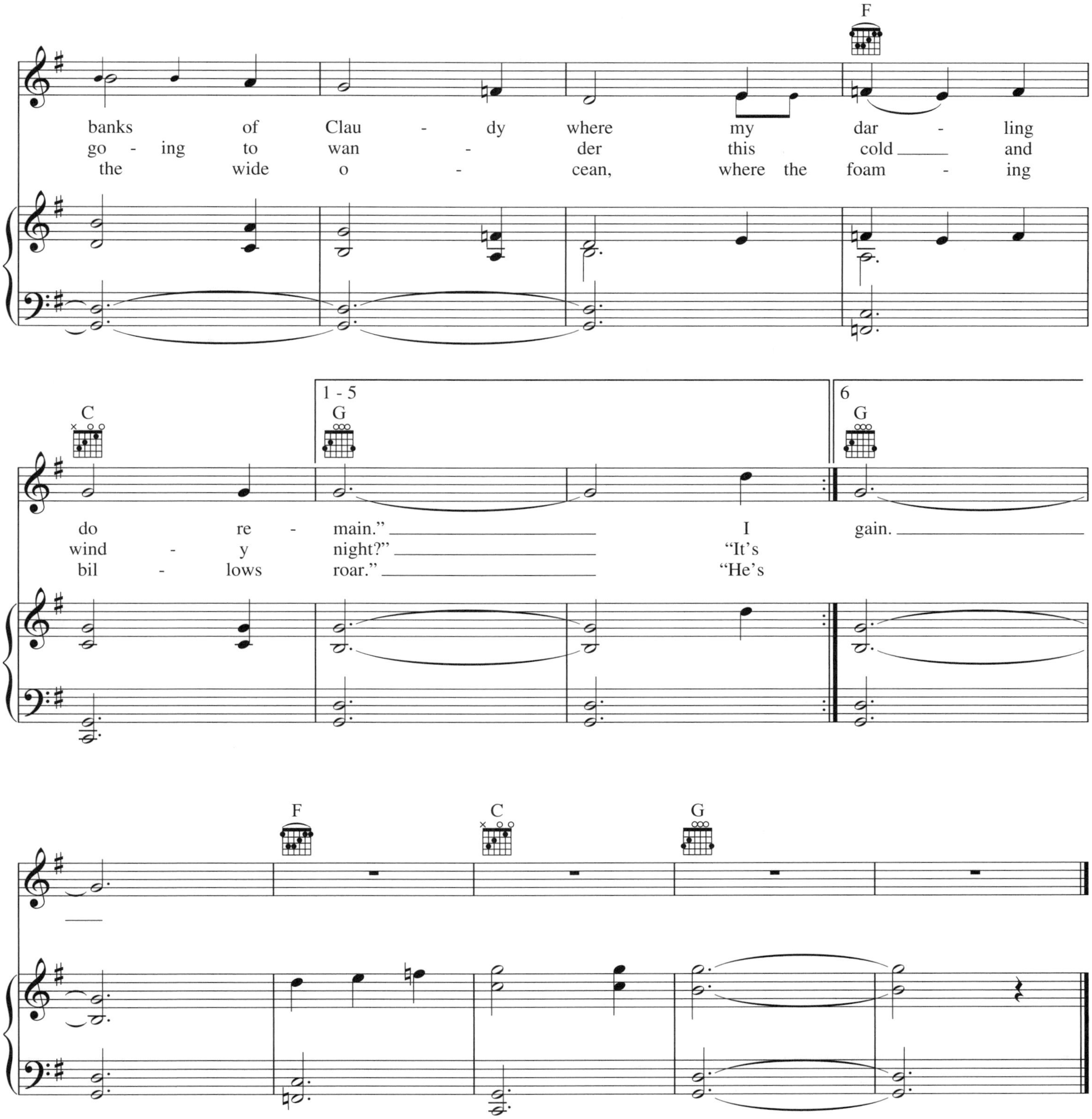
F
banks of Clau - dy where my dar - ling
go - ing to wan - der this cold and
the wide o - cean, where the foam - ing
C
1 - 5
G
6
G
do re - main." I gain.
wind - y night?" "It's
bil - lows roar." "He's
F
C
G

Additional Lyrics

4. "He's crossing the wide ocean for honour and for fame
His ship's been wrecked so I've been told down on the Spanish Main."
"It's on the banks of Claudy fair maiden whereon you stand
Now don't you believe young Johnny, for he's a false young man."

5. Now when she heard this dreadful news she fell into despair
For the wringing of her tender hands and the tearing of her hair
"If Johnny be drowned no man alive I'll take
Through lonesome glens and valleys I'll wander for his sake."

6. Now when he saw her loyalty no longer could he stand
He fell into her arms saying, "Betsy, I'm the man."
Saying, "Betsy, I'm the young man who caused you all the pain
And since we've met on Claudy's banks we'll never part again."

AVONDALE

Traditional Irish Folk Song

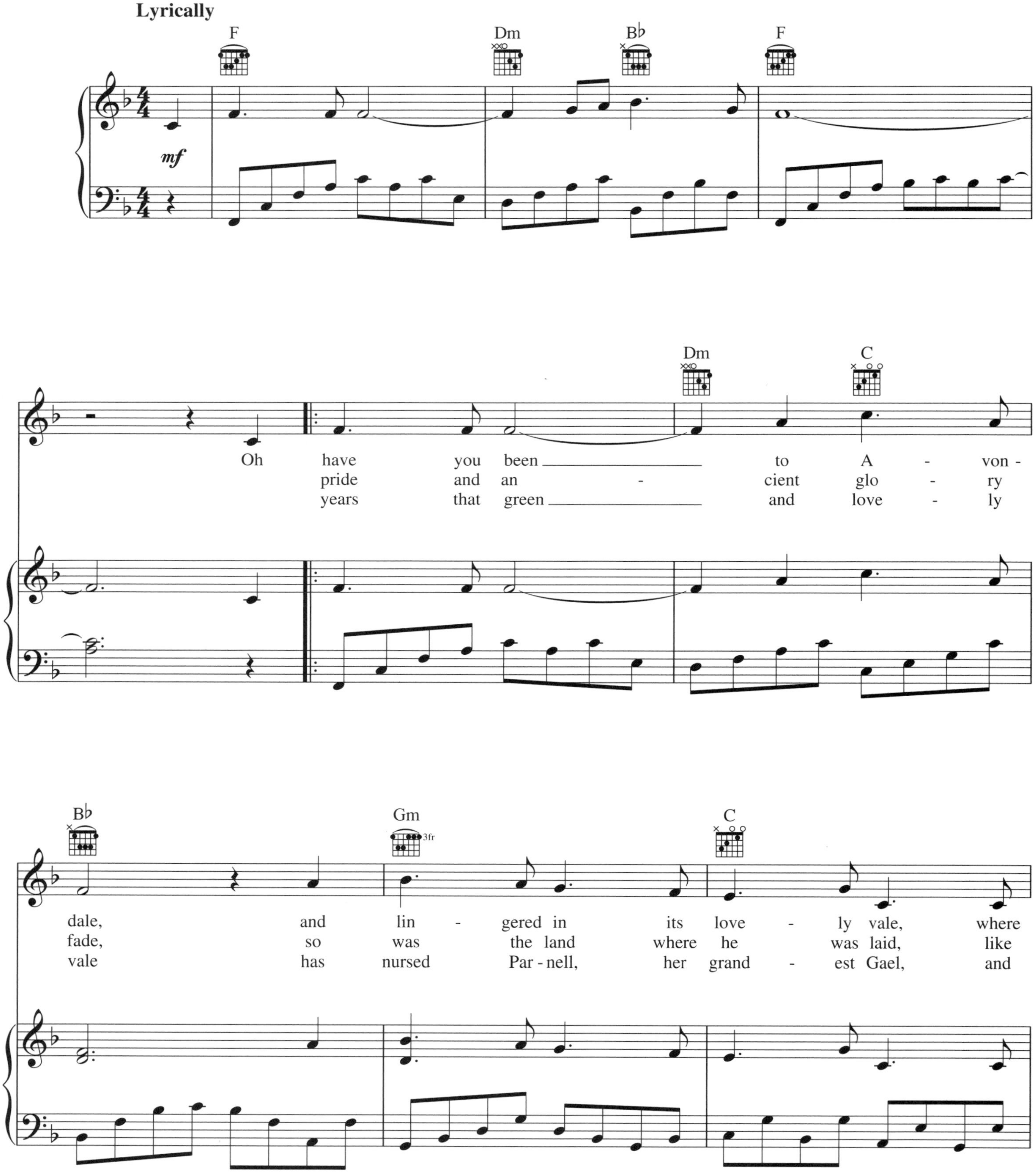
Lyrically
F Dm B♭ F
mf
Dm C
Oh have you been to A - von -
pride and an - cient glo - ry
years that green and love - ly
B♭ Gm C
dale, and lin - gered in its love - ly vale, where
fade, so was the land where he was laid, like
vale has nursed Par - nell, her grand - est Gael, and

Copyright © 2006 by HAL LEONARD CORPORATION
International Copyright Secured All Rights Reserved

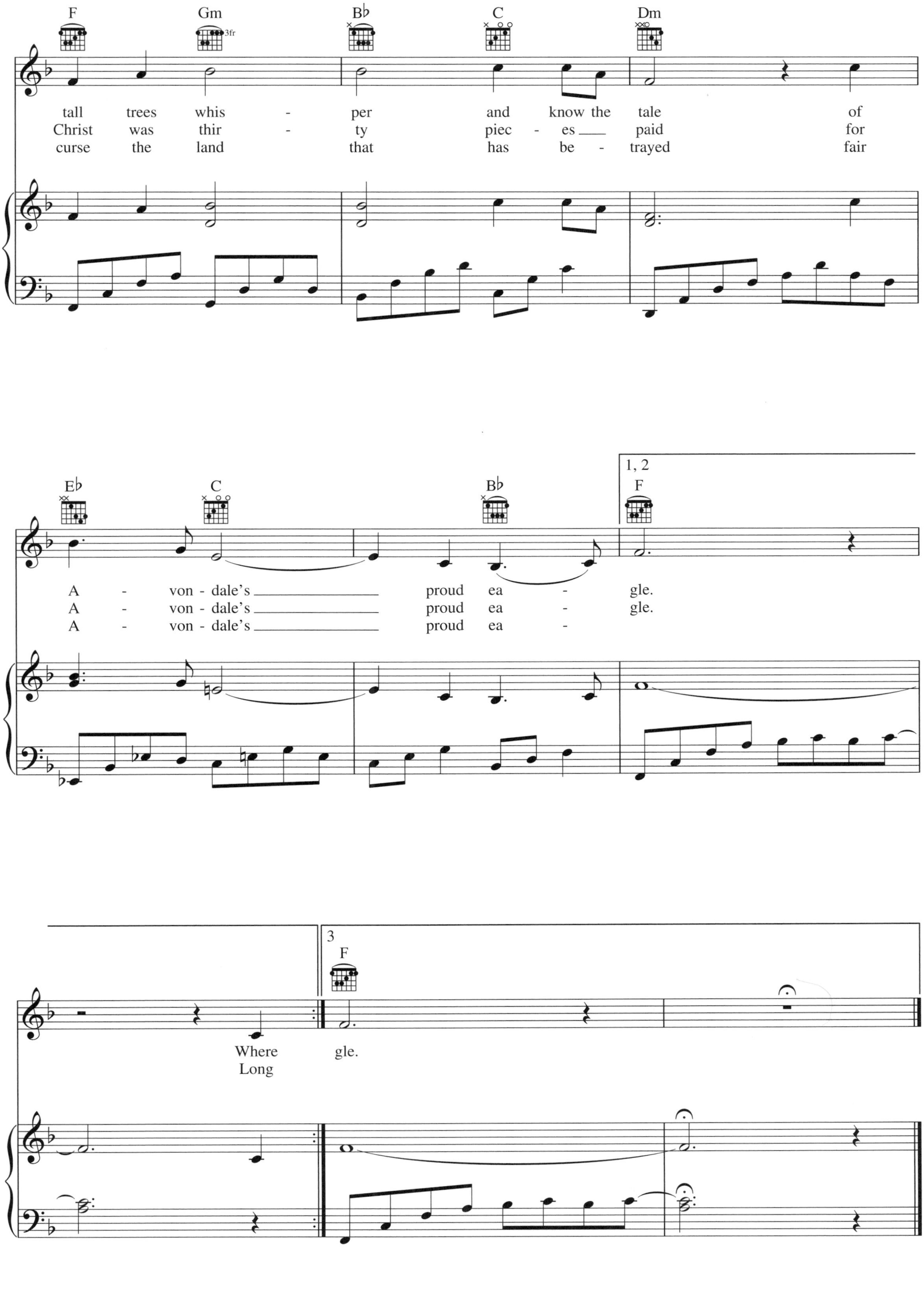
F
Gm
3fr
B♭
C
Dm
tall trees whis - per and know the tale of
Christ was thir - ty piec - es paid for
curse the land that has be - trayed fair
E♭
C
B♭
1, 2
F
A - von - dale's proud ea - gle.
A - von - dale's proud ea - gle.
A - von - dale's proud ea -
3
F
Where gle.
Long

THE BANKS OF MY OWN LOVELY LEE

Traditional Irish Folk Song

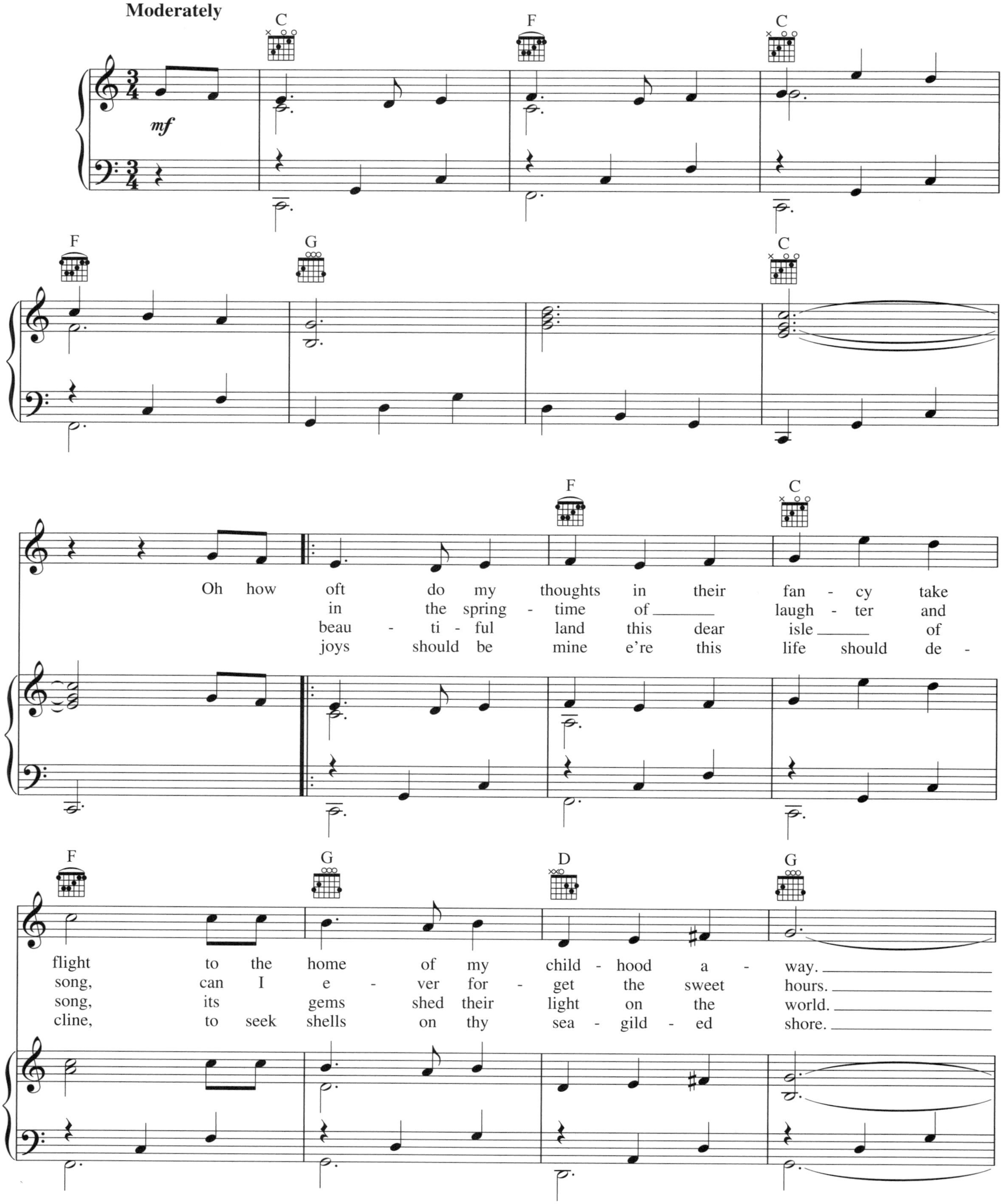
Moderately
C F C
mf
F G C
F C
Oh how oft do my thoughts in their fan - cy take
in the spring - time of laugh - ter and
beau - ti - ful land this dear isle of
joys should be mine e're this life should de -
F G D G
flight to the home of my child - hood a - way.
song, can I e - ver for - get the sweet hours.
song, its gems shed their light on the world.
cline, to seek shells on thy sea - gild - ed shore.

Copyright © 2006 by HAL LEONARD CORPORATION
International Copyright Secured All Rights Reserved

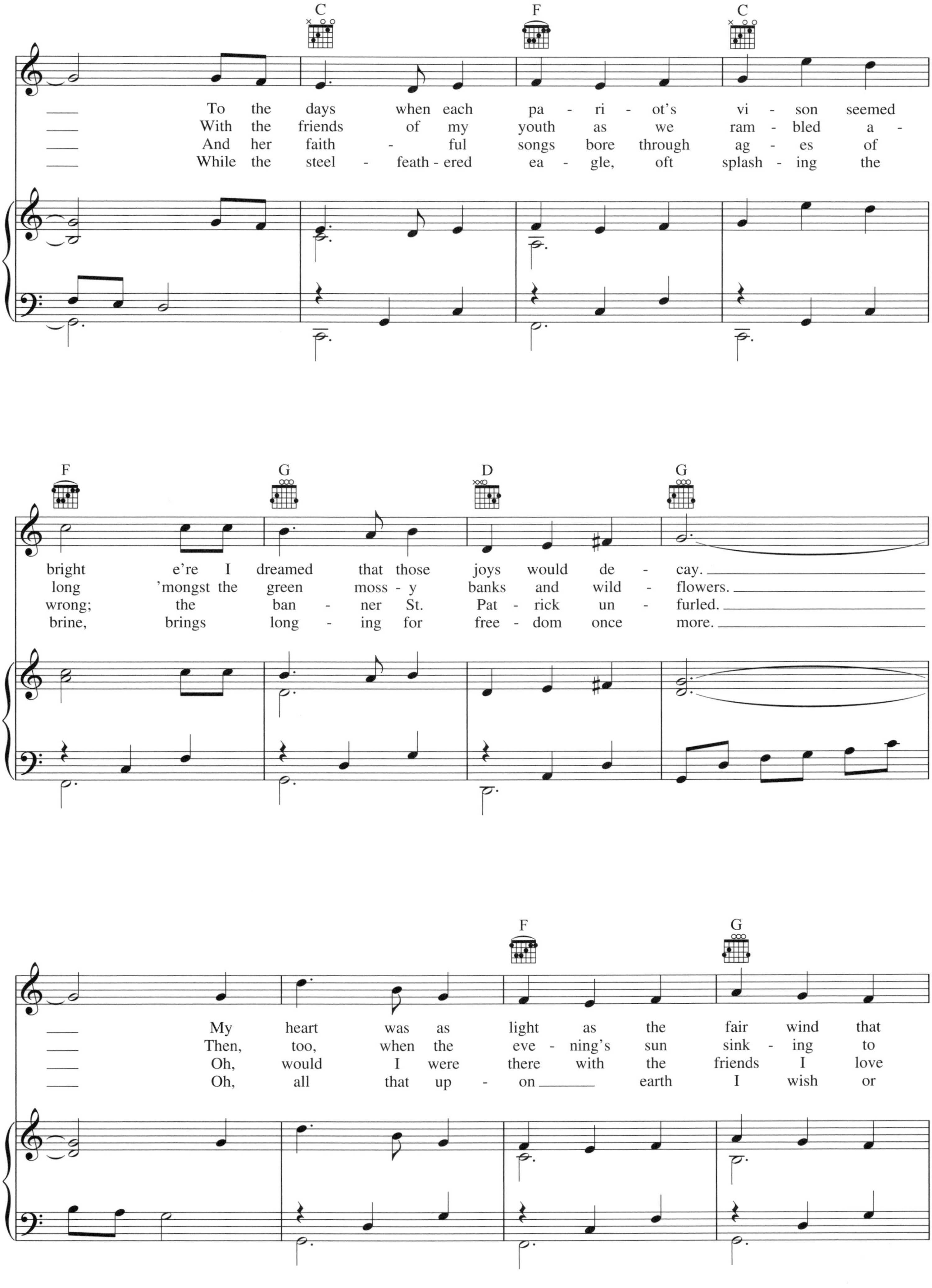
C F C
To the days when each pa - ri - ot's vi - son seemed
With the friends of my youth as we ram - bled a -
And her faith - ful songs bore through ag - es of
While the steel - feath - ered ea - gle, oft splash - ing the
F G D G
bright e're I dreamed that those joys would de - cay.
long 'mongst the green moss - y banks and wild - flowers.
wrong; the ban - ner St. Pat - rick un - furled.
brine, brings long - ing for free - dom once more.
F G
My heart was as light as the fair wind that
Then, too, when the eve - ning's sun sink - ing to
Oh, would I were there with the friends I love
Oh, all that up - on earth I wish or

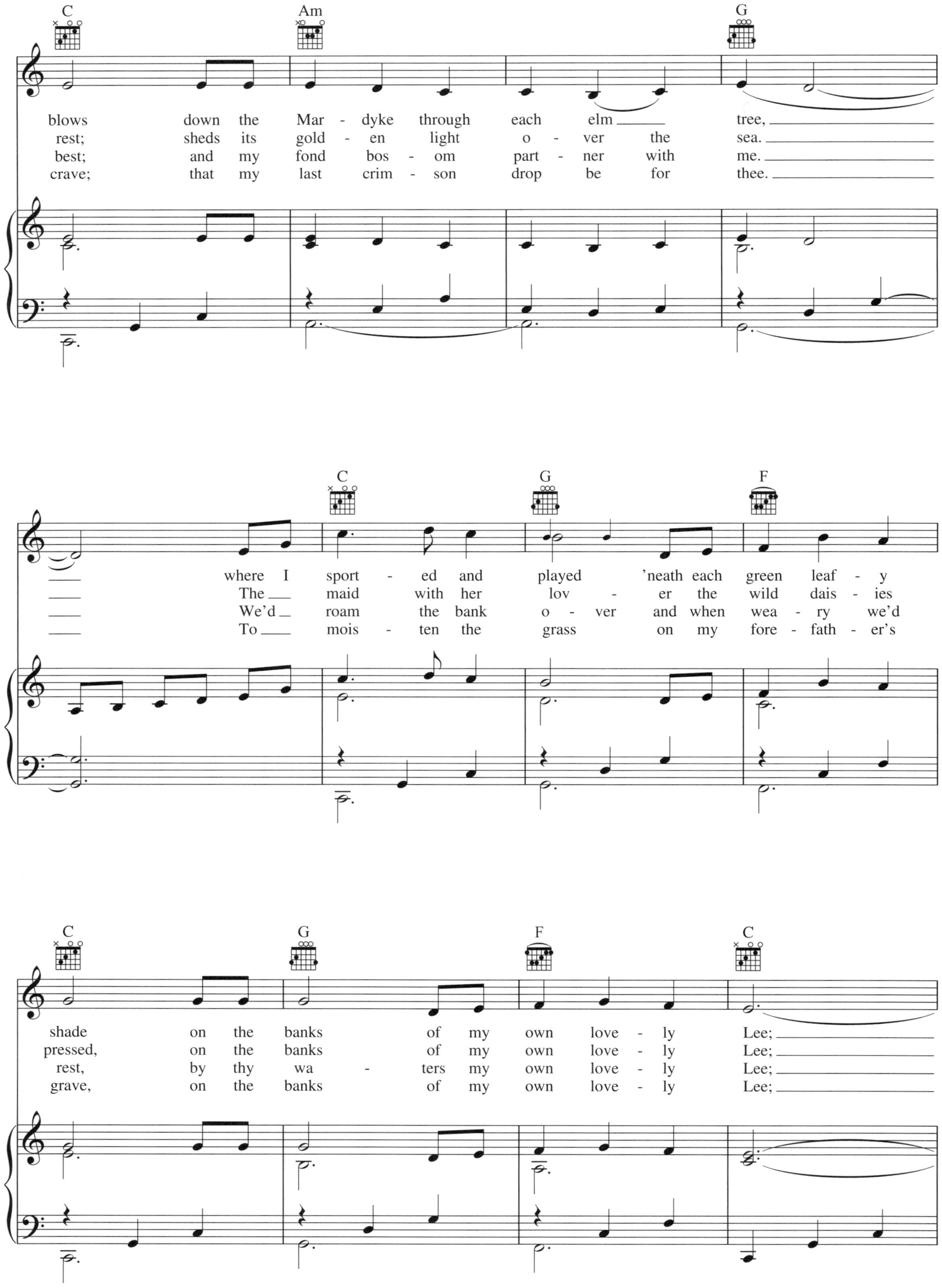
C Am G
blows down the Mar - dyke through each elm tree,
rest; sheds its gold - en light o - ver the sea.
best; and my fond bos - om part - ner with me.
crave; that my last crim - son drop be for thee.
C G F
where I sport - ed and played 'neath each green leaf - y
The maid with her lov - er the wild dais - ies
We'd roam the bank o - ver and when wea - ry we'd
To mois - ten the grass on my fore - fath - er's
C G F C
shade on the banks of my own love - ly Lee;
pressed, on the banks of my own love - ly Lee;
rest, by thy wa - ters my own love - ly Lee;
grave, on the banks of my own love - ly Lee;

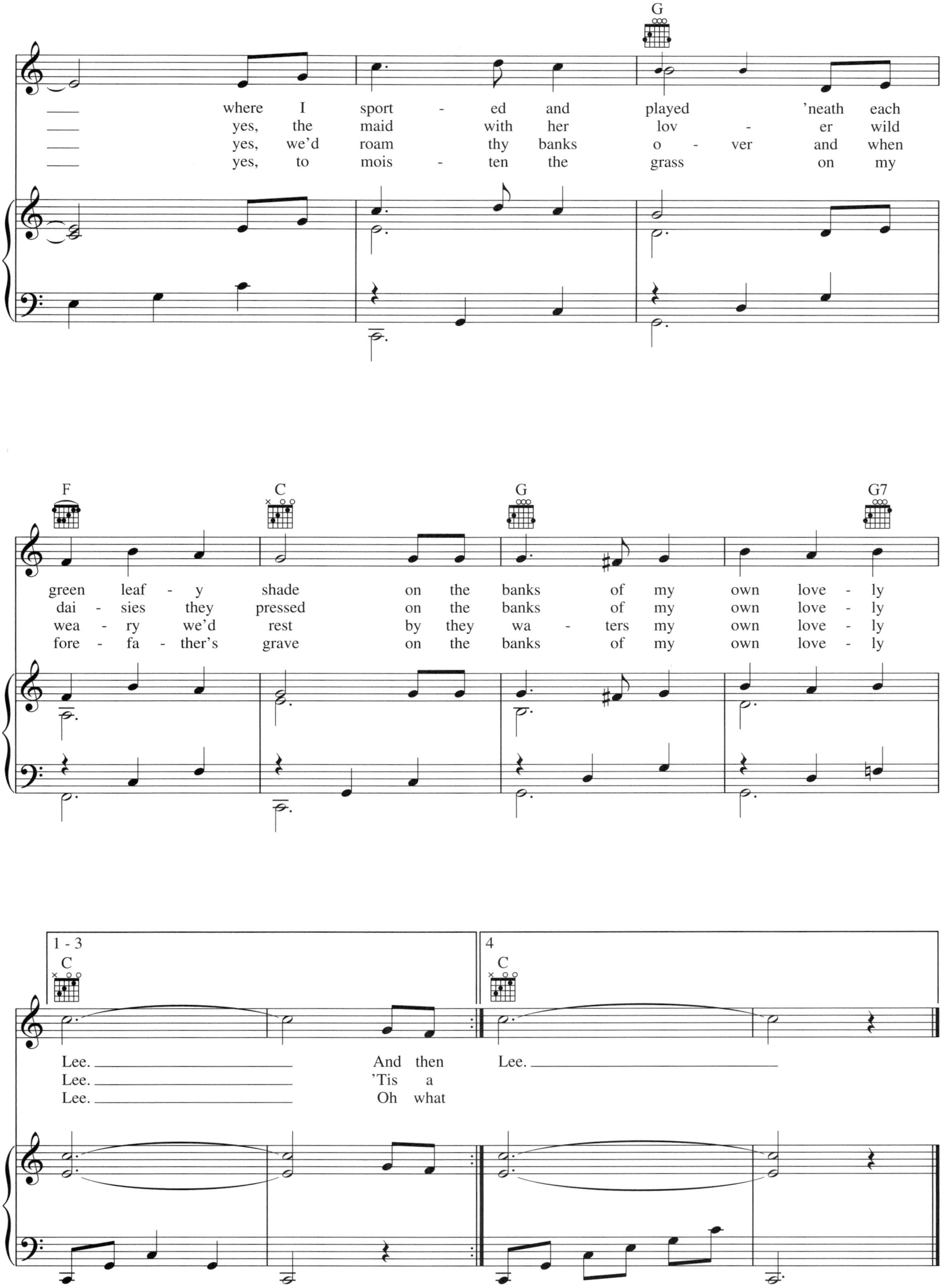
G
where I sport - ed and played 'neath each
yes, the maid with her lov - er wild
yes, we'd roam thy banks o - ver and when
yes, to mois - ten the grass on my
F C G G7
green leaf - y shade on the banks of my own love - ly
dai - sies they pressed on the banks of my own love - ly
wea - ry we'd rest by they wa - ters my own love - ly
fore - fa - ther's grave on the banks of my own love - ly
1 - 3
C
Lee. And then
Lee. 'Tis a
Lee. Oh what
4
C
Lee.

BANNA STRAND

Traditional Irish Folk Song

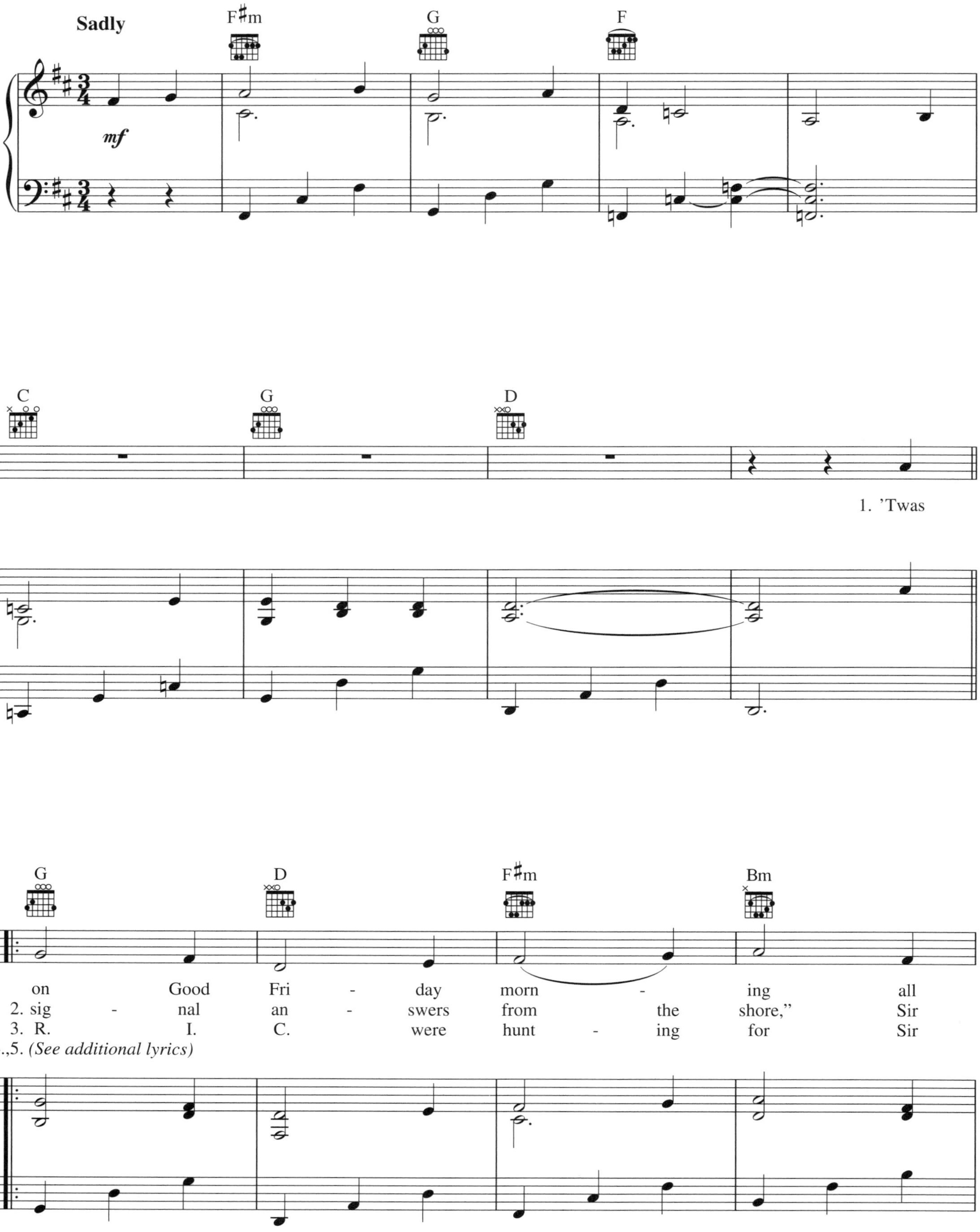
Sadly
F#m
G
F
mf
C
G
D
1. 'Twas
G
D
F#m
Bm
on Good Fri - day morn - ing all
2. sig - nal an - swers from the shore," Sir
3. R. I. C. were hunt - ing for Sir
4.,5. (See additional lyrics)

Copyright © 2006 by HAL LEONARD CORPORATION
International Copyright Secured All Rights Reserved

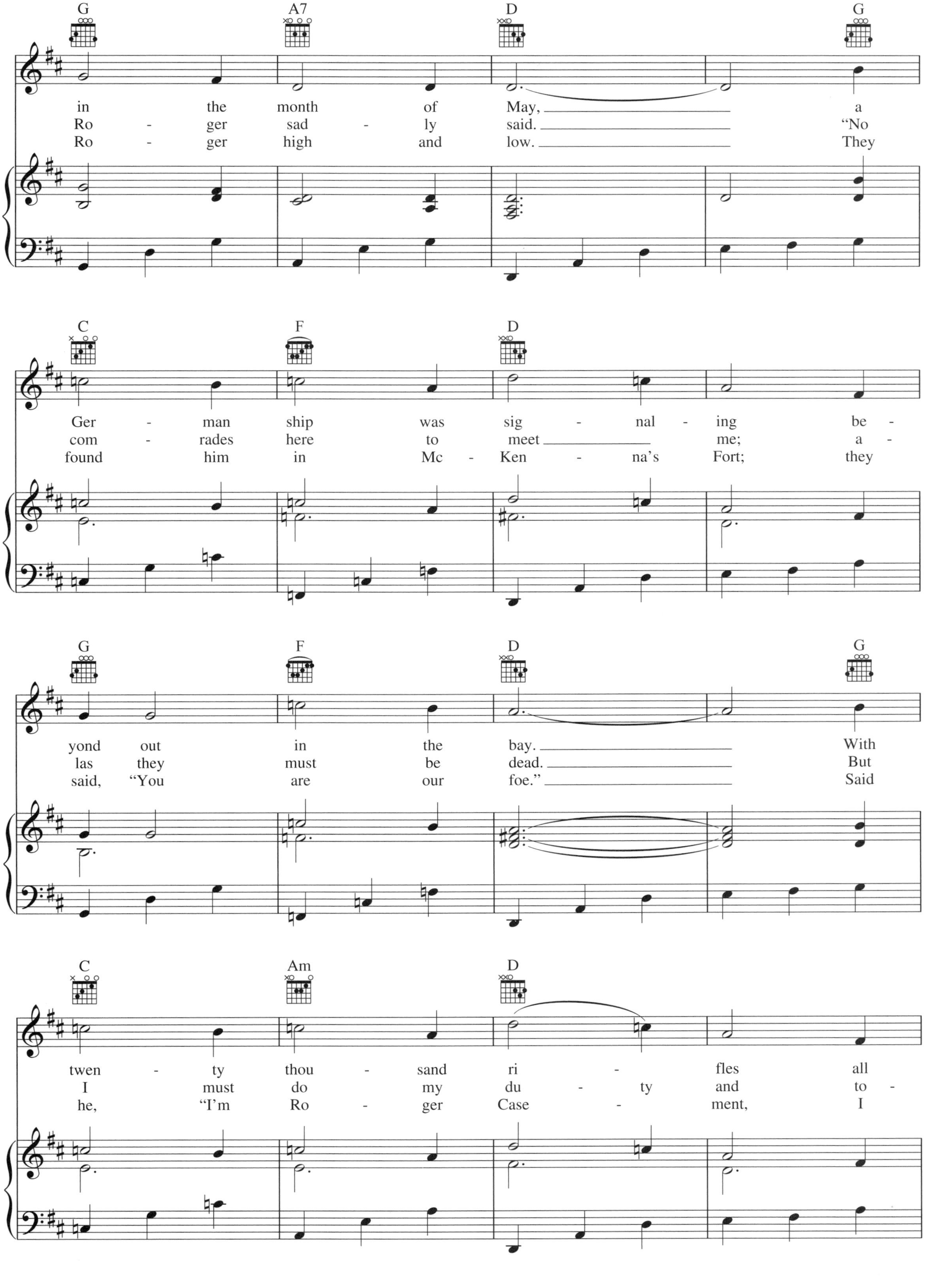
G A7 D G
in the month of May, a
Ro - ger sad - ly said. "No
Ro - ger high and low. They
C F D
Ger - man ship was sig - nal - ing be -
com - rades here to meet me; a -
found him in Mc - Ken - na's Fort; they
G F D G
yond out in the bay. With
las they must be dead. But
said, "You are our foe." Said
C Am D
twen - ty thou - sand ri - fles all
I must do my du - ty and to -
he, "I'm Ro - ger Case - ment, I

G F D
rea - dy for to land, but no
day I mean to land." So in
come to my na - tive land. And I
F♯m G F
an - sw'ring sig - nal did come from the
a small boat rowed a - shore on the
mean to free my coun - try - men on the
C G D
1 - 4
5
lone - ly Ban - na Strand. "No
lone - ly Ban - na Strand. The
lone - ly Ban - na Strand. They

Additional Lyrics

4. They took Sir Roger prisoner and sailed to London Town,
   And in the Tower they locked him up; a traitor to the Crown.
   Said he, "I am no traitor," but on trial he had to stand,
   For bringing German rifles to the lonely Banna Strand.

5. 'Twas in an English prison that they led him to his death.
   "I'm dying for my country," he said with his last breath.
   They buried him in British soil far from his native land,
   And the wild waves sang his requiem on the lonely Banna Stand.

BLACK VELVET BAND

Traditional Irish Folk Song

Lyrically
G
Em
mf
C
D
G
G
Her eyes they shun like dia - monds;
you'd think she was queen of the land.
D

Copyright © 2003 by HAL LEONARD CORPORATION
International Copyright Secured All Rights Reserved

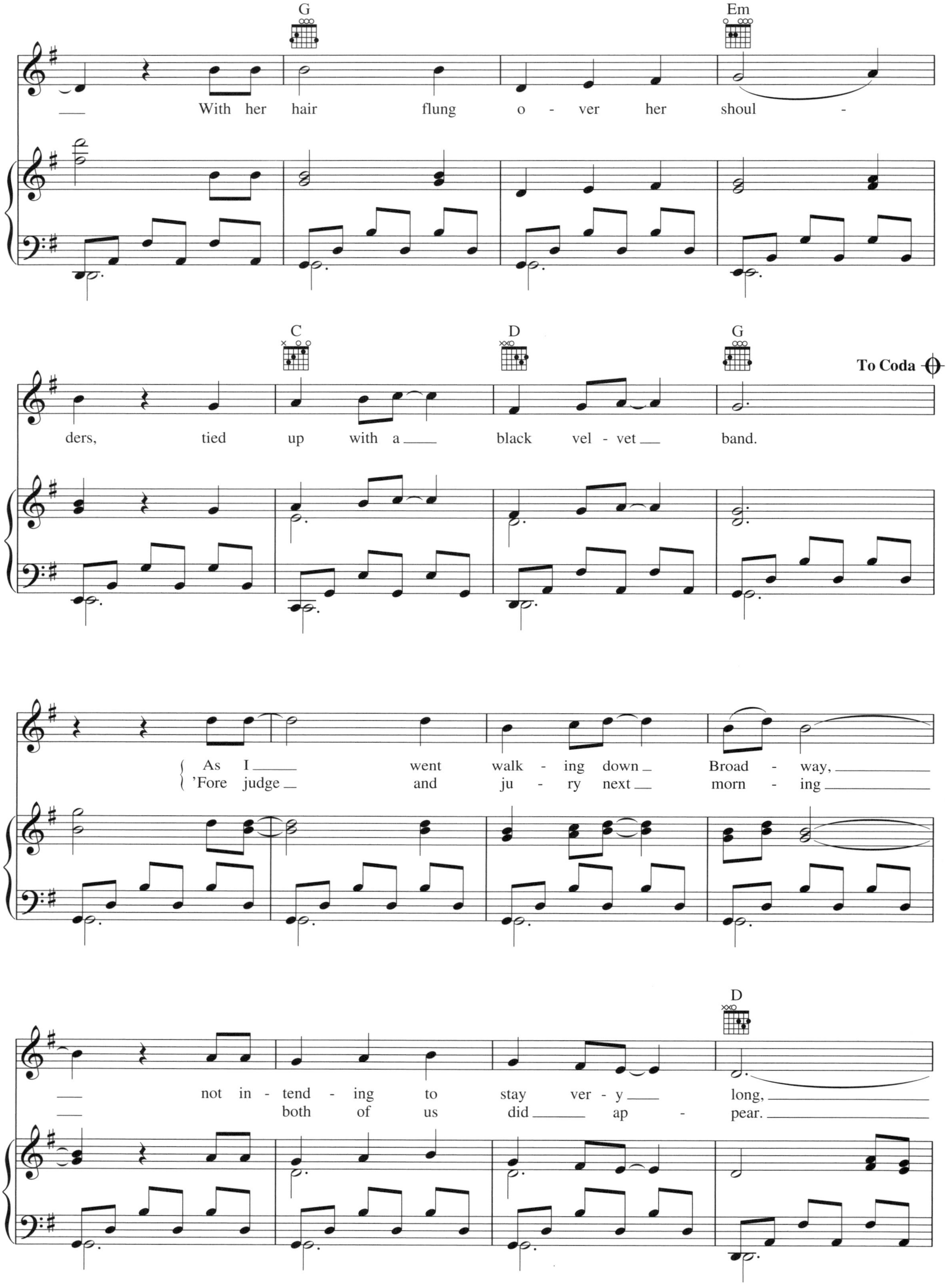
G
Em
With her hair flung o - ver her shoul -
C
D
G
To Coda
ders, tied up with a black vel - vet band.
As I went walk - ing down Broad - way,
'Fore judge and ju - ry next morn - ing
D
not in - tend - ing to stay ver - y long,
both of us did ap - pear.

G
Em
I met with this frol - ick - some dam - sel as she came trip - ping a - long.
A gen - tle - man claimed his jew - el - ry and the case a - gainst us was clear.
C
D
G
A watch she pulled out of her pock - et and slipped it right in - to me hand.
Sev - en long years trans - por - ta - tion right on down to Van Die - men's Land;
D

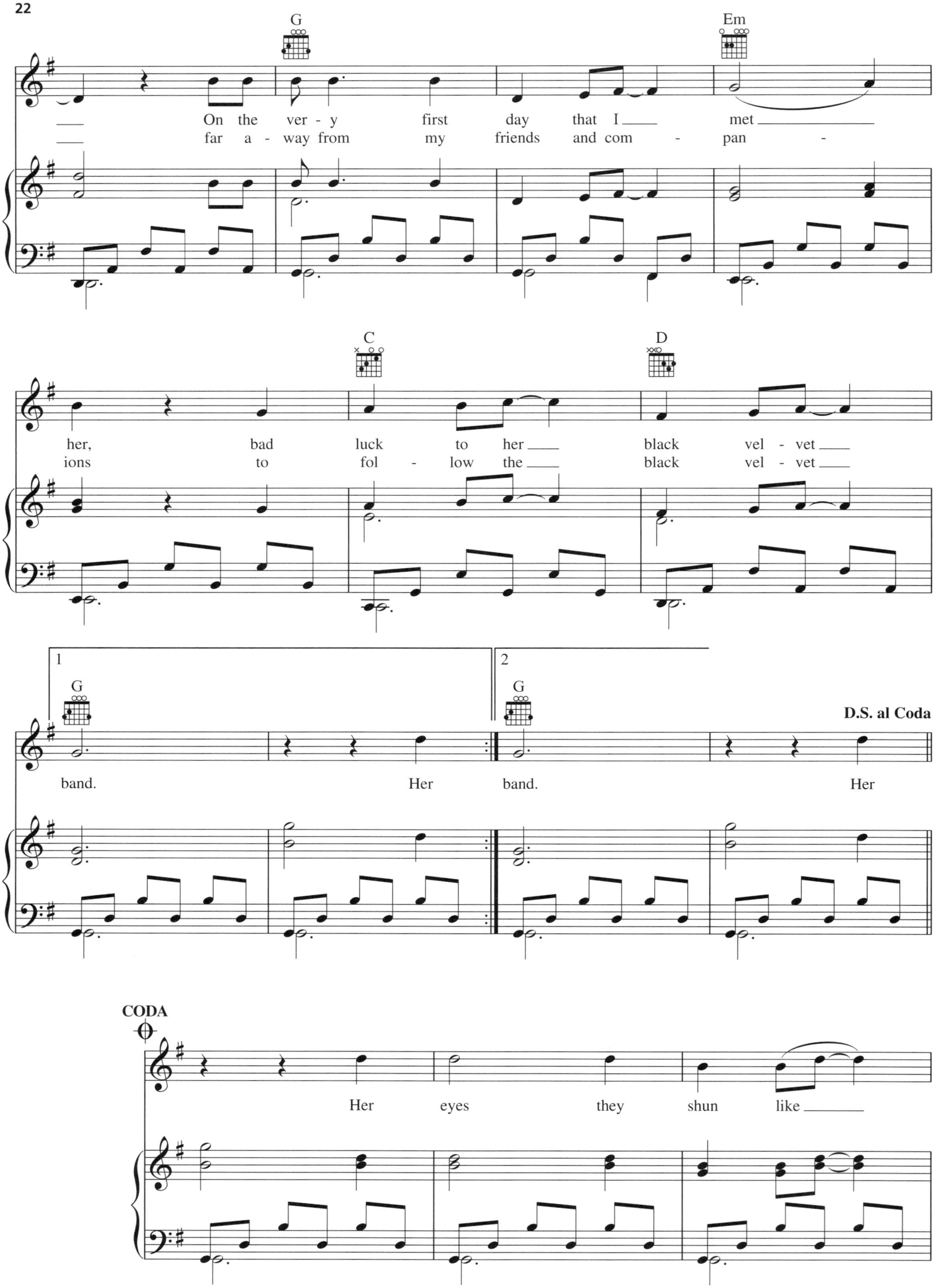
G
Em
On the ver - y first day that I met
far a - way from my friends and com - pan -
C
D
her, bad luck to her black vel - vet
ions to fol - low the black vel - vet
1
2
G
G
D.S. al Coda
band. Her band. Her
CODA
Her eyes they shun like

dia - monds; you'd think she was queen of the
D
G
land. With her hair flung
Em
o - ver her shoul - ders, tied
C
D
G
up with a black vel - vet band.

THE BARD OF ARMAGH

Traditional Irish Folk Song

Gently
D
A7
D
A7
mf
D
G
D
Oh, list to the lay of a poor I - rish
fair or a wake I could twist my shil -
I long to muse on the days of my
Ser - geant Death in his cold arms shall em -
A7
D
A7
D
harp - er and scorn not the strains of his old with - ered
le - lagh or trip through a jig with my brogues bound with
boy - hood, though four - score and three years have flit - ted since
brace me, then lull me to sleep with sweet Er - in go

Copyright © 2006 by HAL LEONARD CORPORATION
International Copyright Secured All Rights Reserved

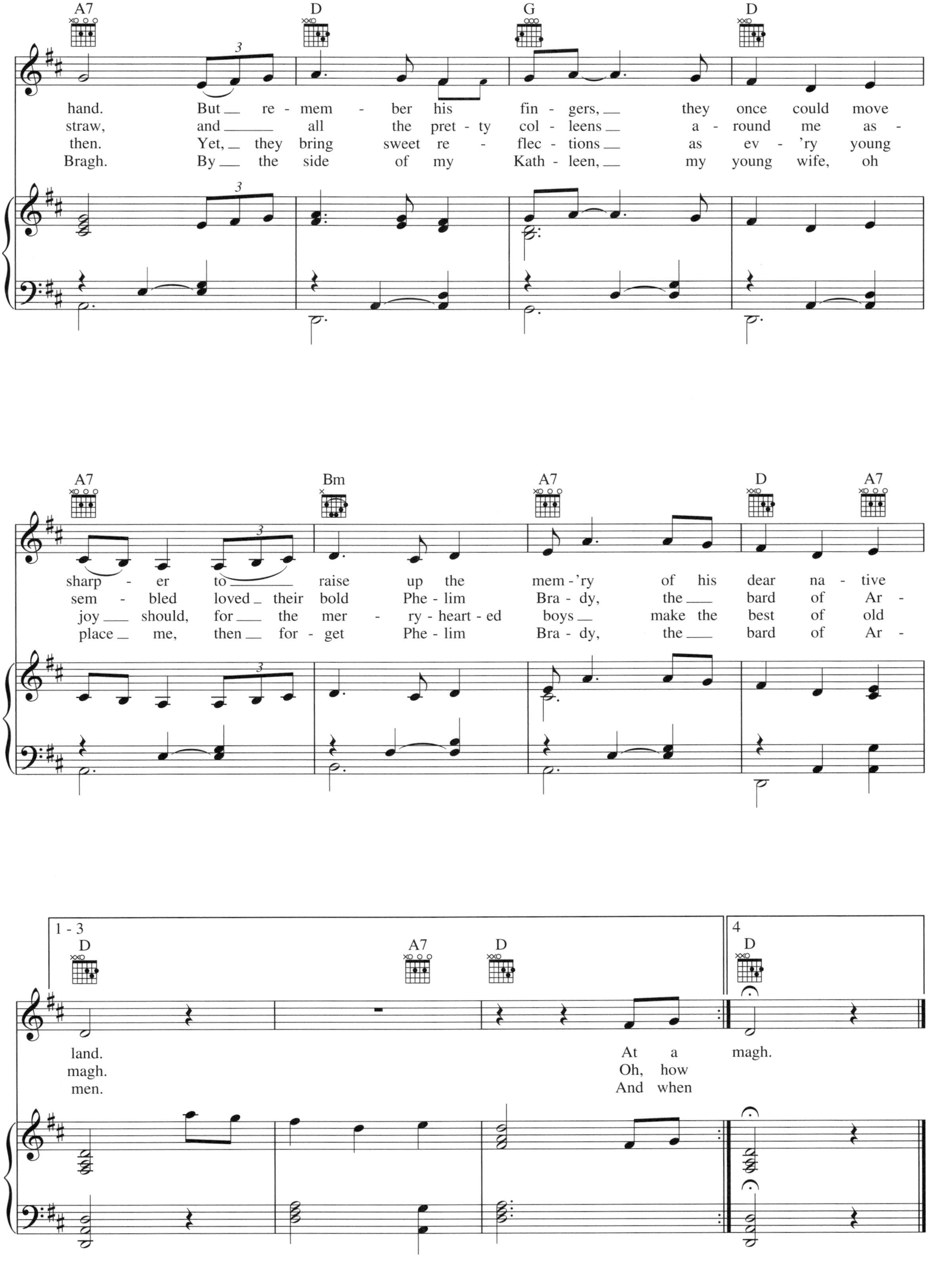
A7 D G D
hand. But re - mem - ber his fin - gers, they once could move
straw, and all the pret - ty col - leens a - round me as -
then. Yet, they bring sweet re - flec - tions as ev - 'ry young
Bragh. By the side of my Kath - leen, my young wife, oh
A7 Bm A7 D A7
sharp - er to raise up the mem - 'ry of his dear na - tive
sem - bled loved their bold Phe - lim Bra - dy, the bard of Ar -
joy should, for the mer - ry - heart - ed boys make the best of old
place me, then for - get Phe - lim Bra - dy, the bard of Ar -
1 - 3
D A7 D
land. At a
magh. Oh, how
men. And when
4
D
magh.

BELIEVE ME, IF ALL THOSE ENDEARING YOUNG CHARMS

Words and Music by
THOMAS MOORE

Moderately
E♭ E♭7 A♭ A♭m6 E♭/B♭ B♭7
mf
E♭ A♭ Adim
Be - lieve me, if all those en - dear - ing young charms which I
not while beau - ty and youth are thine own, and thy
E♭/B♭ B♭7 E♭ B♭7
gaze on so fond - ly to - day, were to
cheeks un - pro - faned by a tear, that the
E♭ A♭ Adim E♭ B♭7
change by to - mor - row, and fleet in my arms, like fair - y gifts fad - ing a -
fer - vor and faith of a soul can be known, to which time will but make thee more

Copyright © 1993 by HAL LEONARD CORPORATION
International Copyright Secured All Rights Reserved

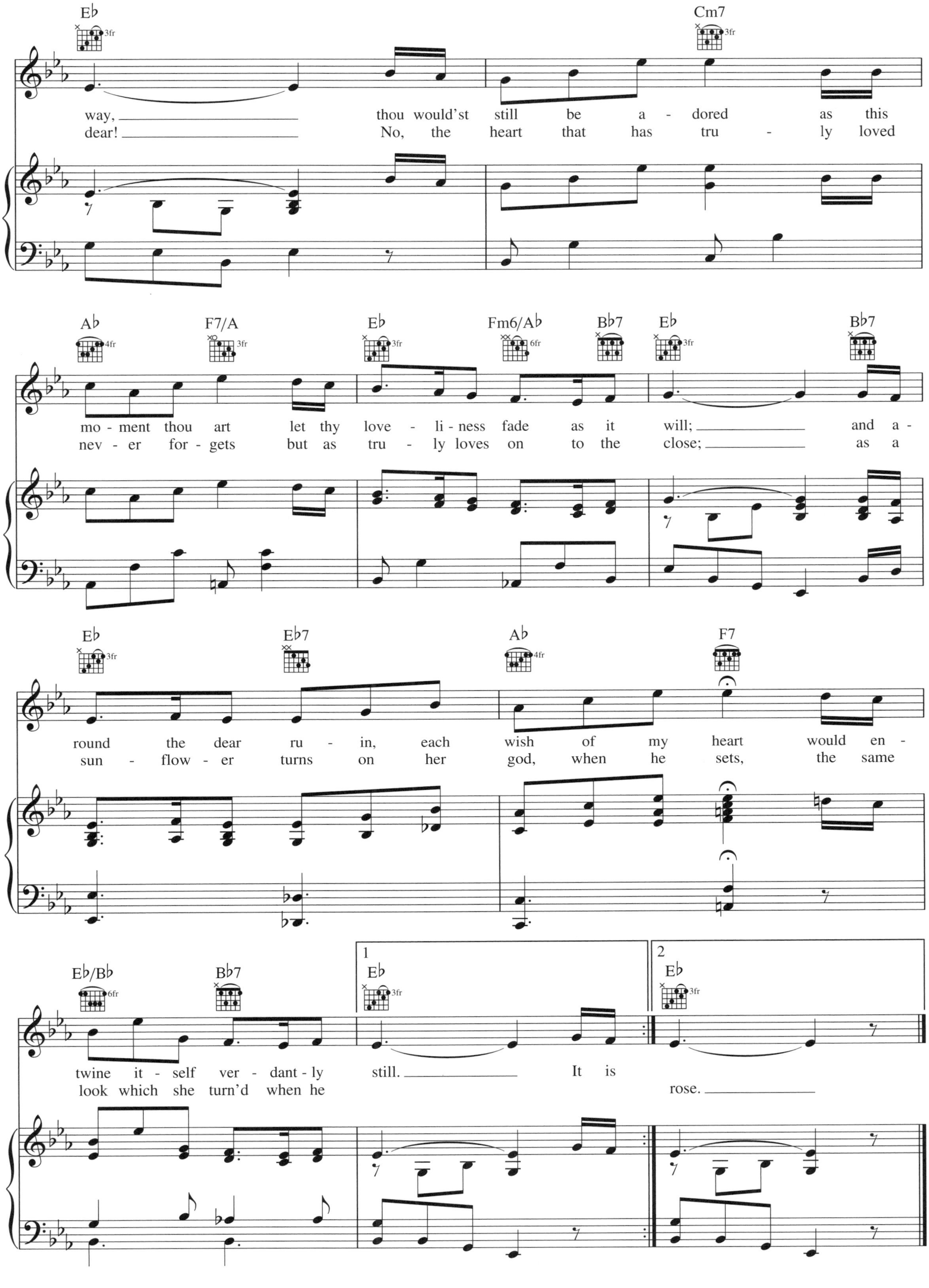
E♭
Cm7
way, thou would'st still be a - dored as this
dear! No, the heart that has tru - ly loved
A♭
F7/A
E♭
Fm6/A♭
B♭7
E♭
B♭7
mo - ment thou art let thy love - li - ness fade as it will; and a -
nev - er for - gets but as tru - ly loves on to the close; as a
E♭
E♭7
A♭
F7
round the dear ru - in, each wish of my heart would en -
sun - flow - er turns on her god, when he sets, the same
E♭/B♭
B♭7
1
E♭
2
E♭
twine it - self ver - dant - ly still. It is
look which she turn'd when he rose.
3fr
4fr
6fr

BOLD FENIAN MEN

Traditional Irish Melody
Words by M. SCANLAN

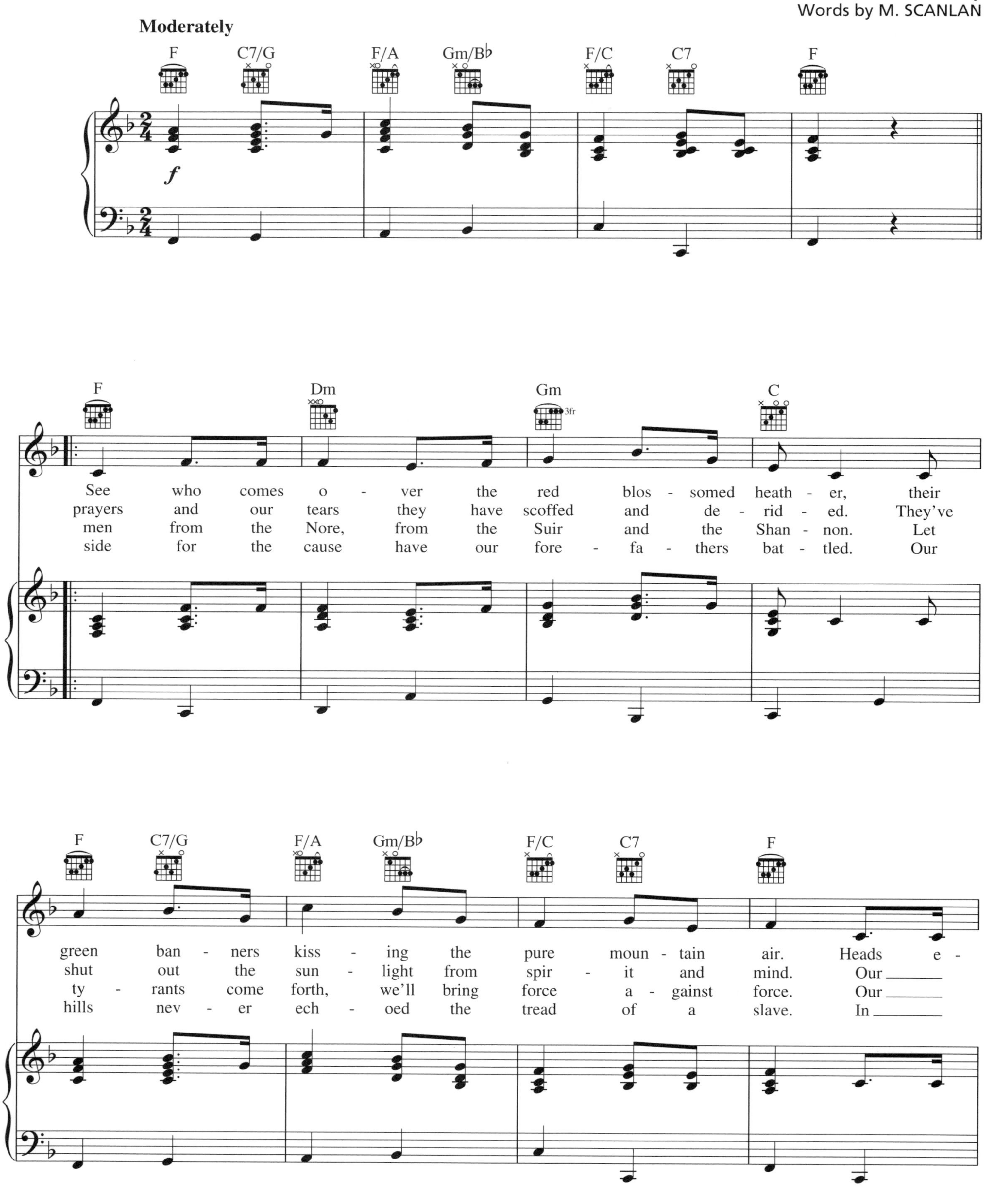
Moderately
F C7/G F/A Gm/B♭ F/C C7 F
f
F Dm Gm C
3fr
See who comes o - ver the red blos - somed heath - er, their
prayers and our tears they have scoffed and de - rid - ed. They've
men from the Nore, from the Suir and the Shan - non. Let
side for the cause have our fore - fa - thers bat - tled. Our
F C7/G F/A Gm/B♭ F/C C7 F
green ban - ners kiss - ing the pure moun - tain air. Heads e -
shut out the sun - light from spir - it and mind. Our
ty - rants come forth, we'll bring force a - gainst force. Our
hills nev - er ech - oed the tread of a slave. In

Copyright © 2006 by HAL LEONARD CORPORATION
International Copyright Secured All Rights Reserved

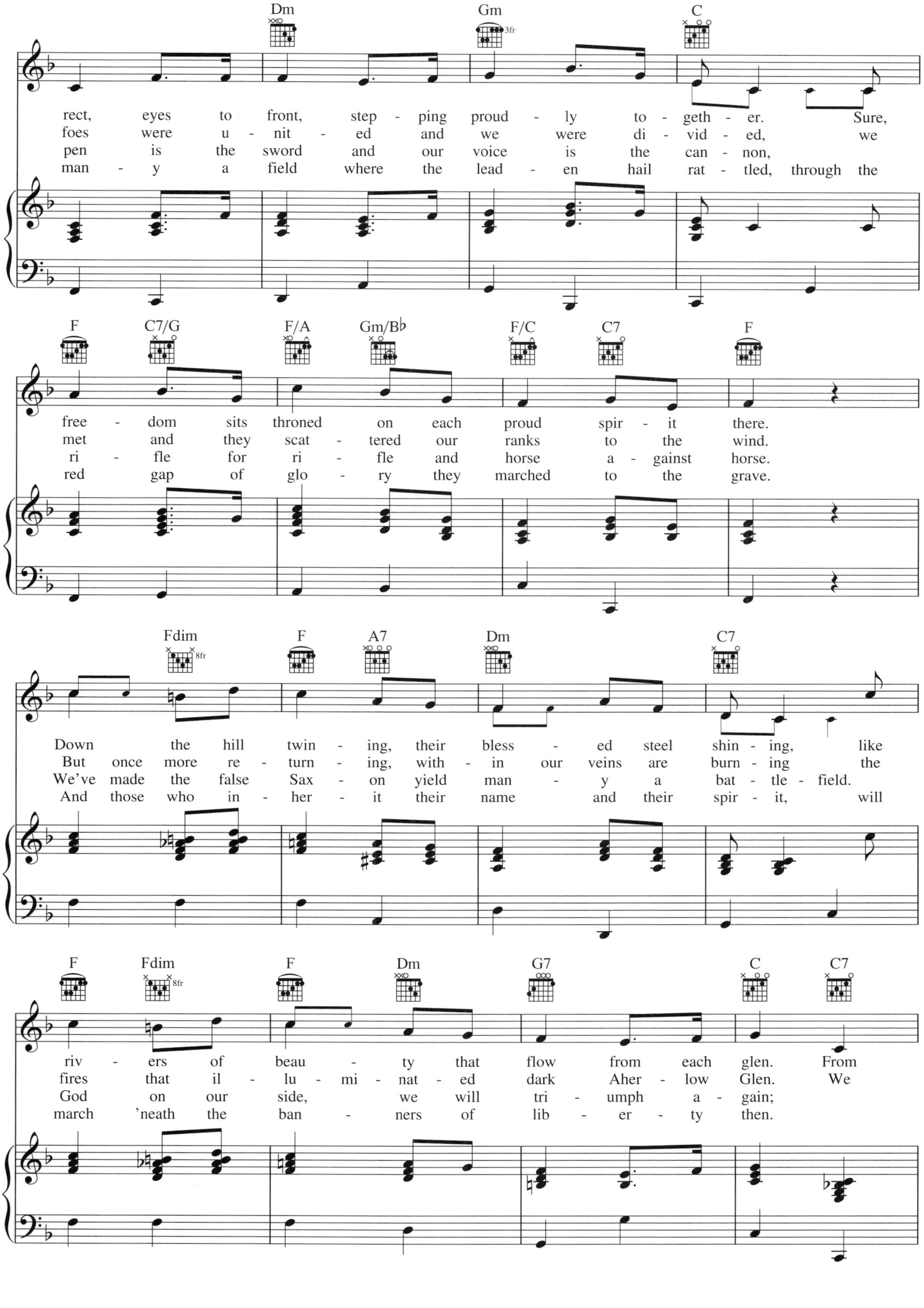
Dm Gm 3fr C
rect, eyes to front, step - ping proud - ly to - geth - er. Sure,
foes were u - nit - ed and we were di - vid - ed, we
pen is the sword and our voice is the can - non,
man - y a field where the lead - en hail rat - tled, through the
F C7/G F/A Gm/B♭ F/C C7 F
free - dom sits throned on each proud spir - it there.
met and they scat - tered our ranks to the wind.
ri - fle for ri - fle and horse a - gainst horse.
red gap of glo - ry they marched to the grave.
Fdim 8fr F A7 Dm C7
Down the hill twin - ing, their bless - ed steel shin - ing, like
But once more re - turn - ing, with - in our veins are burn - ing the
We've made the false Sax - on yield man - y a bat - tle - field.
And those who in - her - it their name and their spir - it, will
F Fdim 8fr F Dm G7 C C7
riv - ers of beau - ty that flow from each glen. From
fires that il - lu - mi - nat - ed dark Aher - low Glen. We
God on our side, we will tri - umph a - gain;
march 'neath the ban - ners of lib - er - ty then.

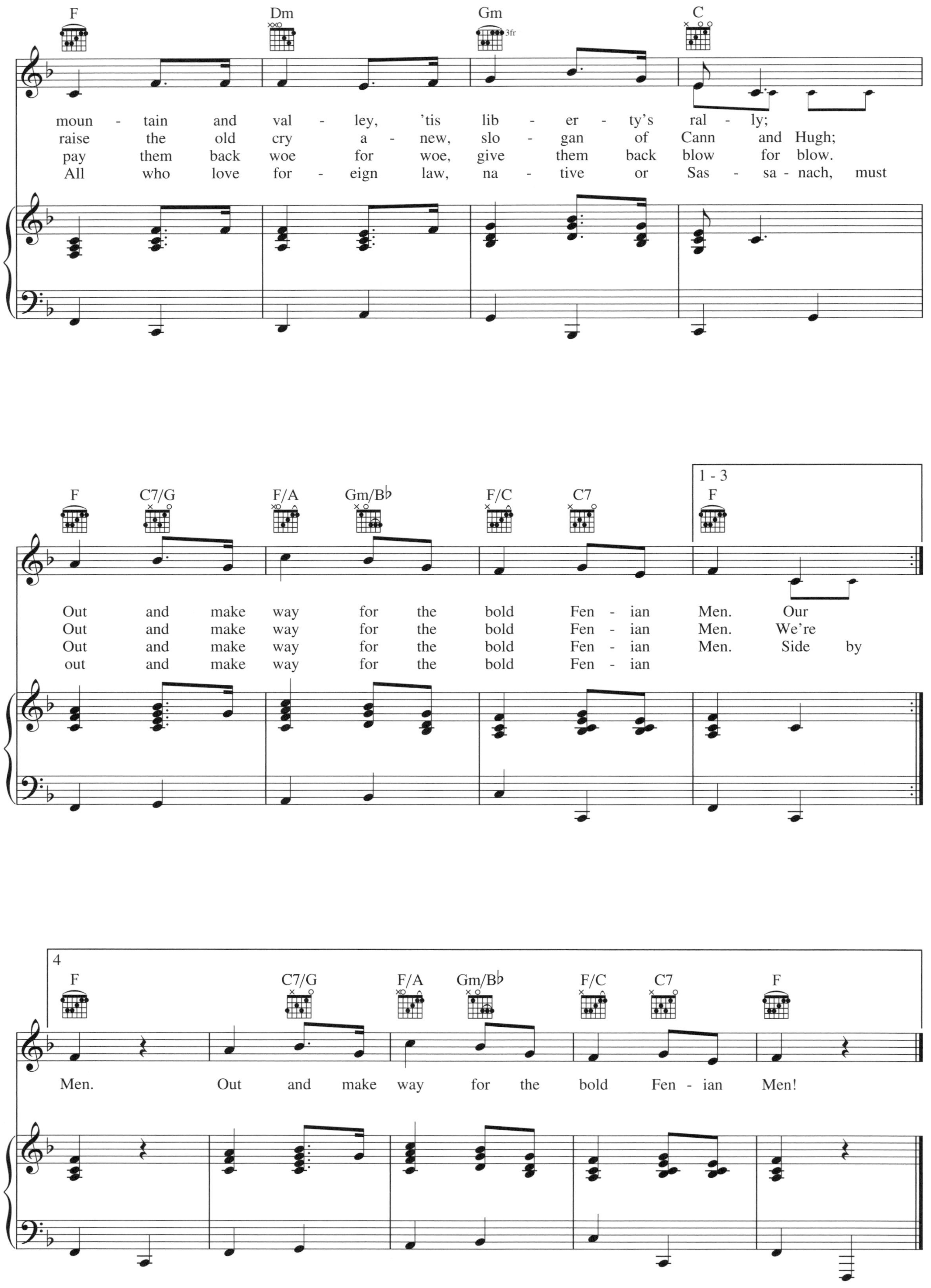
F Dm Gm 3fr C
moun - tain and val - ley, 'tis lib - er - ty's ral - ly;
raise the old cry a - new, slo - gan of Cann and Hugh;
pay them back woe for woe, give them back blow for blow.
All who love for - eign law, na - tive or Sas - sa - nach, must
F C7/G F/A Gm/B♭ F/C C7
1 - 3
F
Out and make way for the bold Fen - ian Men. Our
Out and make way for the bold Fen - ian Men. We're
Out and make way for the bold Fen - ian Men. Side by
out and make way for the bold Fen - ian
4
F C7/G F/A Gm/B♭ F/C C7 F
Men. Out and make way for the bold Fen - ian Men!

THE BOLD TENANT FARMER

Traditional Irish Folk Song

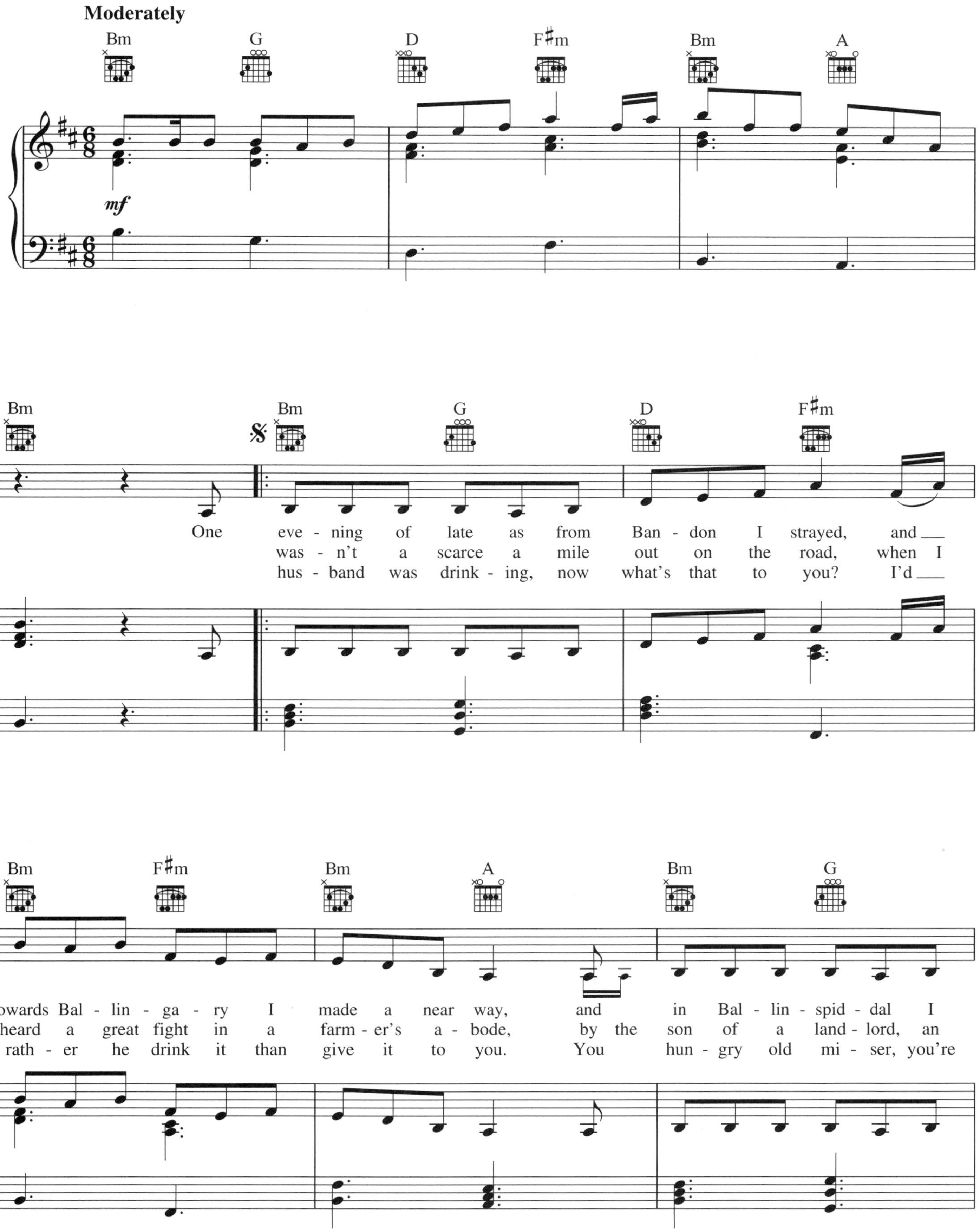
Moderately
Bm G D F#m Bm A
mf
Bm Bm G D F#m
One eve - ning of late as from Ban - don I strayed, and
was - n't a scarce a mile out on the road, when I
hus - band was drink - ing, now what's that to you? I'd
Bm F#m Bm A Bm G
towards Bal - lin - ga - ry I made a near way, and in Bal - lin - spid - dal I
heard a great fight in a farm - er's a - bode, by the son of a land - lord, an
rath - er he drink it than give it to you. You hun - gry old mi - ser, you're

Copyright © 2003 by HAL LEONARD CORPORATION
International Copyright Secured All Rights Reserved

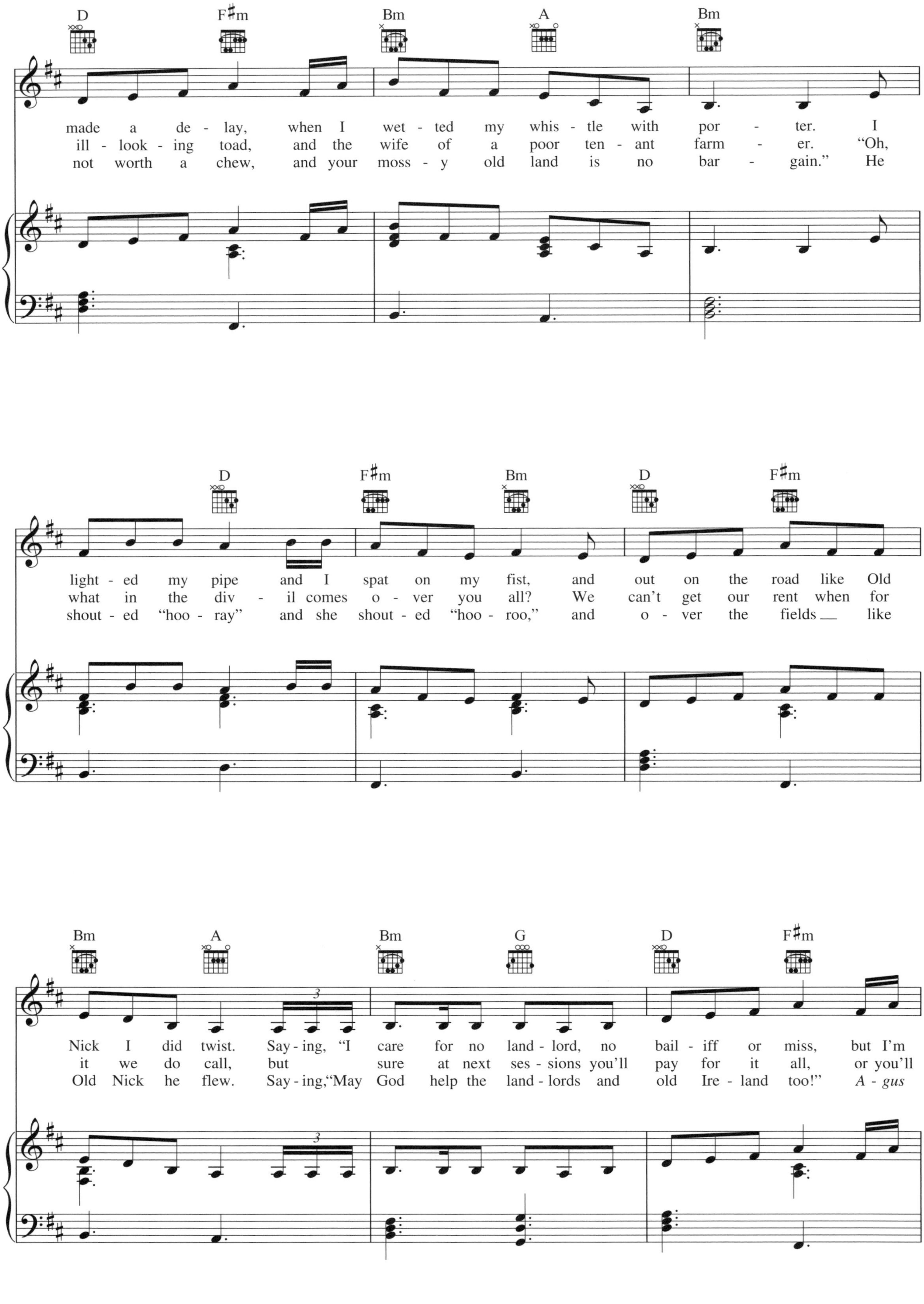
D F♯m Bm A Bm
made a de - lay, when I wet - ted my whis - tle with por - ter. I
ill - look - ing toad, and the wife of a poor ten - ant farm - er. "Oh,
not worth a chew, and your moss - y old land is no bar - gain." He
D F♯m Bm D F♯m
light - ed my pipe and I spat on my fist, and out on the road like Old
what in the div - il comes o - ver you all? We can't get our rent when for
shout - ed "hoo - ray" and she shout - ed "hoo - roo," and o - ver the fields like
Bm A Bm G D F♯m
Nick I did twist. Say - ing, "I care for no land - lord, no bail - iff or miss, but I'm
it we do call, but sure at next ses - sions you'll pay for it all, or you'll
Old Nick he flew. Say - ing, "May God help the land - lords and old Ire - land too!" A - gus

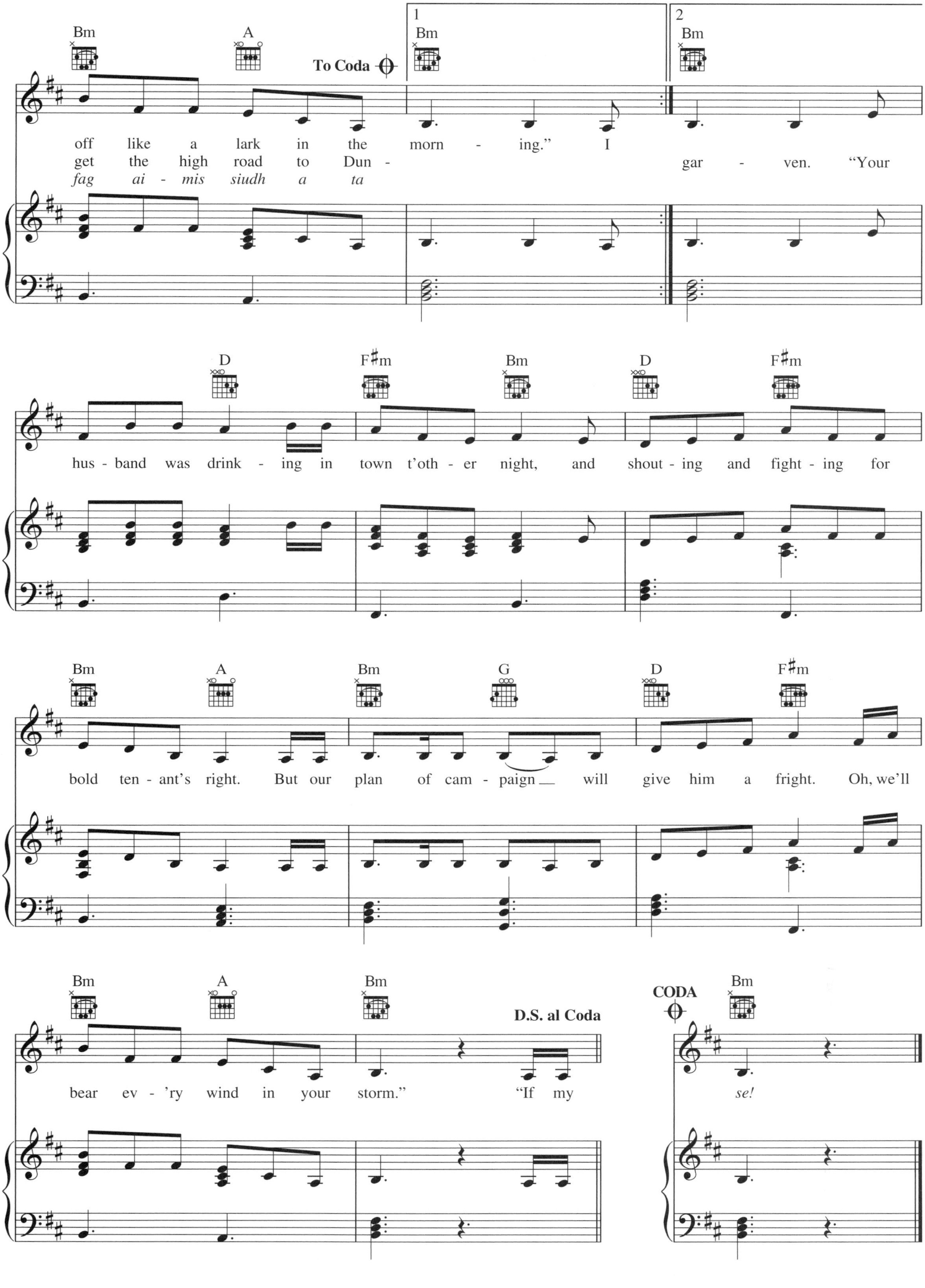
Bm A To Coda 1 Bm 2 Bm
off like a lark in the morn - ing." I
get the high road to Dun - gar - ven. "Your
fag ai - mis siudh a ta
D F♯m Bm D F♯m
hus - band was drink - ing in town t'oth - er night, and shout - ing and fight - ing for
Bm A Bm G D F♯m
bold ten - ant's right. But our plan of cam - paign will give him a fright. Oh, we'll
Bm A Bm D.S. al Coda CODA Bm
bear ev - 'ry wind in your storm." "If my se!

THE BONNY BOY

Traditional Irish Folk Song

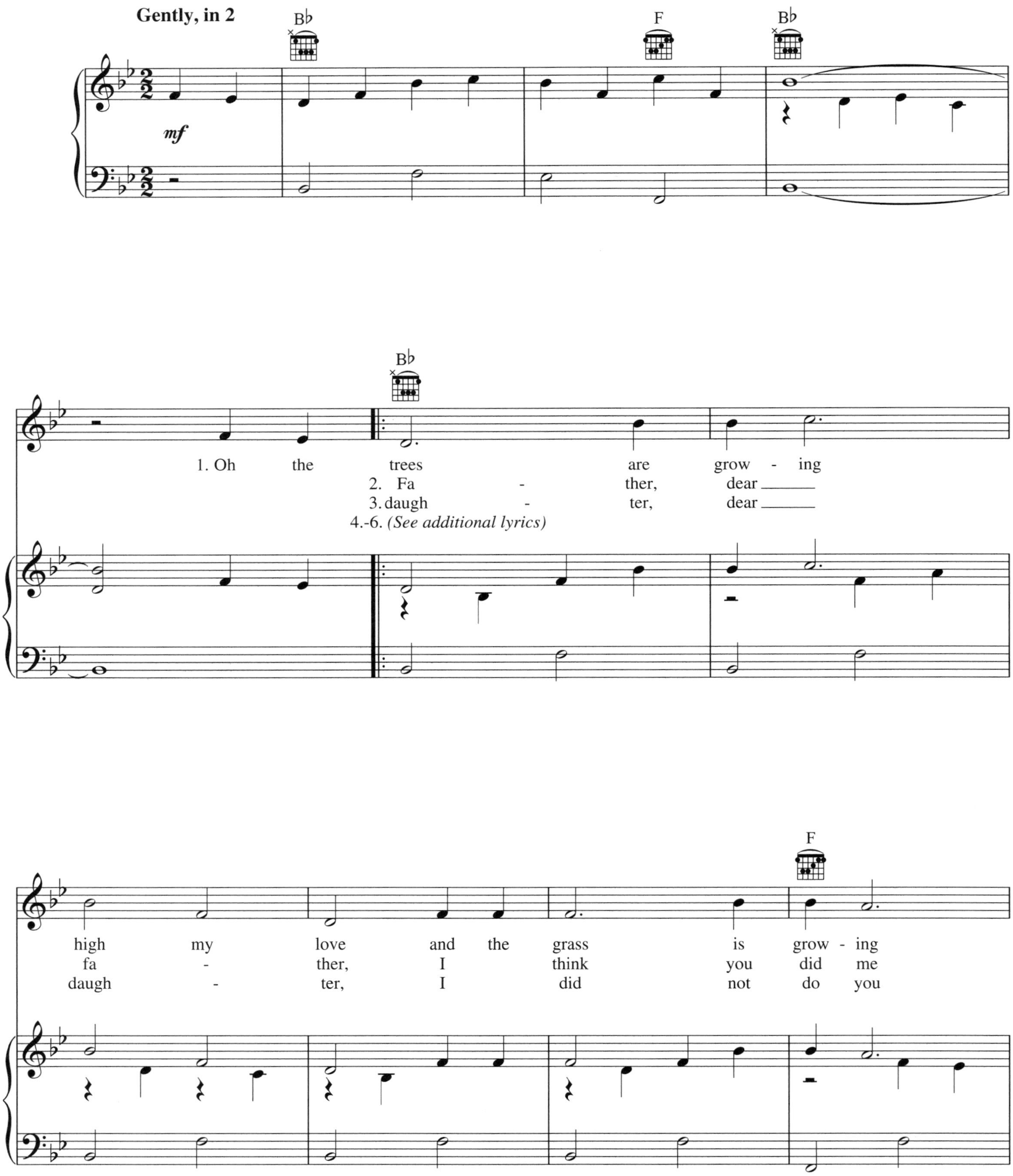
Gently, in 2
B♭
F
B♭
mf
B♭
1. Oh the trees are grow - ing
2. Fa - ther, dear
3. daugh - ter, dear
4.-6. (See additional lyrics)
F
high my love and the grass is grow - ing
fa - ther, I think you did me
daugh - ter, I did not do you

Copyright © 2006 by HAL LEONARD CORPORATION
International Copyright Secured All Rights Reserved

Bb Eb Bb Gm
green. And man - y's the cold and
wrong, for to go and get me
wrong, for to go and get you
Dm Eb F
bit - ter night since I my love have
mar - ried to one who is so
mar - ried to one who is so
Bb Gm
seen. It is a cold and
young. For he is on - ly
young. I know he'll be a
Dm Eb F
bit - ter night that I must lie a -
six - teen years and I am twen - ty -
match for you when I am dead and

E♭
3fr
F
B♭
lone. Oh the bon - ny boy is
one, and the bon - ny boy is
gone, oh the bon - ny boy is
E♭
3fr
B♭
E♭
3fr
young __ but he's grow - ing. ______
young __ and still grow - ing. ______
young __ but he's grow - ing. ______
B♭
1 - 5
6
Oh, ____
Oh, ____
Oh, ____

Additional Lyrics

4. Oh, Father, dear father, I'll tell you what I'll do.
   I'll send my love to college for another year or two,
   And all around his college cap I'll tie a ribbon blue
   Just to show the other girls that he's married.

5. At evening when strolling down by the college wall
   You'd see the young collegiates a-playing at the ball.
   You'd see him in amongst them there, the fairest of them all.
   He's my bonny boy, he's young but he's growing.

6. At the early age of sixteen years he was a married man,
   And at the age of seventeen the father of a son.
   But at the age of eighteen o'er his grave the grass grew strong,
   Cruel death put an end to his growing.

BOTANY BAY

Australian Folk Song

Moderately
C
F/C
C
mf
G7
C
1. Fare - well to old Eng - land for - ev - er,
2. cap - tain as is out Com - mand - er,
3. leav - in' old Eng - land we cares a - bout,
4.-6. (See additional lyrics)
F
G7
fare - well to my rum culls as well.
there's the bo - 'sun and all the ship's crew.
'taint cos we mis - pels what we knows.
G/D
C/E
F
C
Fare - well to the well - known Old Bai - lee
There's the first and sec - ond class pas - sen - gers,
But be - cos all we light fin - gered gen - try

Copyright © 2006 by HAL LEONARD CORPORATION
International Copyright Secured All Rights Reserved

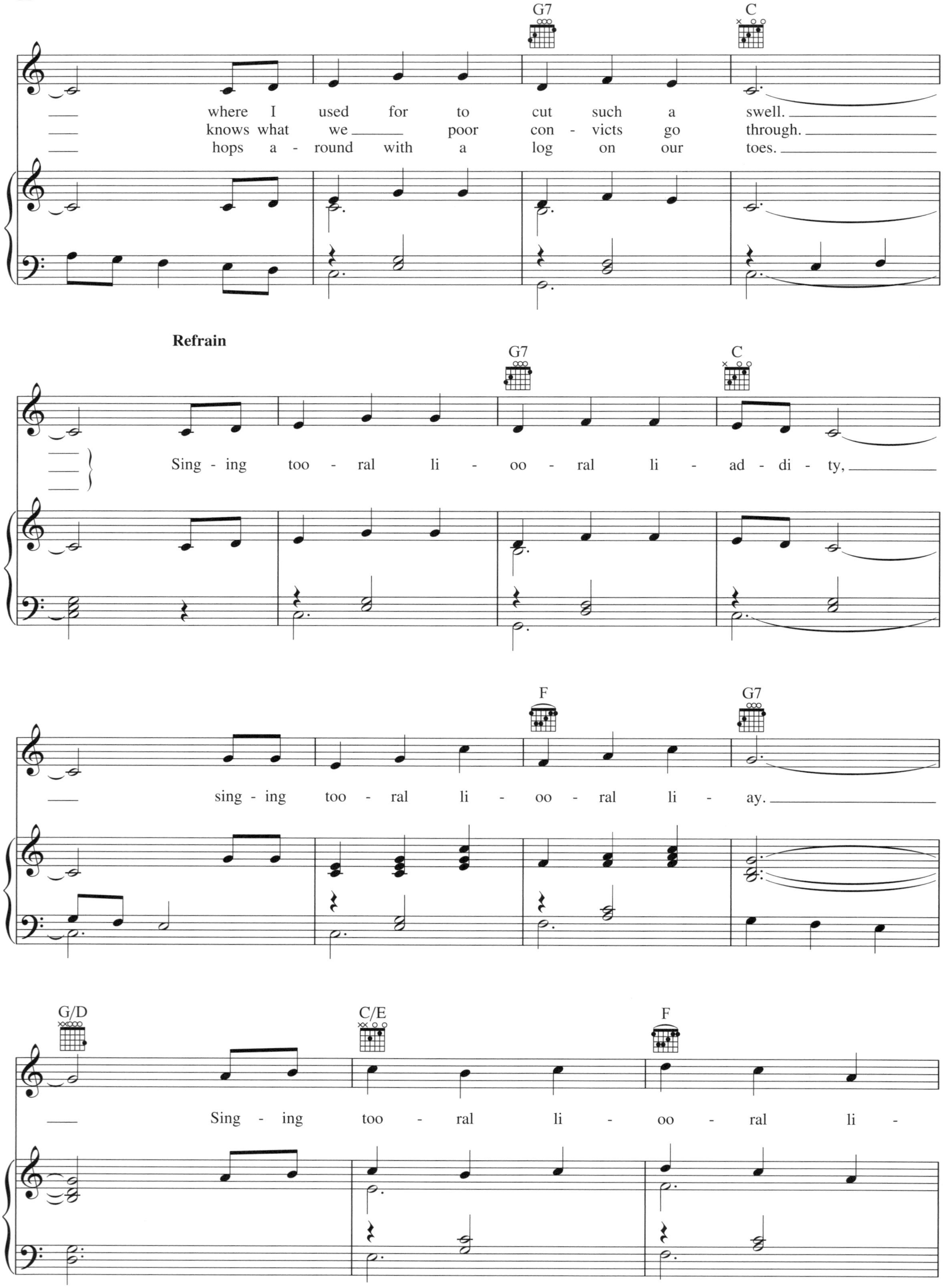
G7
C
where I used for to cut such a swell.
knows what we poor con - victs go through.
hops a - round with a log on our toes.
Refrain
G7
C
Sing - ing too - ral li - oo - ral li - ad - di - ty,
F
G7
sing - ing too - ral li - oo - ral li - ay.
G/D
C/E
F
Sing - ing too - ral li - oo - ral li -

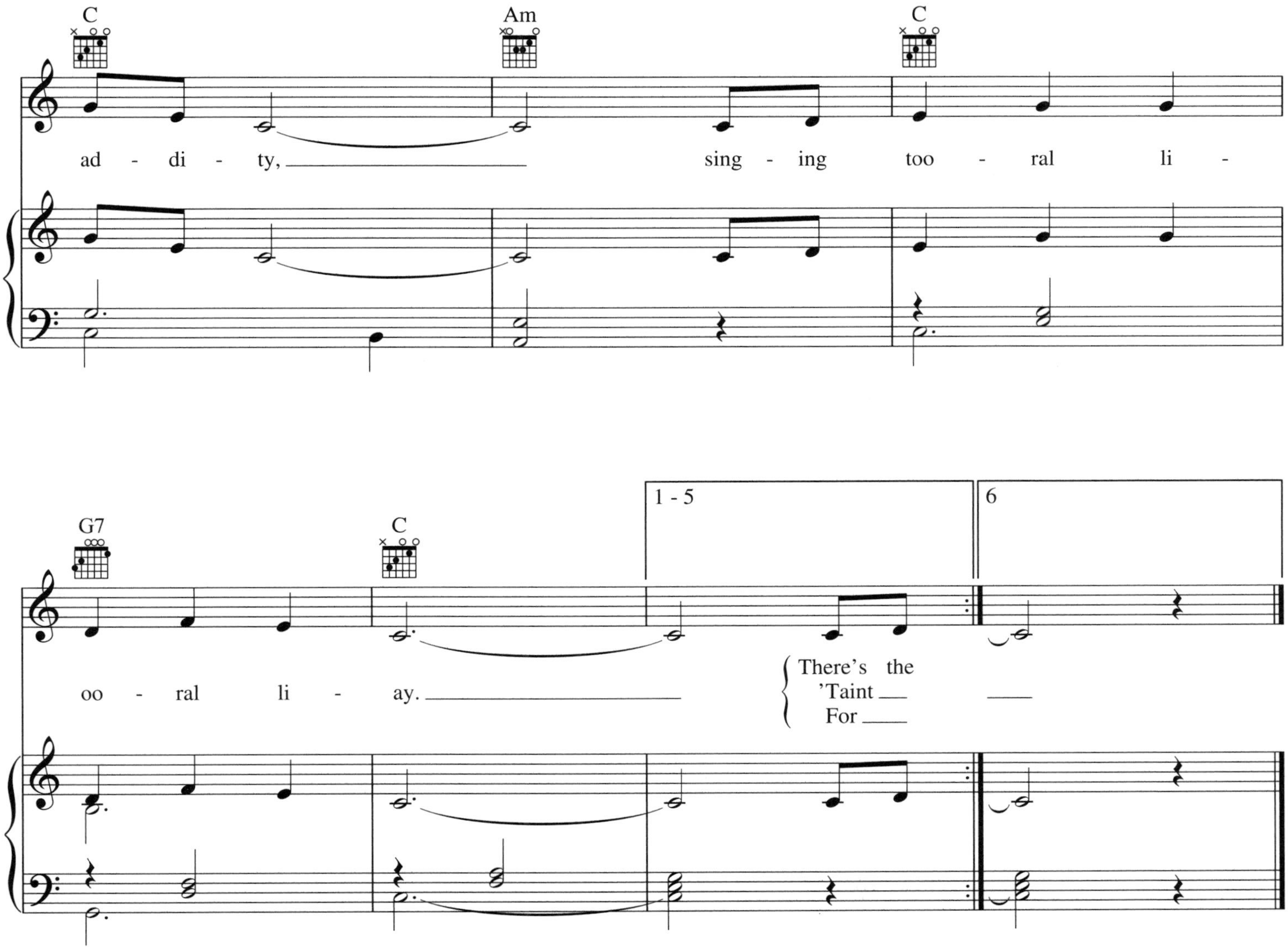
C
Am
C
ad - di - ty, singing too - ral li -
G7
C
1 - 5
6
oo - ral li - ay.
There's the
'Taint
For

Additional Lyrics

4. For seven long years I'll be staying here,
   For seven long years and a day.
   For meeting a cove in an area
   And taking his ticker away.
   Refrain

5. Oh, had I the wings of a turtle dove!
   I'd soar on my pinions so high.
   Slap bang to the arms of my Polly love,
   And in her sweet presence I'd die.
   Refrain

6. Now, all my young Dookies and Duchesses,
   Take warning from what I've to say.
   Mind all is your own as you touchesses.
   Or you'll find us in Botany Bay.
   Refrain

BOSTON BURGLAR

Traditional Irish Folk Song

Brightly
D Bm G D/A A7
mf
D D/C# Bm7 Bm7/A
1. Oh, I was born in Bos - ton, a
2. char - ac - ter was tak - en, and
3. see my ag - ed fa - ther, he's
4.,5. (See additional lyrics)
D Am7 D D/C#
town you all know well, brought up by hon - set
I was sent to jail. My friends found out it
stand - ing at the bar. Like - wise my poor old
Bm7 Bm7/A D A7
par - ents, the truth to you I'll tell. Brought
was in vain to try and set my bail. The
moth - er, tear - ing out her hair. Yes,

Copyright © 2006 by HAL LEONARD CORPORATION
International Copyright Secured All Rights Reserved

D D/C♯ Bm7 Bm7/A D Am7
up by hon - est par - ents, and raised most ten - der -
ju - ry found me guilt - y, the clerk he wrote it
tear - ing out those old grey locks, while tears come pour - ing
D Bm G
ly, 'til I be - came a sport - in' man, at the
down. The judge then passed the sen - tence; I was
down, cry - ing, "Son, oh son, what have you done, to be
D/A A7 1 - 4 D 5 D
age of twen - ty - three. My rum.
sen - tenced to Charles - town. I
sen - tenced to Charles - town?" I was

Additional Lyrics

4. I was put on board an eastern train, one cold December day.
   And ev'ry station that we passed I'd hear the people say,
   "There goes the Boston burglar. In strong chains he is bound.
   For some crime or another, he is going to Charlestown."

5. Now there's a girl in Boston, a girl that I love well.
   And when I gain my freedom, along with her I'll dwell.
   Yes, when I gain my freedom, bad company I'll shun.
   Likewise night walking, rambling, and also drinking rum.

BOULAVOGUE

Irish Folk Song
Words and Music by P.J. McCALL

Moderately, in one
D5
5fr
f
A5
5fr
D
G
At Bou - la - vogue as the sun was set - ting O'er bright May mead - ows of Shel - ma -
led us on 'gainst the com - ing sol - diers, And the cow'rd - ly Yeo - men were put to
took Cam - o - lin and En - ni - scor - thy And Wex - ford storm - ing, drove out our
Vin - e - gar Hill, o'er the pleas - ant Sla - ney, Our he - roes vain - ly stood back to
mf
D
Em

Copyright © 2003 by HAL LEONARD CORPORATION
International Copyright Secured All Rights Reserved

G D Em D/F♯
lier, A reb - el hand set the heath - er
flight. 'Twas at the Bar - row the boys of
foes. 'Twas at Slieve Coill - te our pikes were
back, And the Yeos at Tul - low took Fa - ther
G D/A
blaz - ing And brought the neigh - bors from
Wex - ford Showed Book - ey's reg - i - ment how
reek - ing With the crim - son stream of the
Mur - phy And burned his bod - y up -
A D
far and near. Then Fa - ther
men could fight. Look out for
beat - en Yeos. At Tub - ber -
on the rack. God grant you
G/D D
Mur - phy from old Kil - cor - mack Spurred up the
hire - lings, King George of Eng - land, Search ev - 'ry
neer - ing and Bal - ly - el - lis Full man - y a
glo - ry, brave Fa - ther Mur - phy, And o - pen

G
D
rocks with a warn - ing cry: "Arm, arm," he
king - dom where breathes a slave, For Fa - ther
Hes - sian lay in his gore. Ah, Fa - ther
heav - en to all your men; The cause that
Em
D/F♯
G
D
cried, "For I've come to lead you, For Ire - land's
Mur - phy from the Coun - ty Wex - ford Sweeps o'er the
Mur - phy had aid come o - ver; The green flag
called you may call to - mor - row In an - oth - er
1 - 3
A5
5fr
D5
5fr
free - dom we fight or die."
land like a might - y wave.
float - ed from shore to shore.
fight for the
4
A
D
He green a - gain.
We
At

THE BOYS OF FAIRHILL

Traditional Irish Folk Song

Lively
B♭ Gm E♭ F B♭
mf
Gm E♭ F B♭ Gm E♭ F B♭ Gm E♭ F B♭ Gm
1 - 3 E♭ F7 B♭
4 E♭ F7 B♭
3fr
8fr
Come and have a hol - i - day with our hurl - ing club so gay. Your souls we will charm and your hearts we will thrill. The girls sure they will charm_ you. The boys sure they won't harm_ you.
We'll go down by Sun-day's well, what might hap - pen, who can tell: heads, they might_ roll or some blood it might spill. We'll come back by Black - pool_ way when we've o - ver-come the fray.
Jim - my Bar - ry hooks the ball, we'll hook Jim - my, ball and all. "Here's up them all!" says the boys of Fair - hill. The Rock - ies thought they were the stars till they met the Saint Fin - barr's.
Kath - y Bar - ry sells cru beens, fair - ly burst - ing at the seams, sure for to cure and more sure for to kill. The stench on Pat - rick's Bridge is wick - ed how does Fa - ther Mat-thew stick it.
"Here's up them all," says the boys of Fair - hill.
boys of Fair - hill.

Copyright © 2006 by HAL LEONARD CORPORATION
International Copyright Secured All Rights Reserved

THE BOYS FROM THE COUNTY ARMAGH

Traditional Irish Folk Song

Lively
mf
D
G
C
Am
D
G
C
G
C
Am
There's one fair coun - ty in Ire - land with mem - ories so glor - ious and grand. Where na - ture has lav - ished her beau - ty in the
trav - eled that part of the coun - ty through New - ton, Fork - hill, Cross - ma - glen, a - round by the gap of Mount Nor - ris and

Copyright © 2006 by HAL LEONARD CORPORATION
International Copyright Secured All Rights Reserved

D
G
or - chards of Er - in's green land. I
home by Black - wa - ter a - gain. Where
C
Am
love its Ca - the - der - al cit - y once
girls are so fair and so pret - ty; none
D
G
found - ed by Pat - rick so true, and it
bet - ter you'll find near or far. But
C
Am
bears in the heart of its bos - om the
where are the boys that can court them like the

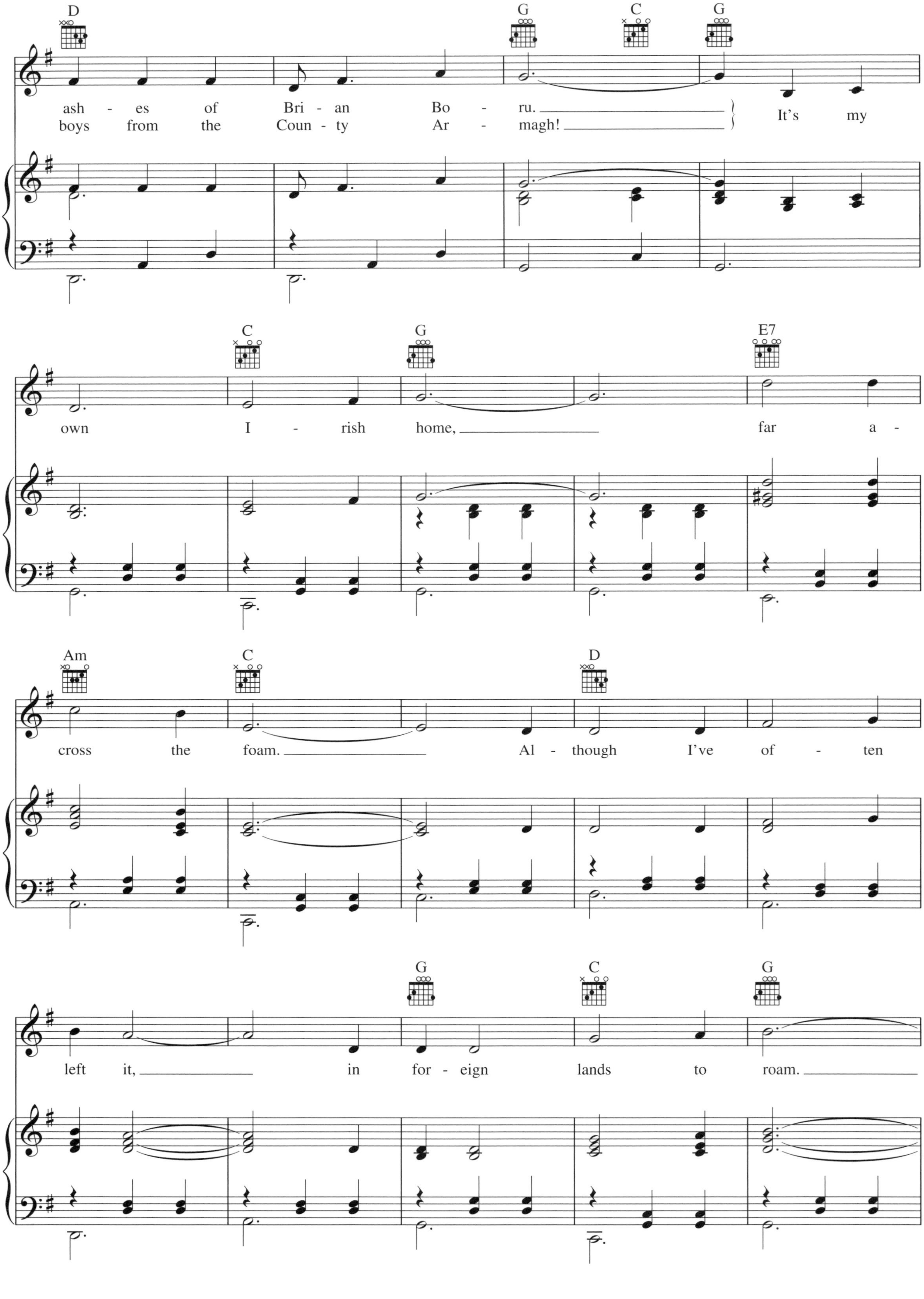
D G C G
ash - es of Bri - an Bo - ru.
boys from the Coun - ty Ar - magh!
It's my
C G E7
own I - rish home, far a -
Am C D
cross the foam. Al - though I've of - ten
G C G
left it, in for - eign lands to roam.

C
G
No matter where I wander through
E7
Am
C
G
cities near or far, sure my heart is at
C
Am
D
home in old Ireland, in the county
1
G
2
G
of Armagh. I've magh.

BRENNAN ON THE MOOR

Traditional Irish Folk Song

Moderately
F
C
F
mf
C
F
1. It's a - bout a fierce high - way - man my sto - ry I will
2. up - on the King's high - way Old Bren - nan he sat
3. Bren - nan's wife had gone to town pro - vi - sions for to
4.-6. (See additional lyrics)
C
F
Am
tell. His name was Wil - ly Bren - nan and in Ire - land he did
down. He met the may - or of Moor - land five miles out - side of
buy, and when she saw her Wil - ly tak - en she be - gan to
C
F
Am
C
dwell. 'Twas up - on the King's own moun - tain he be - gan his wild ca - reer, and
town. Now the may - or, he had heard of Bren - nan and, "I think," says he, "Your
cry. Says he, "Hand me that ten - pen - ny," and as soon as Wil - ly spoke, she

Copyright © 2006 by HAL LEONARD CORPORATION
International Copyright Secured All Rights Reserved

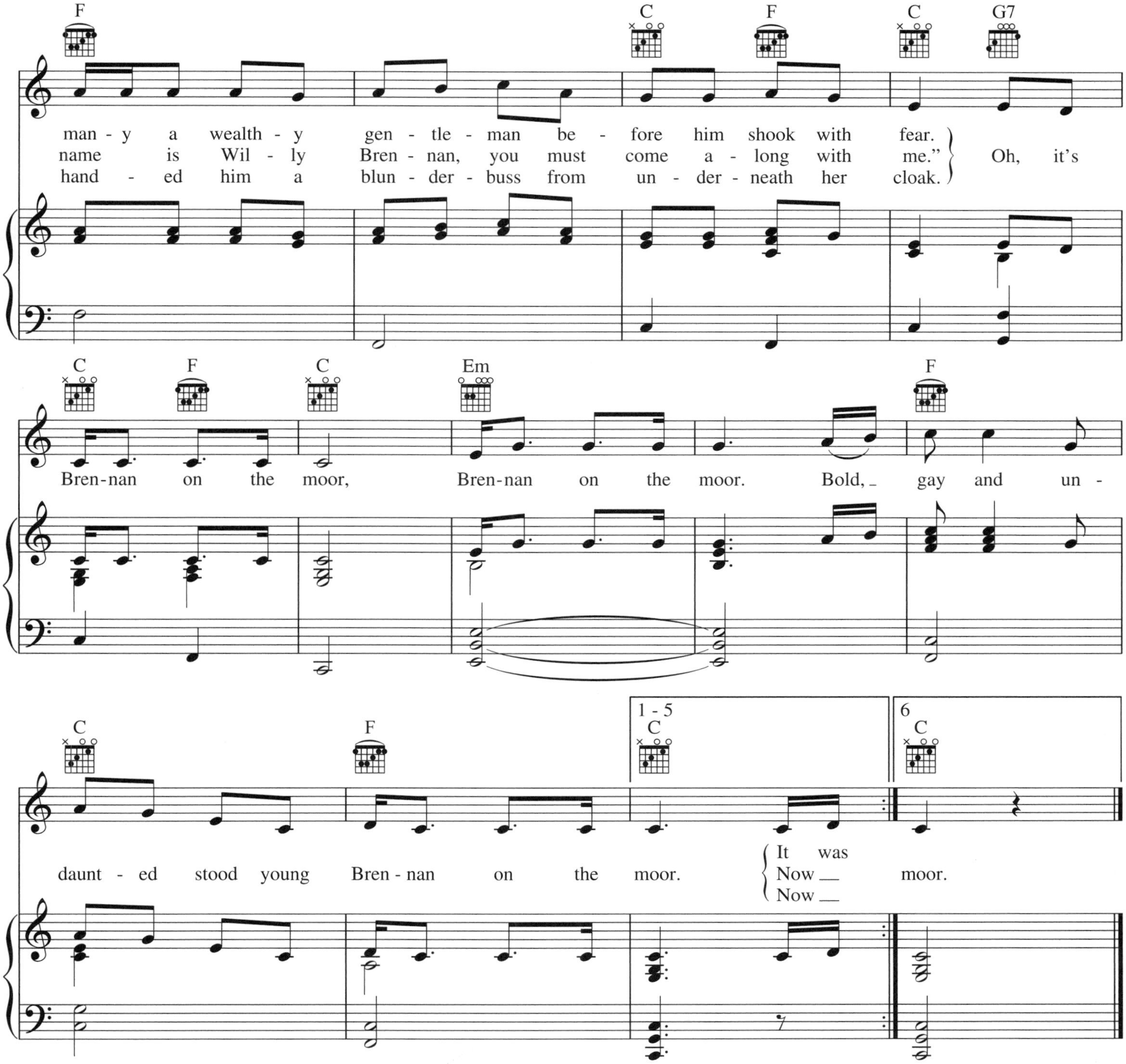
F C F C G7
man - y a wealth - y gen - tle - man be - fore him shook with fear.
name is Wil - ly Bren - nan, you must come a - long with me."
hand - ed him a blun - der - buss from un - der - neath her cloak.
Oh, it's
C F C Em F
Bren - nan on the moor, Bren - nan on the moor. Bold, gay and un -
C F
daunt - ed stood young Bren - nan on the moor.
1 - 5
C
It was
Now
Now
6
C
moor.

Additional Lyrics

4. Now Brennan got his blunderbuss, my story I'll unfold.
   He caused the mayor to tremble and deliver up his gold.
   Five thousand pounds were offered for his apprehension there,
   But Brennan and the peddler to the mountain did repair.
   Oh, it's Brennan on the moor, Brennan on the moor.
   Bold, gay and undaunted stood young Brennan on the moor.

5. Now Brennan is an outlaw all on some mountain high.
   With infantry and cavalry to take him they did try.
   But he laughed at them and he scorned at them until, it was said,
   By a false-hearted woman he was cruelly betrayed.
   Oh, it's Brennan on the moor, Brennan on the moor.
   Bold, gay and undaunted stood young Brennan on the moor.

6. They hung him at the crossroads; in chains he swung and died.
   But still they say that in the night some do see him ride.
   They see him with his blunderbuss in the midnight chill;
   Along, along the king's highway rides Willy Brennan still.
   Oh, it's Brennan on the moor, Brennan on the moor.
   Bold, gay and undaunted stood young Brennan on the moor.

A BUNCH OF THYME

Traditional Irish Folk Song

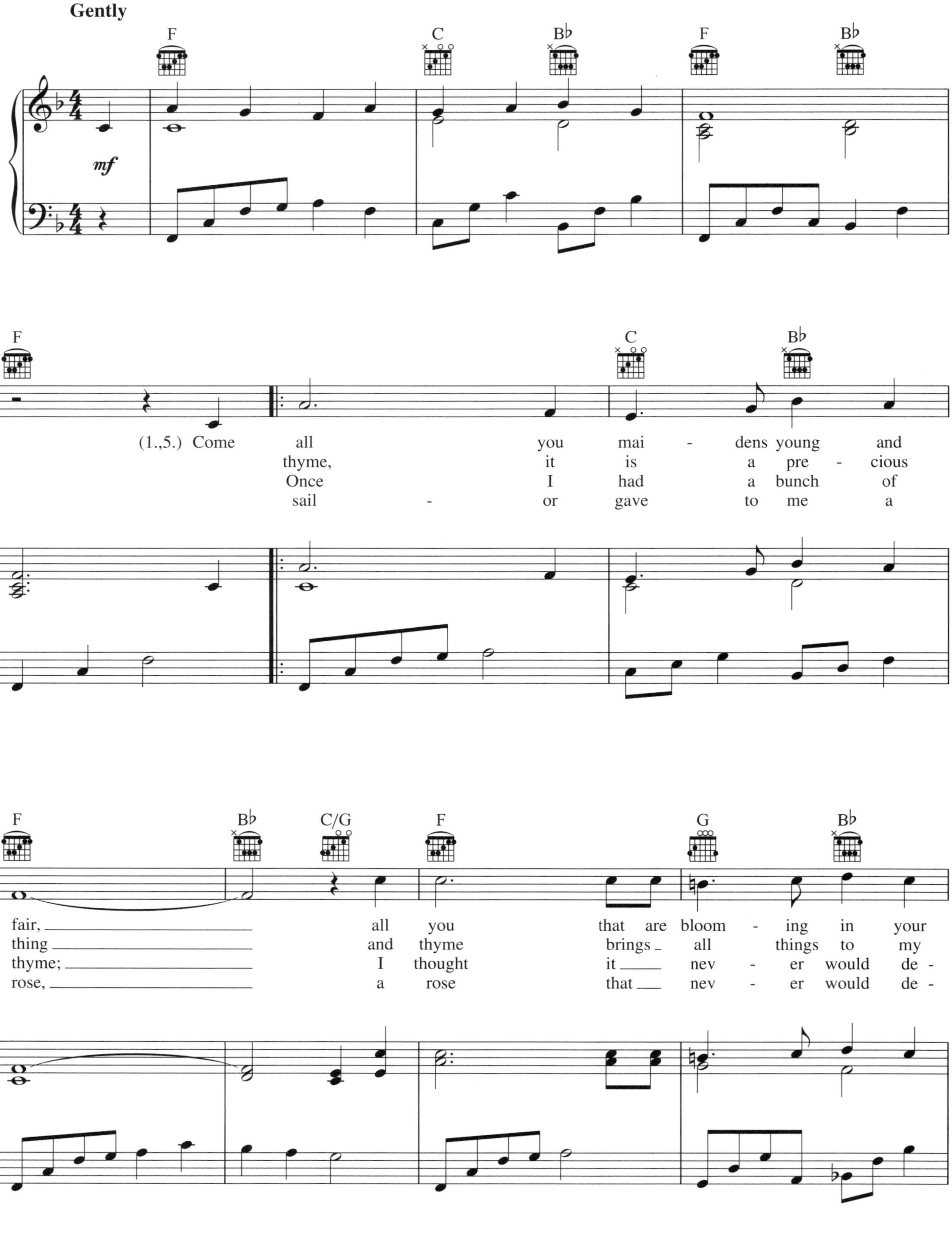
Gently
F C B♭ F B♭
mf
F C B♭
(1.,5.) Come all you mai - dens young and
thyme, it is a pre - cious
Once I had a bunch of
sail - or gave to me a
F B♭ C/G F G B♭
fair, all you that are bloom - ing in your
thing and thyme brings all things to my
thyme; I thought it nev - er would de -
rose, a rose that nev - er would de -

Copyright © 2006 by HAL LEONARD CORPORATION
International Copyright Secured All Rights Reserved

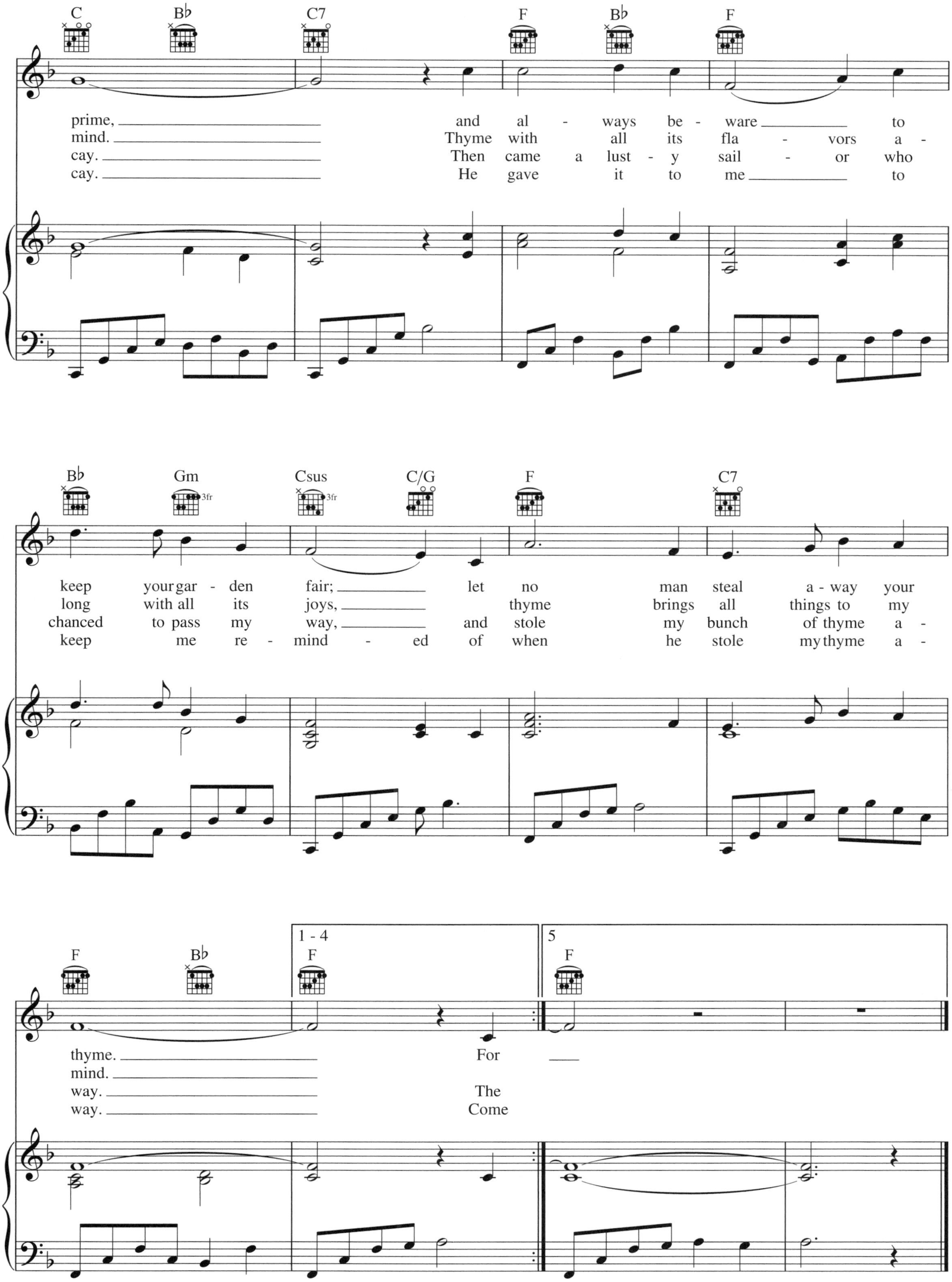

C Bb C7 F Bb F
prime, and always beware to
mind. Thyme with all its flavors a-
cay. Then came a lusty sailor who
cay. He gave it to me to
Bb Gm Csus C/G F C7
keep your garden fair; let no man steal away your
long with all its joys, thyme brings all things to my
chanced to pass my way, and stole my bunch of thyme a-
keep me reminded of when he stole my thyme a-
F Bb 1 - 4 F 5 F
3fr
thyme. For
mind.
way. The
way. Come

BUTCHER BOY

Traditional Irish Folk Song

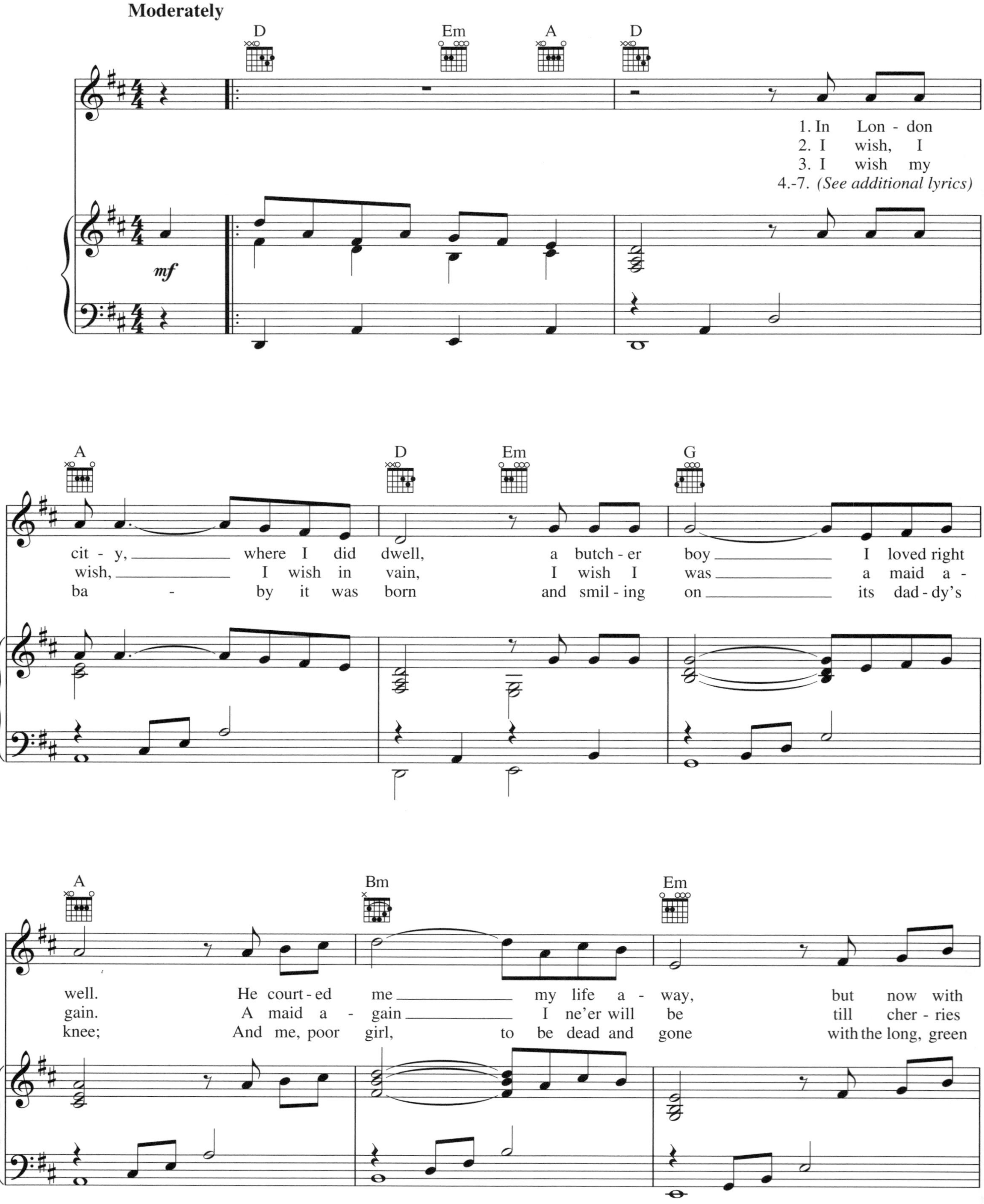
Moderately
D Em A D
1. In London
2. I wish, I
3. I wish my
4.-7. (See additional lyrics)
mf
A D Em G
city, where I did dwell, a butcher boy I loved right
wish, I wish in vain, I wish I was a maid a-
baby it was born and smiling on its daddy's
A Bm Em
well. He courted me my life away, but now with
gain. A maid again I ne'er will be till cherries
knee; And me, poor girl, to be dead and gone with the long, green

Copyright © 2006 by HAL LEONARD CORPORATION
International Copyright Secured All Rights Reserved

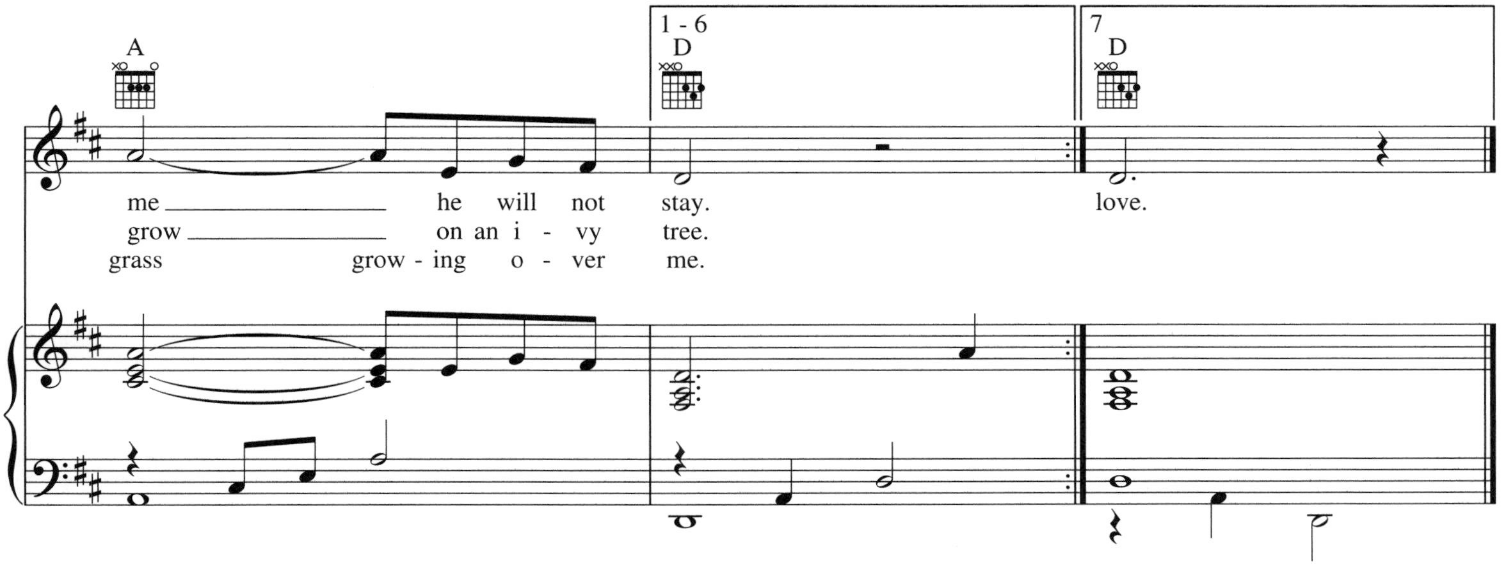
A
1 - 6
D
7
D
me he will not stay.
grow on an i - vy tree.
grass grow - ing o - ver me.
love.

Additional Lyrics

4. She went upstairs to go to bed,
And calling to her mother said,
"Give me a chair till I sit down
And a pen and ink till I write down."

5. At ev'ry word she dropped a tear,
At ev'ry line cried, "Willie, dear,
Oh, what a foolish girl was I
To be led astray by a butcher boy."

6. He went upstairs and the door he broke;
He found her hanging from a rope.
He took his knife and he cut her down,
And in her pocket these words he found:

7. "Oh, make my grave large, wide and deep;
Put a marble stone at my head and feet.
And in the middle a turtledove,
That the world may know that I died for love."

CARRICKFERGUS

Traditional Irish Folk Song

Moderately
D
E7
A
mf
D
E7
I wish I was in Car - rick -
ken - ny it is re -
A
F♯m
Bm
fer - gus, on - ly for nights
port - ed, they've mar - ble stones
E
A
A/C♯
in Bal - ly - grant. I would swim
as black as ink. With gold and

Copyright © 2003 by HAL LEONARD CORPORATION
International Copyright Secured All Rights Reserved

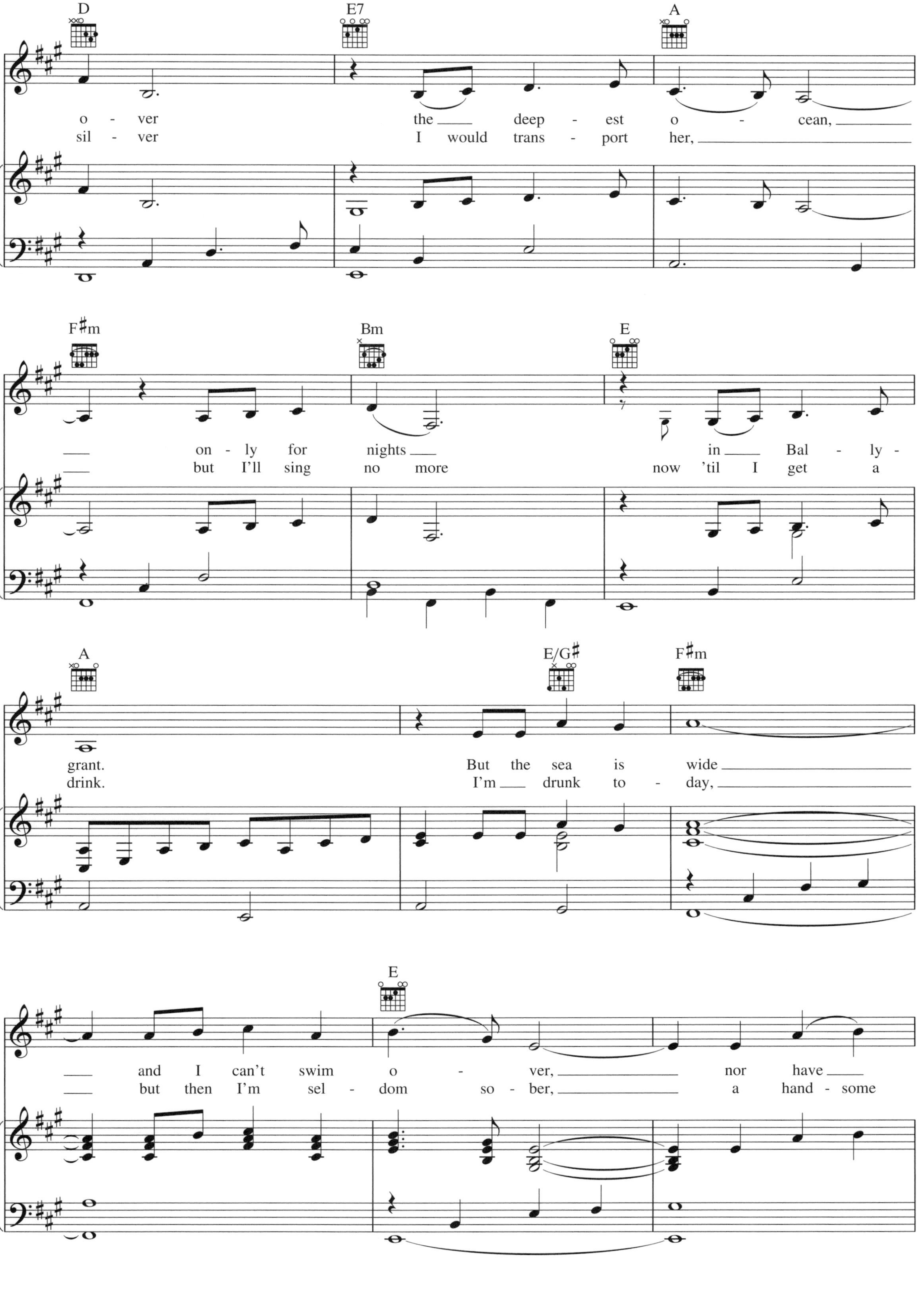
D
E7
A
o - ver the deep - est o - cean,
sil - ver I would trans - port her,
F♯m
Bm
E
on - ly for nights in Bal - ly -
but I'll sing no more now 'til I get a
A
E/G♯
F♯m
grant. But the sea is wide
drink. I'm drunk to - day,
E
and I can't swim o - ver, nor have
but then I'm sel - dom so - ber, a hand - some

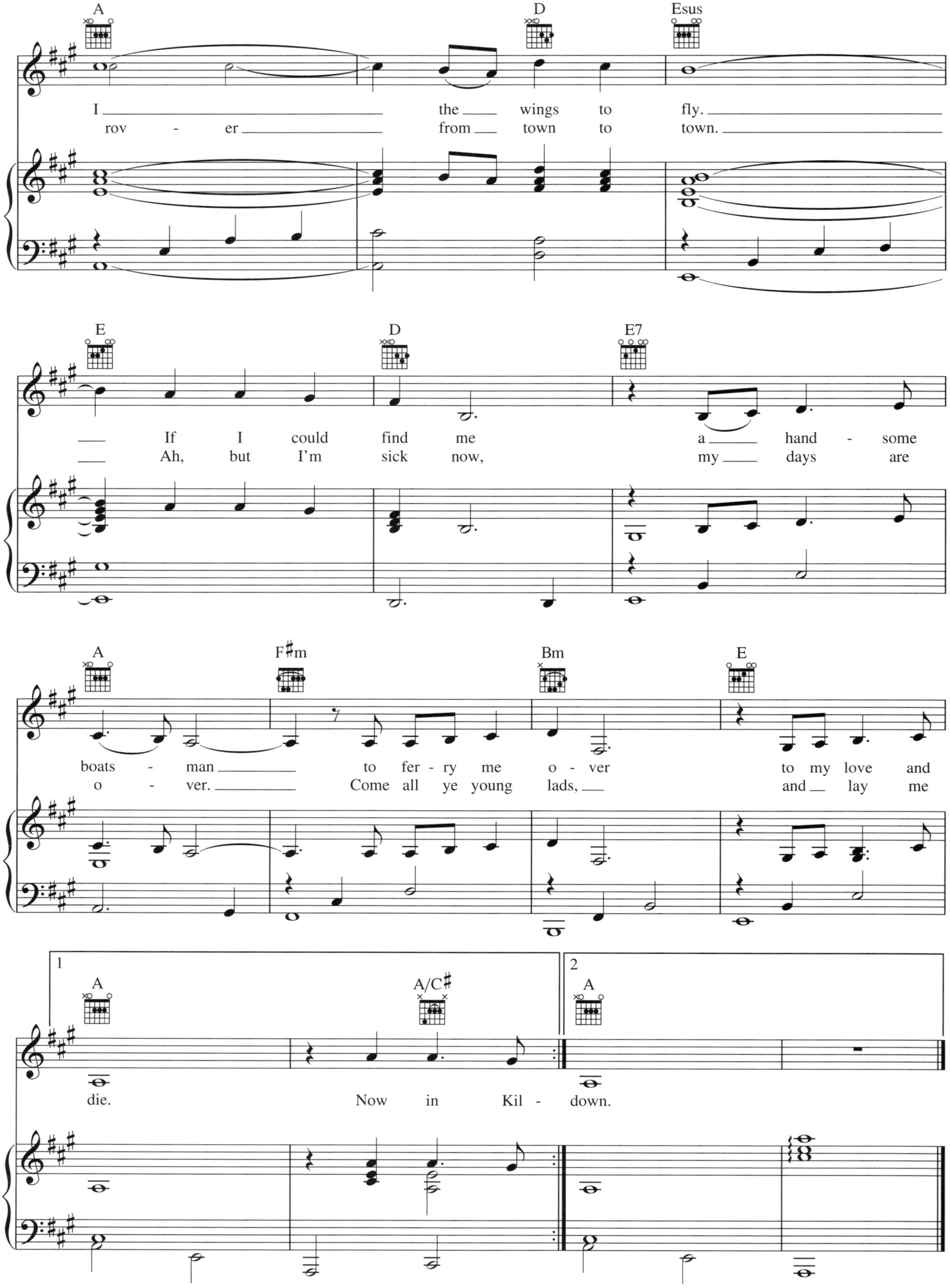
A
D
Esus
I the wings to fly.
rov - er from town to town.
E
D
E7
If I could find me a hand - some
Ah, but I'm sick now, my days are
A
F♯m
Bm
E
boats - man to fer - ry me o - ver to my love and
o - ver. Come all ye young lads, and lay me
1
A
A/C♯
die. Now in Kil -
2
A
down.

CLIFFS OF DONEEN

Traditional Irish Folk Song

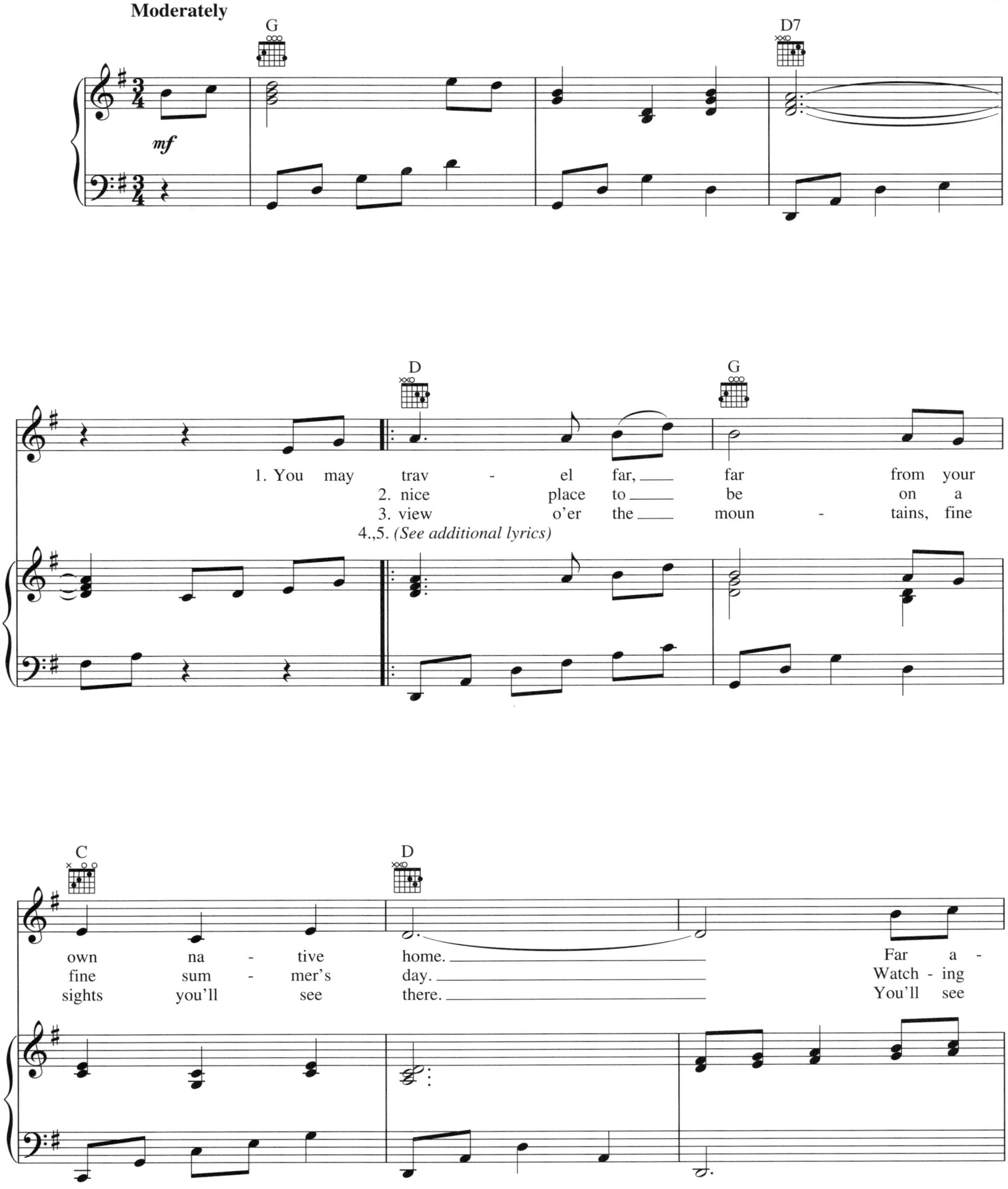
Moderately
G
D7
mf
D
G
1. You may trav - el far, far from your
2. nice place to be on a
3. view o'er the moun - tains, fine
4.,5. (See additional lyrics)
C
D
own na - tive home. Far a -
fine sum - mer's day. Watch - ing
sights you'll see there. You'll see

Copyright © 2006 by HAL LEONARD CORPORATION
International Copyright Secured All Rights Reserved

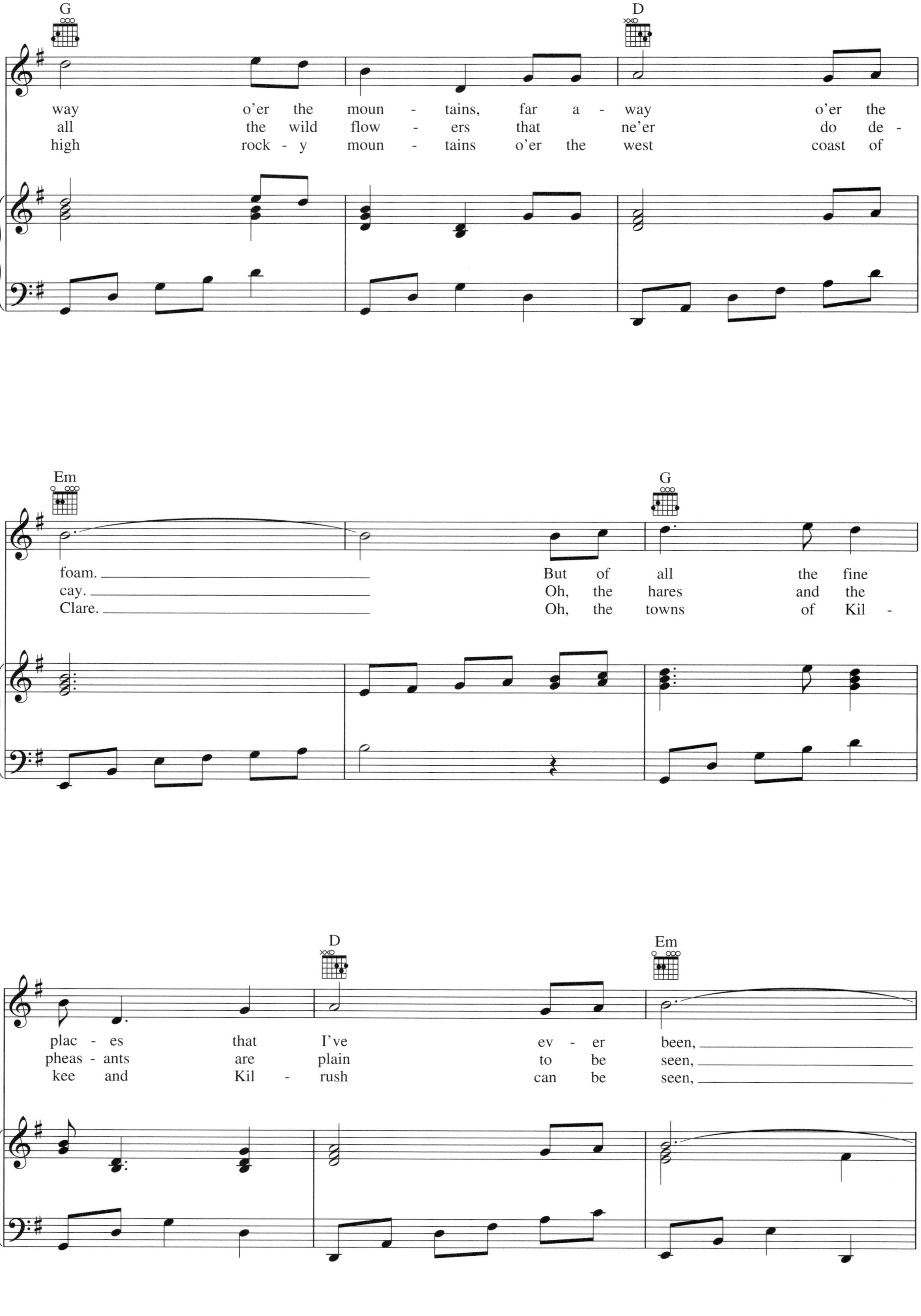
G
D
way o'er the moun - tains, far a - way o'er the
all the wild flow - ers that ne'er do de -
high rock - y moun - tains o'er the west coast of
Em
G
foam. But of all the fine
cay. Oh, the hares and the
Clare. Oh, the towns of Kil -
D
Em
plac - es that I've ev - er been,
pheas - ants are plain to be seen,
kee and Kil - rush can be seen,

C
G
sure there's none to com - pare with the
mak - ing homes for their young 'round the
from the high rock - y slopes 'round the
C
D7
1 - 4
cliffs of Don - een. It's a
cliffs of Don - een. Take a
cliffs of Don - een. Fare thee
5
G
rit.

Additional Lyrics

4. Fare thee well to Doneen, fare thee well for a while
   And to all the kind people I'm leaving behind.
   To the streams and the meadows where late I have been,
   And the high rocky slopes 'round the cliffs of Doneen.

5. Fare thee well to Doneen, fare thee well for a while.
   And although we are parted by the raging sea wild,
   Once again I will walk with my Irish colleen
   'Round the high rocky slopes of the cliffs of Doneen.

CASTLE OF DROMORE

Traditional Irish Folk Song

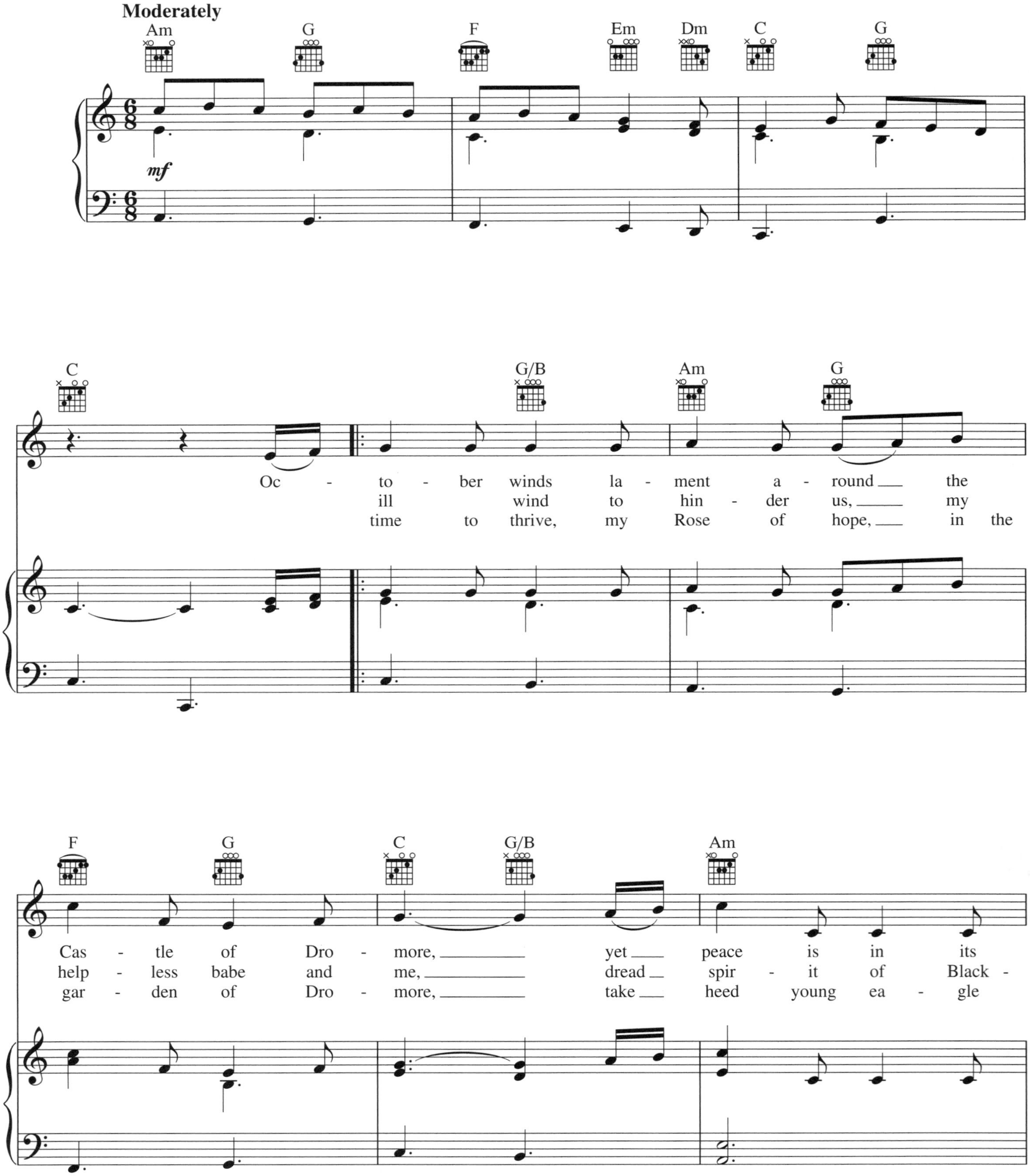
Moderately
Am G F Em Dm C G
mf
C G/B Am G
Oc - to - ber winds la - ment a - round the
ill wind to hin - der us, my
time to thrive, my Rose of hope, in the
F G C G/B Am
Cas - tle of Dro - more, yet peace is in its
help - less babe and me, dread spir - it of Black -
gar - den of Dro - more, take heed young ea - gle

Copyright © 2006 by HAL LEONARD CORPORATION
International Copyright Secured All Rights Reserved

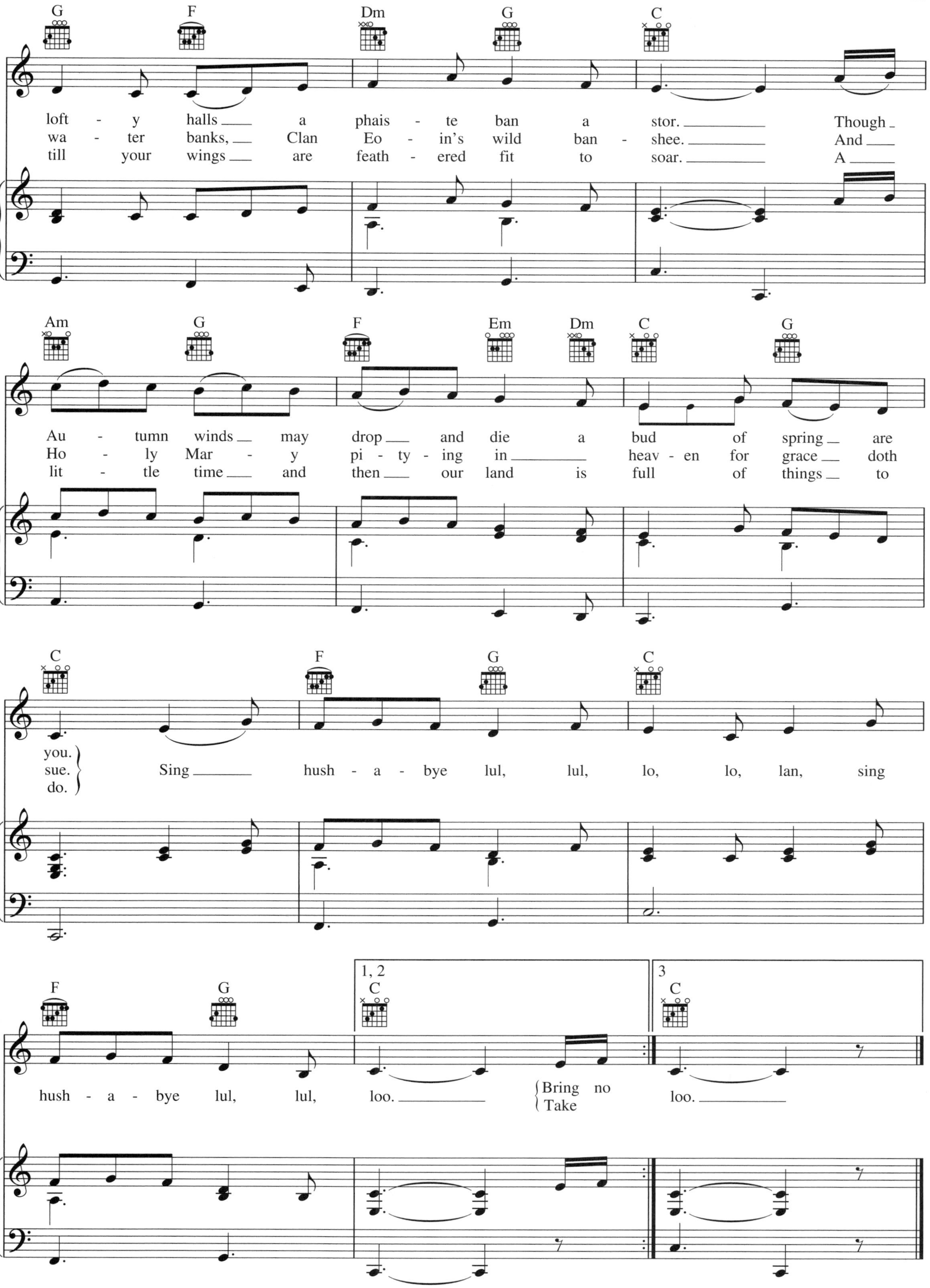
G F Dm G C
loft - y halls a phais - te ban a stor. Though
wa - ter banks, Clan Eo - in's wild ban - shee. And
till your wings are feath - ered fit to soar. A
Am G F Em Dm C G
Au - tumn winds may drop and die a bud of spring are
Ho - ly Mar - y pi - ty - ing in heav - en for grace doth
lit - tle time and then our land is full of things to
C F G C
you.
sue.
do.
Sing hush - a - bye lul, lul, lo, lo, lan, sing
F G
1, 2
C
3
C
hush - a - bye lul, lul, loo.
Bring no
Take
loo.

COCKLES AND MUSSELS
(Molly Malone)

Traditional Irish Folk Song

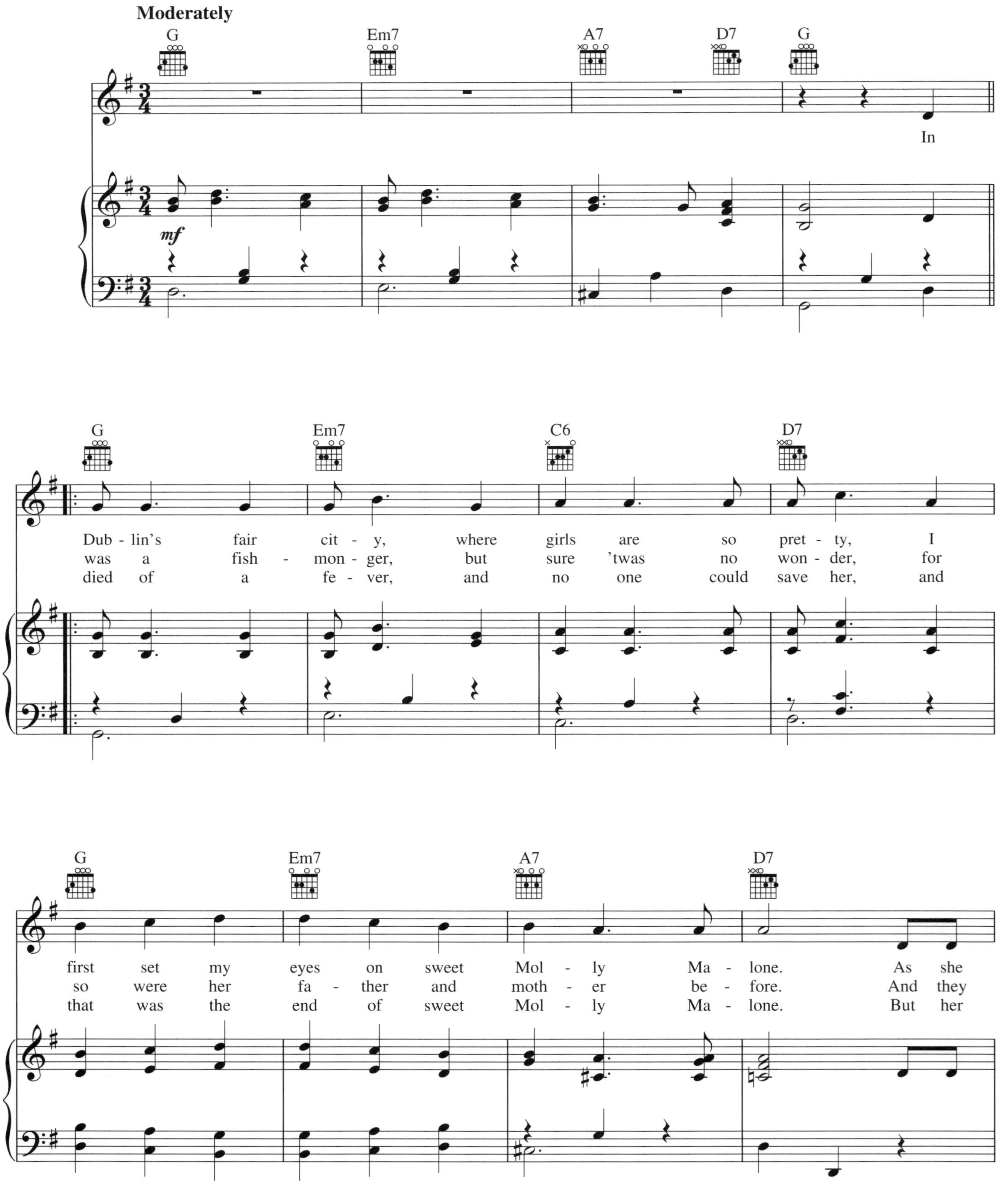
Moderately
G
Em7
A7
D7
G
In
mf
G
Em7
C6
D7
Dub - lin's fair cit - y, where girls are so pret - ty, I
was a fish - mon - ger, but sure 'twas no won - der, for
died of a fe - ver, and no one could save her, and
G
Em7
A7
D7
first set my eyes on sweet Mol - ly Ma - lone. As she
so were her fa - ther and moth - er be - fore. And they
that was the end of sweet Mol - ly Ma - lone. But her

Copyright © 2006 by HAL LEONARD CORPORATION
International Copyright Secured All Rights Reserved

G
G7/F
Am/E
Adim/E♭
pushed her wheel - bar - row thro' streets broad and nar - row cry - ing,
each wheeled their bar - row thro' streets broad and nar - row cry - ing,
ghost wheels her bar - row thro' streets broad and nar - row cry - ing,
G/D
Em7
A7
D7
G
"Cock - les and mus - sels, a - live, a - live, oh!
"Cock - les and mus - sels, a - live, a - live, oh!
"Cock - les and mus - sels, a - live, a - live, oh!
A -
G7/F
Am/E
Adim/E♭
G/D
live, a - live, oh! A - live, a - live, oh!" Cry - ing, "Cock - les and
Em7
A7
D7
1, 2
G
3
G
mus - sels, a - live, a - live, oh!"
She
She
oh!"

COME BACK TO ERIN

Traditional Irish Folk Song

Moderately
C Dm C/G G7 C C Cdim 3fr
mf
Come back to Er - in, Ma-
O - ver the green sea, Ma-
Oh may the an - gels, oh
G7 Cdim 3fr C F D7 G7
vour - neen, Ma-vour - neen. Come back, a-roon, to the land of my birth.
vour - neen, Ma-vour - neen, long shone the white sail that bore thee a-way.
wak - in' and sleep - in', watch o'er my bird in the land far a-way.
C Cdim 3fr G7 Cdim 3fr C Am D7
Come with the sham - rocks and spring - time, Ma-vour - neen, and its Kil-lar - ney shall
Rid - ing the white waves that fair sum-mer morn - in', just like a may - flow'r a-
And it's my prayers will con-sign to their keep - in' care o' my jew - el by

Copyright © 2003 by HAL LEONARD CORPORATION
International Copyright Secured All Rights Reserved

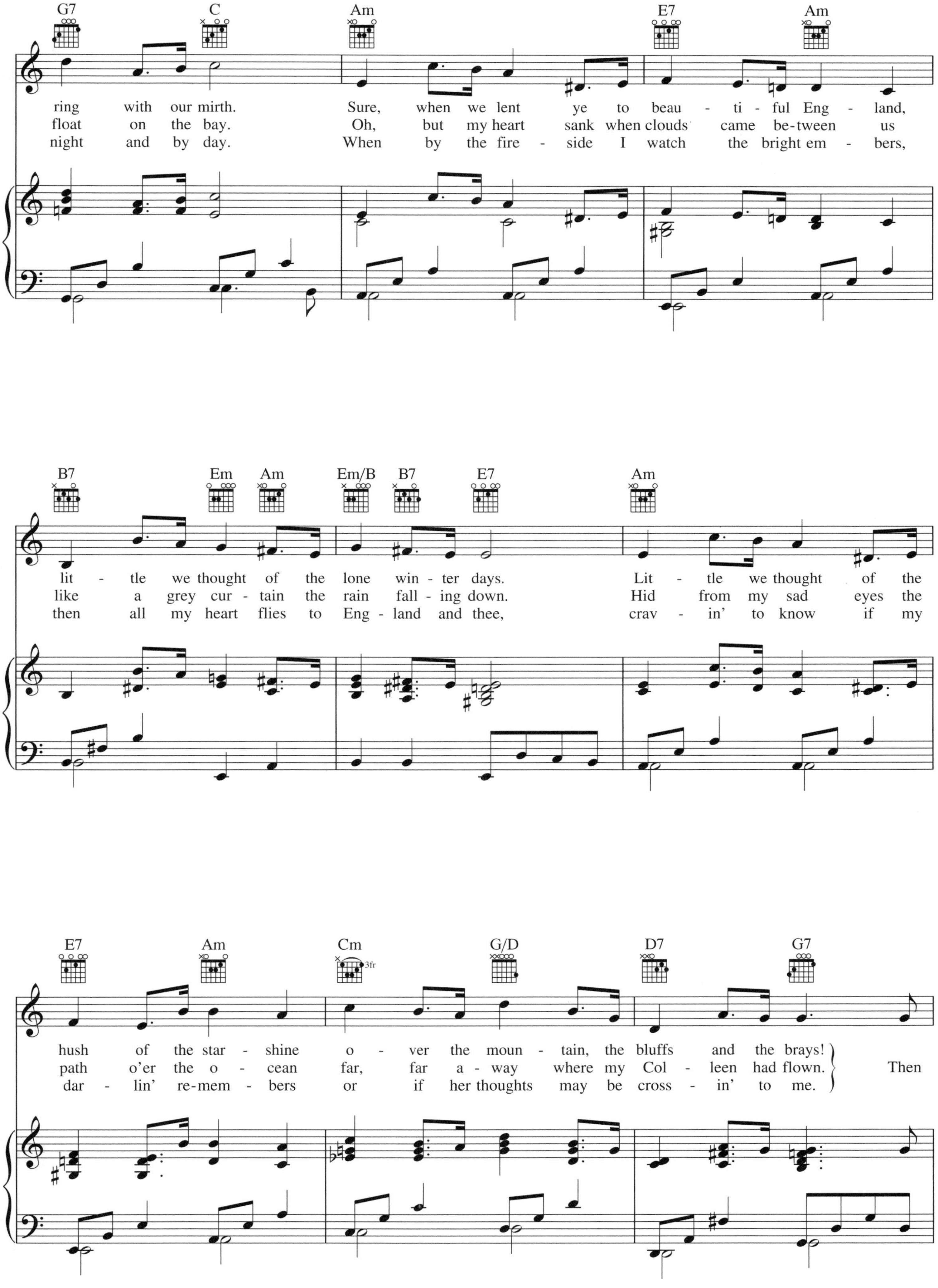
G7 C Am E7 Am
ring with our mirth. Sure, when we lent ye to beau - ti - ful Eng - land,
float on the bay. Oh, but my heart sank when clouds came be-tween us
night and by day. When by the fire - side I watch the bright em - bers,
B7 Em Am Em/B B7 E7 Am
lit - tle we thought of the lone win - ter days. Lit - tle we thought of the
like a grey cur - tain the rain fall - ing down. Hid from my sad eyes the
then all my heart flies to Eng - land and thee, crav - in' to know if my
E7 Am Cm 3fr G/D D7 G7
hush of the star - shine o - ver the moun - tain, the bluffs and the brays!
path o'er the o - cean far, far a - way where my Col - leen had flown.
dar - lin' re-mem - bers or if her thoughts may be cross - in' to me.
Then

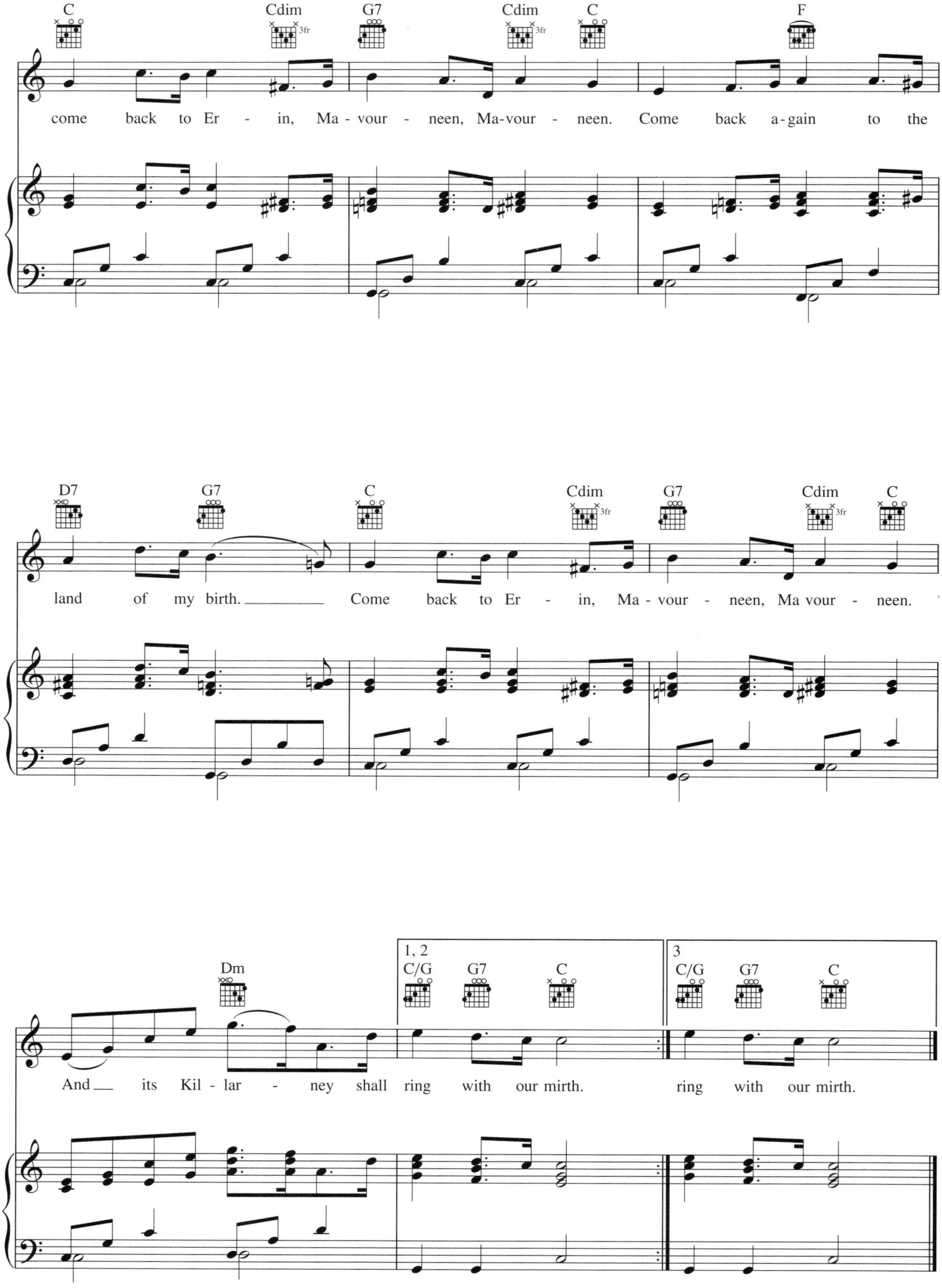
C Cdim G7 Cdim C F
3fr
come back to Er - in, Ma - vour - neen, Ma-vour - neen. Come back a-gain to the
D7 G7 C Cdim G7 Cdim C
land of my birth. Come back to Er - in, Ma - vour - neen, Ma vour - neen.
Dm
1, 2
C/G G7 C
3
C/G G7 C
And its Kil - lar - ney shall ring with our mirth. ring with our mirth.

EASY AND SLOW

Traditional Irish Folk Song

Gently
C
Em
G7
mf
C
Dm
'Twas down by Christ - church that I
long Thom - as Street,
cit - y or coun - ty the
if you should go to the
Am
Em
C
first met with An - nie. A neat lit - tle
down to the Lif - fey, the sun - shine was
girl she's a jew - el, and well made for
town of Dun - gan - non, you search till your
Am
Dm
G7
girl and not a bit shy.
gone and the eve - ning grew dark.
grip - ping the most of them are.
eyes they are wea - ry or blind.

Copyright © 2006 by HAL LEONARD CORPORATION
International Copyright Secured All Rights Reserved

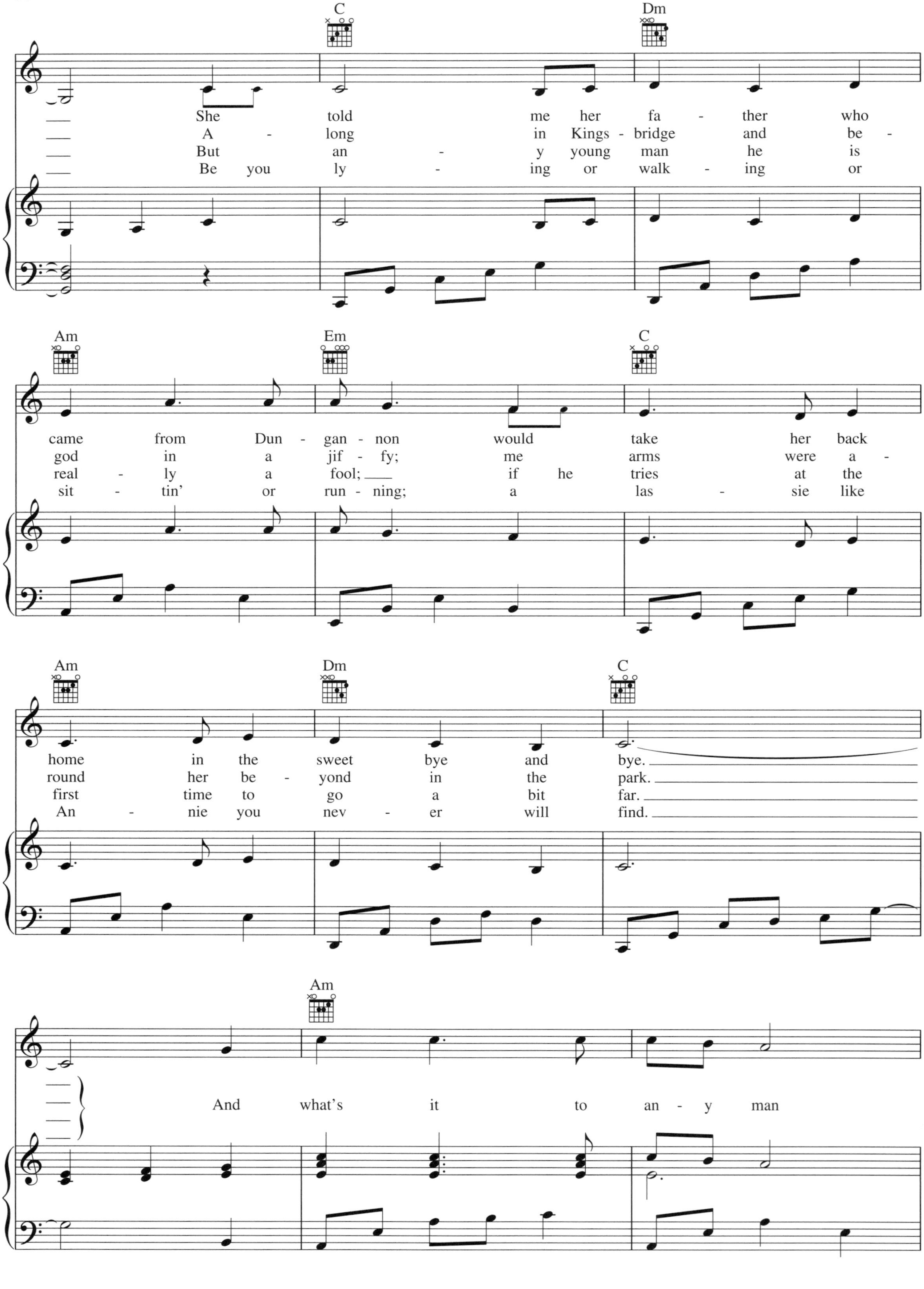
C
Dm
She told me her fa - ther who
A - long in Kings - bridge and be -
But an - y young man he is
Be you ly - ing or walk - ing or
Am
Em
C
came from Dun - gan - non would take her back
god in a jif - fy; me arms were a -
real - ly a fool; if he tries at the
sit - tin' or run - ning; a las - sie like
Am
Dm
C
home in the sweet bye and bye.
round her be - yond in the park.
first time to go a bit far.
An - nie you nev - er will find.
Am
And what's it to an - y man

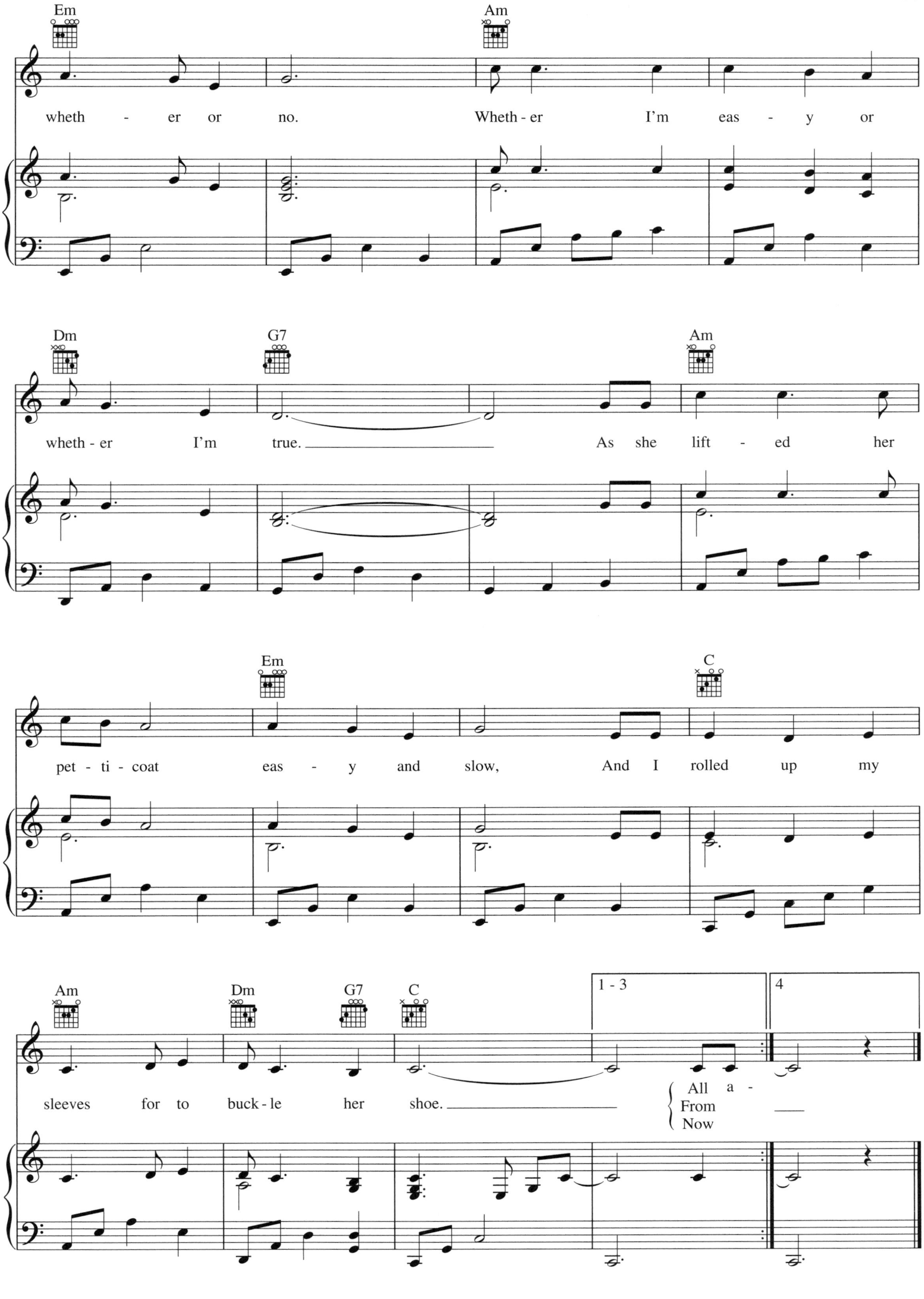
Em
Am
wheth - er or no. Wheth - er I'm eas - y or
Dm
G7
Am
wheth - er I'm true. As she lift - ed her
Em
C
pet - ti - coat eas - y and slow, And I rolled up my
Am
Dm
G7
C
1 - 3
4
sleeves for to buck - le her shoe.
All a -
From
Now

COME TO THE BOWER

Traditional Irish Folk Song

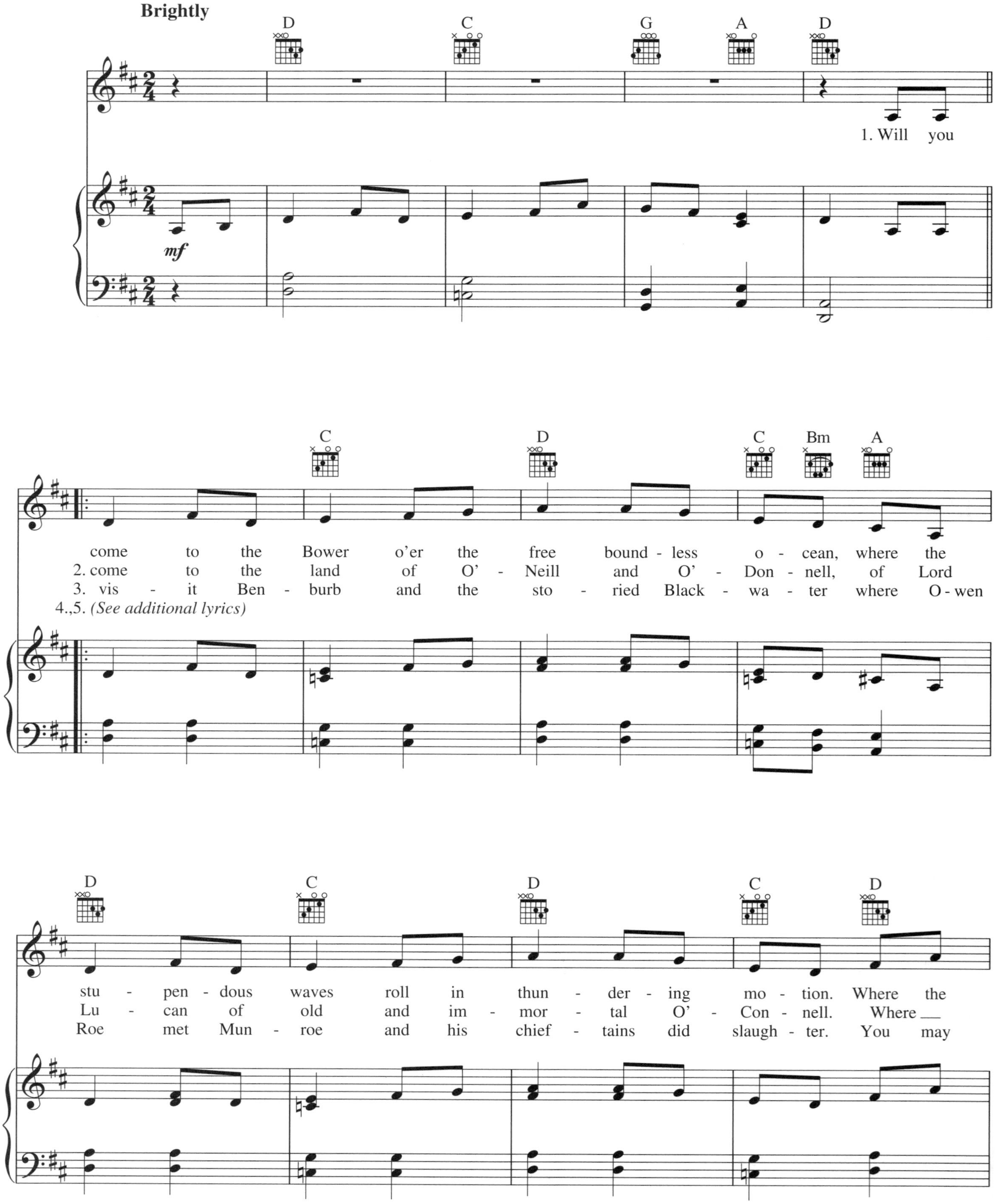
Brightly
D C G A D
mf
1. Will you
C D C Bm A
come to the Bower o'er the free bound - less o - cean, where the
2. come to the land of O' - Neill and O' - Don - nell, of Lord
3. vis - it Ben - burb and the sto - ried Black - wa - ter where O - wen
4.,5. (See additional lyrics)
D C D C D
stu - pen - dous waves roll in thun - der - ing mo - tion. Where the
Lu - can of old and im - mor - tal O' - Con - nell. Where
Roe met Mun - roe and his chief - tains did slaugh - ter. You may

Copyright © 2006 by HAL LEONARD CORPORATION
International Copyright Secured All Rights Reserved

Bm D G A Bm
mer - maids are seen and the fierce tem - pest gath - ers to love Er - in the
Bri - an drove the Danes and St. Pat - rick the ver - min and whose val - leys re -
ride on the tide o'er the broad ma - jes - tic Shan - non you may sail 'round Lough
Refrain
D A C Bm A
Green, the dear land of our fa - thers.
main still most beau - ti - ful and charm - ing.
Neagh and see sto - ried Dun - gan - non.
Will you come, will you,
G A G D
1 - 4
5
will you, will you come to the bow - er.
2. Will you
3. You can
4. You can
5. Will you

Additional Lyrics

4. You can visit New Ross, gallant Wexford and Gorey,
   Where the green was last seen by proud Saxon and Tory,
   Where the soil is sanctified by the blood of each true man,
   Where they died, satisfied, their enemies they would not run from.
   Refrain

5. Will you come and awake our lost land from its slumbers?
   And her fetters we will break; links that long are encumbered.
   And the air will resound with "Hosannas" to greet you
   On the shore will be found gallant Irishmen to meet you.
   Refrain

THE CROPPY BOY

18th Century Irish Folk Song

Moderately
D
C
G
mf
1. 'Twas ear - ly, ear - ly in the spring, the birds did whis - tle and sweet - ly sing,
2. ear - ly, ear - ly in the night, the yeo - man cav - al - ry gave me a fright.
3. in the guard - house where I was laid, and in the par - lor where I was tried.
4.-7. (See additional lyrics)
chang - ing their notes from
The yeo - man cav - al - ry
My sen - tence passed and my

Copyright © 2006 by HAL LEONARD CORPORATION
International Copyright Secured All Rights Reserved

D G/D G D
tree to tree, and the song they sang was
was my down - fall, and tak - en was I by
cour - age low, when to Dun - gan - non I
C
1 - 6
G
7
G
"Old Ire - land Free." 'Twas boy.
the Lord Corn - wall. 'Twas
was forced to go. As

Additional Lyrics

4. As I was passing my father's door, my brother William stood at the door.
   My aged father stood there also, my tender mother her hair she tore.

5. As I was going up Wexford Hill, who could blame me to cry my fill?
   I looked behind and I looked before, my aged mother I shall see no more.

6. As I was mounted on the scaffold high, my aged father was standing by.
   My aged father did me deny, and the name he gave me was the croppy boy.

7. 'Twas in the Dungannon this young man died, and in Dungannon his body lies.
   And you good people that do pass by, oh, shed a tear for the croppy boy.

THE CURRAGH OF KILDARE

Traditional Irish Folk Song

Moderately
A F#m Bm
mf
E A
1. The winter it is past and the summer's come at last and the small birds they sing on ev - 'ry tree; their
2. rose up - on the briar by the wa - ter run - ning clear, gives joy to the lin - net and the bee. Their
3. liv - er - y I'll wear, and I'll comb back my hair and in vel - vet so green I will ap - pear; and
4.-7. (See additional lyrics)
F#m D E
C#m Bm E
4fr

Copyright © 2006 by HAL LEONARD CORPORATION
International Copyright Secured All Rights Reserved

D
A
Bm
lit - tle hearts are glad but mine is ver - y
lit - tle hearts are blest but mine is not at
straight I will re - pair to the Cur - ragh of Kil -
E
A
Bm
sad, since my true love is far a - way from
rest, while my true love is ab - sent from
dare, for it's there I'll find tid - ings of my
E
1 - 6
7
me. The
me. A
dear. I'll

Additional Lyrics

4. I'll wear a cap of black, with a frill around my neck,
   Gold rings on my fingers I wear;
   It's this I undertake, for my true lover's sake,
   He resides at the Curragh of Kildare.

5. I would not think it strange, thus the world for to range,
   If I only got tiding of my dear;
   But here is Cupid's chain, if I'm bound to remain,
   I would spend my whole life in despair.

6. My love is like the sun, that in the firmament does run;
   And always proves constant and true;
   But his is like the moon, that wanders up and down,
   And ev'ry month is new.

7. All you that are in love, and cannot it remove.
   I pit the pains you endure;
   For experience let me know, that your hearts are full of woe,
   And a woe that no mortal can cure.

DANNY BOY
(Londonderry Air)

Words by FREDERICK EDWARD WEATHERLY
Traditional Irish Folk Melody

Slowly
C7 F/C G7♭9 Fm/G
mf
C N.C. C C7 F Fm
Oh, Dan - ny Boy, the pipes, the pipes are call - ing, from glen to
come, when all the flow'rs are dy - ing, and I am
C Am6 Fm6 G7 C C7
glen, and down the moun - tain side. The sum - mer's gone, and all the ros - es
dead, as dead I well may be, ye'll come and find the place where I am
F6 Fm C/G G7 C N.C.
fall - ing. It's you, it's you must go and I must bide. But come ye
ly - ing, and kneel and say an *A - ve* there for me; And I shall

Copyright © 1993 by HAL LEONARD CORPORATION
International Copyright Secured All Rights Reserved

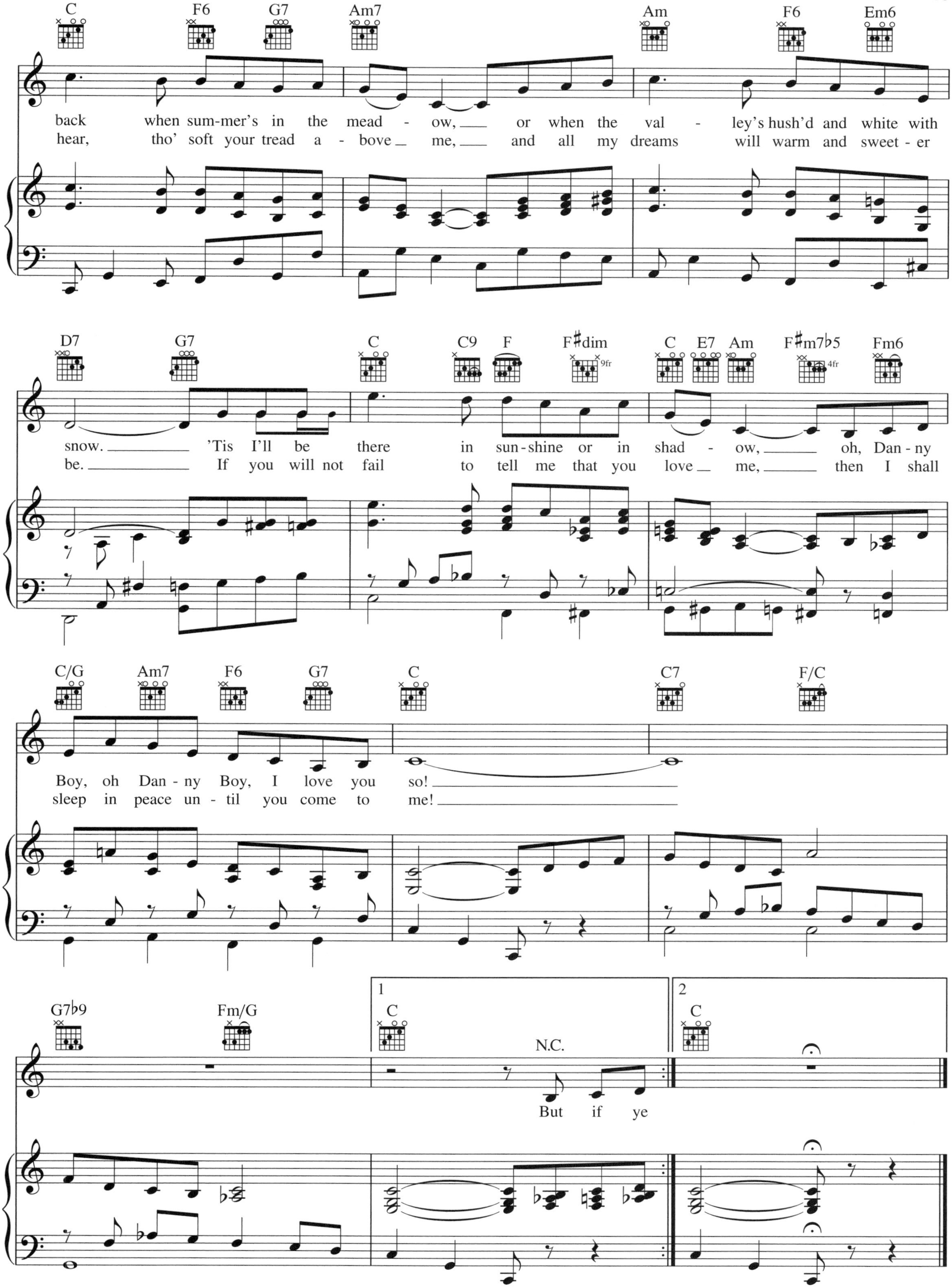
C F6 G7 Am7 Am F6 Em6
back when sum-mer's in the mead - ow, or when the val - ley's hush'd and white with
hear, tho' soft your tread a - bove me, and all my dreams will warm and sweet - er
D7 G7 C C9 F F♯dim C E7 Am F♯m7♭5 Fm6
9fr
4fr
snow. 'Tis I'll be there in sun-shine or in shad - ow, oh, Dan - ny
be. If you will not fail to tell me that you love me, then I shall
C/G Am7 F6 G7 C C7 F/C
Boy, oh Dan - ny Boy, I love you so!
sleep in peace un - til you come to me!
G7♭9 Fm/G
1
C
N.C.
But if ye
2
C

DICEY REILLY

Traditional Irish Folk Song

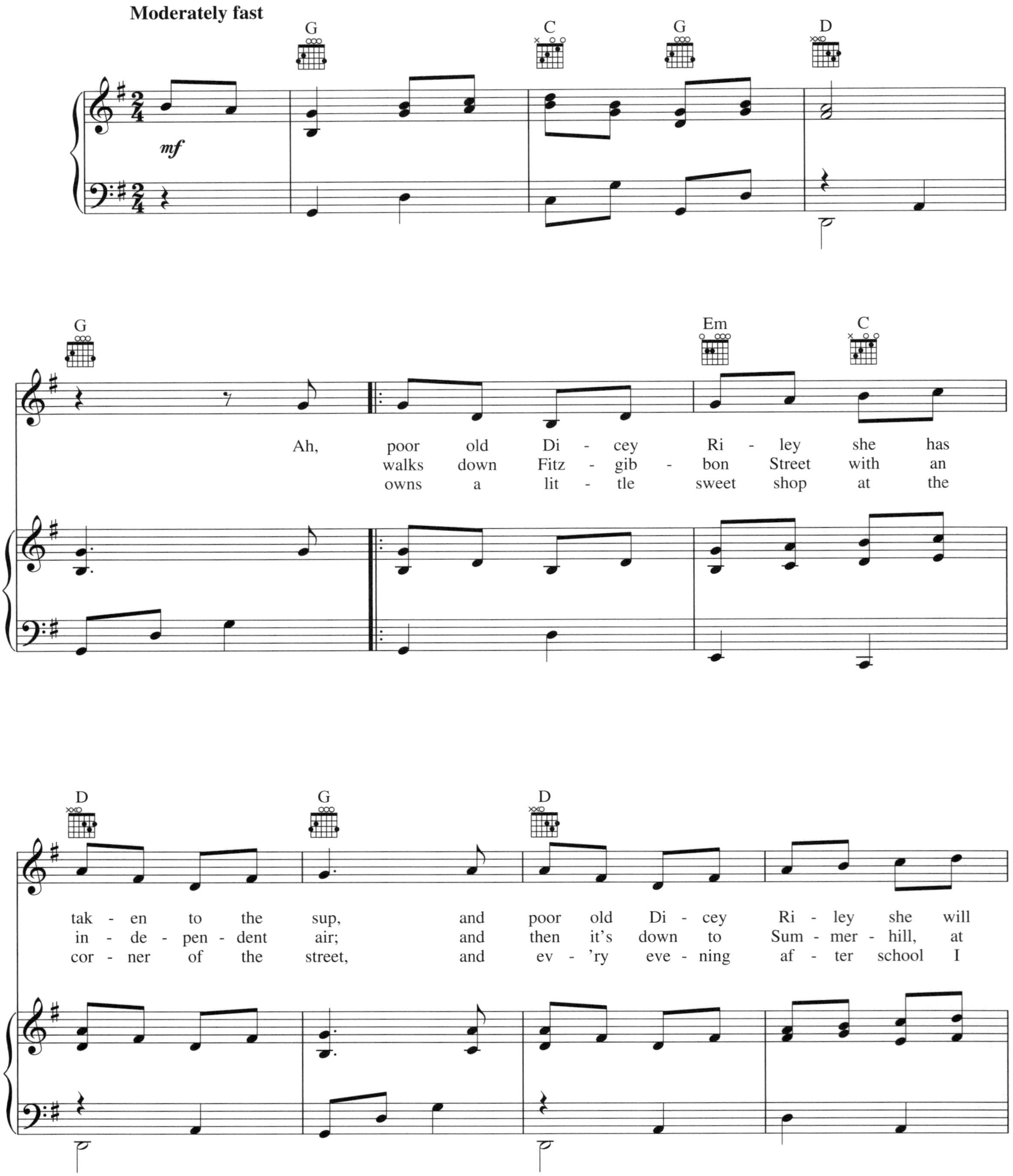
Moderately fast
mf
G C G D
G Em C
Ah, poor old Di - cey Ri - ley she has
walks down Fitz - gib - bon Street with an
owns a lit - tle sweet shop at the
D G D
tak - en to the sup, and poor old Di - cey Ri - ley she will
in - de - pen - dent air; and then it's down to Sum - mer - hill, at
cor - ner of the street, and ev - 'ry eve - ning af - ter school I

Copyright © 2006 by HAL LEONARD CORPORATION
International Copyright Secured All Rights Reserved

G B G C
nev - er give it up, it's off each morn - ing to the pop and
her the peo - ple stare. She says, "It's near - ly half past one, so I'll
go to wash her feet. She leaves me there to mind the shop, while she
D G C G
then she's in for an - oth - er lit - tle drop.
nip in for an - oth - er lit - tle one."
nips in for an - oth - er lit - tle drop.
Ah, the heart of the rowl is Di - cey
D
1, 2
G
3
G
Ri - ley. She She ley.

DO YOU WANT YOUR OLD LOBBY

Traditional Irish Folk Song

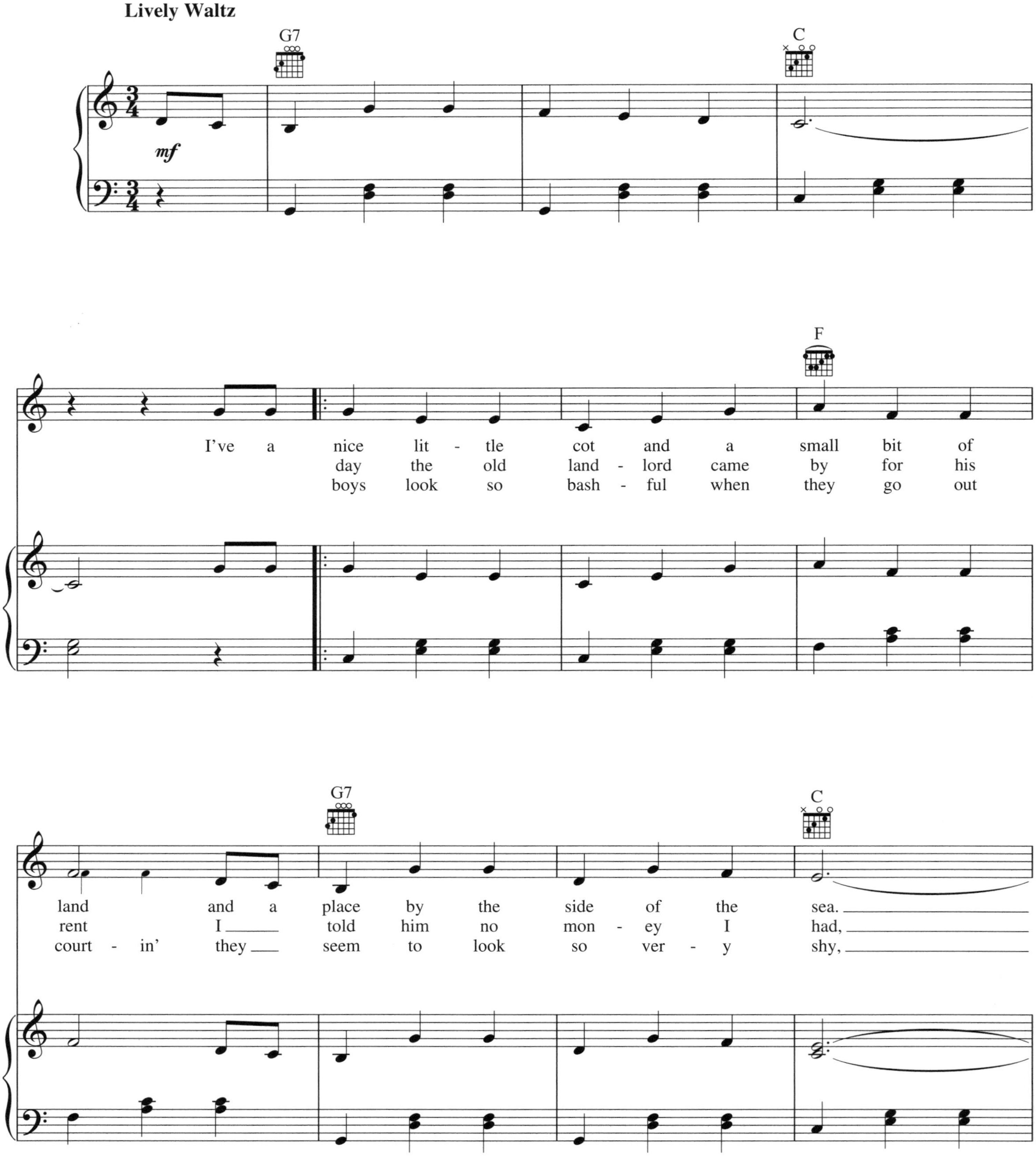
Lively Waltz
G7
C
mf
F
I've a nice lit - tle cot and a small bit of
day the old land - lord came by for his
boys look so bash - ful when they go out
G7
C
land and a place by the side of the sea.
rent I told him no mon - ey I had,
court - in' they seem to look so ver - y shy,

Copyright © 2006 by HAL LEONARD CORPORATION
International Copyright Secured All Rights Reserved

F
And I care a - bout no one, be - cause I be -
be - sides 'twas - n't fair to ask me to
as to kiss a young maid, sure they seem half a -
G7
C
lieve there's no - bod - y cares a - bout me.
pay, the times were so aw - ful - ly bad.
fraid, but they would if they could on the sly.
G7
C
My peace is de - stroyed and I'm fair - ly an -
He felt dis - con - tent at not get - ting his
But me I do things in a dif - fer - ent
D
G7
noyed, by a las - sie who works in the town.
rent, and he shook his big head in a frown,
way, I don't give a nod or a frown.

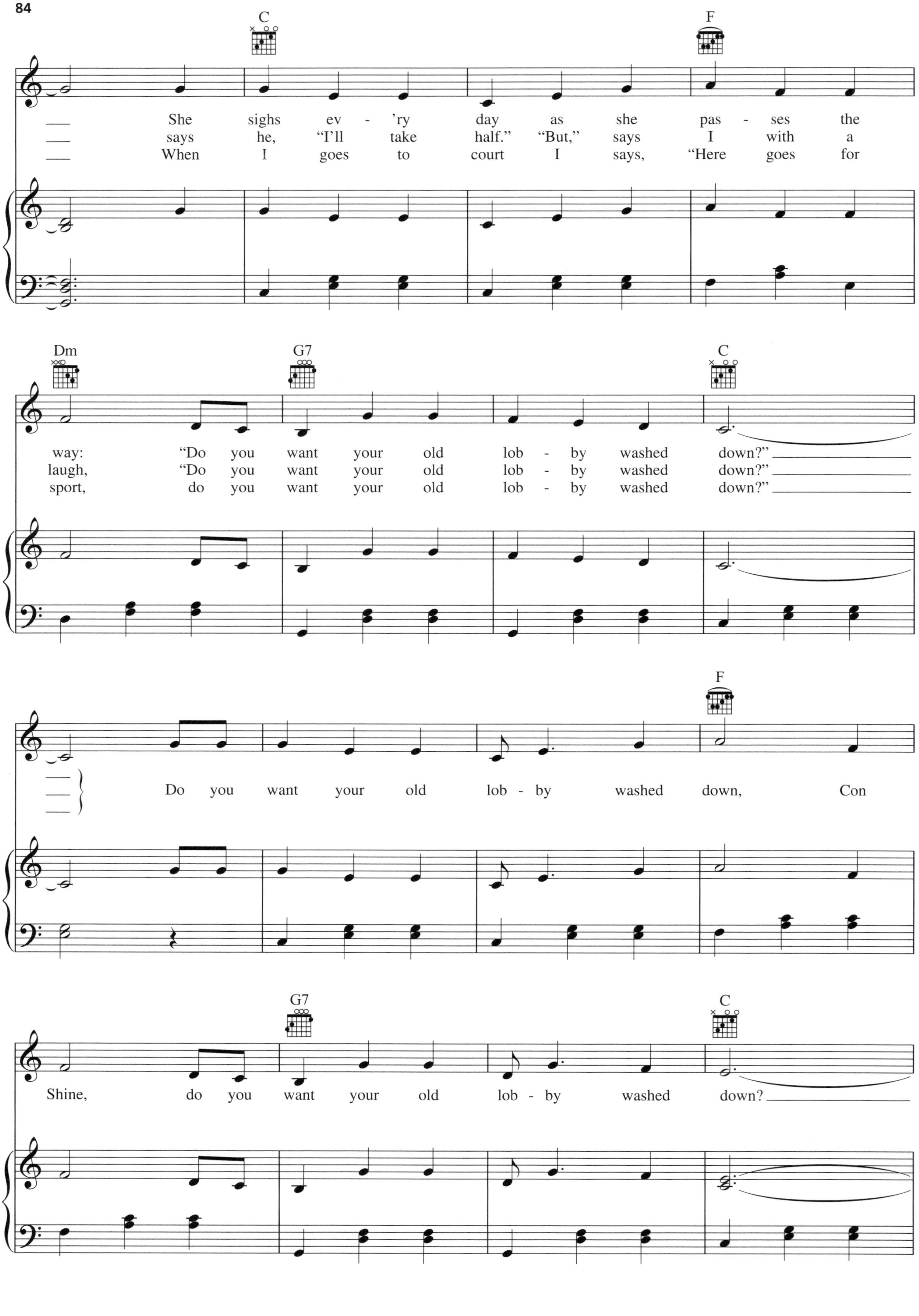
C
F
She sighs ev - 'ry day as she pas - ses the
says he, "I'll take half." "But," says I with a
When I goes to court I says, "Here goes for
Dm
G7
C
way: "Do you want your old lob - by washed down?"
laugh, "Do you want your old lob - by washed down?"
sport, do you want your old lob - by washed down?"
F
Do you want your old lob - by washed down, Con
G7
C
Shine, do you want your old lob - by washed down?

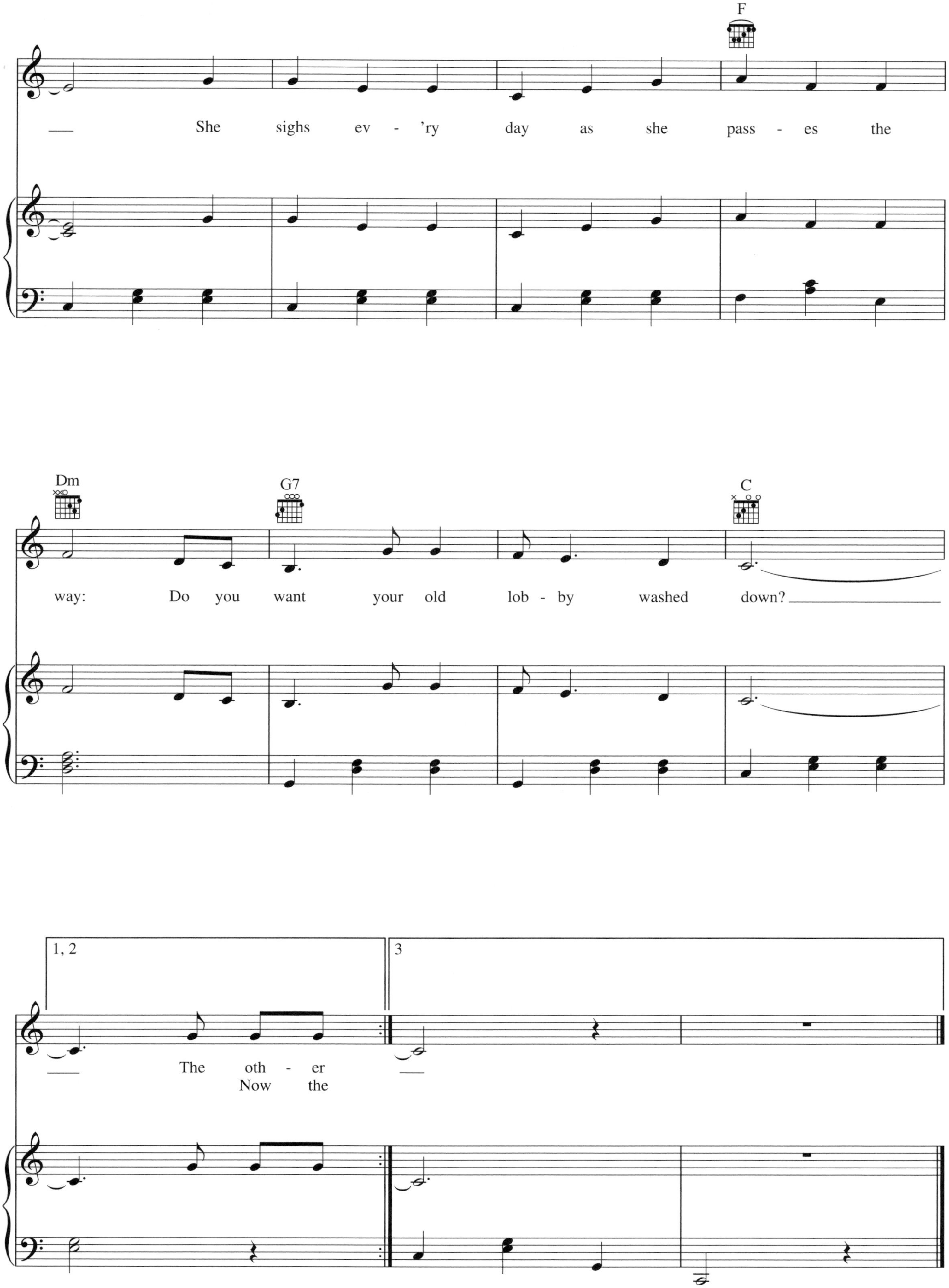
F
She sighs ev - 'ry day as she pass - es the
Dm
G7
C
way: Do you want your old lob - by washed down?
1, 2
3
The oth - er
Now the

DOWN BY THE SALLEY GARDENS

Traditional Irish Folk Song

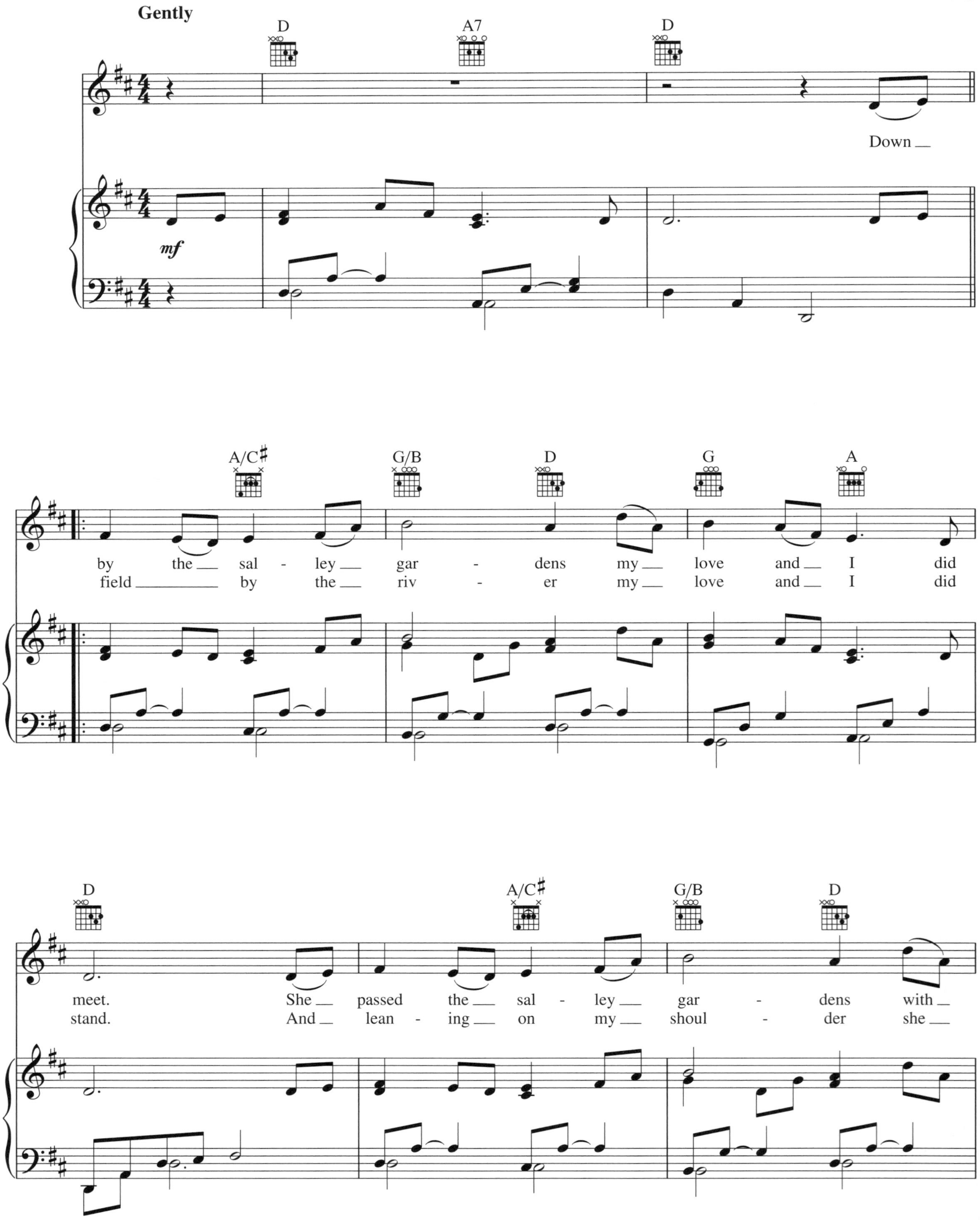
Gently
D A7 D
Down
mf
A/C♯ G/B D G A
by the sal - ley gar - dens my love and I did
field by the riv - er my love and I did
D A/C♯ G/B D
meet. She passed the sal - ley gar - dens with
stand. And lean - ing on my shoul - der she

Copyright © 2006 by HAL LEONARD CORPORATION
International Copyright Secured All Rights Reserved

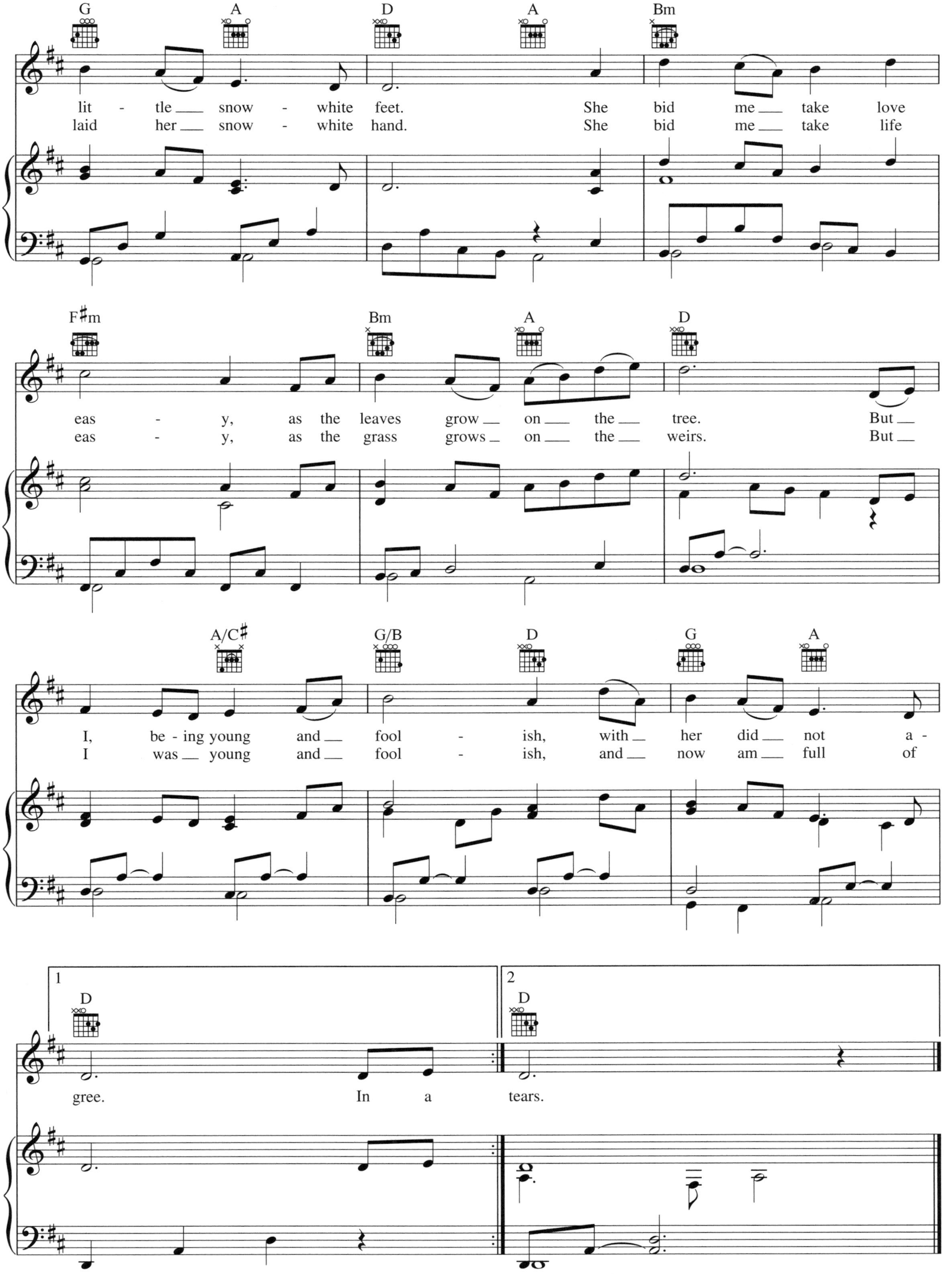
G A D A Bm
lit - tle snow - white feet. She bid me take love
laid her snow - white hand. She bid me take life
F♯m Bm A D
eas - y, as the leaves grow on the tree. But
eas - y, as the grass grows on the weirs. But
A/C♯ G/B D G A
I, be - ing young and fool - ish, with her did not a -
I was young and fool - ish, and now am full of
1 D 2 D
gree. In a tears.

THE ENNISKILLEN DRAGOON

Traditional Irish Folk Song

Lively
D
C
G
A
mf
D
A7
1. Fare thee well, En - nis - kil - len, fare thee
2. were all dressed out just like
3. bright sons of Mars as they
4.-7. (See additional lyrics)
D
Bm
A
G
well for a while. To all your fair wa - ters and
gen - tle - men's sons with their bright shin - ing swords and
stood to the right, their ar - mour did shine like the
C
A7
Bm
ev - 'ry green isle. Your green isle will
new car - bine guns. With their sil - ver mount - ed
bright stars at night. She says, "Love - ly

Copyright © 2006 by HAL LEONARD CORPORATION
International Copyright Secured All Rights Reserved

A G C A7 D
flour - ish and your fair wa - ters flow, while I from old
pis - tols she ob - served them full soon all be - cause that she
Wil - lie, you've en - list - ed too soon to serve as a
A7
1 - 6
D C A7
I - re - land an ex - ile must go.
loved her En - nis - kil - len Dra - goon.
Roy - al En - nis - kil - len Dra - goon.
D
7
D C A7 D
Oh they
The
"Oh
goon.

Additional Lyrics

4. "Oh beautiful Flora, your pardon I crave,
   From now and forever I will act as your slave.
   Your parents insult you both morning and noon
   For fear you should wed your Enniskillen Dragoon."

5. "Oh now, dearest Willie, you should mind what you say
   Until I'm of age my parents I must obey.
   But when you're leaving Ireland they will surely change their tune
   Saying, the Lord be he with you Enniskillen Dragoon."

6. Farewell Enniskillen, fare thee well for a while
   And all around the borders of Erin's green isle
   And when the wars are over I'll return in full bloom
   And they'll all welcome home their Enniskillen Dragoon.

7. Now the war is over, they've returned home at last.
   The regiment's in Dublin and Willie got a pass.
   Last Sunday they were married and bold Willie was the groom
   And now she enjoys her Enniskillen Dragoon.

FIDDLER'S GREEN

Traditional Irish Folk Song

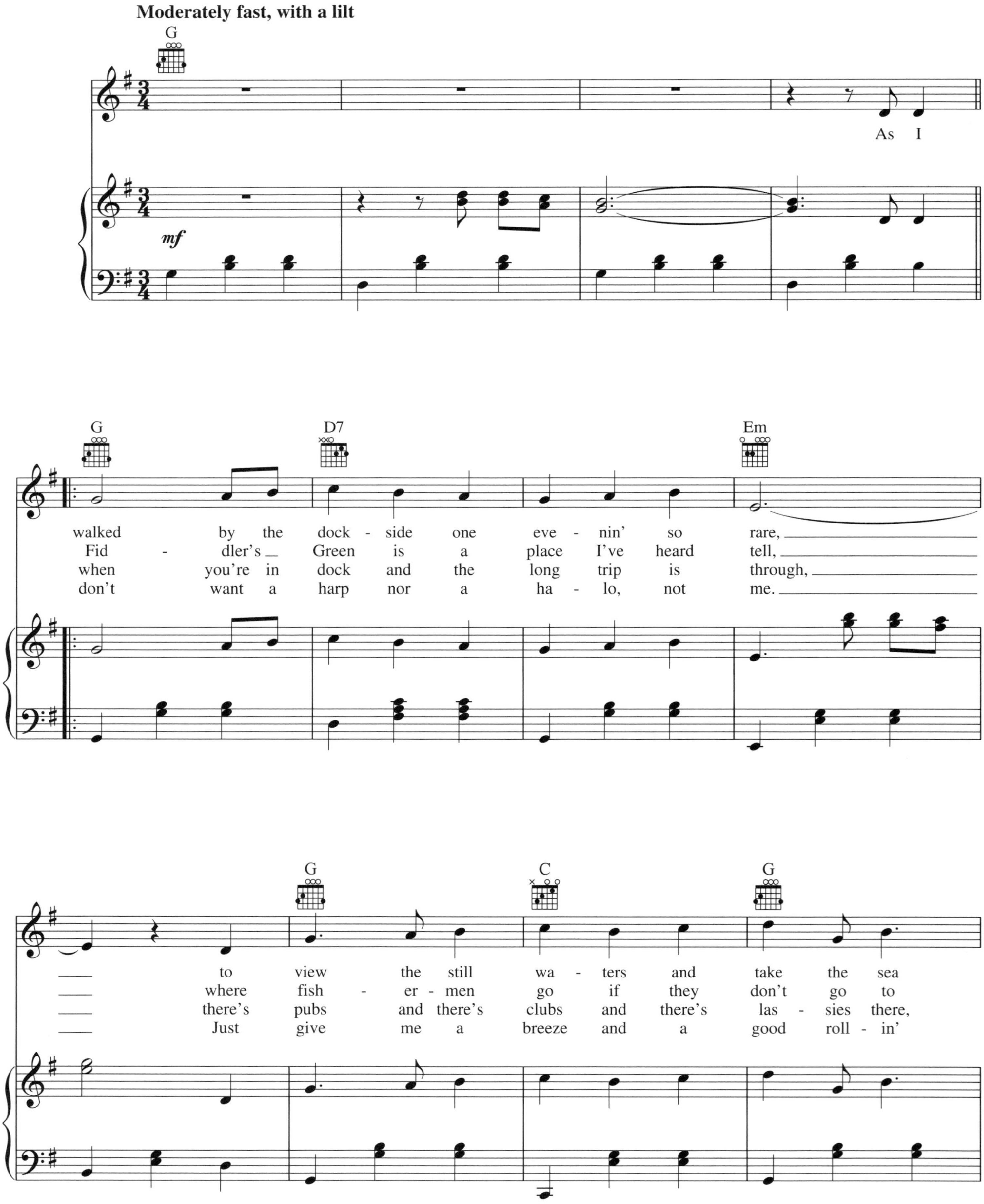
Moderately fast, with a lilt
G
mf
As I
G
D7
Em
walked by the dock - side one eve - nin' so rare,
Fid - dler's Green is a place I've heard tell,
when you're in dock and the long trip is through,
don't want a harp nor a ha - lo, not me.
G
C
G
to view the still wa - ters and take the sea
where fish - er - men go if they don't go to
there's pubs and there's clubs and there's las - sies there,
Just give me a breeze and a good roll - in'

Copyright © 2006 by HAL LEONARD CORPORATION
International Copyright Secured All Rights Reserved

D7
C
air. I spied an old fish - er - man
hell. The weath - er is fair and the
too. The girls are all pret - ty and the
sea. I'll play me old squeeze box as
G
sing - ing this song: Ah, take me a - way,
dol - phins do play, and the cold coast of Fin -
beer is all free, and there's bot - tles o' rum
we sail a - long, with the wind in the rig -
D7
G
D
boys, me time is not long.
- land is far, far a - way.
grow - in' on ev - 'ry tree.
- gin' a - sing - in' this song:
Wrap me
G
D7
G
up in me oil - skin and blan - kets; no

C G D7
more at the docks I'll be seen. Just
C G
tell me old ship - mates I'm tak - ing a trip, mates.
D7
1 - 3
G
I'll see ya some - day at Fid - dl - er's Green.
4
G
Now,
And
Now, I
Green.

FINNEGAN'S WAKE

Traditional Irish Folk Song

Moderately
N.C.
Em
Bm7
Em
Bm7
Em
Bm7
1. Tim Fin - ne - gan lived in
2. One morn - in' Tim was
3. His friends as - sem - bled
4.,5. (See additional lyrics)
Em
D
G
D
Walk - in' Street, a gen - tle I - rish - man, might - y odd. He
rath - er full; his head felt heav - y, which made him shake. He
at the wake, and Mis - sus Fin - ne - gan called for lunch.

Copyright © 2003 by HAL LEONARD CORPORATION
International Copyright Secured All Rights Reserved

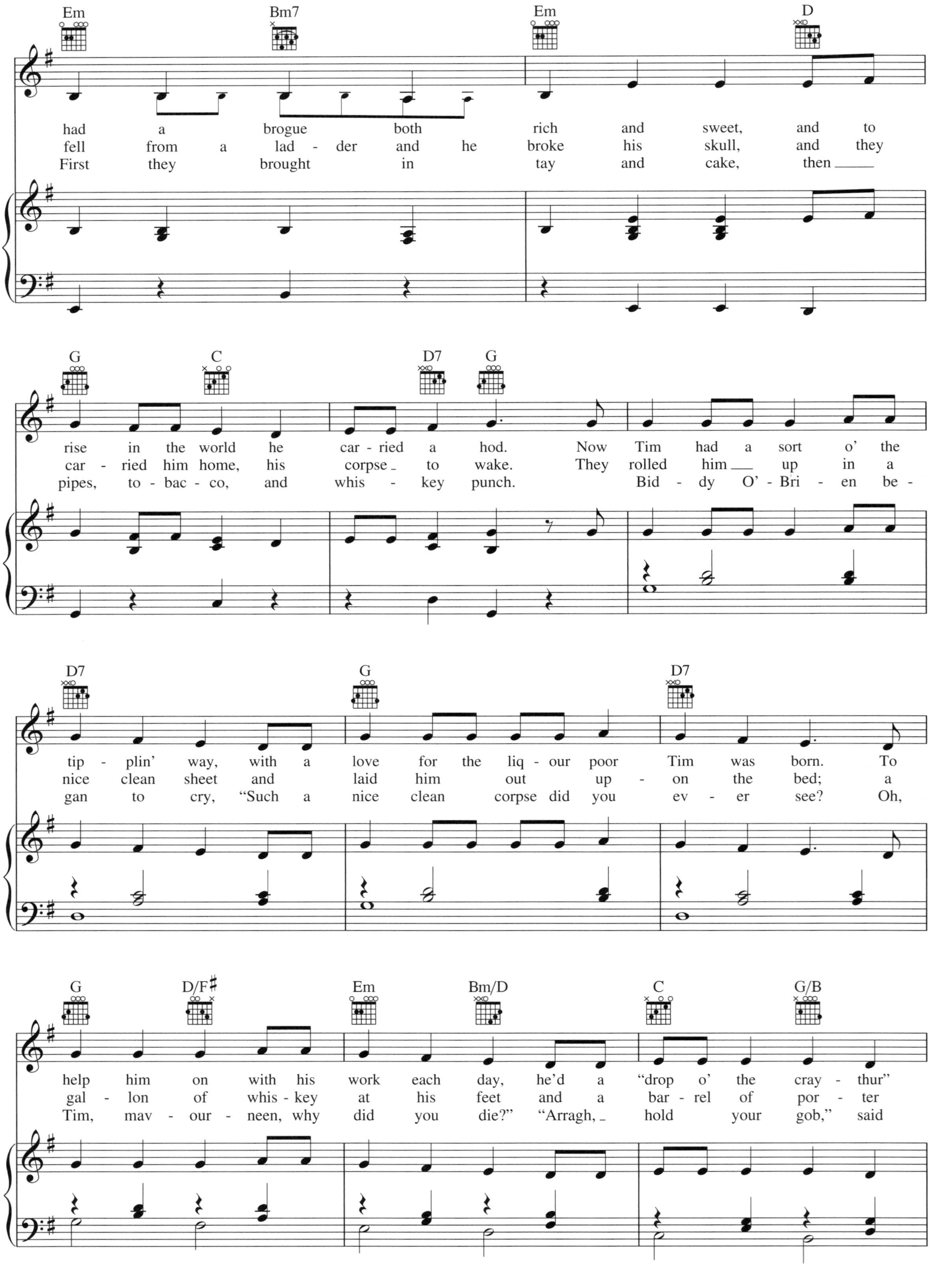
Em Bm7 Em D
had a brogue both rich and sweet, and to
fell from a lad - der and he broke his skull, and they
First they brought in tay and cake, then
G C D7 G
rise in the world he car - ried a hod. Now Tim had a sort o' the
car - ried him home, his corpse to wake. They rolled him up in a
pipes, to - bac - co, and whis - key punch. Bid - dy O' - Bri - en be -
D7 G D7
tip - plin' way, with a love for the liq - our poor Tim was born. To
nice clean sheet and laid him out up - on the bed; a
gan to cry, "Such a nice clean corpse did you ev - er see? Oh,
G D/F♯ Em Bm/D C G/B
help him on with his work each day, he'd a "drop o' the cray - thur"
gal - lon of whis - key at his feet and a bar - rel of por - ter
Tim, mav - our - neen, why did you die?" "Arragh, hold your gob," said

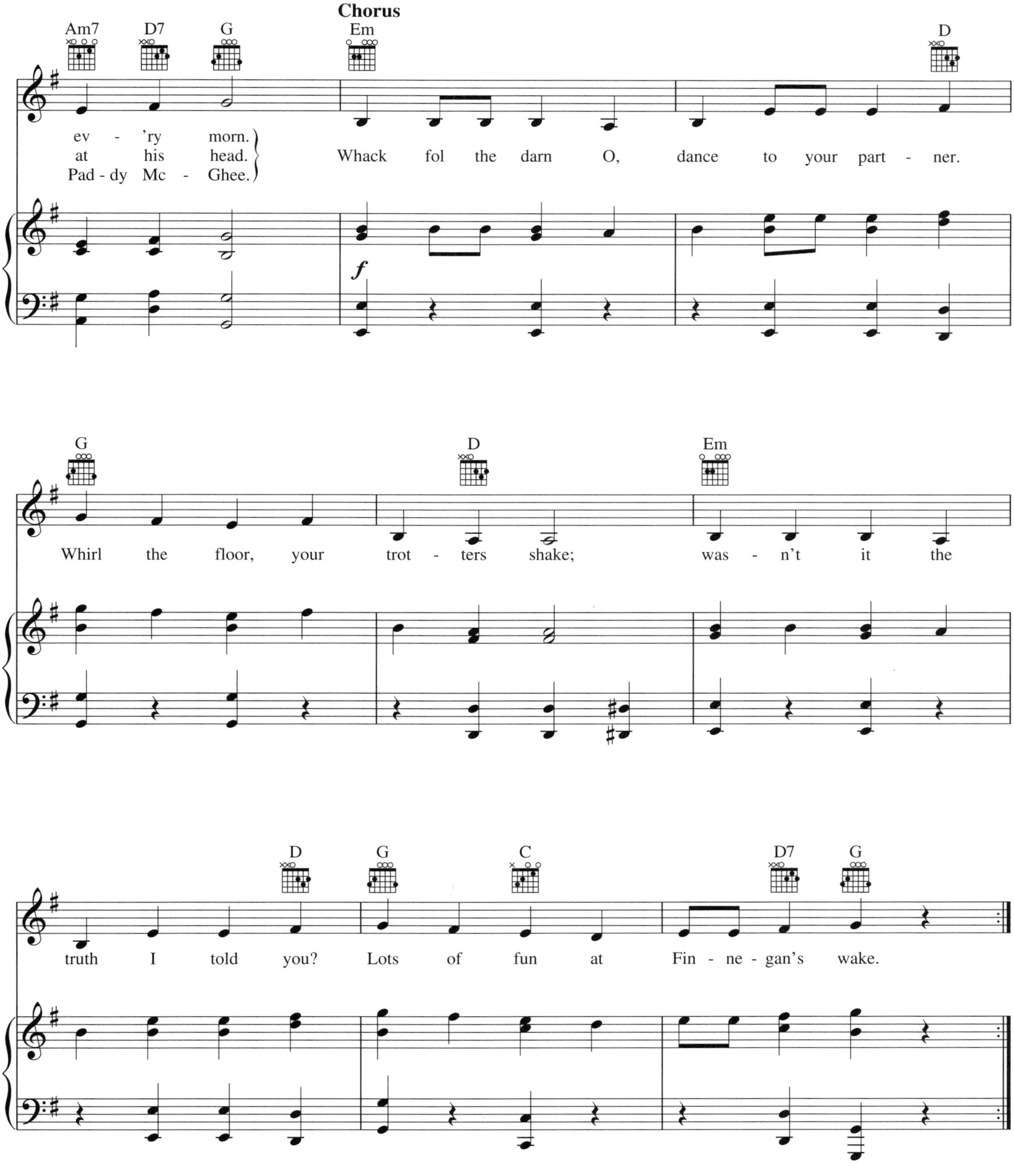
Chorus
Am7 D7 G Em D
ev - 'ry morn.
at his head.
Pad - dy Mc - Ghee.
Whack fol the darn O, dance to your part - ner.
G D Em
Whirl the floor, your trot - ters shake; was - n't it the
D G C D7 G
truth I told you? Lots of fun at Fin - ne - gan's wake.

Additional Lyrics

4. Then Maggie O'Connor took up the job,
"Oh Biddy," says she, "you're wrong, I'm sure."
Biddy, she gave her a belt in the gob
And left her sprawlin' on the floor.
And then the war did soon engage,
'Twas woman to woman and man to man.
Shillelaigh law was all the rage,
And a row and ruction soon began.
Chorus

5. Then Mickey Maloney ducked his head
When a noggin of whiskey flew at him.
It missed, and falling on the bed,
The liquor scattered over Tim!
The corpse revives; see how he rises!
Timothy, rising from the bed,
Said, "Whirl your whiskey around like blazes,
Thanum an Dhul! Do you think I'm dead?"
Chorus

THE FOGGY DEW

Traditional Irish Folk Song

Moderately slow
Bm Em F#m Bm
mp
Em A Bm
O - ver the hills I went one day; a love - ly
O - ver the hills I went one morn, a - sing - ing
Em F#m Bm
maid I spied. With her coal - black hair and her
I did go. Met this love - ly maid with her
Em A Bm Em F#m Bm
man - tle so green, an im - age to per - ceive.
coal - black hair, and she an - swered soft and low.

Copyright © 2003 by HAL LEONARD CORPORATION
International Copyright Secured All Rights Reserved

D G D A
Says I, "Dear girl, will you be my bride?" And she
Said she, "Young man, I'll be your bride, if I
Bm Em F♯m Bm
lift - ed her eyes of blue. She smiled and
know that you'll be true." Oh, in my
Em A Bm
said, "Young man, I'm to wed; I'm to meet him in the
arms, all of her charms were cast - ed in the
Em F♯m 1 Bsus Bm 2 Bm
fog - gy dew.
fog - gy dew.

FOLLOW ME UP TO CARLOW

Traditional Irish Folk Song

Moderately fast, with a lilt
Gm Dm Gm F Gm
mf
Gm Dm Gm
Lift, Mac - Ca - hir Oge, your face, brood - ing o'er the
See the swords of Glen Im - aal, Flash - ing o'er the
From Tas - sa - gart to Clon - more flows a stream of
B♭ Gm Dm
old dis - grace, that old Fitz - wil - liam stormed your place, and
Eng - lish Pale! See all the chil - dren of the Gael be -
Sax - on gore! O, great is Ror - y Oge O More at
Gm Dm Gm
drove you to the fern, O! Grey said vic - to -
neath O' - Byrne's ban - ners! Roos - ter of a
send - ing loons to Ha - des! White is sick and

Copyright © 2006 by HAL LEONARD CORPORATION
International Copyright Secured All Rights Reserved

Dm Gm B♭
3fr
ry was sure, soon the fire - brand he'd se - cure, un -
fight - ing stock, would you let a Sax - on cock crow
Lane is fled! Now for Fitz - wil - liam's head. We'll
Gm Dm Gm Dm
til he met at Glan - ma - lure, Feagh Mac - Hugh O' -
out up - on an I - rish rock? Fly up and teach him
send it o - ver drip - ping red to Li - za and her
Gm B♭
Byrne, O!
man - ners.
la - dies!
Curse and swear, Lord Kil - dare!
Dm F B♭
Feagh will do what Feagh will dare; and now Fitz - wil - liam

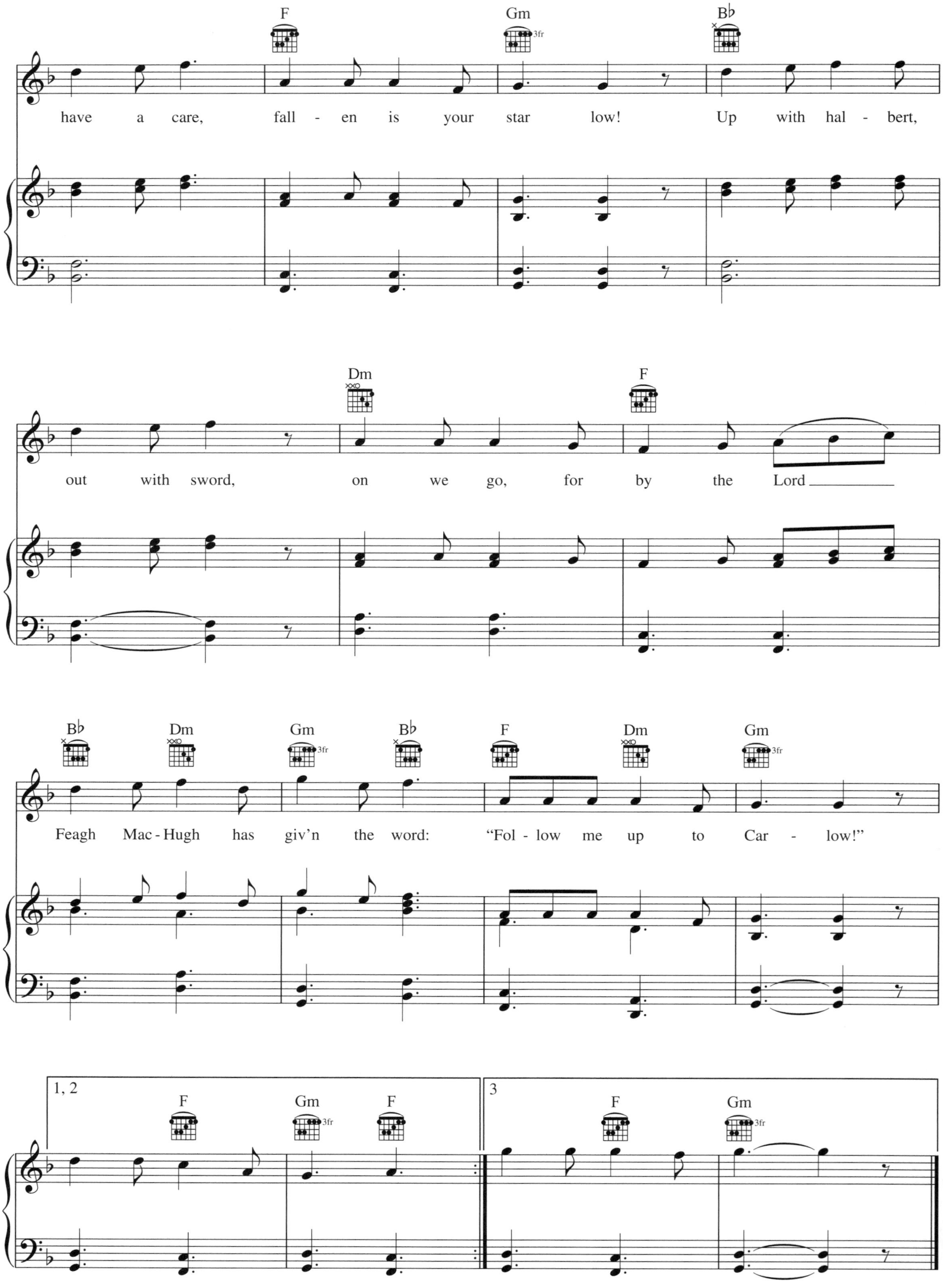
F Gm Bb
have a care, fall - en is your star low! Up with hal - bert,
Dm F
out with sword, on we go, for by the Lord
Bb Dm Gm Bb F Dm Gm
Feagh Mac - Hugh has giv'n the word: "Fol - low me up to Car - low!"
1, 2
F Gm F
3
F Gm

THE GALWAY SHAWL

Traditional Irish Folk Song

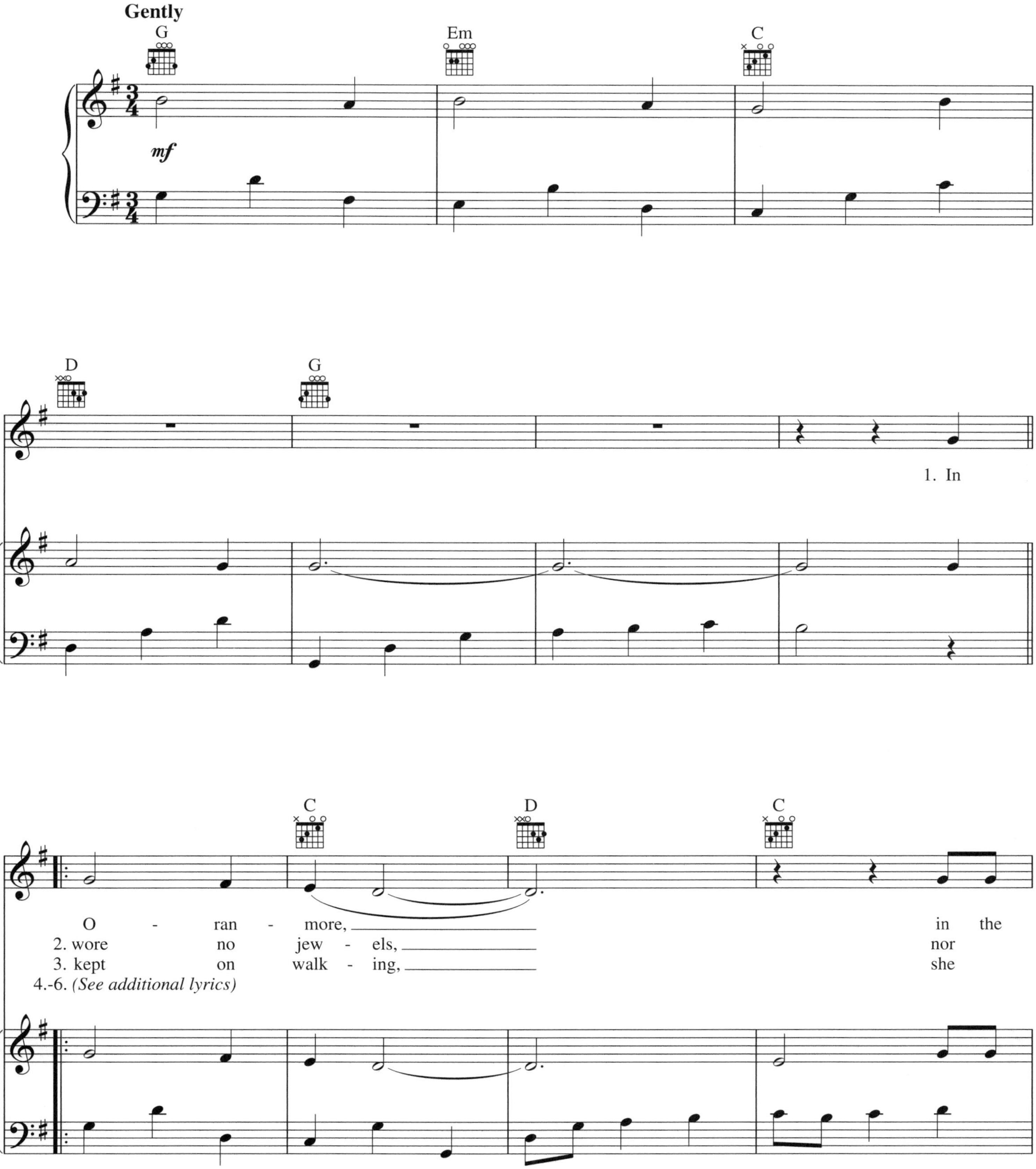
Gently
G
Em
C
mf
D
G
1. In
C
D
C
O - ran - more,
in the
2. wore no jew - els,
nor
3. kept on walk - ing,
she
4.-6. (See additional lyrics)

Copyright © 2006 by HAL LEONARD CORPORATION
International Copyright Secured All Rights Reserved

D Em C
Coun - ty Gal - way one
cost - ly dia - monds, no
kept on talk - ing till her
Bm Em D C G
pleas - ant eve - ning, in the
paint or pow - der, no,
fa - ther's cot - tage came
Am C G D
month of May, I
none at all. She
in - to view. Says
G C
spied a dam - sel she was
wore a bon - net with a
she, "Come in, sir, and

Em D Bm C
young and hand - some, her
rib - bon on it, and
meet my fa - ther, and
G Em D C D
beau - ty fair - ly took my breath a -
'round her shoul - der was the Gal - way
for to please him play 'The Fog - gy
G
1 - 5
6
way. She
shawl. We
Dew.'"

Additional Lyrics

4. She sat me down beside the fire,
   I could see her father, he was six feet tall.
   And soon her mother had the kettle singing,
   All I could think of was the Galway shawl.

5. I played "The Blackbird" and "The Stack of Barley,"
   "Rodney's Glory," and "The Foggy Dew."
   She sang each note like an Irish linnet
   Whilst the tears stood in her eyes of blue.

6. 'Twas early, early, all in the morning,
   When I hit the road for old Donegal.
   She said, "Goodbye, Sir," she cried and kissed me,
   And my heart remained with the Galway shawl.

THE GALWAY RACES

Traditional Irish Folk Song

Spirited
A E F♯m C♯m F♯m A C♯m
4fr
mf
1. As I rode out to Gal-way town to
2. pas-sen-gers from Lim-er-ick and
3. mul-ti-tudes from Ar-an and mem-
4.-8. (See additional lyrics)
A C♯m F♯m D E A
seek for re-cre-a-tion, on the sev-en-teenth of Au-gust my mind was e-le-vat-ed, there were
pas-sen-gers from Nen-agh, and pas-sen-gers from Dub-lin and sports-men from Tip-p'rar-y. There were
bers from New Quay shore, the boys from Con-ne-ma-ra and the Clare un-mar-ried maid-ens. There were
C♯m E D A F♯m D
mul-ti-tudes as-sem-bled with their tick-ets at the sta-tion, my eyes be-gan to daz-zle and they're
pas-sen-gers from Ker-ry and all the quar-ters of the na-tion, and our mem-ber, Mis-ter Has-set for to
peo-ple from Cork cit-y who were loy-al, true, and faith-ful, that brought home Fen-ian pris-on-ers from

Copyright © 2006 by HAL LEONARD CORPORATION
International Copyright Secured All Rights Reserved

1 - 7
E A E F♯m C♯m F♯m
goin' to see the rac - es.
join the Gal - way Bla - zers.
dy - ing in for - eign na - tions.
With me whack, fol the do, fol the did - de - ly, i - dle ay.
4fr
C♯m F♯m
8
F♯m C♯m F♯m
There were
There were
It is
did - de - ly, i - dle ay.

Additional Lyrics

4. It is there you'll see confectioners with sugar sticks and dainties,
The lozenges and oranges and lemonade and raisins,
And gingerbread and spices to accommodate the ladies,
And a big crubeen for threepence to be picking while you're able.
With me whack, fol the do, fol the diddely, idle ay.

5. It is there you'll see the gamblers, the thimbles and the garters,
And the sporting Wheel-of-Fortune with the four and twenty quarters.
There were others without scruple pelting wattles at poor Maggy,
And her father well contented to be looking at his daughter.
With me whack, fol the do, fol the diddely, idle ay.

6. It is there you'll see the pipers and the fiddlers competing,
And the nimble-footed dancers, and they trippin' on the daisies,
And others cryin' cigars and bill for all the races,
With the colors of the jockeys and the prize and horse's ages.
With me whack, fol the do, fol the diddely, idle ay.

7. It's there you'd see the jockeys and they mounted on most stately,
The pink and blue, the red and green, the emblem of our nation,
When the bell was rung for starting all the horses seemed impatient,
I thought they never stood on ground, their speed was so amazing.
With me whack, fol the do, fol the diddlely, idle ay.

8. There was half a million people there of all denominations,
The Catholic, the Protestant, the Jew and Presbyterian.
There was yet no animosity, no matter what persuasion,
But fortune and hopitality inducing fresh acquaintance.
With me whack, fol the do, fol the diddely, idle ay.

GREEN GROW THE RASHES, O

Traditional Irish Folk Song

Lively
Dm C Dm C Am
There's
mf
C Am Dm
naught but care on ev - 'ry han' in ev - 'ry hour that pass - es, O; what
world - ly race may rich - es chase, an' rich - es still may fly them, O; an'
me a can - nie hour at e'en, my arms a - round my dear - ie, O; an'
you sae douce, ye sneer at this, ye're naught but sense - less ass - es, O; the
na - ture swears the love - ly dears, her no - blest work she class - es, O; her
F C Dm C Am
sig - ni - fies that life o' man, an' 'twere not for the lass - es, O?
though at last they catch them fast, their hearts can ne'er en - joy them, O.
world - ly cares an' world - ly men may a' gae tap - sal - teer - ie, O!
wis - est man the world e'er saw, he dear - ly loved the lass - es, O.
pren - tice han' she tried on man, an' then she made the lass - es, O.

Copyright © 2006 by HAL LEONARD CORPORATION
International Copyright Secured All Rights Reserved

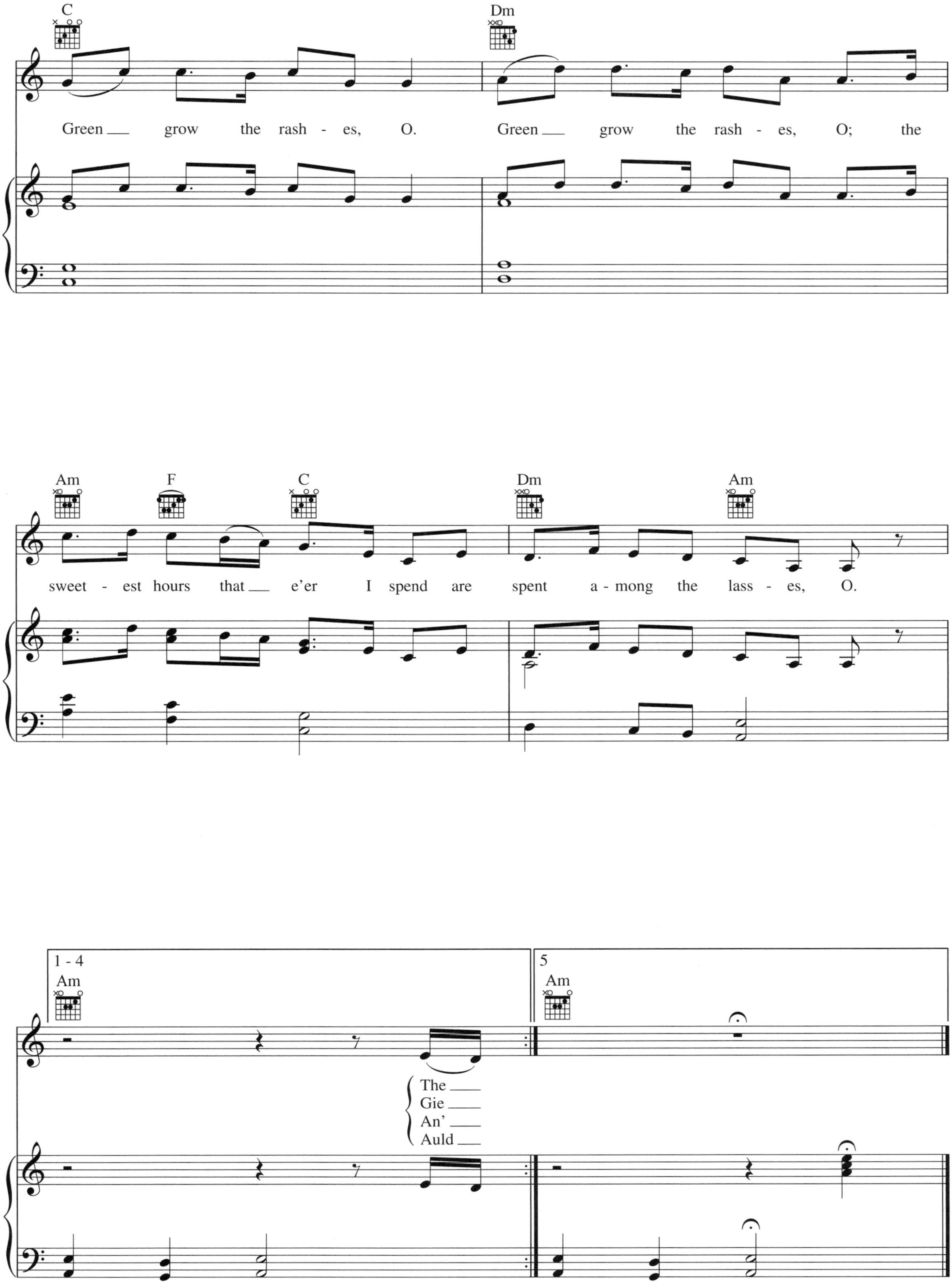
C
Dm
Green grow the rash - es, O. Green grow the rash - es, O; the
Am
F
C
Dm
Am
sweet - est hours that e'er I spend are spent a - mong the lass - es, O.
1 - 4
Am
The
Gie
An'
Auld
5
Am

HENRY MY SON

Traditional Irish Folk Song

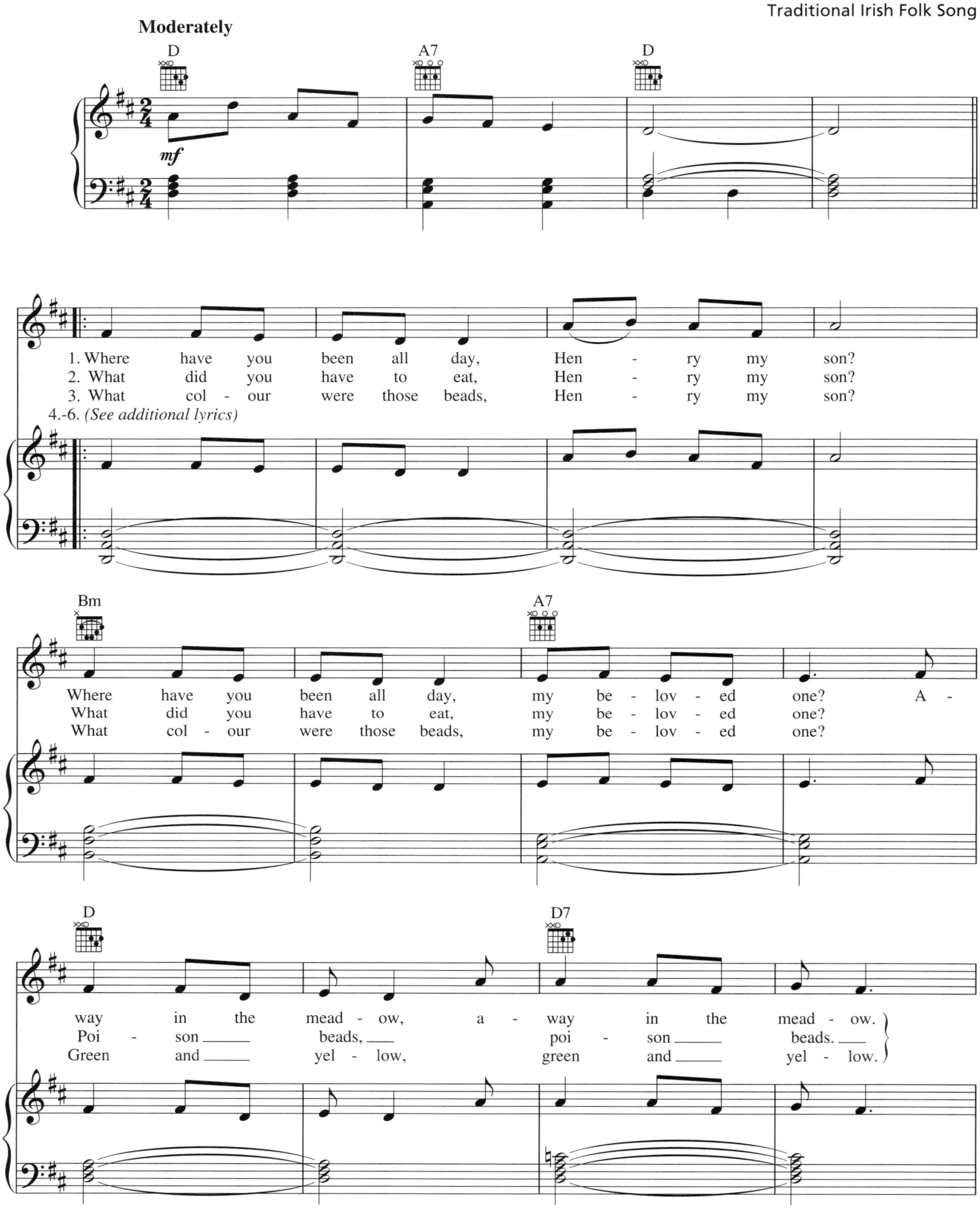
Moderately
D
A7
D
mf
1. Where have you been all day, Hen - ry my son?
2. What did you have to eat, Hen - ry my son?
3. What col - our were those beads, Hen - ry my son?
4.-6. (See additional lyrics)
Bm
A7
Where have you been all day, my be - lov - ed one? A -
What did you have to eat, my be - lov - ed one?
What col - our were those beads, my be - lov - ed one?
D
D7
way in the mead - ow, a - way in the mead - ow.
Poi - son beads, poi - son beads.
Green and yel - low, green and yel - low.

Copyright © 2006 by HAL LEONARD CORPORATION
International Copyright Secured All Rights Reserved

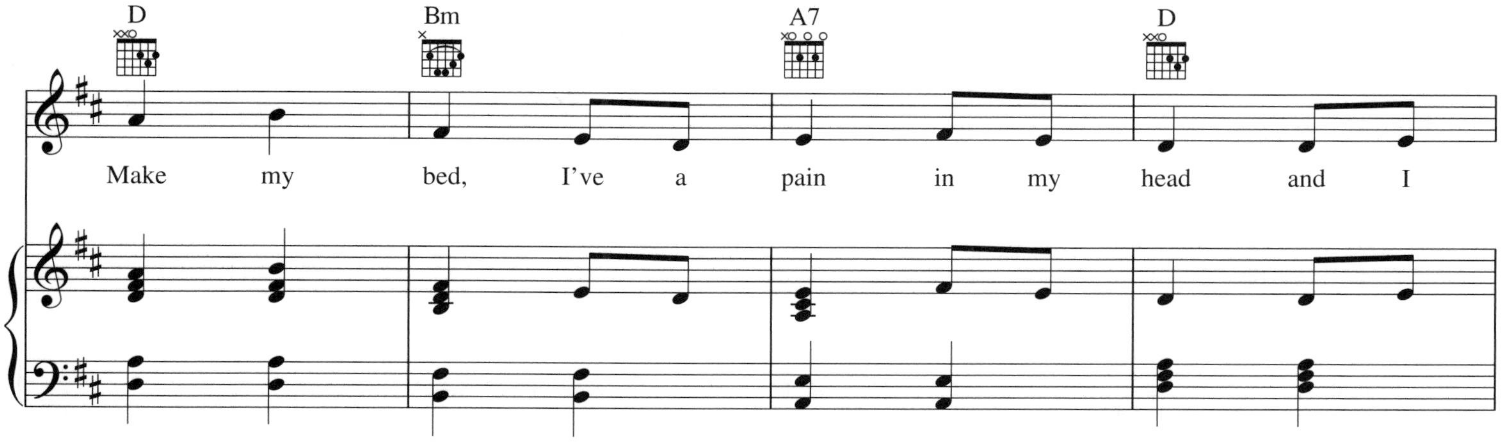
D
Bm
A7
D
Make my bed, I've a pain in my head and I

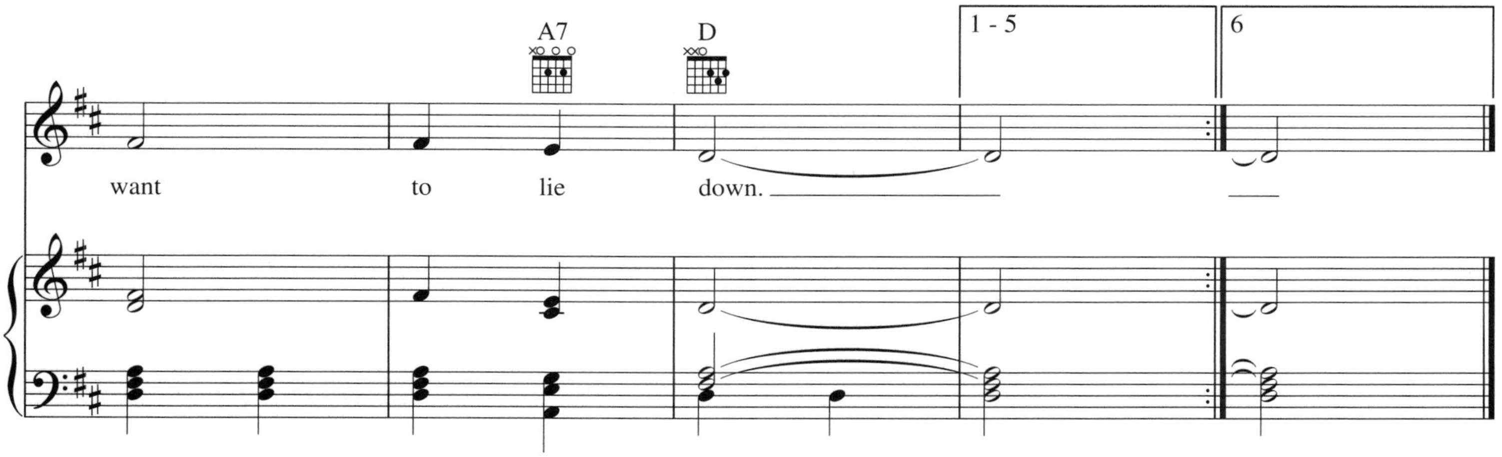
A7
D
1 - 5
6
want to lie down.

Additional Lyrics

4. What will you leave your mother, Henry my son?
   What will you leave your mother, my beloved one?
   A woolen blanket, a woolen blanket.
   Make my bed, I've a pain in my head and I want to lie down.

5. What will you leave your children, Henry my son?
   What will you leave your children, my beloved one?
   The keys of heaven, the keys of heaven.
   Make my bed, I've a pain in my head and I want to lie down.

6. And what will you leave your sweetheart, Henry my son?
   What will you leave your sweetheart, my beloved one?
   A rope to hang her, a rope to hang her.
   Make my bed, I've a pain in my head and I want to lie down.

HIGH GERMANY

Traditional Irish Folk Song

Moderately
mf
Em C Bm
Em
Oh, Col - leen love, oh Col - leen, the
buy for you a horse, me love, and
curs - ed be those cruel wars that
friends I do not val - ue, and my
Am Em G
rout has now be - gun, and I must go a -
on it you will ride, and all of my de -
ev - er did they rise, and out of mer - ry
foes I do not fear, for now my fine love's
Bm C G Am G
march - ing to the beat - ing of a drum. Come
light will be in rid - ing by your side. We'll
Eng - land pass man - y a man like - wise. They
left me and wan - ders far and near. And

Copyright © 2006 by HAL LEONARD CORPORATION
International Copyright Secured All Rights Reserved

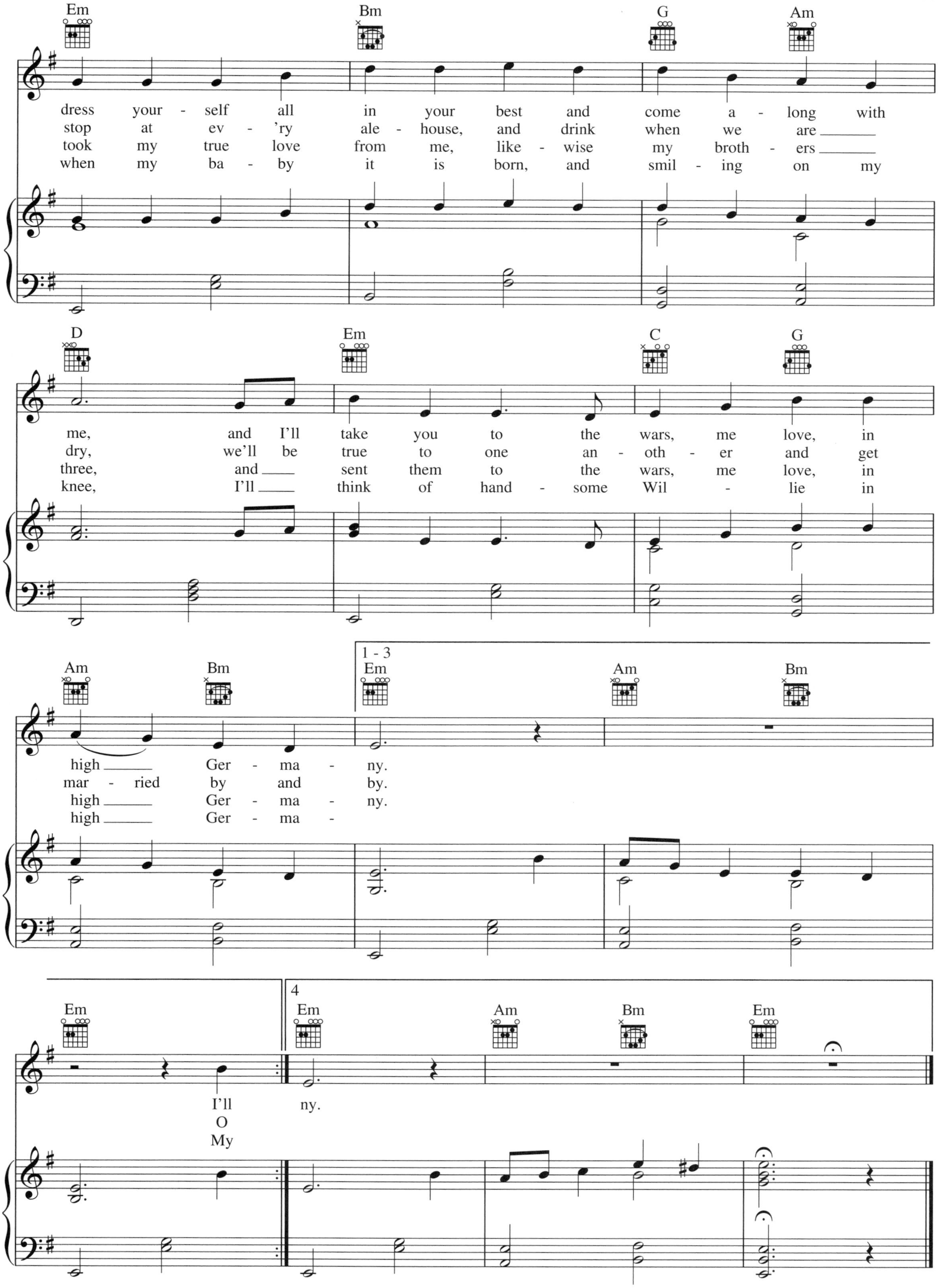
Em
Bm
G
Am
dress your - self all in your best and come a - long with
stop at ev - 'ry ale - house, and drink when we are
took my true love from me, like - wise my broth - ers
when my ba - by it is born, and smil - ing on my
D
Em
C
G
me, and I'll take you to the wars, me love, in
dry, we'll be true to one an - oth - er and get
three, and sent them to the wars, me love, in
knee, I'll think of hand - some Wil - lie in
Am
Bm
1 - 3
Em
Am
Bm
high Ger - ma - ny.
mar - ried by and by.
high Ger - ma - ny.
high Ger - ma -
Em
4
Em
Am
Bm
Em
I'll ny.
O
My

HIGHLAND PADDY

Traditional Irish Folk Song

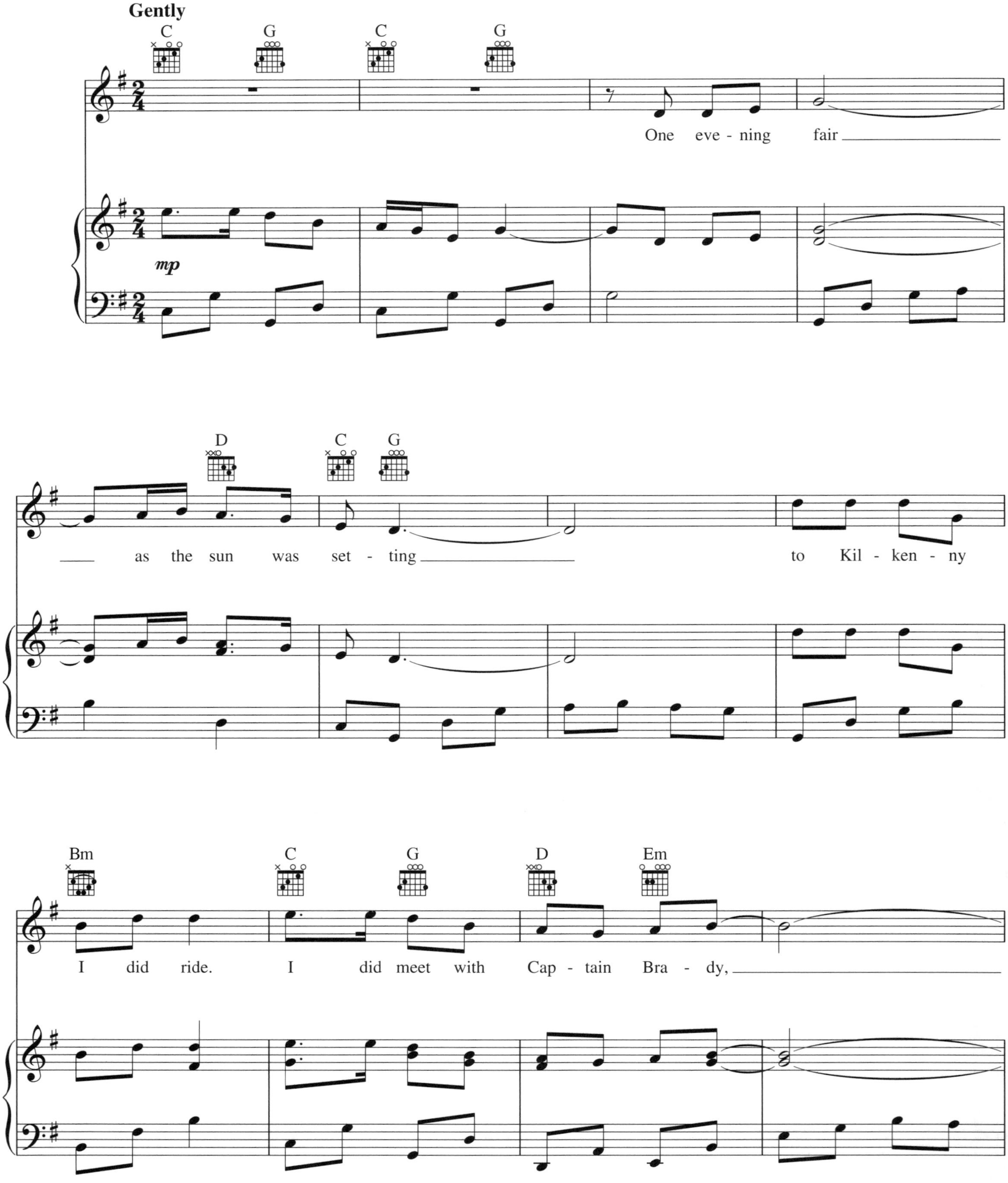
Gently
C G C G
mp
One eve - ning fair
D C G
as the sun was set - ting
to Kil - ken - ny
Bm C G D Em
I did ride. I did meet with Cap - tain Bra - dy,

Copyright © 2006 by HAL LEONARD CORPORATION
International Copyright Secured All Rights Reserved

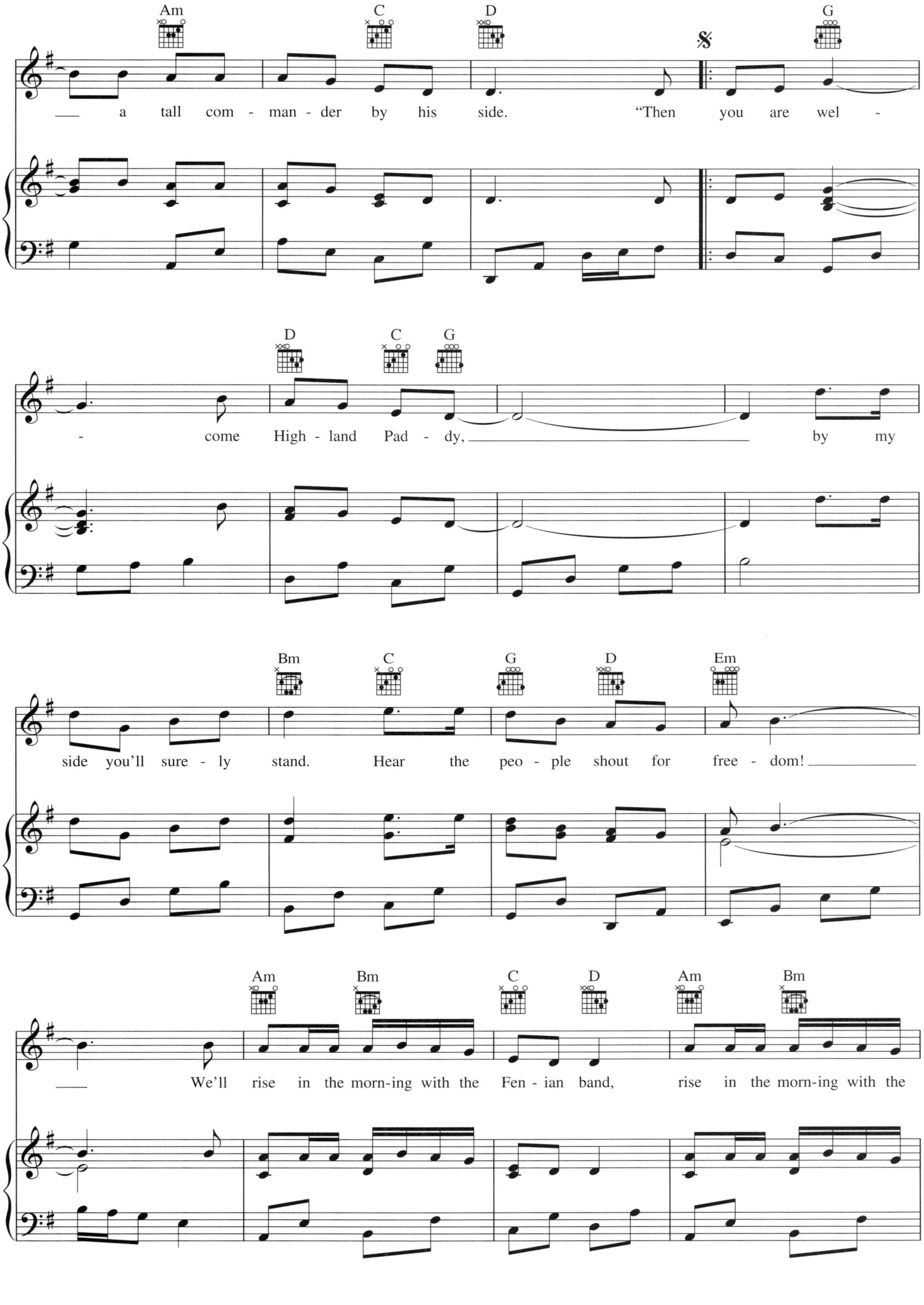
Am C D G
a tall com - man - der by his side. "Then you are wel -
D C G
- come High - land Pad - dy, by my
Bm C G D Em
side you'll sure - ly stand. Hear the peo - ple shout for free - dom!
Am Bm C D Am Bm
We'll rise in the morn-ing with the Fen - ian band, rise in the morn-ing with the

C D G D
And in the morn - ing we rose
Fen - ian band." There is a glen be - side a
For all my life I will re -
C G Bm
ear - ly. just be - fore the break of dawn,
riv - er, just out - side Kil - ken - ny town,
mem - ber I'll re - mem - ber night and day that
C G D Em Am
black - birds sing - ing in the bush - es greet - ings
there we met this no - ble cap - tain, men lay
I once rode in - to Kil - ken - ny and I heard the
To Coda
C D G
to a smil - ing morn. Gath - er 'round
dy - ing on the ground. There is a grave
no - ble Cap - tain

D C G
me men of Ire - land, all ye Fen - ians
down by the riv - er, a mile out - side Kil -
Bm C G D Em
gath - er 'round, Hand to hand with sword and mus - ket,
ken - ny town. There we laid our no - ble Cap - tain,
Am C 1 D 2 D
D.S. al Coda
spill the blood up - on this ho - ly ground. "Then
birds were si - lent when this Fen - ian died. "Then
CODA
D G D C G
say, "Then you are wel - come High - land Pad - dy,

Bm C
by my side you'll sure - ly stand. Hear the
G D Em Am Bm
peo - ple shout for free - dom! We'll rise in the morn-ing with the
C D Am Bm C D
Fen - ian band, rise in the morn - ing with the Fen - ian band."
C G

THE HILLS OF KERRY

Traditional Irish Folk Song

Copyright © 2006 by HAL LEONARD CORPORATION
International Copyright Secured All Rights Reserved

Bm
G
dieu the Hills of Ker -
gone off to a for - eign
hear our reap - er sing -
D
Bm
Em
ry I ne'er will see no
land where the wild can - yons
ing in a gold - en field of
A7
D
more. Oh, why did I
roar. No more shall they
corn. There's a balm for
G
D
leave my home? Oh,
see the sham - rock, the
ev - 'ry woe and a

G
A7
D
why did I cross the sea
plant so dear to me,
cure for ev - 'ry pain,
Bm
and leave the small birds
or hear the small birds
but the hap - pi - ness of my
G
A7
D
sing - ing a - round you
sing - ing a - round you
dar - ling girl I will nev - er
A7
D
1, 2
3
sweet Tra - lee? The
sweet Tra - lee. No
see a - gain.

THE HOLY GROUND

Traditional Irish Folk Song

Brightly
C G C
mf
G C
A - dieu my love - ly dar - ling, a thou - sand times a - dieu.
now the storm is rag - ing, and we are far from shore.
now the storm is o - ver and we are safe and well.
Am C G C
Am F
We are sail - ing a - way from the Ho - ly
And the night is dark and drear -
We will go in - to a pub - lic

Copyright © 2006 by HAL LEONARD CORPORATION
International Copyright Secured All Rights Reserved

G C Am G
Ground and the girls we all love true.
y and our hap - py thoughts no more.
house and we'll eat and drink our fill.
G7 C G C
We will sail the salt seas o -
And the good ship she is tossed a -
And we'll drink strong ale and por -
Am C Am F
ver and we'll re - turn for shore
bout and the rig - ging is all torn.
ter we'll make the raft - ers roar.
G F G Am G F G
to see a - gain the girls we
But still I live in hope to
And when our mon - ey is all

C G7 C
love and the Ho - ly Ground once more. Fine
see the Ho - ly Ground once more. Fine
spent, we'll go to sea once more. Fine
F C Am F
girl you are!
girl you are! You're the girl I do a - dore
girl you are!
G F G Am G Am G C
and still I live in hope to see the
G7 C
Ho - ly Ground once more.
1, 2
3
And
And

I KNOW WHERE I'M GOIN'

English Folk Song

Gently
F Bb/D F C7 F F/E Dm7 Dm7/C
mp
I know where I'm go - ing, and I know who's go - ing with me. I know who I love, but the Lord knows who I'll mar - ry.
I'll wear stock-ings of silk, and shoes of bright green leath - er, combs to buck-le my hair, and a ring for ev - 'ry fin - ger.
Feath - er beds are soft, and paint - ed rooms are bon - nie, but I would trade them all for my hand - some, win - some John - ny.
Some say he's poor, but I say he's bon - nie, fair - est of them all is my hand - some, win - some John - ny.
F Dm Bb/D C7 F F/E Dm7
Bb
1 - 3
C7
4
C7 F

Copyright © 2006 by HAL LEONARD CORPORATION
International Copyright Secured All Rights Reserved

THE HUMOUR IS ON ME NOW

Traditional Irish Folk Song

Moderately
A
A7
mf
D
E
A
G
D
E
1. As I went out one morn - ing, it be - ing the month of May, a farm - er and his daugh - ter I spied up - on my way. And the girl sat down quite calm - ly to the milk - ing of her
2. qui - et you fool - ish daugh - ter, and hold your sim - ple tongue. You're bet - ter free and sin - gle, and hap - py while you're young. But the daugh - ter shook her shoul - ders and milked her pat - ient
3. who are you to turn me, that mar - ried young your - self, and took my dar - ling moth - er from off the sin - gle shelf? Ah sure, daugh - ter dear, so ais - y, and milk your pa - tient
4. deed I'll tell my moth - er the aw - ful things you say, in - deed I'll tell my moth - er this ver - y bless - ed day. Och, now daugh - ter, have a heart, dear, you'll start a fear - ful
5.-8. (See additional lyrics)

Copyright © 2006 by HAL LEONARD CORPORATION
International Copyright Secured All Rights Reserved

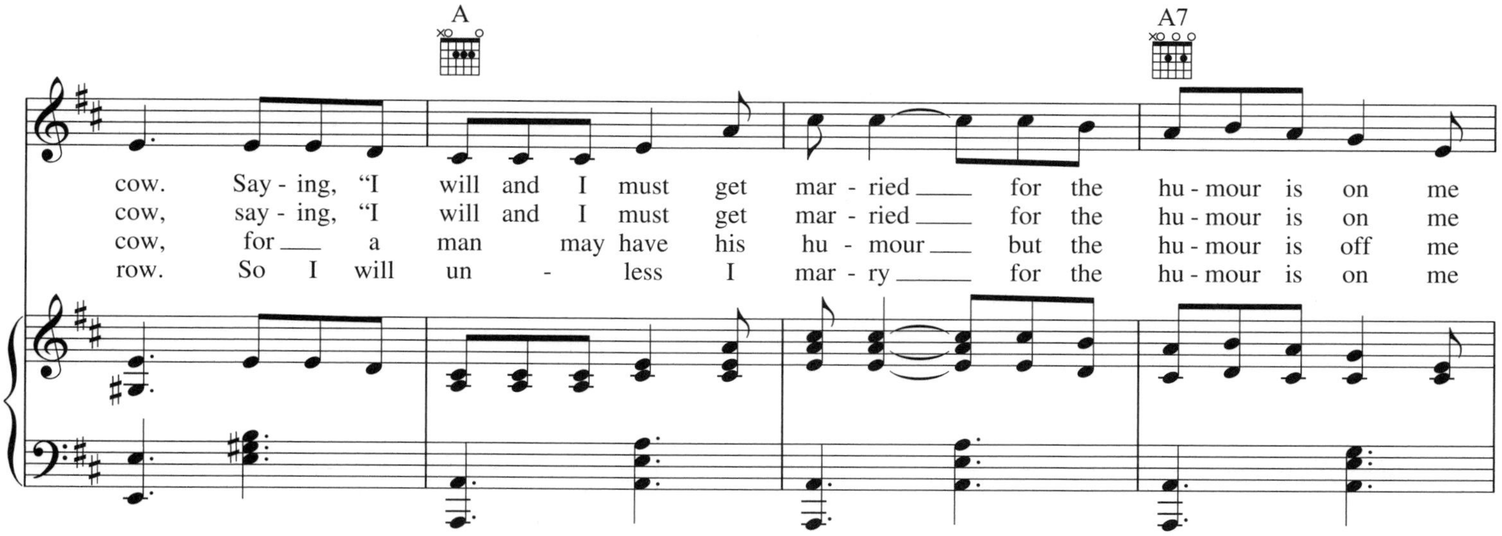
A
A7
cow. Say - ing, "I will and I must get mar - ried for the hu - mour is on me
cow, say - ing, "I will and I must get mar - ried for the hu - mour is on me
cow, for a man may have his hu - mour but the hu - mour is off me
row. So I will un - less I mar - ry for the hu - mour is on me

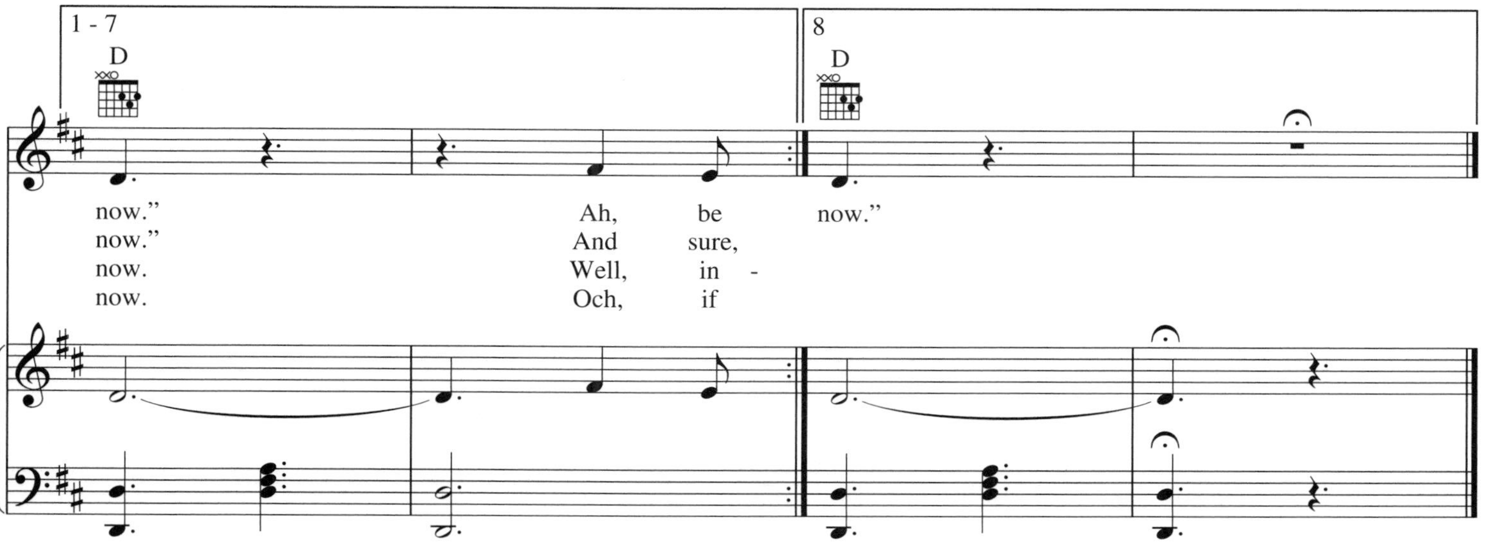
1 - 7
D
8
D
now." Ah, be now."
now." And sure,
now. Well, in -
now. Och, if

Additional Lyrics

5. Och, if you must be married will you tell me who's the man?
And quickly she did answer, "There's William, James and John,
A carpenter, a tailor, and a man to milk the cow,
For I will and I must get married and the humour is on me now."

6. A carpenter's a sharp man, and a tailor's hard to face,
With his legs across the table and his threads about the place.
And sure John's a fearful tyrant and never lacks a row,
But I will and I must be married for the humour is on me now.

7. Well, if you must be married, wiil you tell me what you'll do?
"Sure I will," the daughter answered, "just the same as you.
I'll be mistress of my dairy and my butter and my cow."
And your husband too, I'll venture, for the humour is on you now.

8. So at last the daughter married and married well-to-do,
And loved her darling husband for a month, a year or two.
But John was all a tyrant and she quickly rued her vow,
Saying, "I'm sorry that I married for the humour is off me now."

I KNOW MY LOVE

Traditional Irish Folk Song

Moderately
Bm/F♯ F♯m Em G/D D A7 D
mf
I / There / If / I
G A7
know my love by his way o' walk - in' and I know my love by his
is a dance house in Mar - a - dyke, and there my true love goes
my love know I could wash and wring, if my love knew I could
know my love is an ar - rant rov - er, I know he'll wan - der the
D A7 D
way o' talk - in'. And I know my love in a suit of blue, and if
ev - 'ry night. He takes a strange one up - on his knee, and
weave and spin, I'd make a coat of all the fin - est kind, but the
wild world o - ver. In for - eign parts he may chance to stray, where

Copyright © 2006 by HAL LEONARD CORPORATION
International Copyright Secured All Rights Reserved

Bm A7 D A7
my love leaves me, what will I do?
don't you know, now, that vex - es me?
love of mon - ey leaves me be - hind.
all the girls are so bright and gay.
And still she cried, "I love
D Bm A7 D
him the best, and a trou - bled mind, sure, can know no rest." And
A7 D Bm Em
1 - 3
A7 D
still she cried, "Bon - ny boys are few, and if my love leaves me, what will I do?"
4
A7 D Bm/F♯ F♯m Em G/D D A7 D
will I do?"
rit.

I NEVER WILL MARRY

Traditional Folk Song

Copyright © 2006 by HAL LEONARD CORPORATION
International Copyright Secured All Rights Reserved

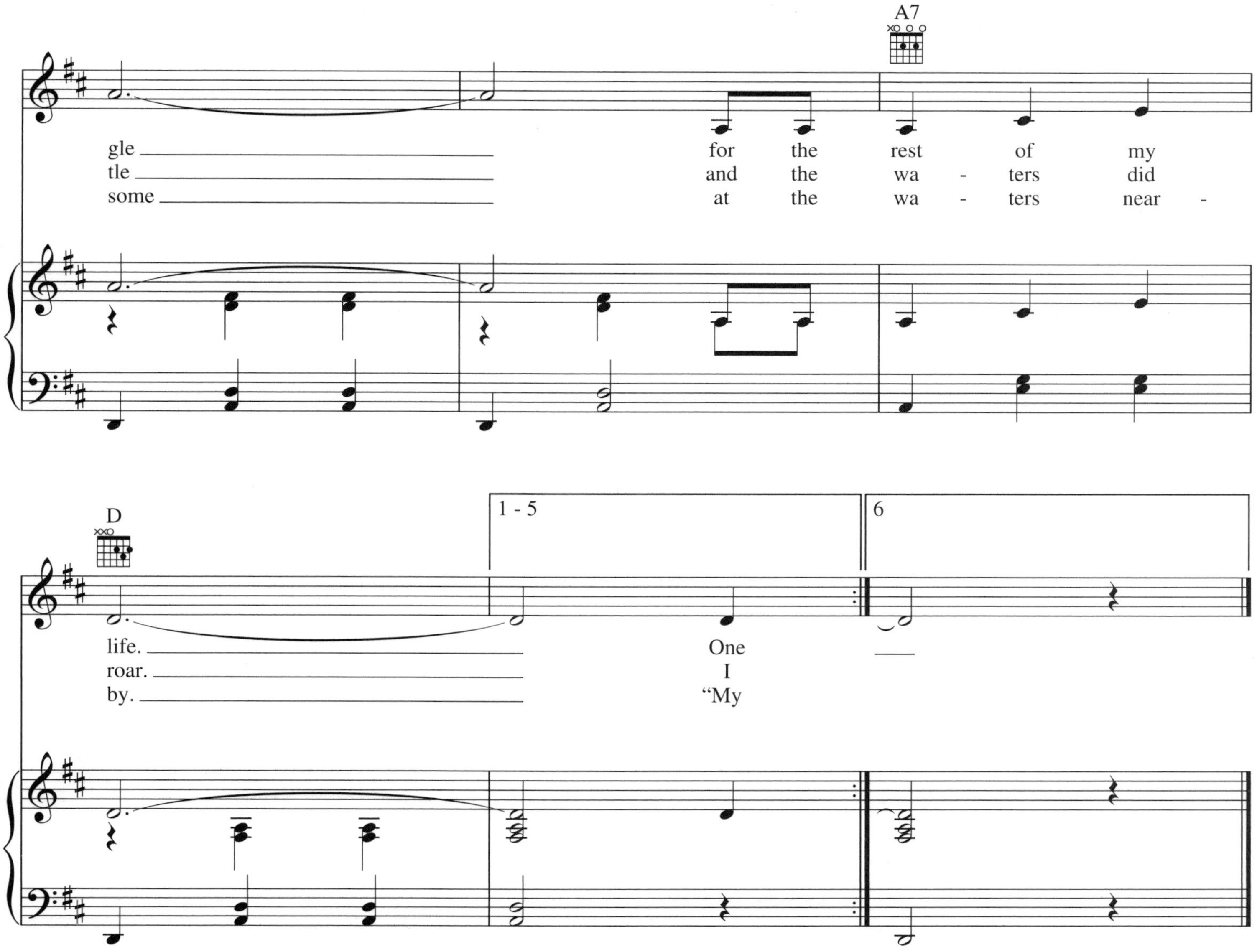
A7
gle for the rest of my
tle and the wa - ters did
some at the wa - ters near -
D
1 - 5
6
life. One
roar. I
by. "My

Additional Lyrics

4. "My love's gone and left me, he's the one I adore.
   I never will see him, no never, no more."

5. "The shells in the ocean will be my deathbed,
   And the fish in the water swim over my head."

6. She plunged her fair body in the water so deep.
   And she closed her pretty blue eyes in the water to sleep.

I ONCE LOVED A LASS

Traditional Irish Folk Song

Sadly
F C G C
mp
G Em
1. I once loved a lass and I
2. I saw my love walk
3. I saw my love sit
4.-6. (See additional lyrics)
C Am G
loved her so well that I ha - ted all
through the church door with groom and bride
down for to dine I sat down be -
C F D
oth - ers that spoke of her ill. But
maid - ens they made a fine show. And
side her and poured out the wine. I

Copyright © 2006 by HAL LEONARD CORPORATION
International Copyright Secured All Rights Reserved

G C G Bm
now she's re - ward - ed me well for my love
I followed them in with my heart full of woe
drank to the las - sie that should have been mine
F C
for she's gone to be wed with an - oth - er.
for now she is wed to an - oth - er.
but now she is wed to an - oth - er.
1 - 5
G C
G
When
When
The
6
G C G
got - ten.
rit.

Additional Lyrics

4. The men in yon forest, they ask it of me
   How many strawberries grow in the salt sea?
   And I ask of them back with a tear in my eye
   How many ships sail in the forest?

5. So dig me a grave and dig it so deep
   And cover me over with flowers so sweet
   And I will turn in for to take a long sleep
   And maybe in time I'll forget her.

6. They dug him a grave and they dug it so deep
   They covered him over with flowers so sweet
   And he has turned in for to take a long sleep
   And maybe by now he's forgotten.

I'LL TAKE YOU HOME AGAIN, KATHLEEN

Words and Music by
THOMAS WESTENDORF

Moderately
F/A Ab dim7 Gm7 C7 F C7 G#dim7
mf
I'll take you home a - gain, Kath-
that dear home be - yond the
F/A C7 F C7
leen, A - cross the o - cean wild and wide, To
sea My Kath - leen shall a - gain re - turn And
F C7 G#dim7 F/A
where your heart has ev - er been Since
when thy old friends wel - come thee Thy

Copyright © 1995 by HAL LEONARD CORPORATION
International Copyright Secured All Rights Reserved

C
G7
C7
first you were my bon - ny bride.
The
lov - ing heart will cease to yearn,
Where
Gm7
C7
F
ros - es all have left your cheek,
I've
laughs the lit - tle sil - ver stream
Be -
C7
F
watched them fade a - way and die,
Your
side your moth - er's hum - ble cot
And
Dm
Dm♯5
A7/E
A7/E♭
D7
voice is sad when - e'er you speak
And
bright - est rays of sun - shine gleam,
There

G7
C7
tears be - dim your lov - ing eyes.
all your grief will be for - got.
Oh,
F
C7/G
G♯dim7
F/A
C7
I will take you back, Kath - leen, To where your heart will feel no
F
C7
F
F7
B♭
Bdim7
pain. And when the fields are fresh and green I'll
F/C
C7
1
F
2
F
take you to your home, Kath - leen. To leen.

ISN'T IT GRAND, BOYS?

Traditional Irish Folk Song

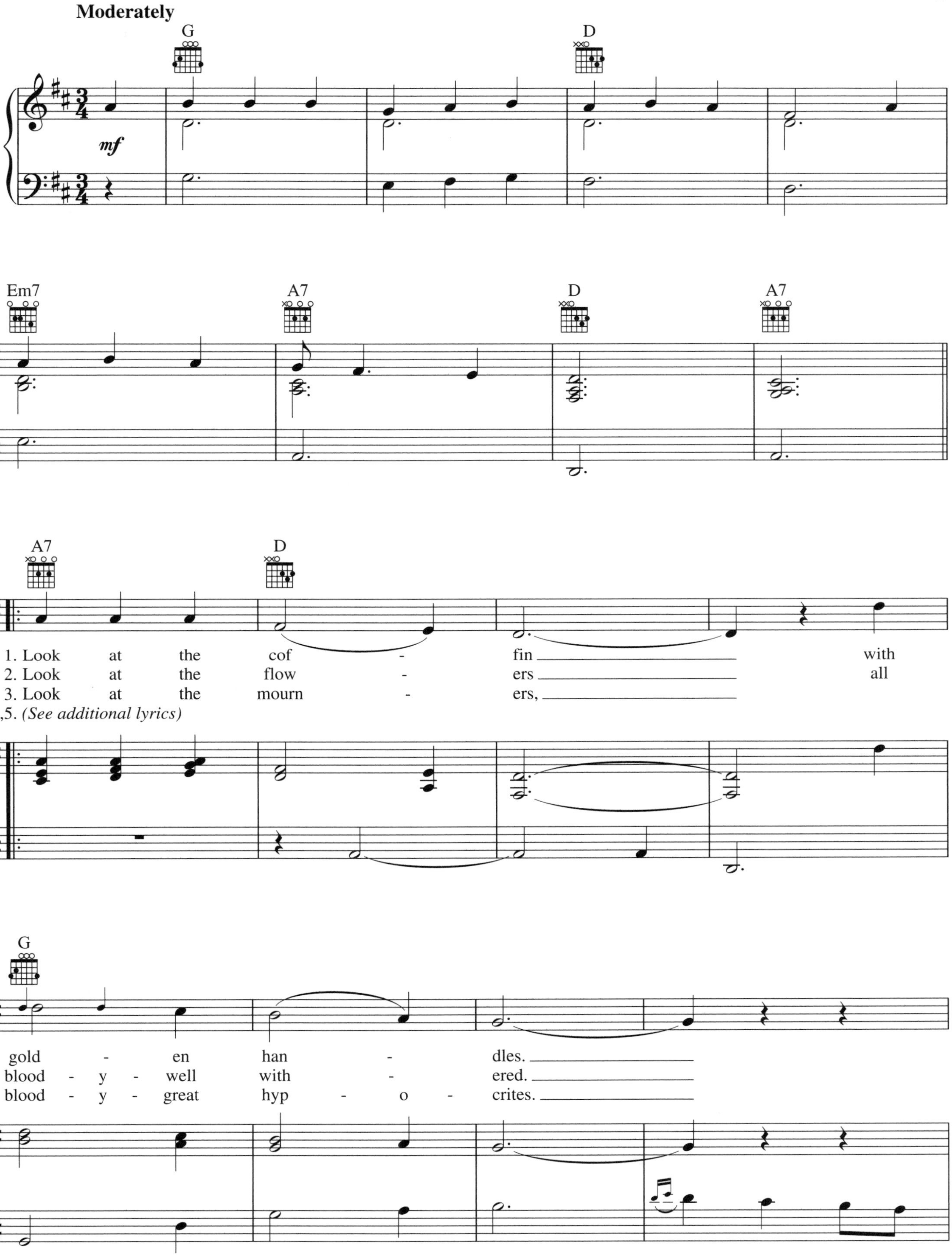
Moderately
G
D
mf
Em7
A7
D
A7
A7
D
1. Look at the cof - fin with
2. Look at the flow - ers all
3. Look at the mourn - ers,
4.,5. (See additional lyrics)
G
gold - en han - dles.
blood - y - well with - ered.
blood - y - great hyp - o - crites.

Copyright © 2006 by HAL LEONARD CORPORATION
International Copyright Secured All Rights Reserved

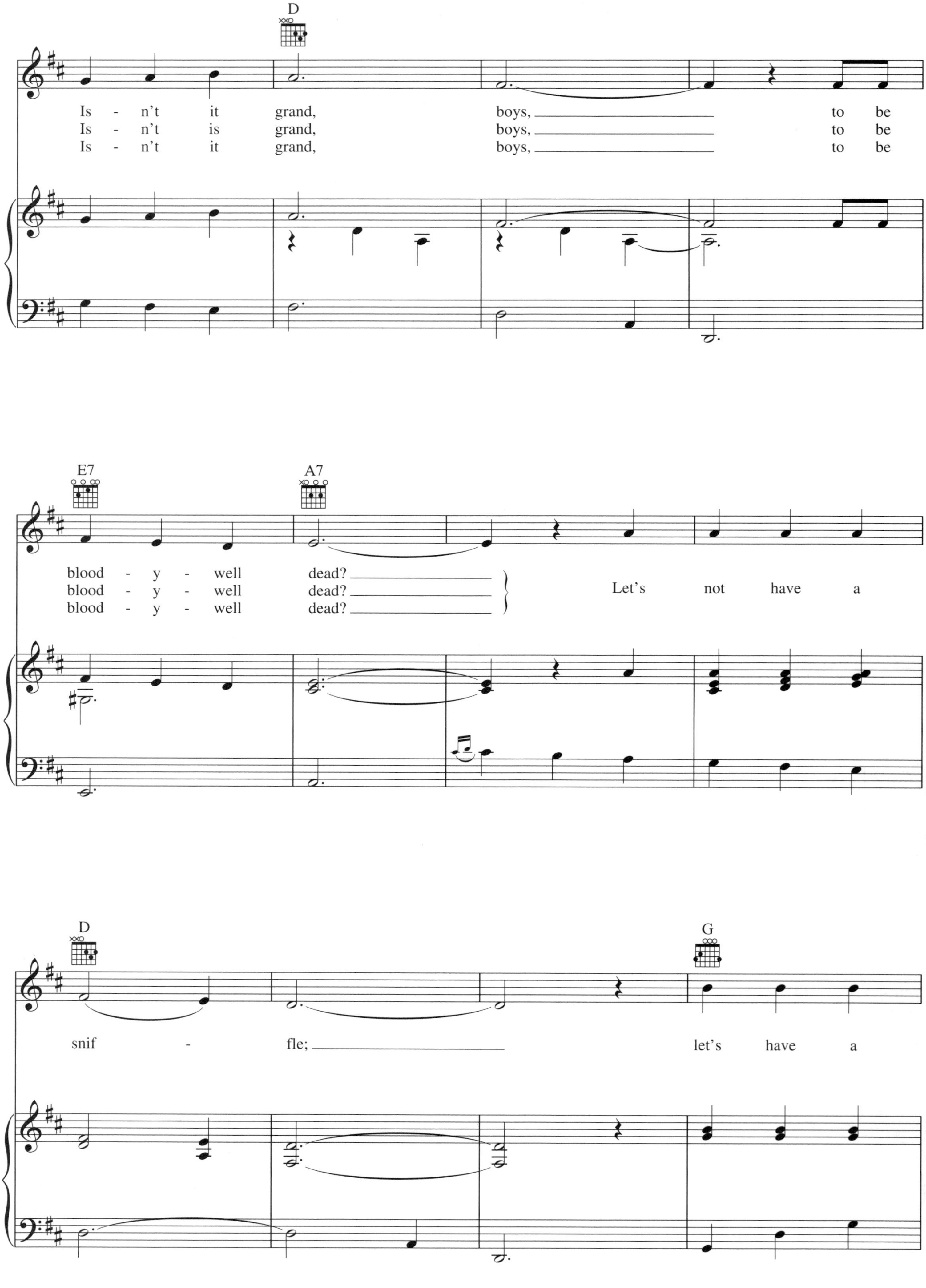
D
Is - n't it grand, boys, to be
Is - n't is grand, boys, to be
Is - n't it grand, boys, to be
E7
A7
blood - y - well dead?
blood - y - well dead?
blood - y - well dead?
Let's not have a
D
G
snif - fle; let's have a

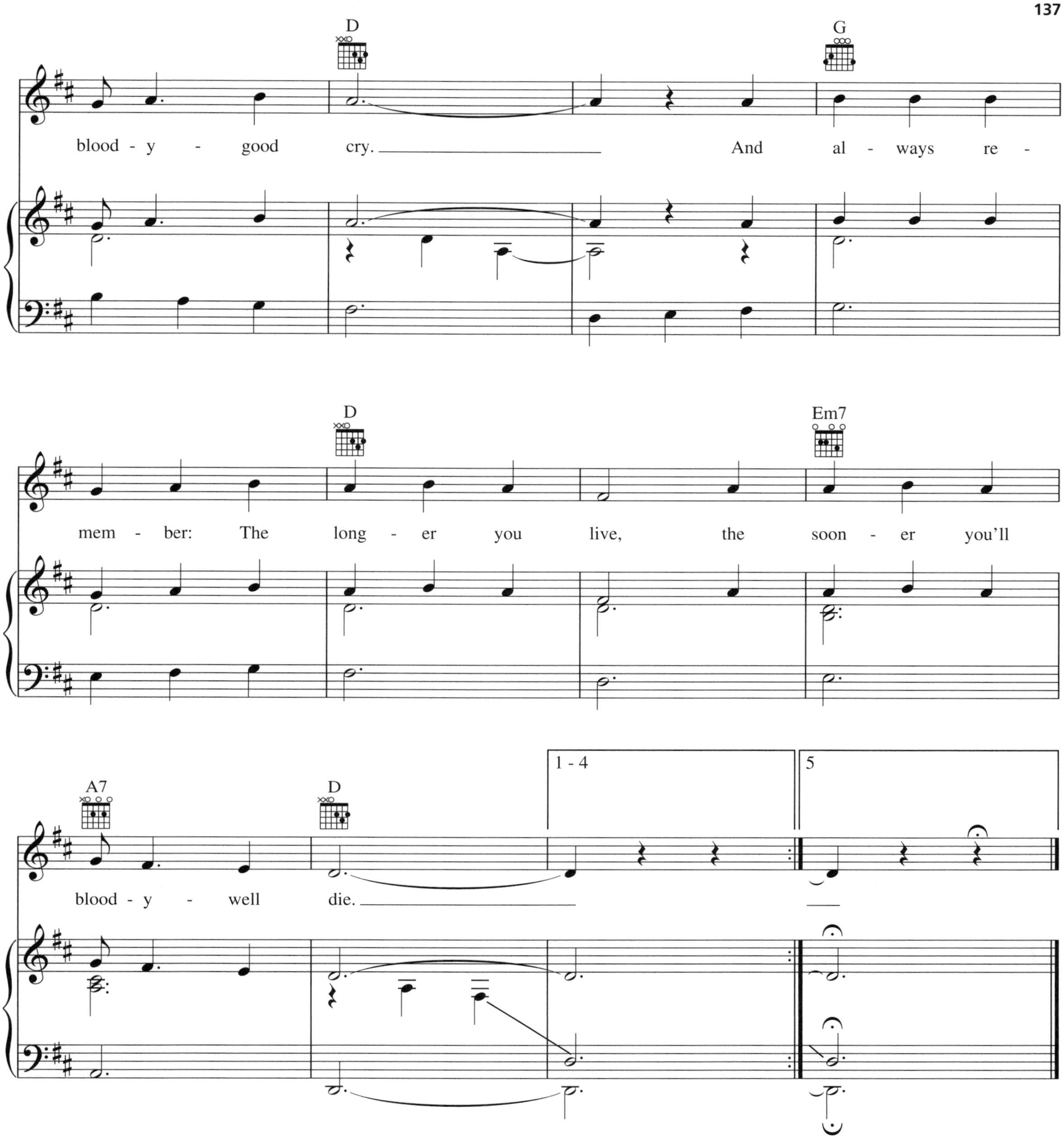
D
G
blood - y - good cry.
And al - ways re -
D
Em7
mem - ber: The long - er you live, the soon - er you'll
A7
D
1 - 4
5
blood - y - well die.

Additional Lyrics

4. Look at the preacher,
   Bloody-nice fellow.
   Isn't it grand, boys,
   To be bloody-well dead?

5. Look at the widow,
   Bloody-great female.
   Isn't it grand, boys,
   It be bloody-well dead?

I'LL TELL ME MA

Traditional Irish Folk Song

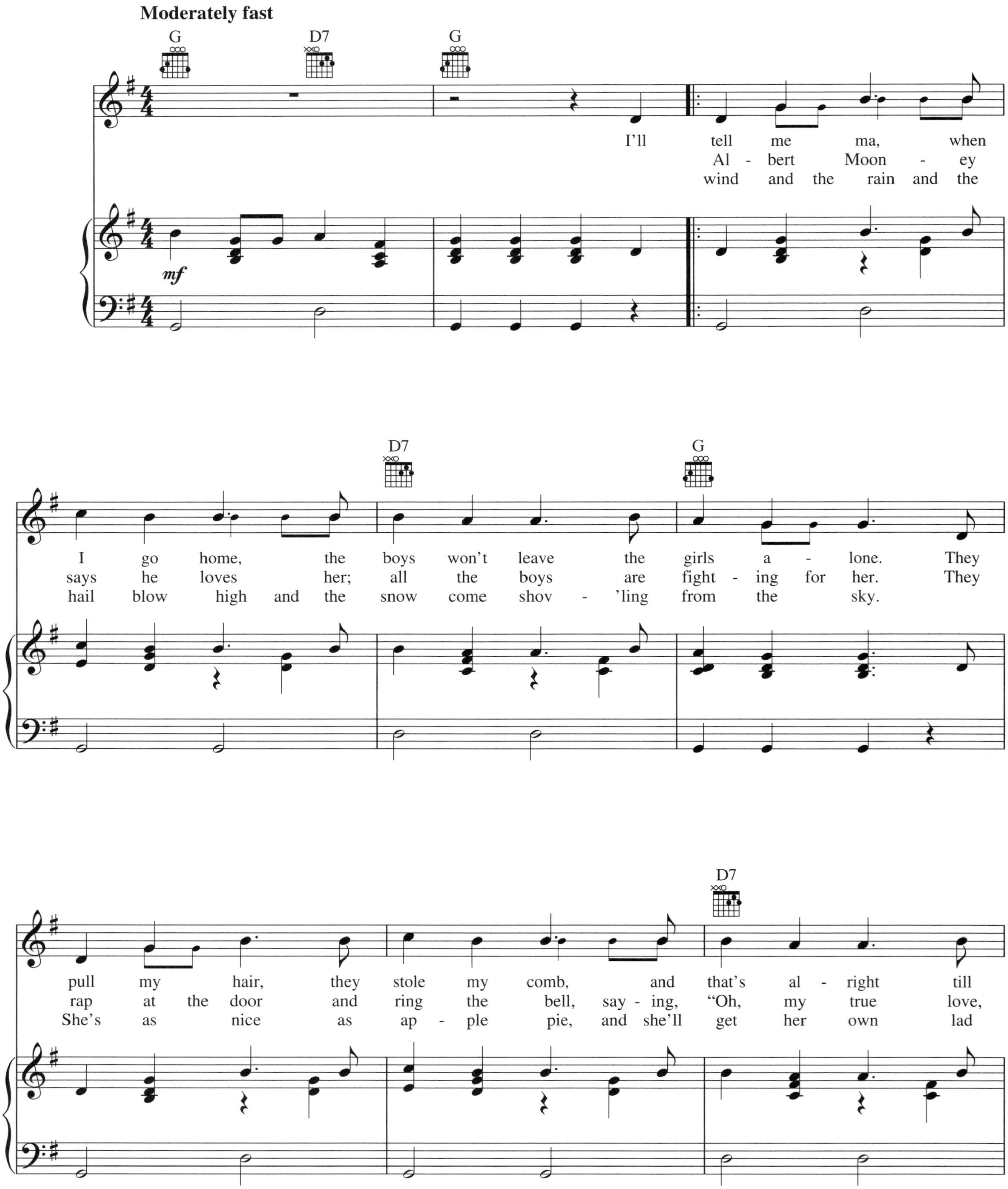
Moderately fast
G
D7
G
mf
I'll tell me ma, when
Al - bert Moon - ey
wind and the rain and the
D7
G
I go home, the boys won't leave the girls a - lone. They
says he loves her; all the boys are fight - ing for her. They
hail blow high and the snow come shov - 'ling from the sky.
D7
pull my hair, they stole my comb, and that's al - right till
rap at the door and ring the bell, say - ing, "Oh, my true love,
She's as nice as ap - ple pie, and she'll get her own lad

Copyright © 2003 by HAL LEONARD CORPORATION
International Copyright Secured All Rights Reserved

G
G7
C
D7
I go home. She is hand - some, she is pret - ty,
are you well?" Out she comes, as white as snow,
by and by. When she gets a lad of her own,
G
A7
D7
G
G7
she's the belle of Bel - fast cit - y. She is court - in',
rings on her fin - gers, bells on her toes. Old Jen - ny Mur - phy
she won't tell her ma when she gets home. Let them all come
C
Cm
3fr
G
D7
one, two, three. Please won't you tell me
says she'll die, if she does - n't get the fel - low
as they will, but it's Al - bert Moon - ey
1, 2
G
3
G
who is she? Now she loves still.
with the rov - ing eye. Let the

I'M A ROVER AND SELDOM SOBER

Traditional Irish Folk Song

Moderately
G D7 G C
I'm a rov - er and sel - dom
mf
G D7 G D7
so - ber, I'm a rov - er o' high de - gree. It's when I'm drink - ing I'm al - ways
G D7 G C
think - ing how to gain my love's com - pa - ny.
1. Though the night be as dark as
2. He step - pit up to her bed - room
3. She raised her heid on her snaw - white
4.-7. (See additional lyrics)

Copyright © 2003 by HAL LEONARD CORPORATION
International Copyright Secured All Rights Reserved

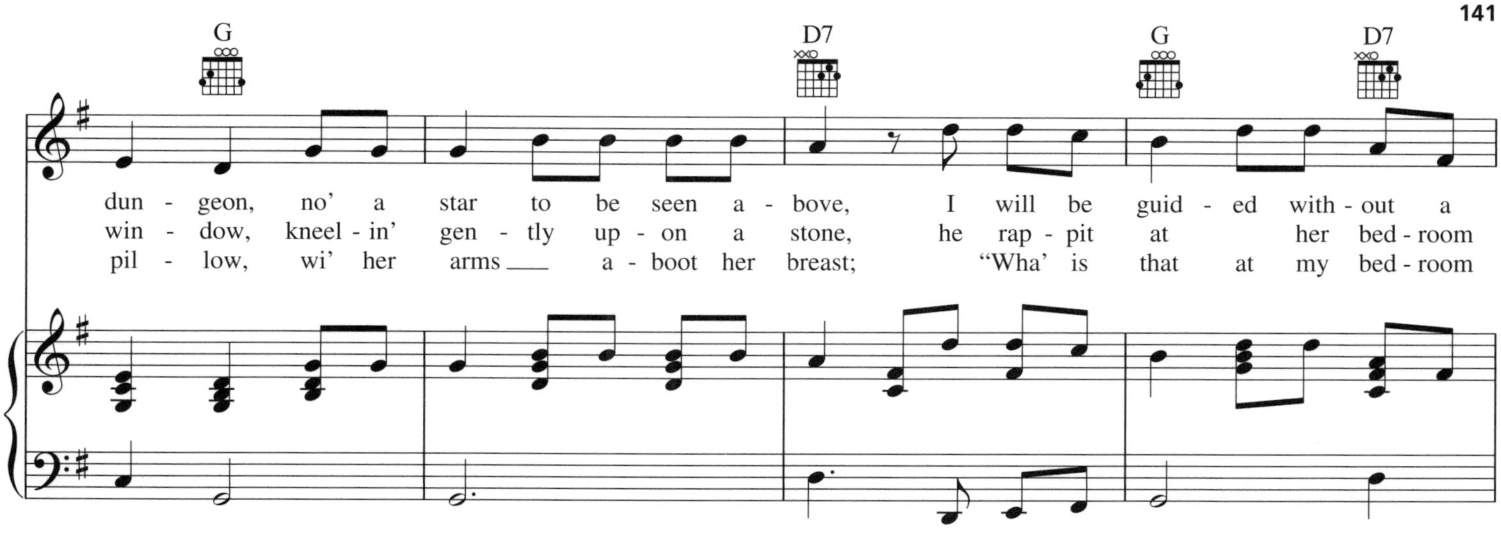
G
D7
G
D7
dun - geon, no' a star to be seen a - bove, I will be guid - ed with - out a
win - dow, kneel - in' gen - tly up - on a stone, he rap - pit at her bed - room
pil - low, wi' her arms ___ a - boot her breast; "Wha' is that at my bed - room

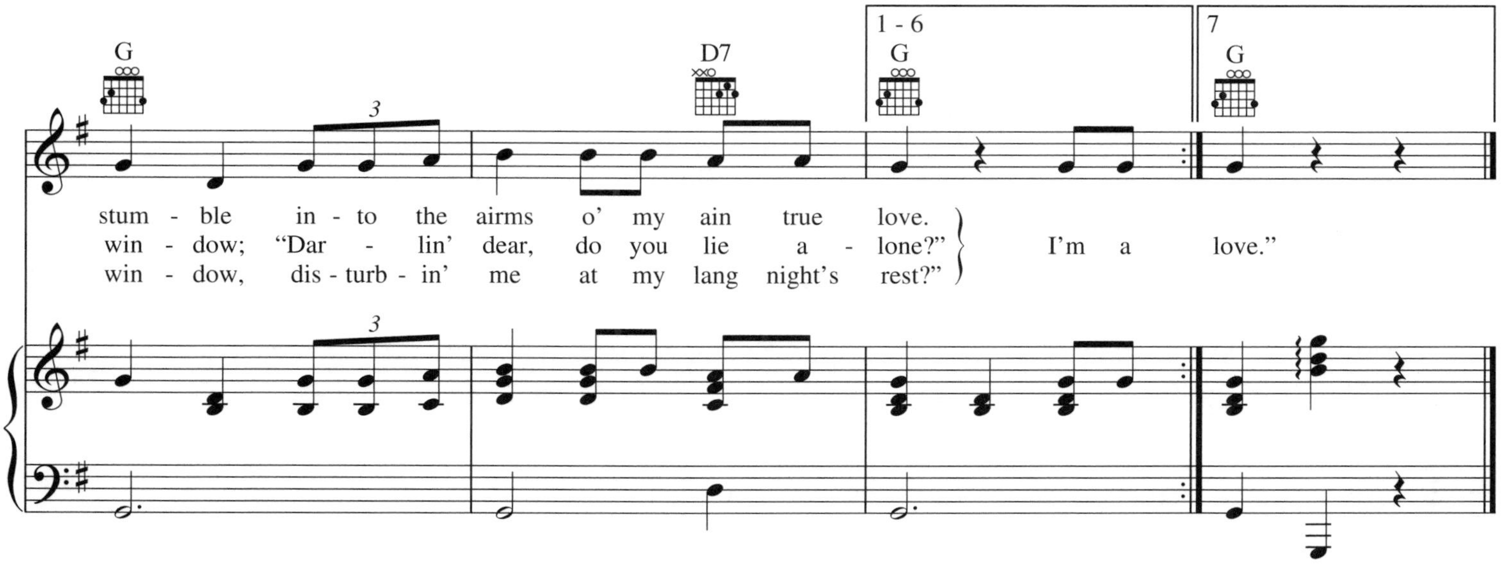
1 - 6
7
G
D7
G
G
3
stum - ble in - to the airms o' my ain true love.
win - dow; "Dar - lin' dear, do you lie a - lone?"
win - dow, dis - turb - in' me at my lang night's rest?"
I'm a love."

Additional Lyrics

4. "It's only me, your ain true lover;
   Open the door and let me in,
   For I hae come on a lang journey
   And I'm near drenched to the skin."

5. She opened the door wi' the greatest pleasure,
   She opened the door and she let him in;
   They baith shook hands and embraced each other,
   Until the mornin' they lay as one.

6. The cocks were crawin', the birds were whistlin',
   The burns they ran free abune the brae;
   "Remember, lass, I'm a ploughman laddie
   And the fairmer I must obey."

7. "Noo, my lass, I must gang and leave thee,
   And though the hills they are high above,
   I will climb them wi' greater pleasure
   Since I been in the airms o' my love."

THE IRISH ROVER

Traditional Irish Folk Song

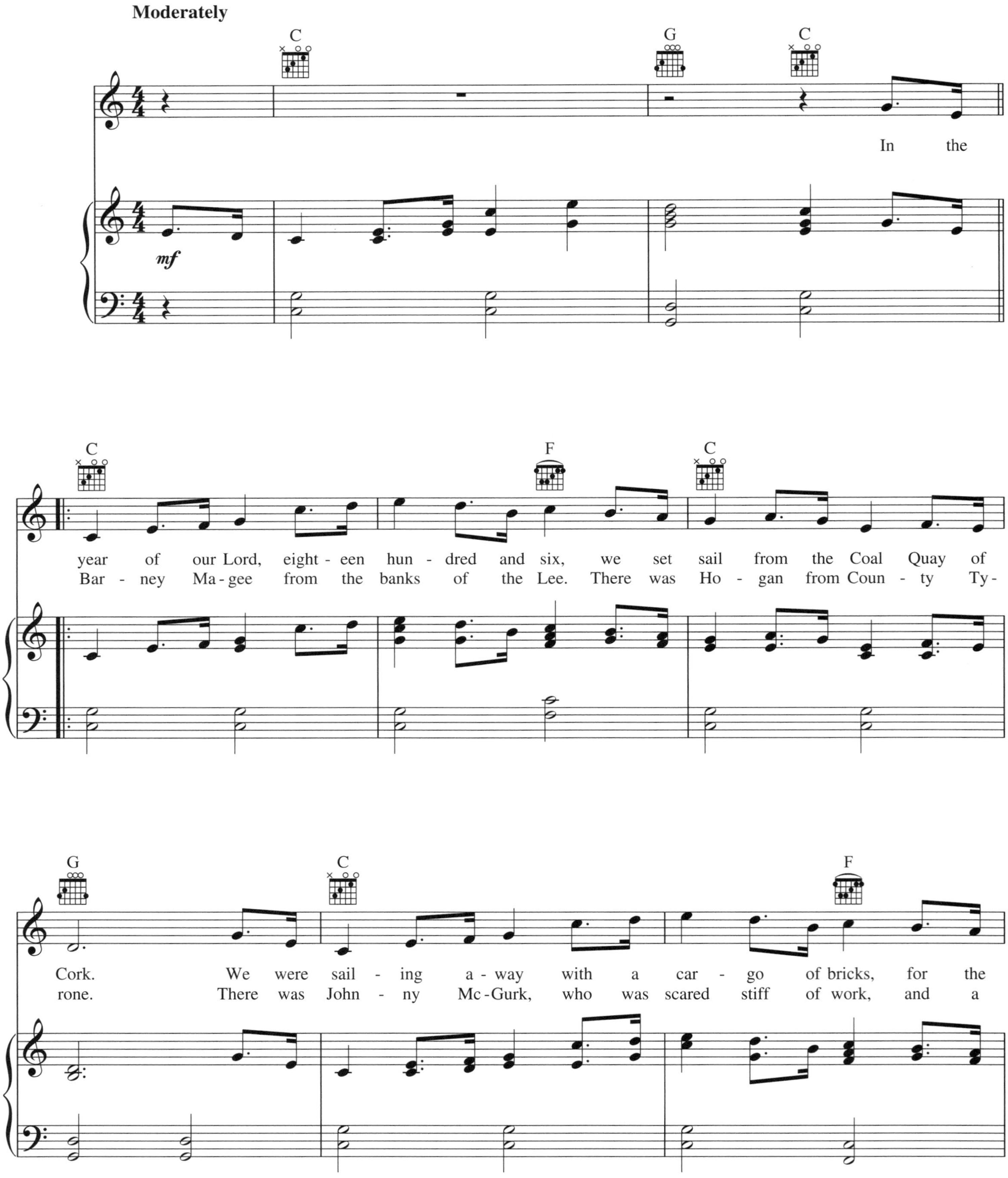
Moderately
C
G
C
mf
In the
C
F
C
year of our Lord, eight - een hun - dred and six, we set sail from the Coal Quay of
Bar - ney Ma - gee from the banks of the Lee. There was Ho - gan from Coun - ty Ty-
G
C
F
Cork. We were sail - ing a - way with a car - go of bricks, for the
rone. There was John - ny Mc - Gurk, who was scared stiff of work, and a

Copyright © 2003 by HAL LEONARD CORPORATION
International Copyright Secured Used by Permission

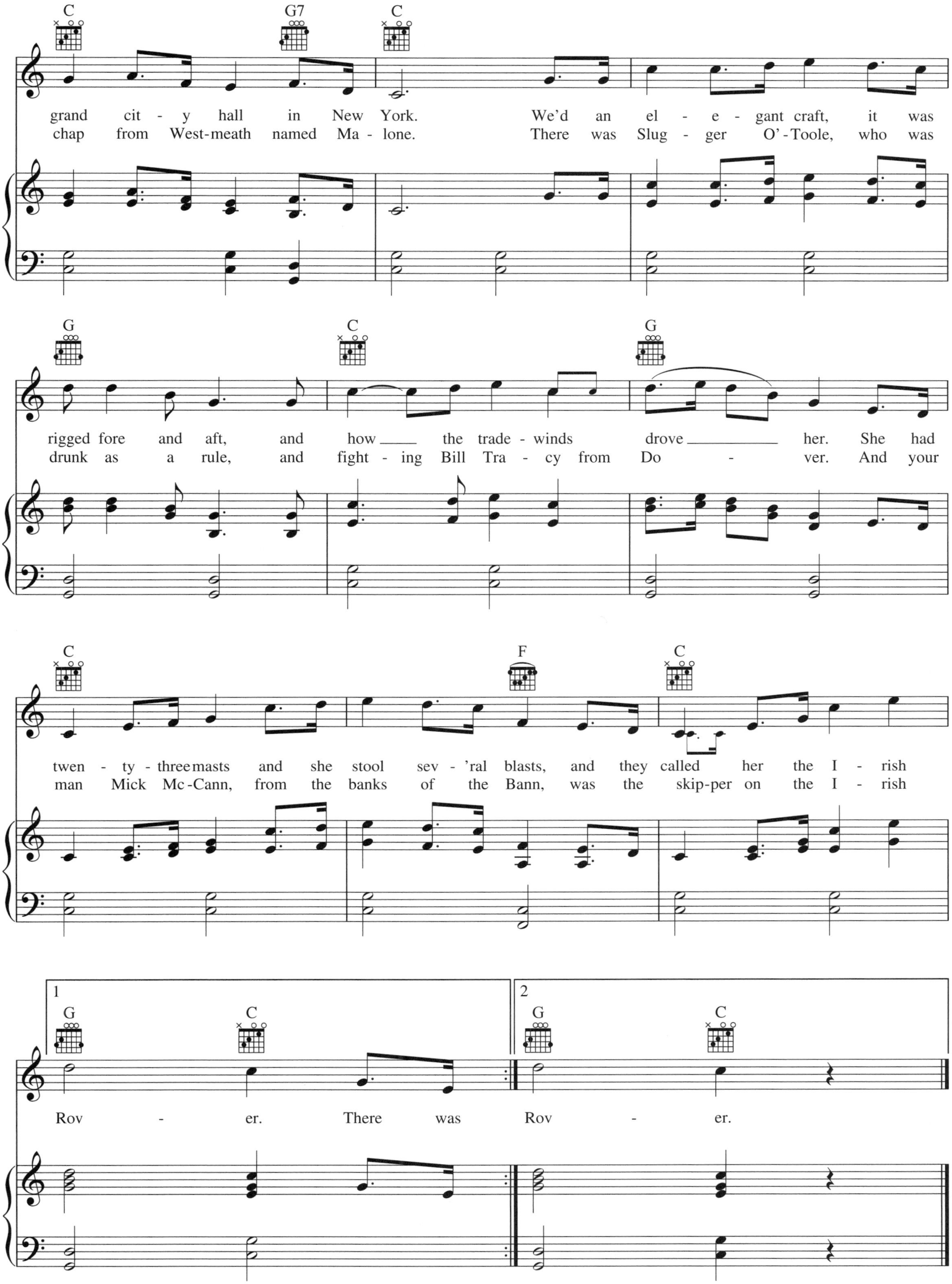
C G7 C
grand cit - y hall in New York. We'd an el - e - gant craft, it was
chap from West-meath named Ma - lone. There was Slug - ger O'-Toole, who was
G C G
rigged fore and aft, and how the trade - winds drove her. She had
drunk as a rule, and fight - ing Bill Tra - cy from Do - ver. And your
C F C
twen - ty - three masts and she stool sev - 'ral blasts, and they called her the I - rish
man Mick Mc-Cann, from the banks of the Bann, was the skip-per on the I - rish
1 G C
Rov - er. There was
2 G C
Rov - er.

JAMES CONNOLLY

Traditional Irish Folk Song

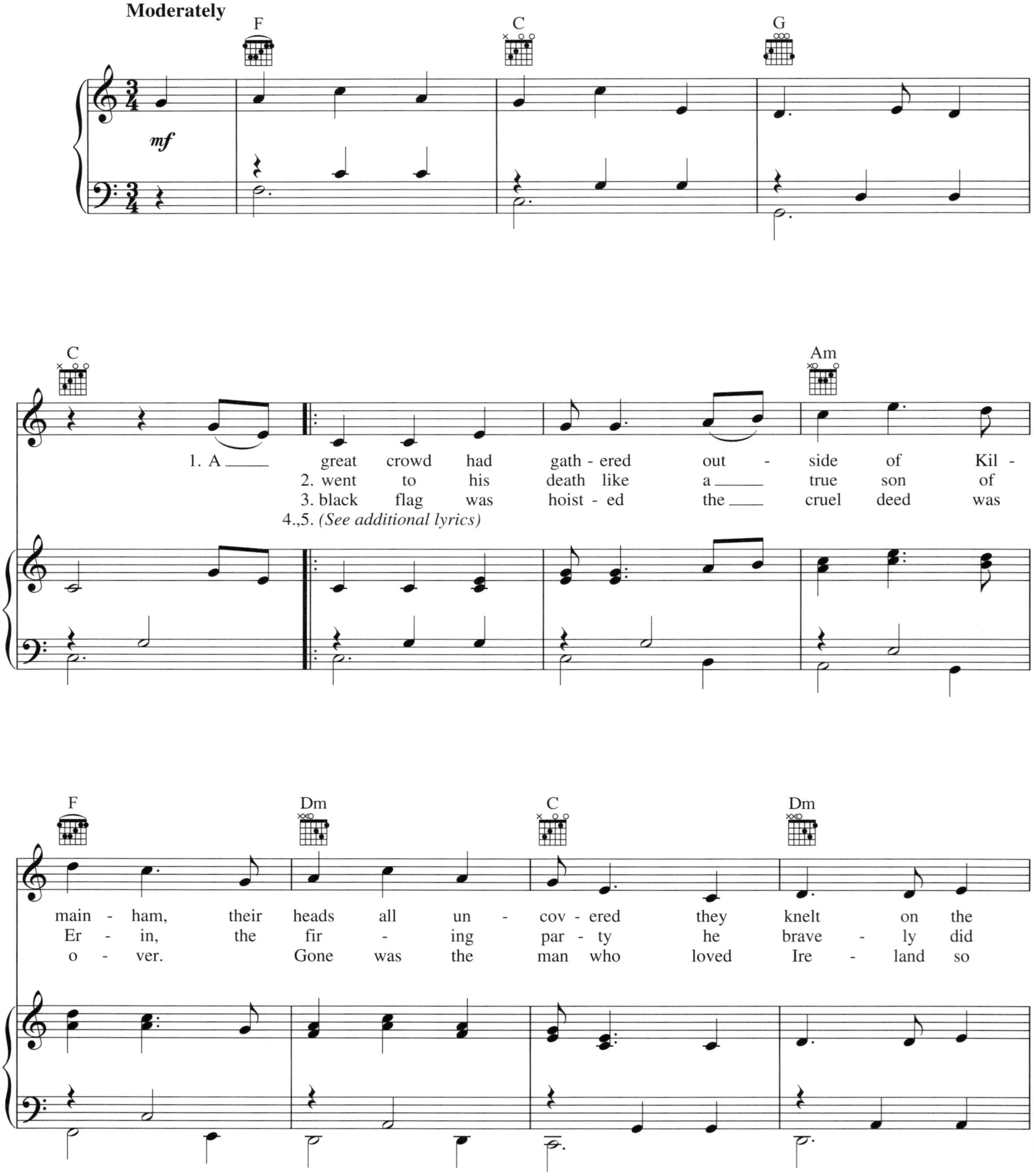
Moderately
F C G
mf
C Am
1. A great crowd had gath - ered out - side of Kil - main - ham, their heads all un - cov - ered they knelt on the
2. went to his death like a true son of Er - in, the fir - ing par - ty he brave - ly did
3. black flag was hoist - ed the cruel deed was o - ver. Gone was the man who loved Ire - land so
4.,5. (See additional lyrics)
F Dm C Dm

Copyright © 2006 by HAL LEONARD CORPORATION
International Copyright Secured All Rights Reserved

G
C
ground. For in - side that grim pris - on, lay a
face. Then the or - der rang out "Pre - sent
well. There was man - y a sad heart in
Am
F
Dm
C
true I - rish sol - dier, his life for his coun - try a -
arms" and "Fire!" James Con - bol - ly fell in - to a
Dub - lin that morn - ing when they mur - dered James Con - nol - ly the
Dm
C
1 - 4
5
bout to lay down. He
read - y - made grave. The
I - rish reb - el. Man - y

Additional Lyrics

4. Many years have rolled by since the Irish Rebellion
   When the guns of Britannia they loudly did speak.
   And the bold IRA they stood shoulder to shoulder
   And the blood from their bodies flowed down Sackville Street.

5. The Four Courts of Dublin the English bombarded
   The spirit of freedom they tried hard to quell.
   But above all the din came the cry "No Surrender!"
   'Twas with voice of James Connolly, the Irish rebel.

JOHNNY I HARDLY KNEW YE

Traditional Irish Folk Song

Lively
Em D C B Em Am
mf
Em
1. While go - in' the road to sweet Ath - y,
2. drums and guns and drums and guns,
3. Where are your eyes that were so mild,
hur -
4.-6. (See additional lyrics)
G Em
roo, hur - roo!
While go - in' the road to
With your drums and guns and
Where are your eyes that
G B
sweet Ath - y,
drums and guns,
were so mild,
hur - roo, hur - roo!
While
With your

Copyright © 2006 by HAL LEONARD CORPORATION
International Copyright Secured All Rights Reserved

Em D Em
go- in' the road to sweet Ath - y a stick in me hand and a
guns and drums and guns and drums, the en - e- my near - ly
Where are your eyes that were so mild when my heart you
B Em D C B
drop in me eye, a dole - ful dam - sel I heard cry:
slew me. Oh, my dar - ling dear, ye look so queer.
so be - guiled? Why did ye run from me and the child?
Em Am
1 - 5
Em Am Em
6
Em
John- ny I hard - ly knew ye.
With your
knew ye.

Additional Lyrics

4. Where are your legs that used to run, hurroo, hurroo!
Where are your legs that used to run, hurroo, hurroo!
Where are your legs that used to run
When you went for to carry a gun?
Indeed your dancing days are done.
Johnny I hardly knew ye.

5. I'm happy for to see you home, hurroo, hurroo!
I'm happy for to see you home, hurroo, hurroo!
I'm happy for to see you home
All from the island of Sulloon,
So low in flesh, so high in bone.
Johnny I hardly knew ye.

6. Ye haven't an arm, ye haven't a leg, hurroo, hurroo!
Ye haven't an arm, ye haven't a leg, hurroo, hurroo!
Ye haven't an arm, ye haven't a leg,
Ye're an armless, boneless, chickenless egg,
Ye'll have to put with a bowl out to beg.
Johnny I hardly knew ye.`

JOHNSON'S MOTOR CAR

Traditional Irish Folk Song

Brightly
mf
C Am G F G C G/B Am G F G C G/B Am F G C G/B
1. 'Twas down by Bran - ni - gan's Cor - ner, one morn - ing I did stray. I met a fel - low reb - el, and to me he did say, "We've or - ders from the
2. Bar - ney dear, be of good cheer, I'll tell you what we'll do. The spe - cials they are plen - ti - ful, the I. R. A. are few. We'll send a wire to
3. Dr. John - son heard the news he soon put on his shoes. He says this is an ur - gent case there is no time to lose. He then put on his
4-6. (See additional lyrics)

Copyright © ---- by HAL LEONARD CORPORATION
International Copyright Secured All Rights Reserved

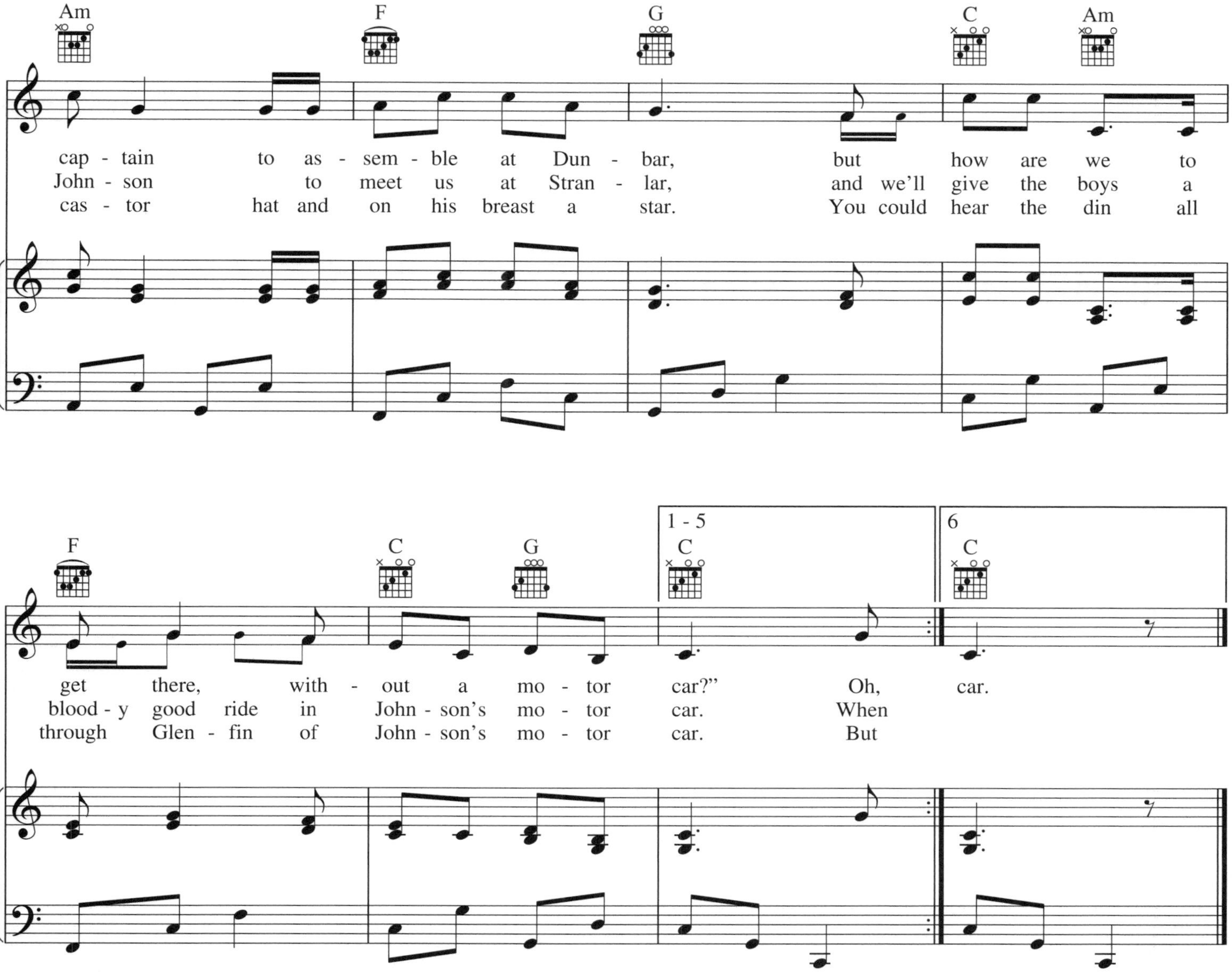
Am F G C Am
cap - tain to as - sem - ble at Dun - bar, but how are we to
John - son to meet us at Stran - lar, and we'll give the boys a
cas - tor hat and on his breast a star. You could hear the din all
F C G
1 - 5 C
6 C
get there, with - out a mo - tor car?" Oh, car.
blood - y good ride in John - son's mo - tor car. When
through Glen - fin of John - son's mo - tor car. But

Additional Lyrics

4. But when he got to the railway bridge, some rebels he saw there.
   Old Johnson knew the game was up, for at him they did stare.
   He said, "I have a permit, to travel near and far."
   "To hell with your English permit, we want your motor car."

5. "What will my loyal brethren think, when they hear the news,
   My car it has been commandeered, by the rebels at Dunluce."
   "We'll give you a receipt for it, all signed by Captain Barr.
   And when Ireland gets her freedom, boy, you'll get your motor car."

6. Well, we put that car in motion and filled it to the brim,
   With guns and bayonets shining which made old Johnson grim,
   And Barney hoisted a Sinn Fein flag, and it fluttered like a star,
   And we gave three cheers for the I.R.A. and Johnson's motor car.

THE JOLLY BEGGARMAN

Traditional Irish Folk Song

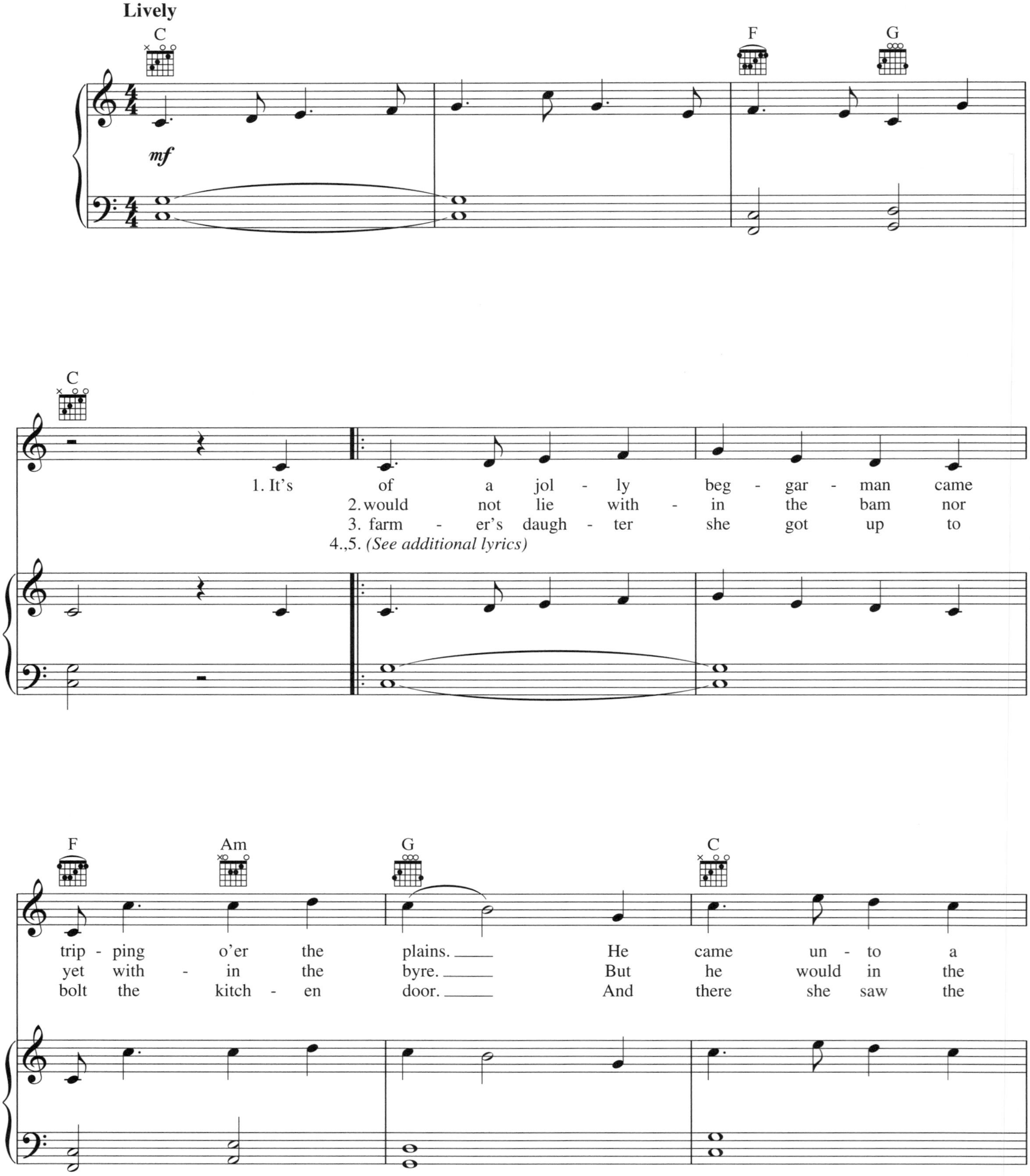
Lively
C F G
mf
C
1. It's of a jol - ly beg - gar - man came
2. would not lie with - in the bam nor
3. farm - er's daugh - ter she got up to
4.,5. (See additional lyrics)
F Am G C
trip - ping o'er the plains. He came un - to a
yet with - in the byre. But he would in the
bolt the kitch - en door. And there she saw the

Copyright © 2006 by HAL LEONARD CORPORATION
International Copyright Secured All Rights Reserved

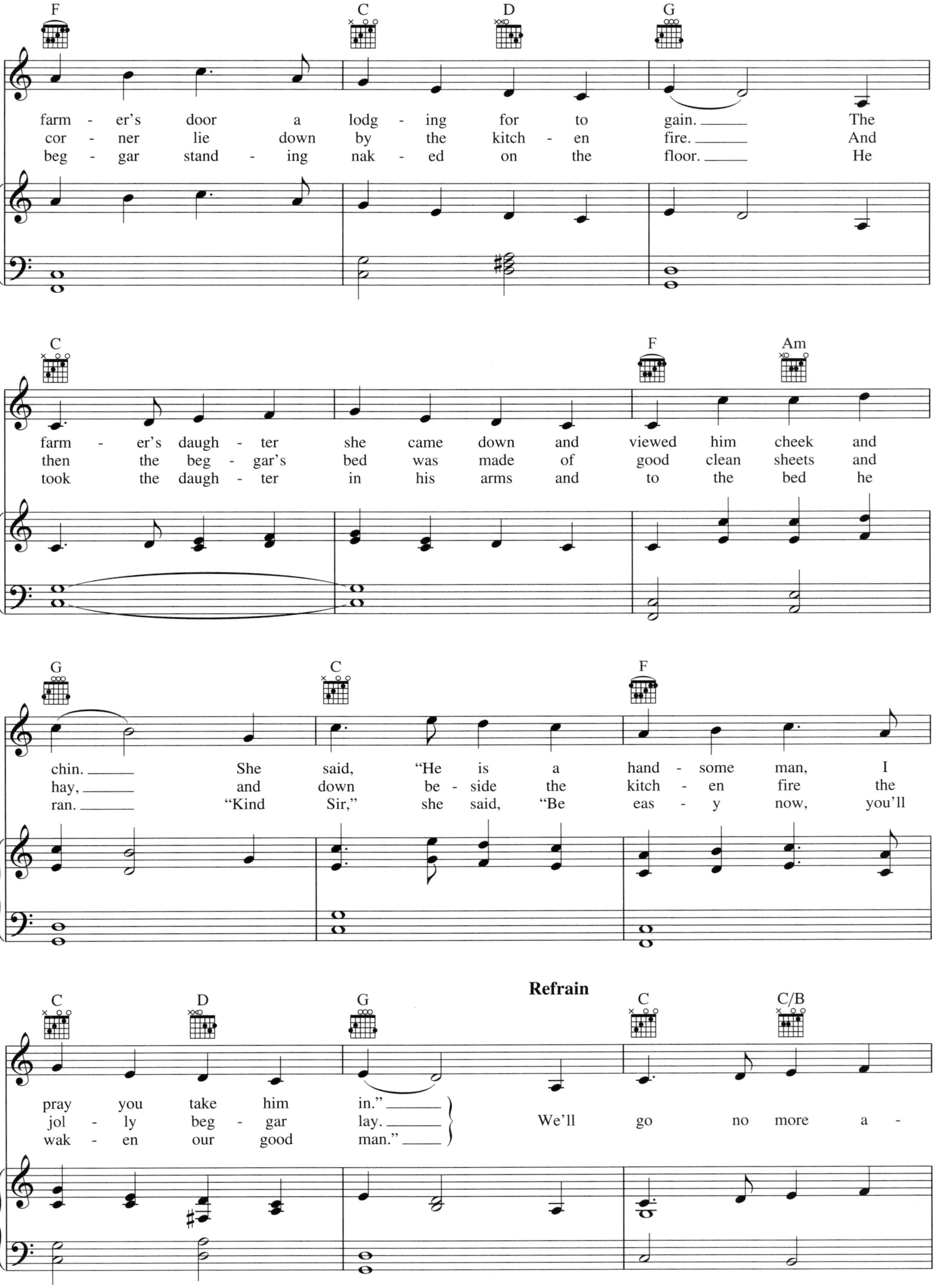
F C D G
farm - er's door a lodg - ing for to gain. The
cor - ner lie down by the kitch - en fire. And
beg - gar stand - ing nak - ed on the floor. He
C F Am
farm - er's daugh - ter she came down and viewed him cheek and
then the beg - gar's bed was made of good clean sheets and
took the daugh - ter in his arms and to the bed he
G C F
chin. She said, "He is a hand - some man, I
hay, and down be - side the kitch - en fire the
ran. "Kind Sir," she said, "Be eas - y now, you'll
C D G
Refrain
C C/B
pray you take him in."
jol - ly beg - gar lay.
wak - en our good man."
We'll go no more a -

C/A C/G F Am Am/G
rov - ing, a - rov - ing in the night, we'll
C C/B F/A F/G C C/F
3fr
go no more a - rov - ing let the moon shine so
G G/D C F
1 - 4
C
5
C
bright. We'll go no more a - rov - ing.
He
The
"O
rov - ing.

Additional Lyrics

4. "O no, you are no beggar man, you are some gentleman
For you have stole my maidenhead and I am quite undone."
"I am no lord, I am no squire, of beggars I be one
And beggars they be robbers all and you are quite undone."
Refrain

5. The farmer's wife came down the stairs, awakened from her sleep.
She saw the beggar and the girl and she began to weep.
She took the bed in both her hands and threw it at the wall
Saying, "Go you with the beggarman, your maidenhead and all!"
Refrain

KELLY OF KILLANE

Traditional Irish Folk Song

March tempo
C G7 C
mf
Am
"What's the news, what's the news, O my
who is that giant with the
cor - thy's in flames and old
gold sun of free - dom grew
C F C
bold Shel - ma - lier; with your long bar - relled
gold curl - ing hair; he who rides at the
Wex - ford is won; and the Bar - row, tom -
dark - ened at Ross; and it set by the
G7 C
gun of the sea? Say what
head of your band. Sev - en
mor - row we will cross. On a
Slan - ey's red waves. And poor

Copyright © 2006 by HAL LEONARD CORPORATION
International Copyright Secured All Rights Reserved

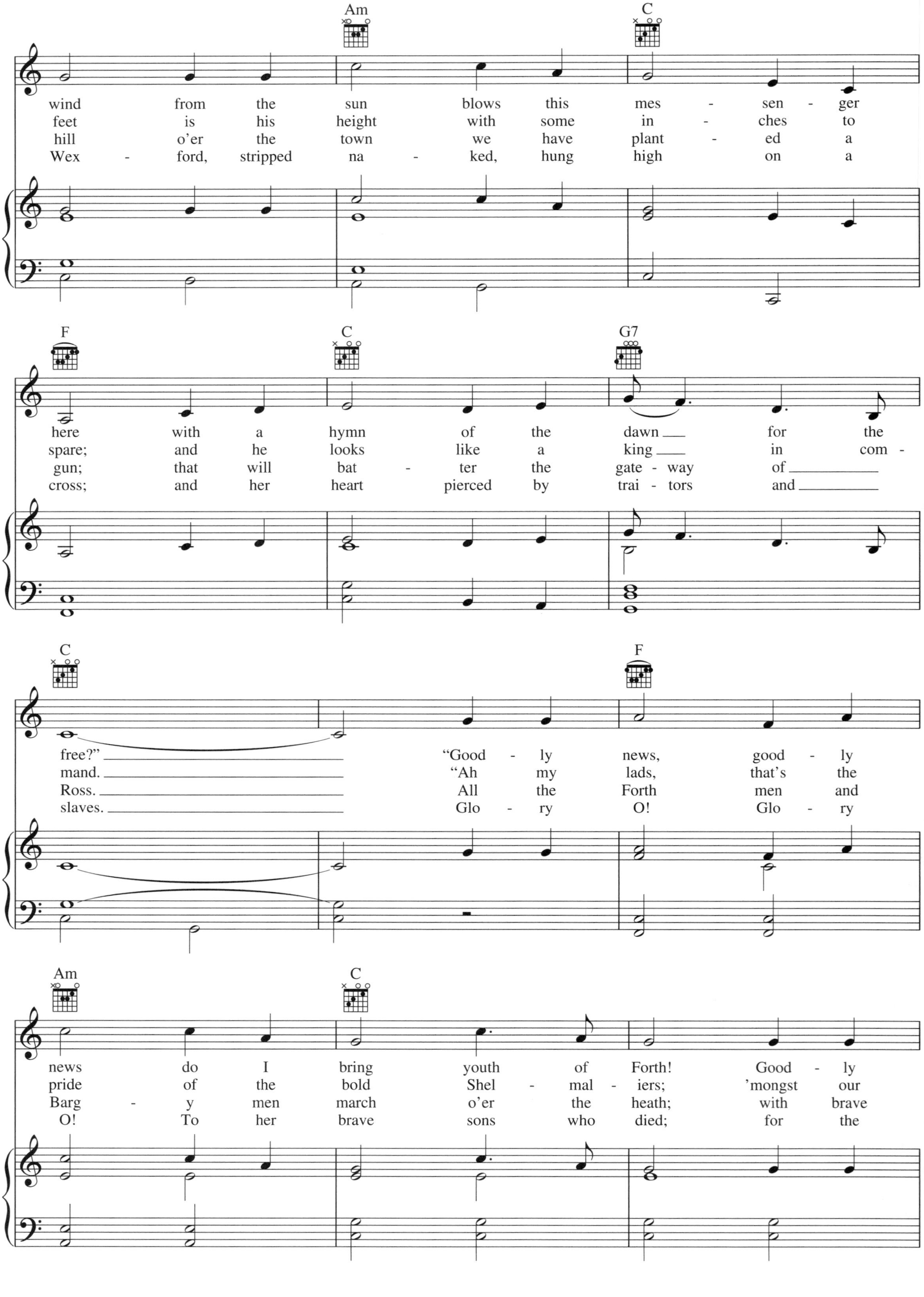
Am C
wind from the sun blows this mes - sen - ger
feet is his height with some in - ches to
hill o'er the town we have plant - ed a
Wex - ford, stripped na - ked, hung high on a
F C G7
here with a hymn of the dawn for the
spare; and he looks like a king in com -
gun; that will bat - ter the gate - way of
cross; and her heart pierced by trai - tors and
C F
free?" "Good - ly news, good - ly
mand. "Ah my lads, that's the
Ross. All the Forth men and
slaves. Glo - ry O! Glo - ry
Am C
news do I bring youth of Forth! Good - ly
pride of the bold Shel - mal - iers; 'mongst our
Barg - y men march o'er the heath; with brave
O! To her brave sons who died; for the

F
G7
news shall you hear, Bar - gy man!
great - est of he - roes a man.
Har - vey to lead on the van.
cause of long down - trod - den man.
C
Am
For the boys march at morn from the
Fling your beav - ers a - loft and give
But the fore - most of all in that
Glo - ry O! To Mount Lein - ster's own
C
F
C
South to the North, led by Kel - ly the
three ring - ing cheers; for John Kel - ly, the
grim gap of death; will be Kel - ly, the
dar - ling and pride; daunt - less Kel - ly, the
G7
C
1 - 3
4
boy from Kil - lane." Tell me
boy from Kil - lane." En - nis -
boy from Kil - lane. But the
boy from Kil - lane.

JUG OF PUNCH

Ulster Folk Song

Brightly
D
'Twas ver - y
mf
D
A
D
ear - ly in the month of June I was sit - ting with my glass and spoon. A
ver - sion can a man de - sire, than to court a girl by a neat turf fire? A
mor - tal Lords drink your nec - tar wine, and the no - ble folks drink their clar - et fine. I'll
when I'm dead and in my grave, no cost - ly tomb - stone will I crave. Just
Em
A
D
A7
small bird sat on an i - vy bunch, and the song he sang was "The Jug of Punch."
Ker - ry pip - pin and the crack and crunch, and on the ta - ble a jug of punch.
give them all the grapes in the bunch for a jol - ly pull at the jug of punch.
lay me down in my na - tive peat with a jug of punch at my head and feet.
Too - rah-

Copyright © 2003 by HAL LEONARD CORPORATION
International Copyright Secured All Rights Reserved

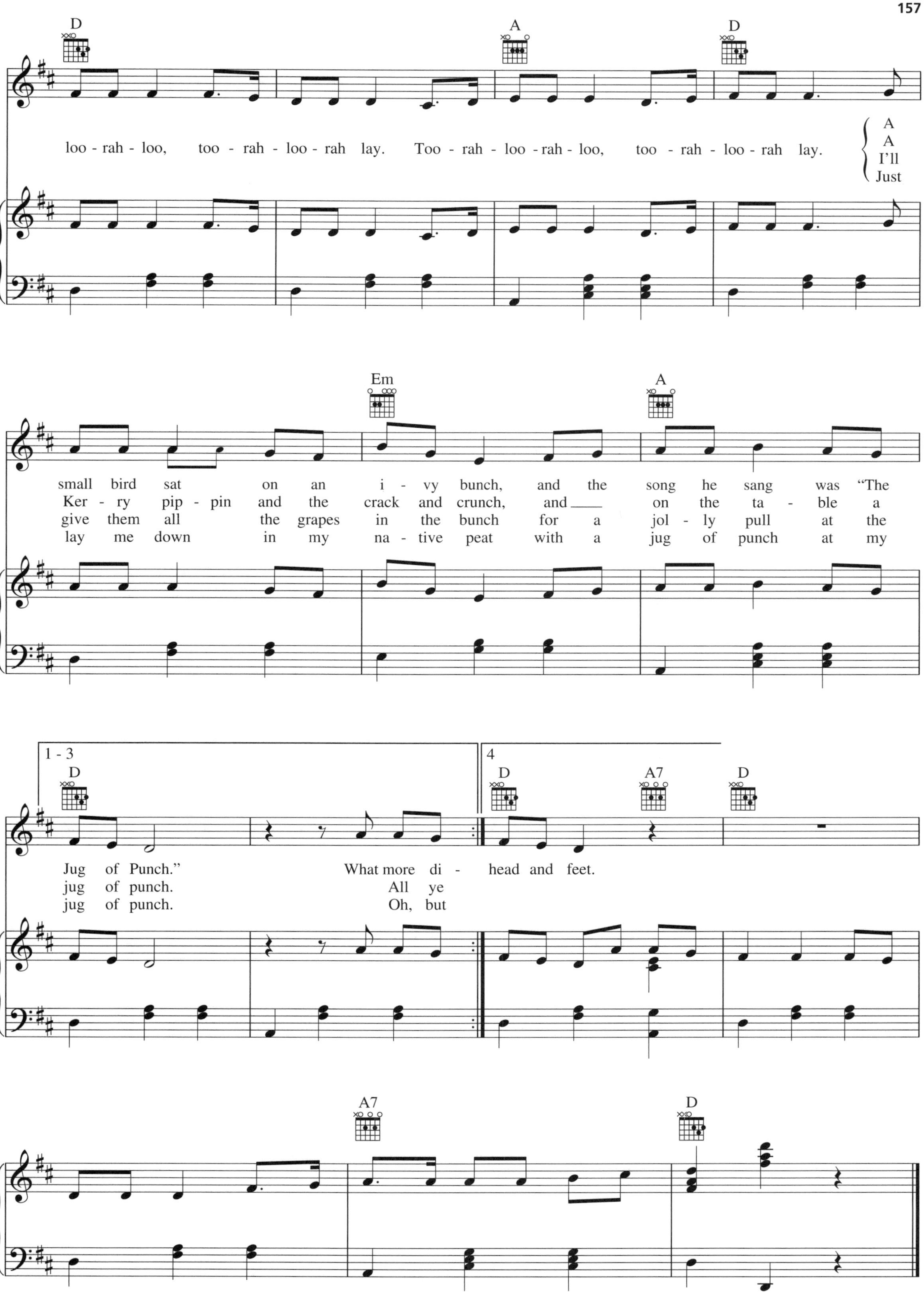
D
A
D
loo - rah - loo, too - rah - loo - rah lay. Too - rah - loo - rah - loo, too - rah - loo - rah lay.
A
A
I'll
Just
Em
A
small bird sat on an i - vy bunch, and the song he sang was "The
Ker - ry pip - pin and the crack and crunch, and on the ta - ble a
give them all the grapes in the bunch for a jol - ly pull at the
lay me down in my na - tive peat with a jug of punch at my
1 - 3
4
D
A7
D
Jug of Punch." What more di -
jug of punch. All ye
jug of punch. Oh, but
head and feet.
A7
D

THE JUICE OF THE BARLEY

Traditional Irish Folk Song

Moderately
mf
D A7 D
Bm G
1. In the sweet Coun - ty Lim - erick one cold win - ter's
2. I was a gas - soon of eight years or
3. learn - ing I wasn't such a gen - ius I'm
4.-6. (See additional lyrics)
A7 D Bm G
night, all the turf fires were burn - ing when I saw the
so, with me turf and me pri - mer to school I did
think - ing but I soon bet the mas - ter en - tirely at drink -
A7 D G Bm
light, and a drunk - en old mid - wife was tip - sy with
go, to a dust - y old school - house with - out an - y
ing, not a wake nor a wed - ding for five miles a -

Copyright © 2006 by HAL LEONARD CORPORATION
International Copyright Secured All Rights Reserved

F♯m Bm G Em
joy as she danced 'round the floor with her slip of a
door where _ lay the school - mas - ter blind drunk on the
round, but me - self in the cor - ner was sure to be
Chorus
A7 D Bm G A7
boy, floor, found, sing - ing, "Ban - ye na mo is an gow - na, and the
D A7 D
1 - 5
6
juice of the bar - ley for me." ________
Well when
At the
One _ ___
So the
Well from

Additional Lyrics

4. One Sunday the priest read me out from the altar
   Saying, "You'll end up your days with your neck in a halter.
   And you'll dance a fine jig betwixt heaven and hell."
   And the words they did frighten, the truth for to tell.
   Chorus

5. So the very next morning as the dawn it did break,
   I went down to the vestry the pledge for to take
   And there in that room sat the priests in a bunch
   'Round a big roaring fire drinking tumblers of punch.
   Chorus

6. Well from that day to this I have wandered alone
   I'm a Jack of all Trades and a master of none.
   With the sky for me roof and the earth for me floor
   And I'll dance out me days drinking whiskey galore.
   Chorus

THE KERRY RECRUIT

Traditional Irish Folk Song

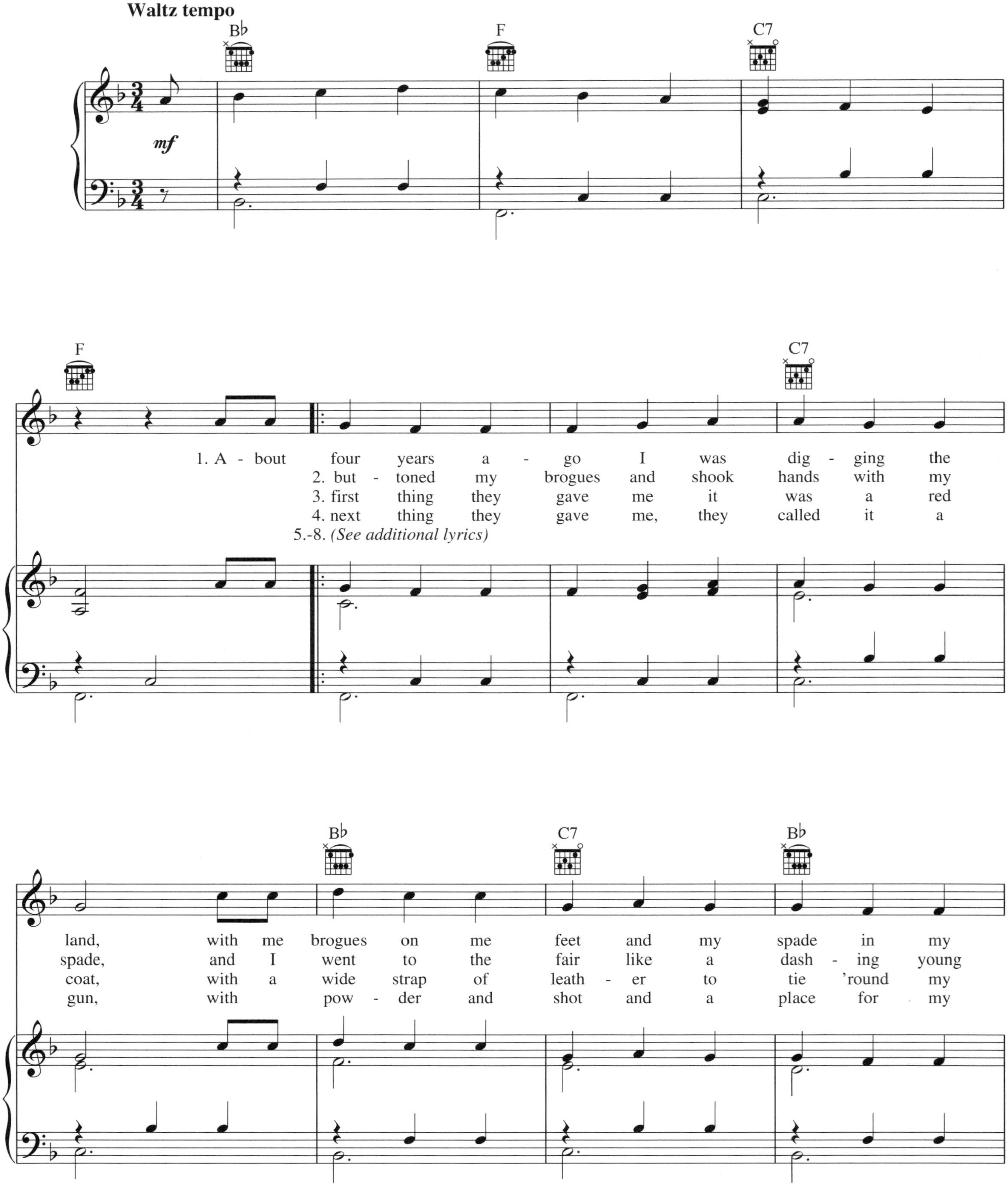
Waltz tempo
B♭
F
C7
mf
F
C7
1. A - bout four years a - go I was dig - ging the
2. but - toned my brogues and shook hands with my
3. first thing they gave me it was a red
4. next thing they gave me, they called it a
5.-8. (See additional lyrics)
B♭
C7
B♭
land, with me brogues on me feet and my spade in my
spade, and I went to the fair like a dash - ing young
coat, with a wide strap of leath - er to tie 'round my
gun, with pow - der and shot and a place for my

Copyright © 2006 by HAL LEONARD CORPORATION
International Copyright Secured All Rights Reserved

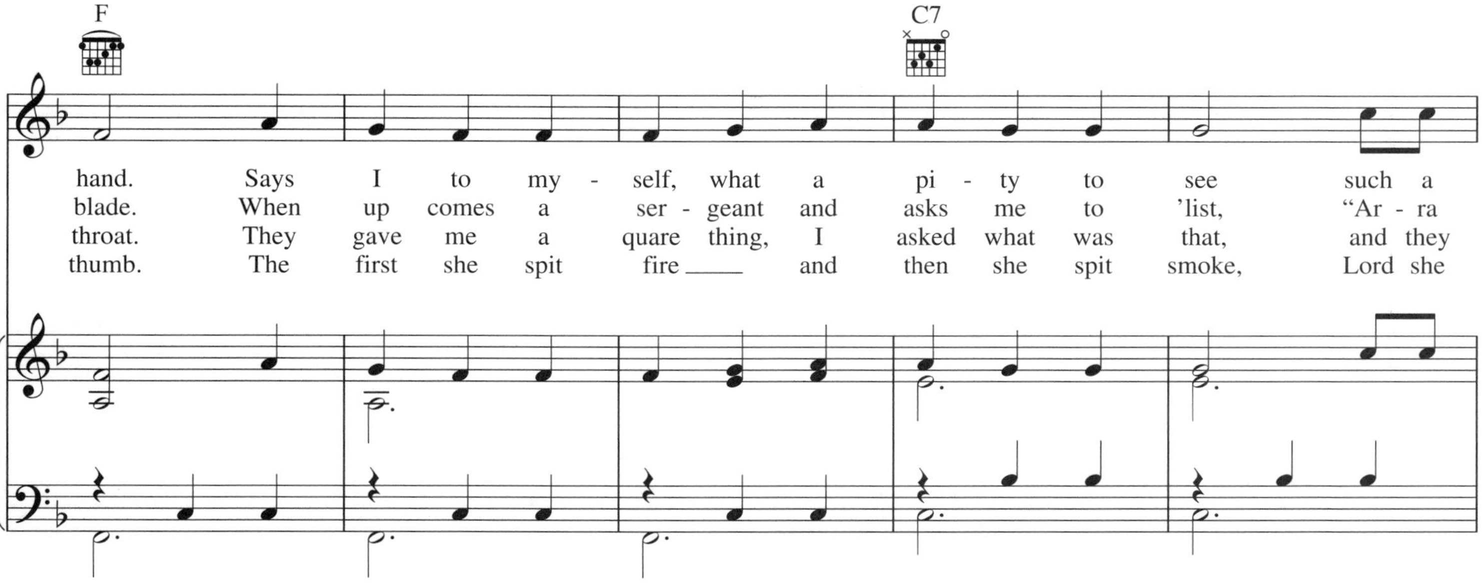
F
C7
hand. Says I to my - self, what a pi - ty to see such a
blade. When up comes a ser - geant and asks me to 'list, "Ar - ra
throat. They gave me a quare thing, I asked what was that, and they
thumb. The first she spit fire ___ and then she spit smoke, Lord she

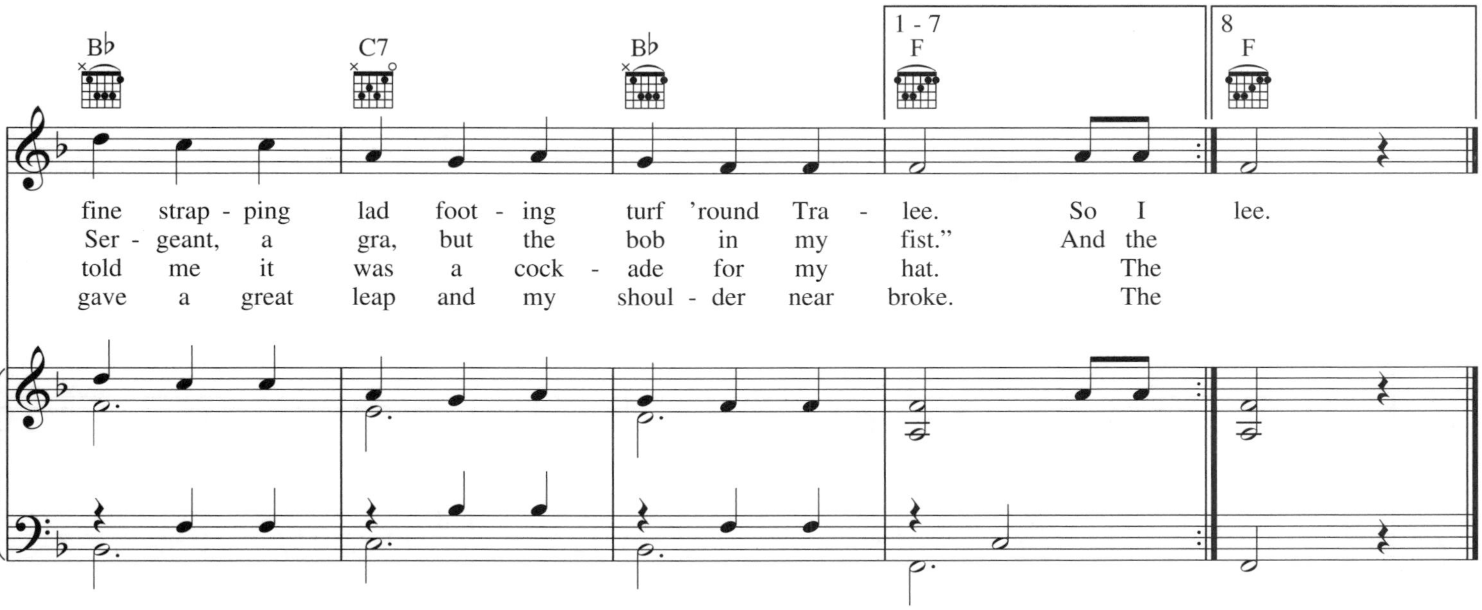
B♭
C7
B♭
1 - 7
F
8
F
fine strap - ping lad foot - ing turf 'round Tra - lee. So I lee.
Ser - geant, a gra, but the bob in my fist." And the
told me it was a cock - ade for my hat. The
gave a great leap and my shoul - der near broke. The

Additional Lyrics

5. The next place they sent me was down to the sea,
On board of a warship bound for the Crimea.
Three sticks in the middle all rowled 'round with sheets.
Faith, she walked through the water without any feet.

6. We fought at the Alma, likewise Inkermann,
But the Russians they whaled us at the Redan.
In scaling the walls there myself lost my eye,
And a big Russian bullet ran off with my thigh.

7. It was there I lay bleeding, stretched on the cold ground,
Heads, legs, and arms were scattered all around.
Says I, if my man or my cleavens were nigh,
They'd bury me decent and raise a loud cry.

8. They brought me the doctor, who soon staunched my blood,
And he gave me an elegant leg made of wood.
They gave me a medal and tenpence a day,
Contented with Sheila, I'll live on half pay.

LANIGAN'S BALL

Traditional Irish Folk Song

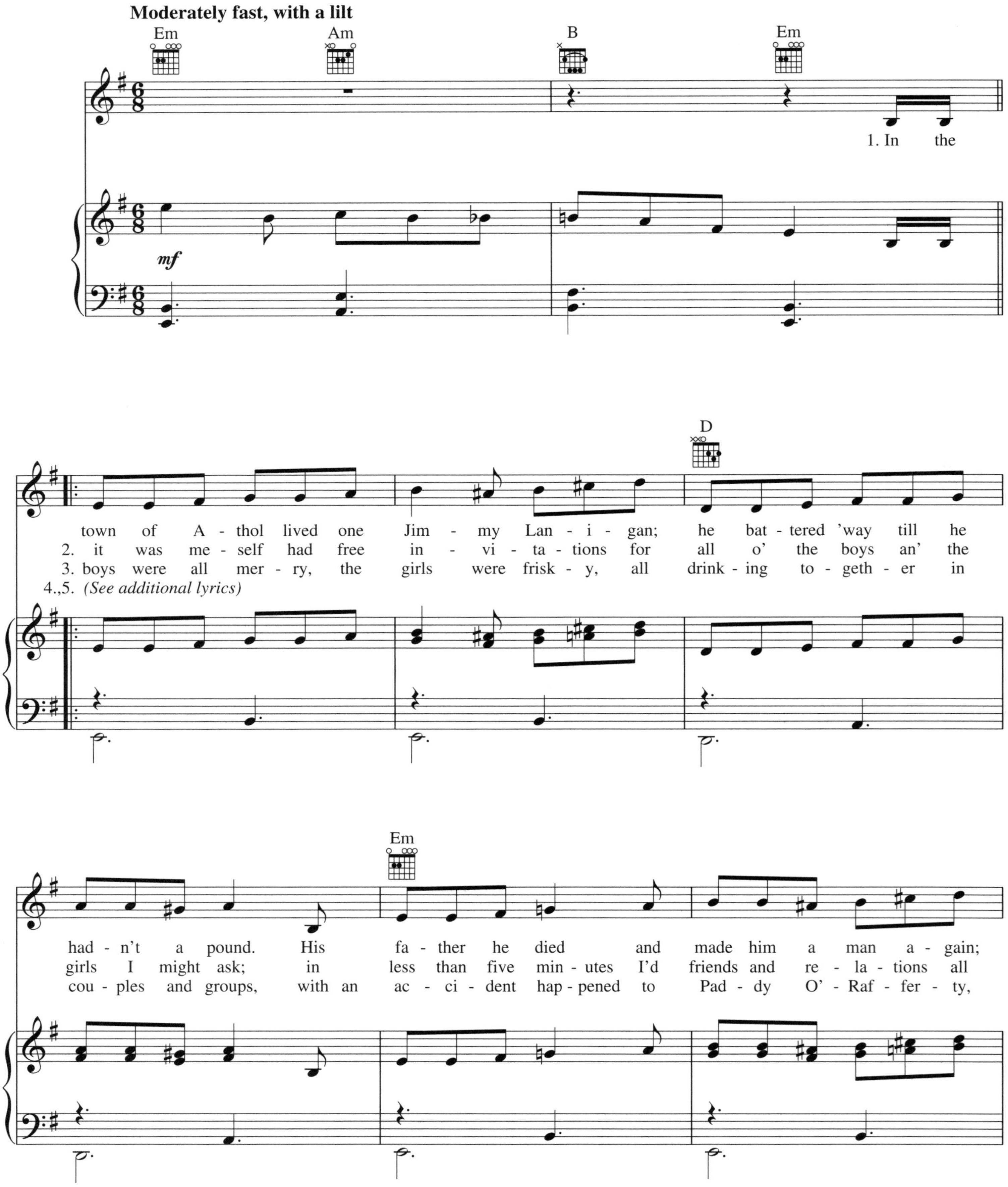
Moderately fast, with a lilt
Em Am B Em
mf
1. In the
D
town of A - thol lived one Jim - my Lan - i - gan; he bat - tered 'way till he
2. it was me - self had free in - vi - ta - tions for all o' the boys an' the
3. boys were all mer - ry, the girls were frisk - y, all drink - ing to - geth - er in
4.,5. (See additional lyrics)
Em
had - n't a pound. His fa - ther he died and made him a man a - gain;
girls I might ask; in less than five min - utes I'd friends and re - la - tions all
cou - ples and groups, with an ac - ci - dent hap - pened to Pad - dy O' - Raf - fer - ty,

Copyright © 2006 by HAL LEONARD CORPORATION
International Copyright Secured All Rights Reserved

Am B Em
left him a farm of ten a - cres of ground. He
sing - ing as mer - ry as flies 'round a cask. Now
he stuck his foot through Miss Flan - i - gan's hoops. The
B Em
gave a large par - ty to all his re - la - tions that stood be - side him when he
Kit - ty O' - Ha - ra, a nate lit - tle mil - li - ner, tipt me the wink and then
cray - thur she faint - ed and roared, "Mil - lia mur - ther!" Then called for her friends and
B Em
went to the wall. So if you but lis - ten, I'll
asked me to call, and when I ar - rived with
gath - ered them all. Tim Der - mod - y swore that he'd
B Em Am
make your eyes glis - ten with the rows and the 'rup - tions at
Tim - o - thy Gal - li - gan, just in time for
go no fur - ther, but have sat - is - fac - tion at

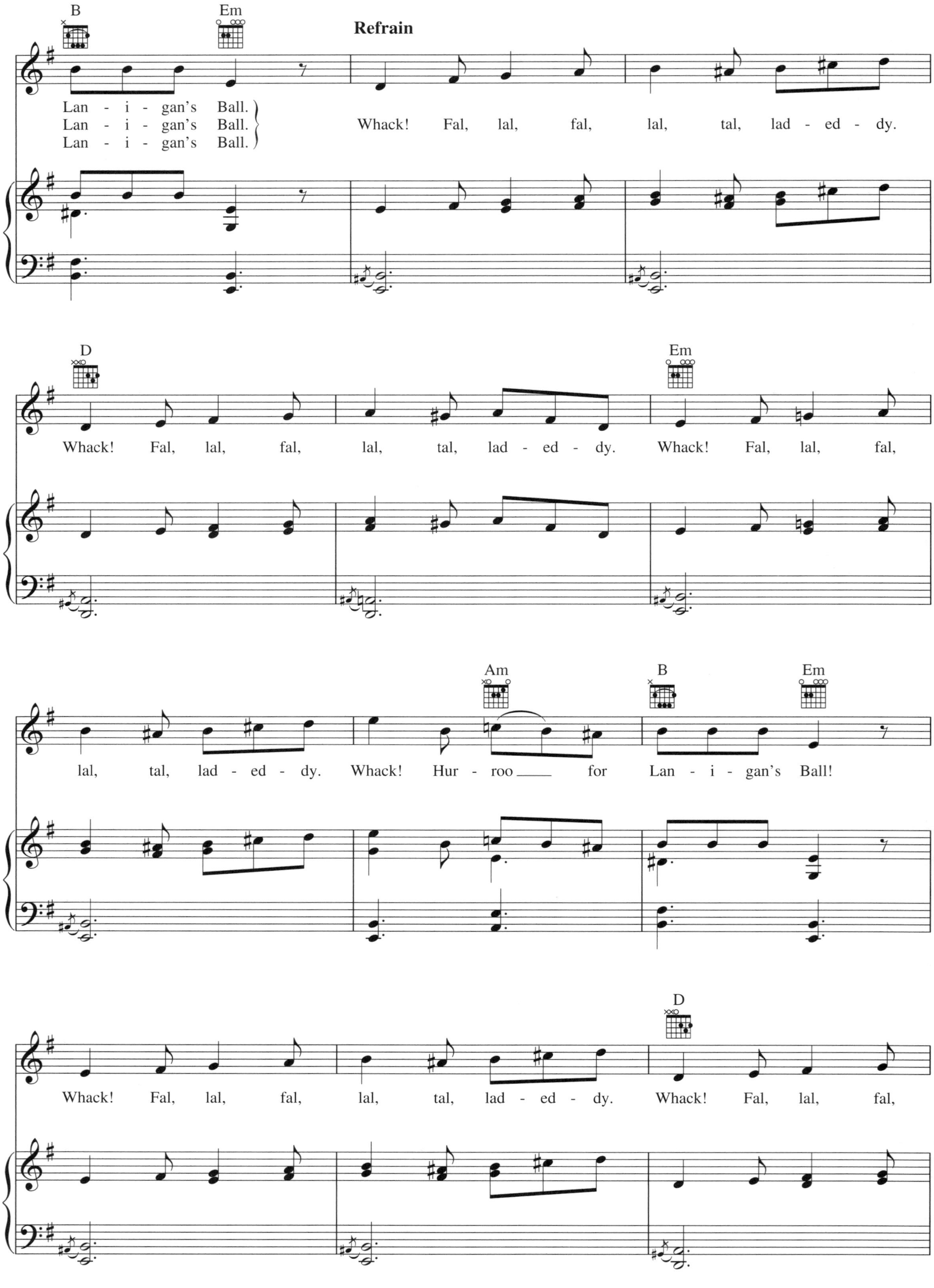
B
Em
Refrain
Lan - i - gan's Ball.
Lan - i - gan's Ball.
Lan - i - gan's Ball.
Whack! Fal, lal, fal, lal, tal, lad - ed - dy.
D
Em
Whack! Fal, lal, fal, lal, tal, lad - ed - dy. Whack! Fal, lal, fal,
Am
B
Em
lal, tal, lad - ed - dy. Whack! Hur - roo for Lan - i - gan's Ball!
D
Whack! Fal, lal, fal, lal, tal, lad - ed - dy. Whack! Fal, lal, fal,

Em
lal, tal, lad - ed - dy. Whack! Fal, lal, fal, lal, tal, lad - ed - dy.
Am B Em
1 - 4
B
Whack! Hur - roo for Lan - i - gan's Ball!
Em
5
B Em
Sure and
The

Additional Lyrics

4. Oh, arrah, boys, but thin was the 'ruption; meself got a wollop from Phelim McCoo.
Soon I replied to his nate introduction and we kicked up the divil's own phililaloo.
Casey, the piper, he was nearly strangled; he squeezed up his bags, chaunters and all.
The girls in their ribbons all got entangled, and that put a stop to Lanigan's Ball.
Refrain

5. In the midst of the row, Miss Kavanagh fainted; her face all the while was as red as the rose.
The ladies declared her cheeks they were painted, but she'd taken a drop too much, I suppose.
Paddy McCarty, so hearty and able, when he saw his dear colleen stretched out in the hall,
He pulled the best leg from out under the table and broke all the chiney at Lanigan's Ball.
Refrain

THE LARK IN THE CLEAR AIR

Words and Music by
SIR SAMUEL FERGUSON

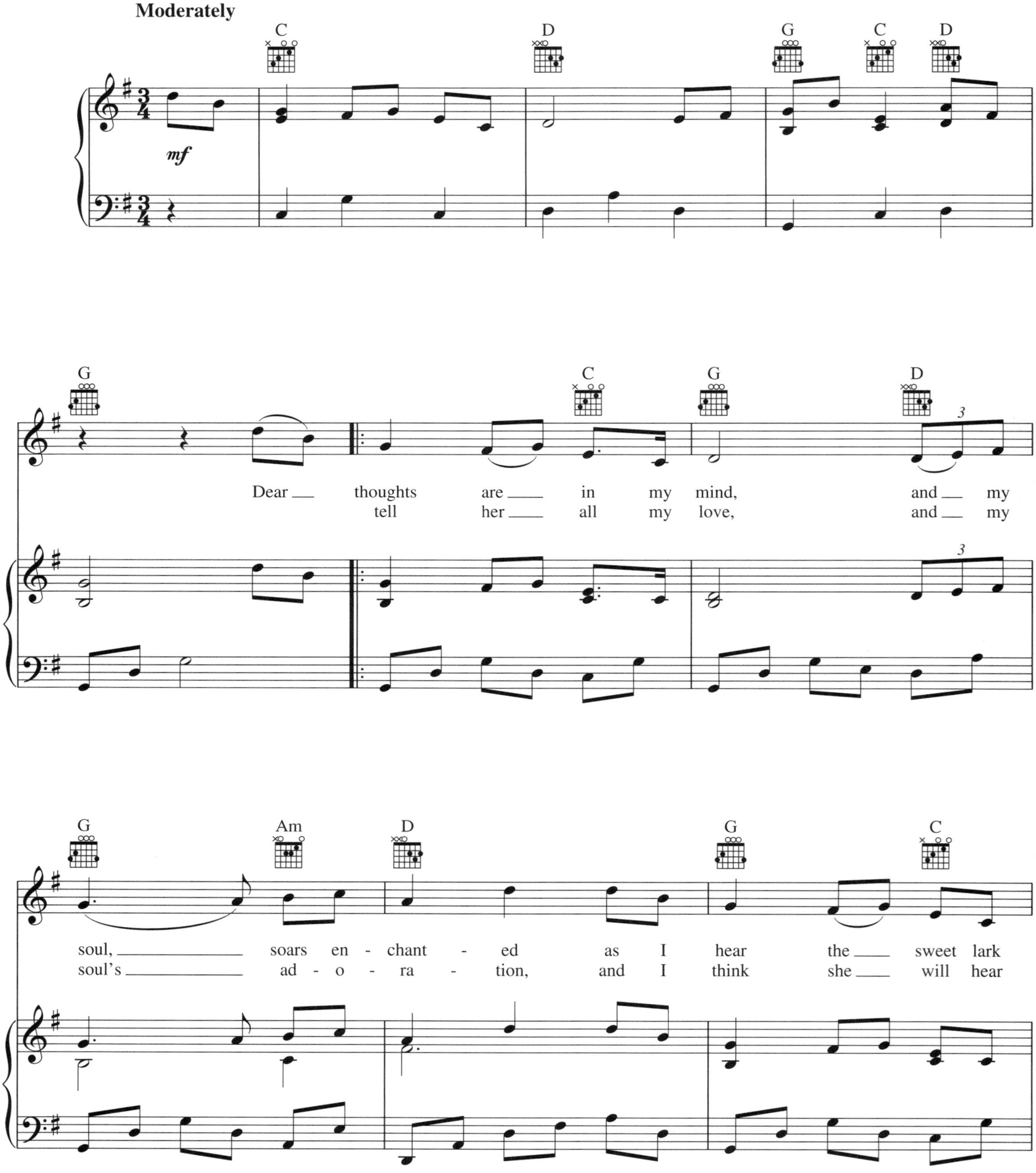
Moderately
C
D
G
C
D
mf
G
C
G
D
3
Dear thoughts are in my mind, and my
tell her all my love, and my
G
Am
D
G
C
soul, soars en - chant - ed as I hear the sweet lark
soul's ad - o - ra - tion, and I think she will hear

Copyright © 2006 by HAL LEONARD CORPORATION
International Copyright Secured All Rights Reserved

G D G C D7 G
sing in the clear air of the day. For a
me, and will not say me nay. It is
Em Bm C G Em
ten - der, beam - ing smile to my hope has been
this that gives my soul all its joy - ous e -
Am D G C Am G D
grant - ed, and to - mor - row she shall hear all my
la - tion, as I hear the sweet lark sing in the
G C D G G
fond heart would say. I shall
clear air of the day.

LARK IN THE MORNING

Traditional Irish Folk Song

Lively
Dm F Dm C
mf
Dm F
1. The lark in the morn - ing she
2. Rog - er, the plough - boy, he
3. they were com - ing home from the
4.,5. (See additional lyrics)
C Am Dm
ris - es off her nest and she flies up to the
is a dash - ing blade. He goes whis - tling and
rakes of the town. The mead - ow be - ing
F Dm C Dm
heav - ens with the dew all on her breast.
sing - ing in yon - der leaf - y shade. He
all mown and the grass had been cut down.

Copyright © 2006 by HAL LEONARD CORPORATION
International Copyright Secured All Rights Reserved

C
Am
Like the jol - ly plough - boy she whis - tles and she sings and she
met with dark - eyed Su - san; she's hand - some I de - clare, and she
And as they should chance to tum - ble all in the new - mown hay, "Oh, it's
Dm
F
Dm
C
comes home in the eve - nings with the dew all on her
is far more en - tic - ing than the birds all in the
kiss me now or nev - er," this bon - nie lass would
1 - 4
5
Dm
C
Dm
Dm
wings.
air.
say.
Oh,
As
When

Additional Lyrics

4. When twenty long weeks were over and had passed,
Her mammy asked the reason why she thickened 'round the waist.
"It was the pretty ploughboy," this lassie then did say,
"For he asked me for to tumble all in the new-mown hay."

5. Here's a health to you ploughboys wherever you may be
That like to have a bonnie lass a-sitting on each knee.
With a pint of good strong porter he'll whistle and he'll sing,
And the ploughboy is as happy as a prince or as a king.

'TIS THE LAST ROSE OF SUMMER

Words by THOMAS MOORE
Music by RICHARD ALFRED MILLIKEN

Sweetly
D G D G D/A Em/A
mp
D N.C. D D/F♯ G A D
'Tis the last rose of summer left
leave thee, thou lone one to
soon may I fol - low, when
D/A A7 D N.C. D Bm G A
bloom - ing a - lone. All her love - ly com -
pine on a stem. Since the love - ly are
friend - ships de - cay and from love's shin - ing
D G/B Gm/B♭ D/A A7 D N.C.
pan - ions are fad - ed and gone. No
sleep - ing, go sleep thou with them. Thus,
cir - cle the gems drop a - way. When

Copyright © 2003 by HAL LEONARD CORPORATION
International Copyright Secured All Rights Reserved

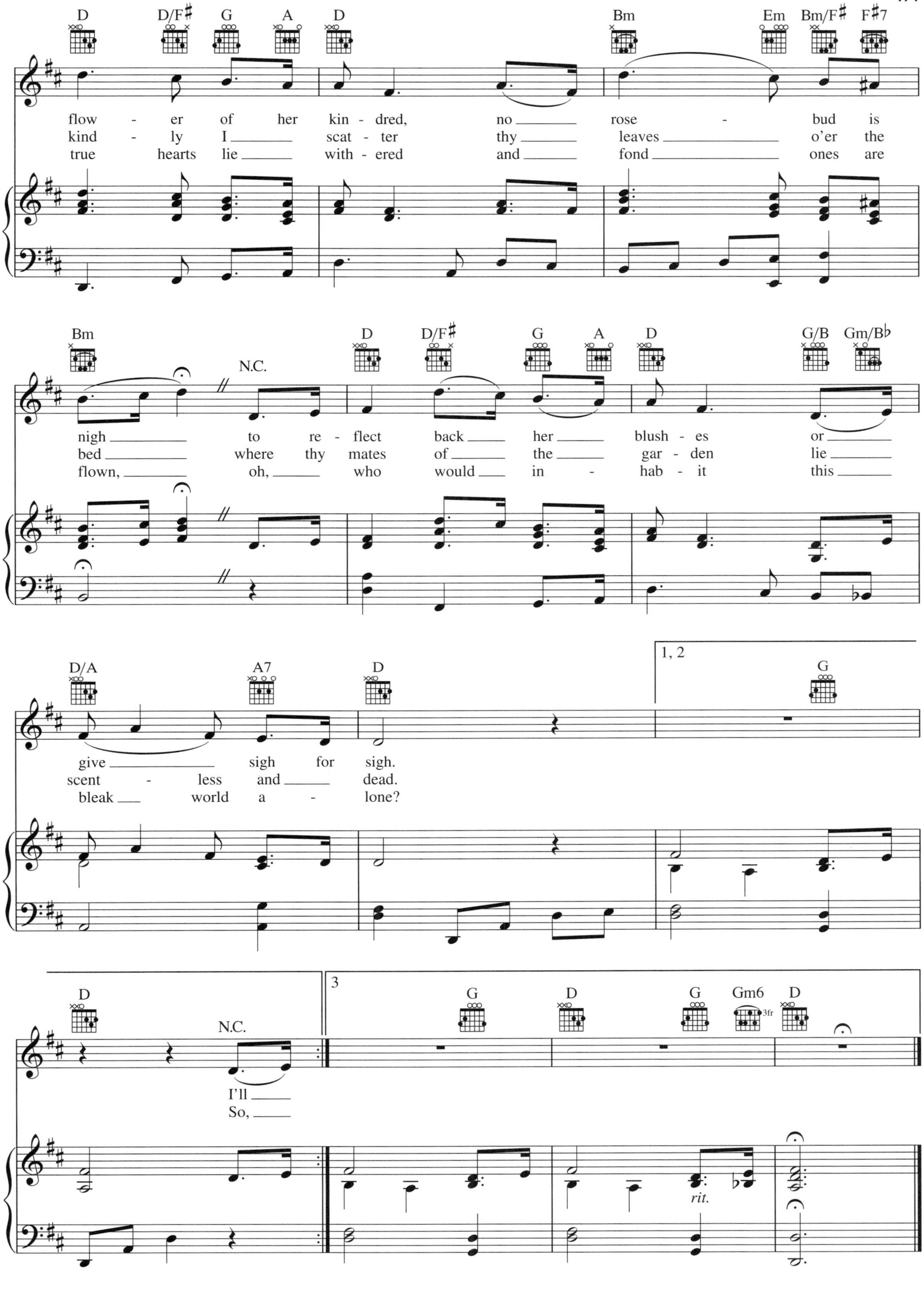
D D/F♯ G A D Bm Em Bm/F♯ F♯7
flow - er of her kin - dred, no rose - bud is
kind - ly I scat - ter thy leaves o'er the
true hearts lie with - ered and fond ones are
Bm N.C. D D/F♯ G A D G/B Gm/B♭
nigh to re - flect back her blush - es or
bed where thy mates of the gar - den lie
flown, oh, who would in - hab - it this
D/A A7 D 1, 2 G
give sigh for sigh.
scent - less and dead.
bleak world a - lone?
D N.C. 3 G D G Gm6 D
3fr
I'll
So,
rit.

LEAVING OF LIVERPOOL

Irish Sea Chantey

Moderately
A
E
A
mp
A
D
Fare - well to you, my own true
shipped on a Yan - kee sail - ing
sun is on the har - bour,
A
C♯m
F♯m
Bm
E
love; I am go - ing far a - way. I am
ship; Da - vy Crock - ett is her name. And
love, and I wish I could re - main, for I
A
D
A
A/E
bound for Cal - i - for - ni - a, but I know that I'll re -
Bur - gess is the cap - tain of her, and they say she is a
know it will be some long time be - fore I see

Copyright © 2003 by HAL LEONARD CORPORATION
International Copyright Secured All Rights Reserved

E A E
turn some day.
float - ing hell.
you a - gain.
So fare thee well, my
D A C♯m B7
own true love, and when I re - turn, u - nit - ed we will be.
E A D A
It's not the leav - ing of Liv - er - pool that grieves me, but my
E A
dar - ling when I think of thee.
1, 2
I have
Oh, the
3

THE LITTLE BEGGARMAN

Traditional Irish Folk Song

With a lilt
D G D C
mf
D
I am a lit - tle beg - gar - man, a -
slept last night in a
must be get - in' home for it's
A G D
beg - ging I have been. For fif - ty years or
barn at Cur - ra - bawn. A wet night came
get - in' late at night, the fire's all raked
A C
more in this lit - tle isle of green, and
on and I slippped through the door. Holes
and there is - n't an - y light. And now

Copyright © 2006 by HAL LEONARD CORPORATION
International Copyright Secured All Rights Reserved

D A
up to the Lif - fey and down to Tes - sa -
in my shoes and the toes peep - in'
you've heard me sto - ry of the old rig - a -
G D G
gue, and I'm known by the name of the
through, sing - in' skid - dy - me re - me dood - lum for
doo. It's good - night and God bless you from
D C D C
bold John - ny Dhu.
ould John - ny Dhu.
ould John - ny Dhu.
Of all the trades of
F D G D
liv - ing sure beg - ging is the best. For when a man is

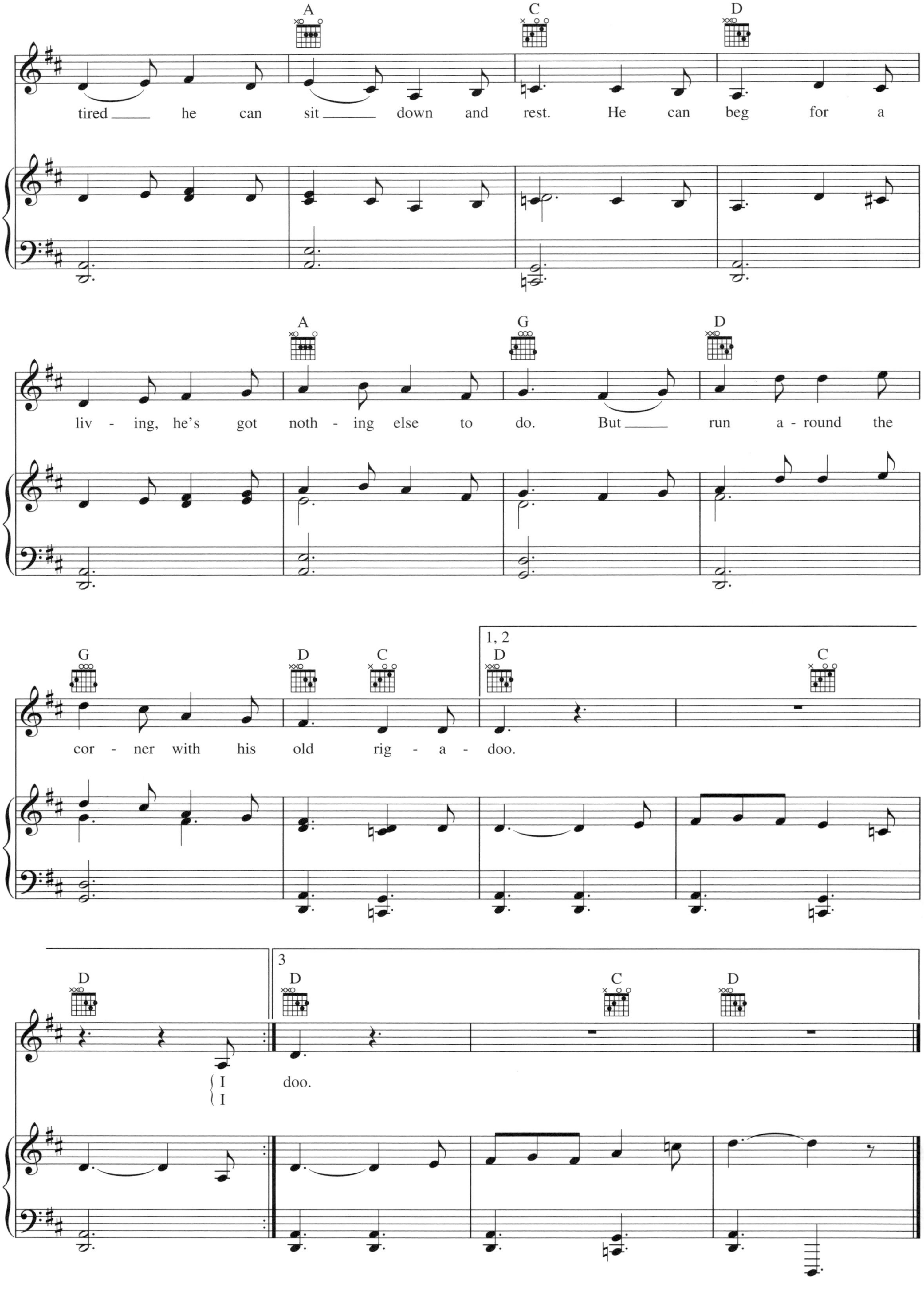
A C D
tired he can sit down and rest. He can beg for a
A G D
liv - ing, he's got noth - ing else to do. But run a - round the
G D C
cor - ner with his old rig - a - doo.
1, 2
D C
D
I
I
3
D C D
doo.

THE MERRY PLOUGHBOY

Traditional Irish Folk Song

March
C G F G C
mf
Am G
Well, I am a mer - ry plough - boy
F G C
and I plow the fields all day,
G F C
till a sud - den thought came to my

Copyright © 2006 by HAL LEONARD CORPORATION
International Copyright Secured All Rights Reserved

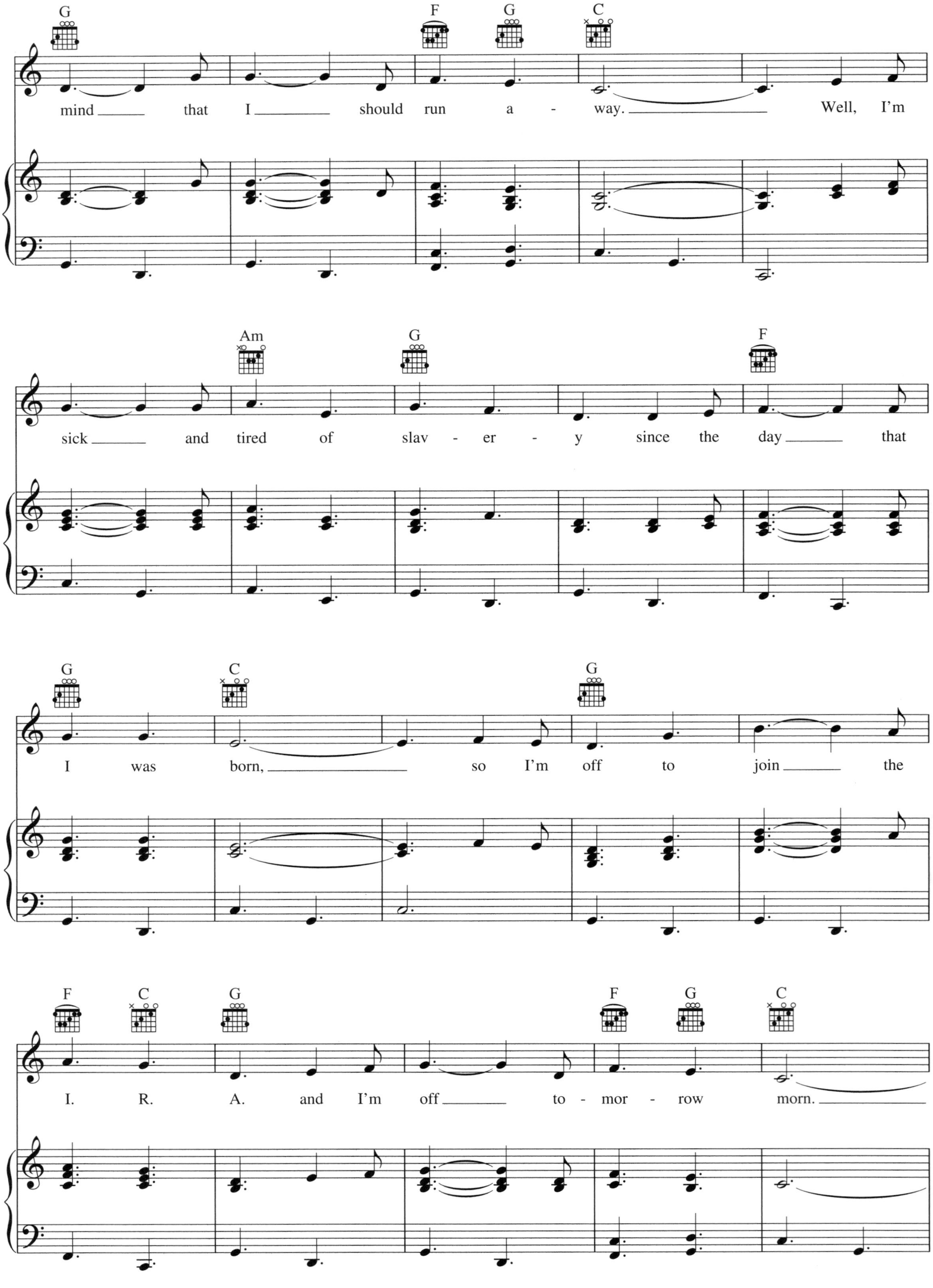
G F G C
mind that I should run a - way. Well, I'm
Am G F
sick and tired of slav - er - y since the day that
G C G
I was born, so I'm off to join the
F C G F G C
I. R. A. and I'm off to - mor - row morn.

Am G
So I'm off to Dub - lin in the
F G C
green, in the green; where the hel - mets glis - ten in the
G F C
sun. Where the bay - onets flash and the ri - fles
G F G C
crash; to the ech - o of a Thomp - son gun.
To Coda

Am G
I'll leave a - side my pick and
And I'll leave a - side my Mar -
F G C
spade, I'll leave a - side my plough. I'll
y, she's the girl that I a - dore. And I'll
G F C G
leave a - side my old grey mare for no more I'll
won - der if she'll think of me when she hears the
F G 1 C 2 C
need them now. So I'm
can - nons roar. And

Am G
when the war is o - ver, and
F G C G
dear old Ire - land's free I will take her
F C G
to the church to wed and a reb - el's
F G C
wife she'll be. So I'm
D.S. al Coda
CODA

LOVE IS TEASING

Traditional Irish Folk Song

Moderately fast
F
C
Am
G
mf
C
Oh love is teas - ing and love is pleas - ing,
and love is a pleas - ure when
Am
F
G
F

Copyright © 2006 by HAL LEONARD CORPORATION
International Copyright Secured All Rights Reserved

G
C
first it's new. But as love grows
Am
F
G
old - er sure love grows cold -
er and fades a - way
To Coda
F
G
C
like the morn - ing dew.
I
And
The
I

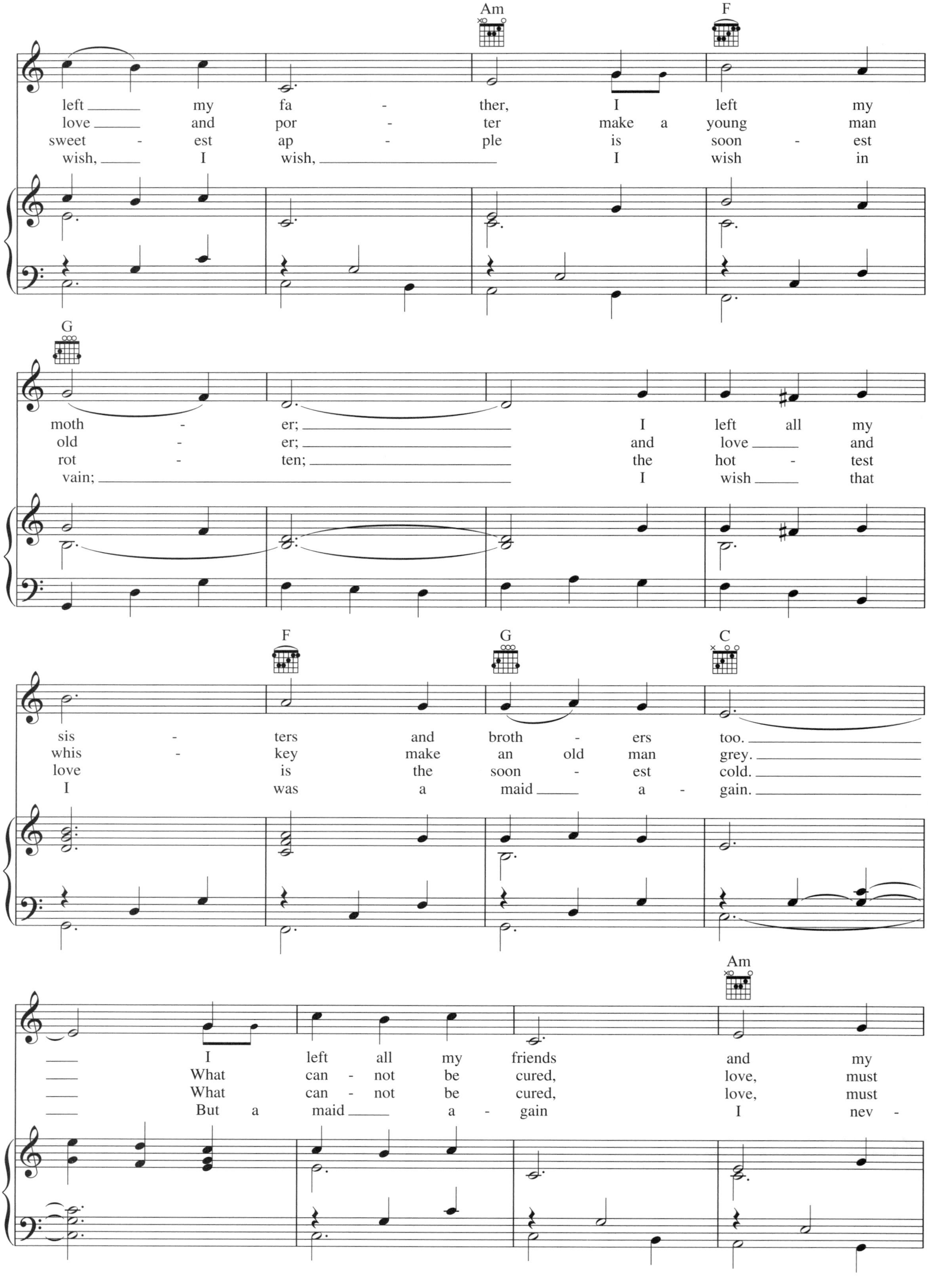
Am
F
left my fa - ther, I left my
love and por - ter make a young man
sweet - est ap - ple is soon - est
wish, I wish, I wish in
G
moth - er; I left all my
old - er; and love and
rot - ten; the hot - test
vain; I wish that
F
G
C
sis - ters and broth - ers too.
whis - key make an old man grey.
love is the soon - est cold.
I was a maid a - gain.
Am
I left all my friends and my
What can - not be cured, love, must
What can - not be cured, love, must
But a maid a - gain I nev -

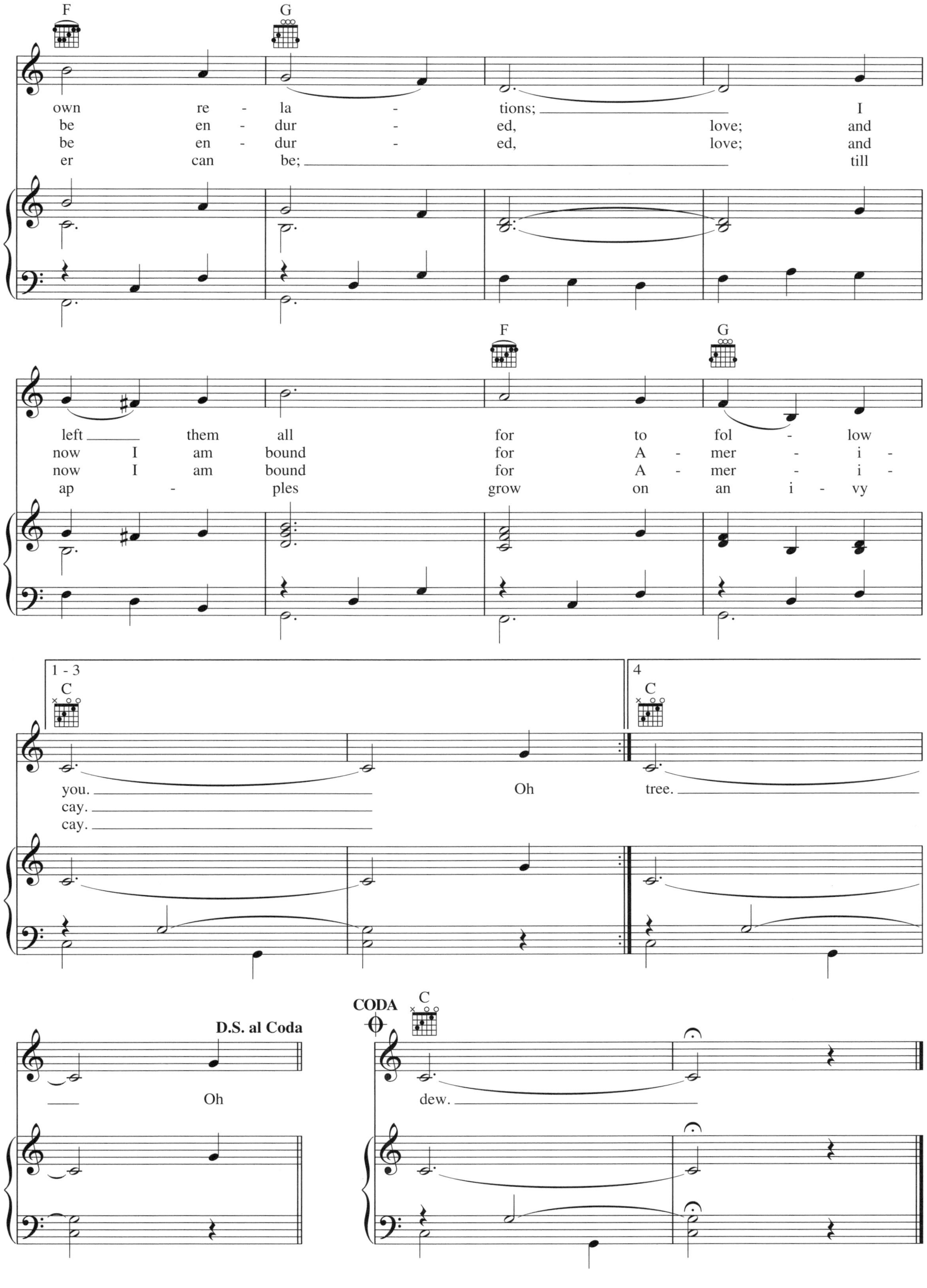
F
G
own re - la - tions; I
be en - dur - ed, love; and
be en - dur - ed, love; and
er can be; till
F
G
left them all for to fol - low
now I am bound for A - mer - i -
now I am bound for A - mer - i -
ap - ples grow on an i - vy
1 - 3
C
4
C
you. Oh tree.
cay.
cay.
D.S. al Coda
Oh
CODA
C
dew.

LOWLANDS LOW

Traditional Irish Folk Song

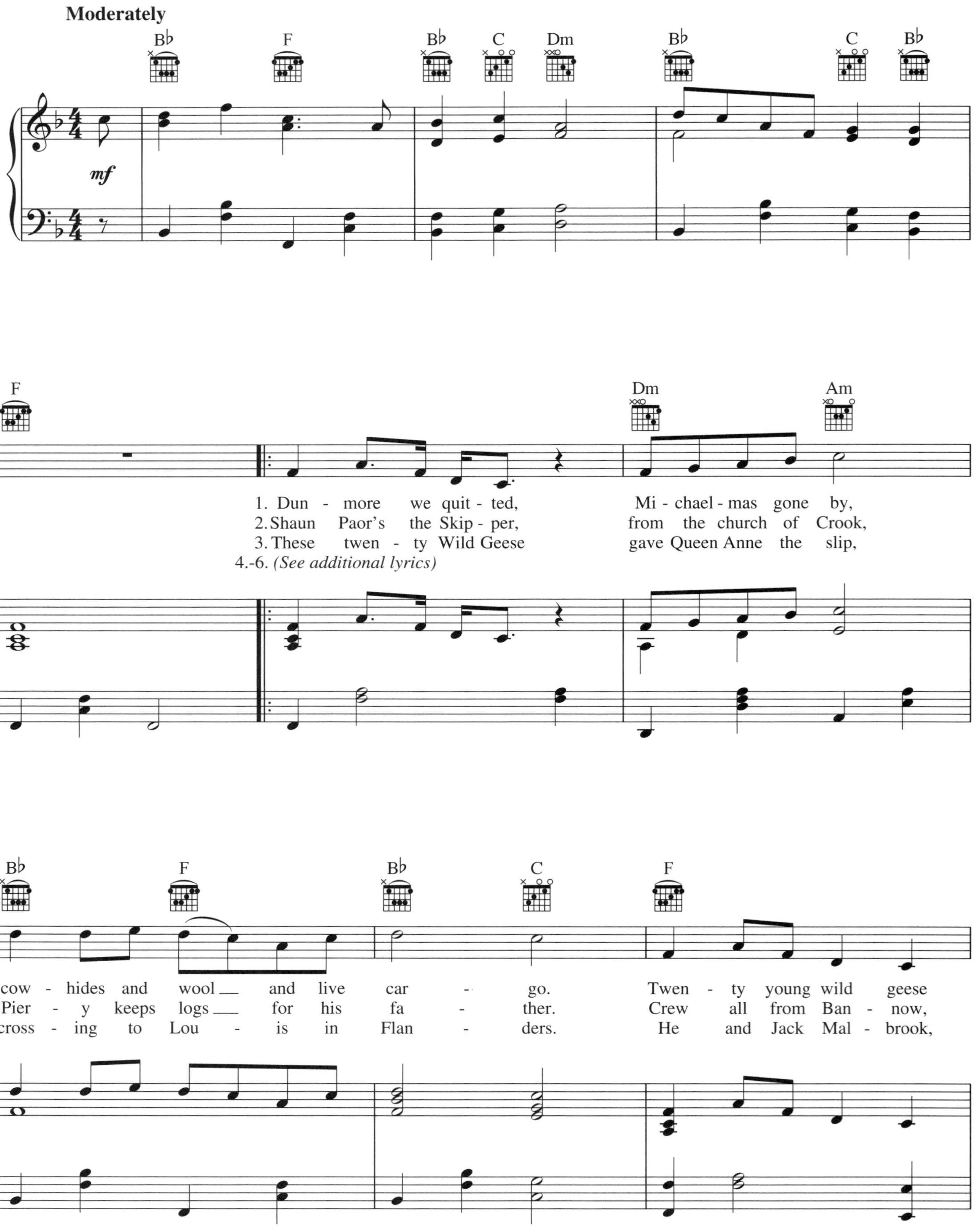
Moderately
B♭ F B♭ C Dm B♭ C B♭
mf
F Dm Am
1. Dun - more we quit - ted, Mi - chael - mas gone by,
2. Shaun Paor's the Skip - per, from the church of Crook,
3. These twen - ty Wild Geese gave Queen Anne the slip,
4.-6. (See additional lyrics)
B♭ F B♭ C F
cow - hides and wool ___ and live car - go. Twen - ty young wild geese
Pier - y keeps logs ___ for his fa - ther. Crew all from Ban - now,
cross - ing to Lou - is in Flan - ders. He and Jack Mal - brook,

Copyright © 2006 by HAL LEONARD CORPORATION
International Copyright Secured All Rights Reserved

Dm Am Dm C
rea - dy fledged to fly, sail - ing for the Low - lands
Fet - hard and the Hook, sail - ing for the Low - lands
both are in a grip, fight - ing in the Low - lands
Refrain
F B♭ F B♭ F Gm Dm
3fr
low.
low.
low.
The Low - lands low, the Low - lands low,
B♭ F C
1 - 5
F
6
F
sail - ing for the Low - lands low.
low.

Additional Lyrics

4. Close lay a rover, off the Isle of Wight,
   Either a Salce or Saxon.
   Out through a sea mist we bade them good night,
   Sailing for the Lowlands low.
   Refrain

5. Ready with priming we'd our galliot gun,
   Muskets and pikes in good order.
   We should be riddled, captives would be none.
   Death! Or else the Lowlands low.
   Refrain

6. Pray, holy Brendan, Turk or Algerine,
   Dutchman nor Saxon may sink us.
   We'll bring back Geneva Rack and Rhenish wine,
   Safely from the Lowlands low.
   Refrain

MacNAMARA'S BAND

Words by JOHN J. STAMFORD
Music by SHAMUS O'CONNOR

March tempo
N.C.
D7
Oh! Me
G A7/C♯ D7sus G Am7 D7
name is Mac-Na-ma-ra, I'm the lead-er of the band, Al-though we're few in
Now we are re-hears-in' for a ver-y swell af-fair, The an-nual cel-e-
G/B Em7 A9 G/B Cm A7/C♯ D7 G
num-ber, we're the fin-est in the land. We play at wakes and wed-dings and at
bra-tion, all the gen-try will be there. When Gen-'ral Grant to Ire-land came he
A7/C♯ D7sus G G/F C/E Cm/E♭ G/D Em7 A9 D7
ev-'ry fan-cy ball, And when we play at fun-er-als we play the march from
took me by the hand, Says he, "I nev-er saw the likes of Mac-Na-ma-ra's

Copyright © 2006 by HAL LEONARD CORPORATION
International Copyright Secured All Rights Reserved

G D7 G D7
Saul. band." Oh! The drums go bang, and the cym - bals clang and the horns they blaze a -
G Am7 D7 G/B Em7 A9 5fr D7
way; Mc - Car - thy pumps the old ba - zoon while I the pipes do play; And,
G D7 G G/F
Hen - nes - sey Ten - nes - see toot - les the flute, and the mu - sic is some - thing grand; A
C/E Cm/E♭ 3fr G/D Em7 A9 5fr D7 1 G D7 2 G
cre - dit to old I - re - land is Mac - Na - ma - ra's band. band.

THE MEETING OF THE WATERS

Traditional Irish Folk Song

Gently
mf
G C D7
G C
There is not in this wide world a
was not that na - ture had
friends, the be - loved of my
vale of A - vo - ca how
D7 G C
val - ley so sweet, as the vale in whose
shed o'er the scene her pur - est of
bos - om were near, who mad e - 'rey dear
calm could I rest in thy bos - om of
F Em D7
bos - om the bright wa - ters meet. Oh, the
crys - tal and bright - est of green. 'Twas
scene of en - chant - ment more dear. And who
shade with the friends I love best. Where the

Copyright © 2006 by HAL LEONARD CORPORATION
International Copyright Secured All Rights Reserved

C G Em
last rays of feel - ing and life must de -
not her soft mag - ic of stream - let or
felt how the best charms of na - ture im -
storms that we feel in this cold world should
D7 G C D7
part, e'er the bloom of that val - ley shall fade from my
hill. Oh, no, it was some - thing more ex - qui - site
prove when we see them re - flect - ed from looks that we
cease, and our hearts like thy wa - ters be min - gled in
Am G C D7
heart. E'er the bloom of that val - ley shall fade from my
still. Oh no, it was some - thing more ex - qui - site
love. When we see them re - flect - ed from looks that we
peace. And our hearts like thy wa - ters be min - gled in
1 - 3
G
heart. Yet it
still. 'Twas that
love. Sweet
4
G
peace.

THE MERMAID

18th Century Sea Chantey

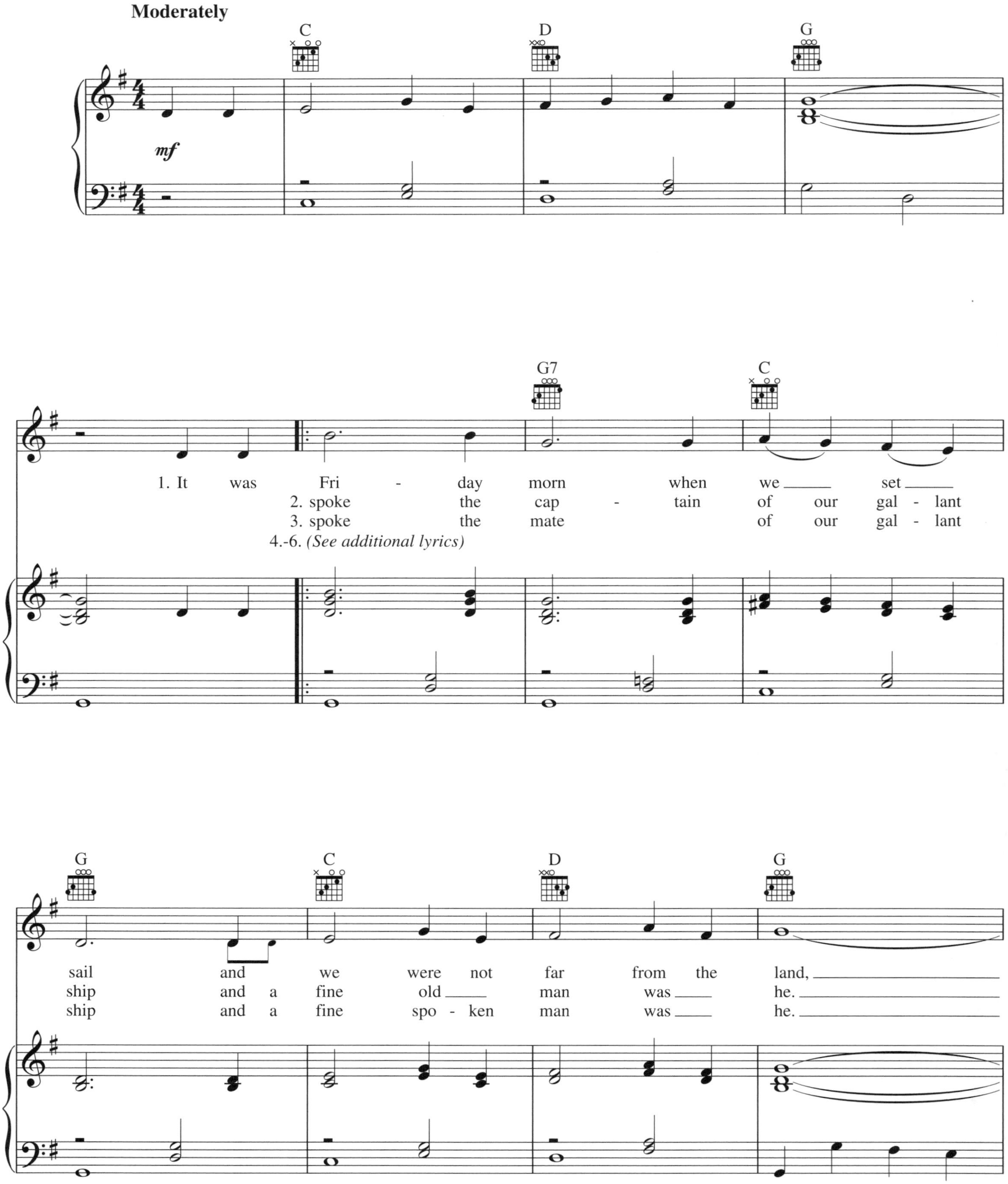
Moderately
C
D
G
mf
G7
C
1. It was Fri - day morn when we set
2. spoke the cap - tain of our gal - lant
3. spoke the mate of our gal - lant
4.-6. (See additional lyrics)
G
C
D
G
sail and we were not far from the land,
ship and a fine old man was he.
ship and a fine spo - ken man was he.

Copyright © 2006 by HAL LEONARD CORPORATION
International Copyright Secured All Rights Reserved

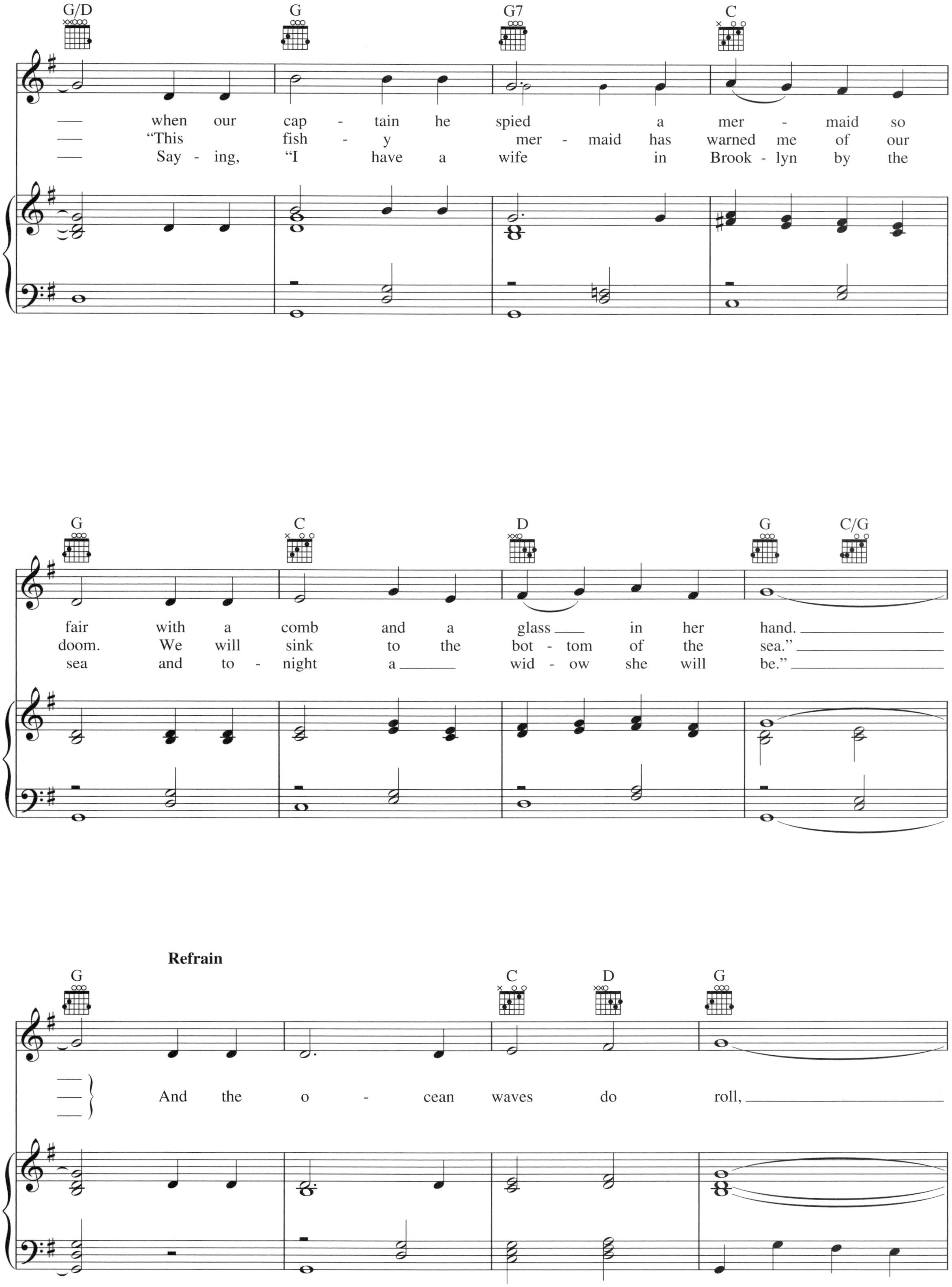
G/D G G7 C
— when our cap - tain he spied a mer - maid so
— "This fish - y mer - maid has warned me of our
— Say - ing, "I have a wife in Brook - lyn by the
G C D G C/G
fair with a comb and a glass in her hand.
doom. We will sink to the bot - tom of the sea."
sea and to - night a wid - ow she will be."
Refrain
G C D G
And the o - cean waves do roll,

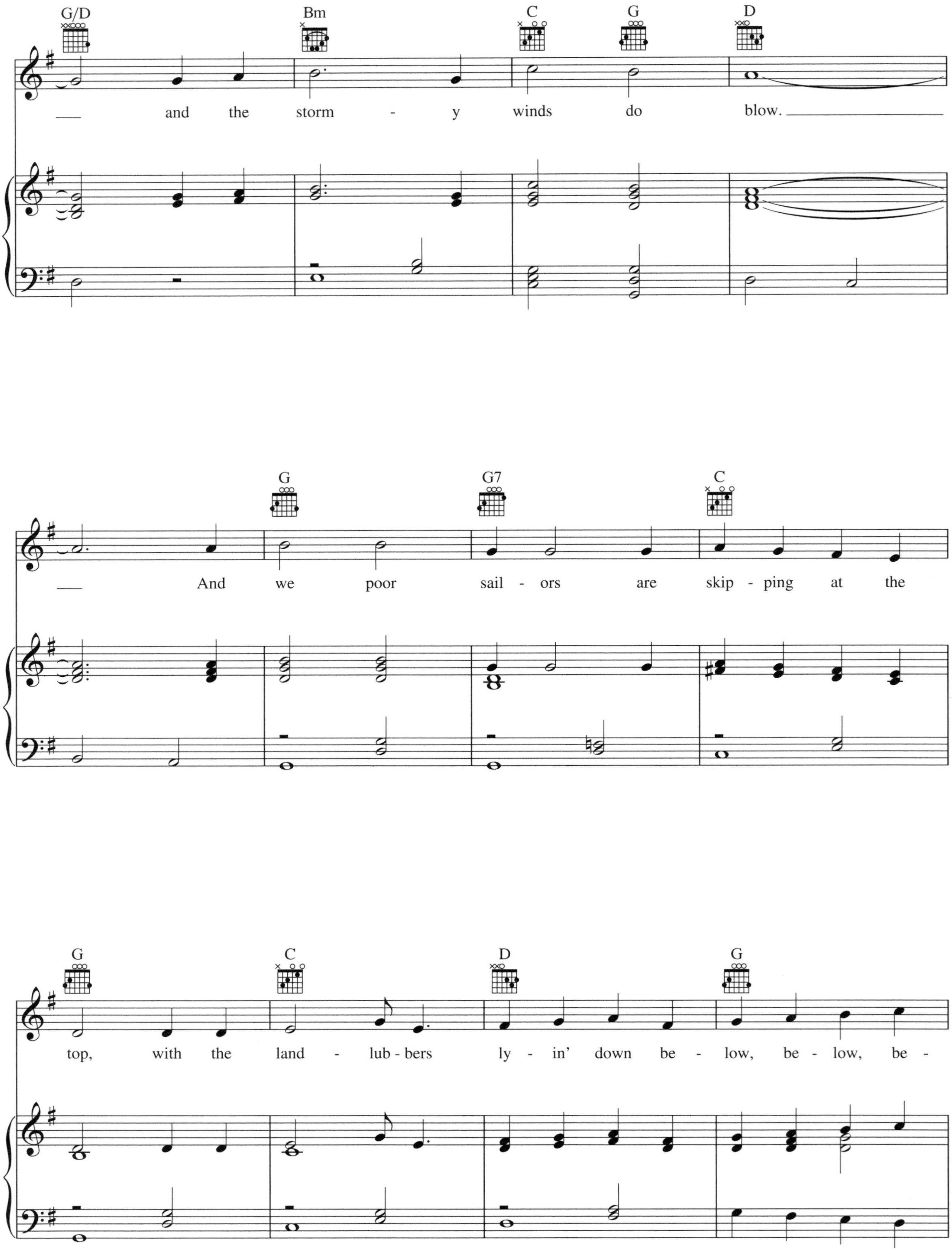
G/D Bm C G D
and the storm - y winds do blow.
G G7 C
And we poor sail - ors are skip - ping at the
G C D G
top, with the land - lub - bers ly - in' down be - low, be - low, be -

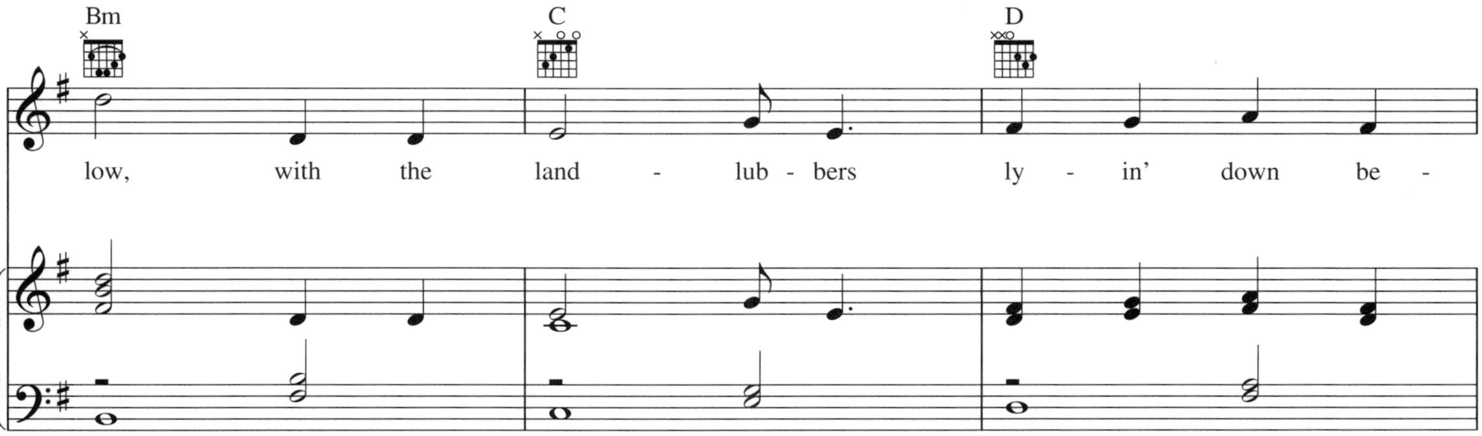
Bm
C
D
low, with the land - lub - bers ly - in' down be -

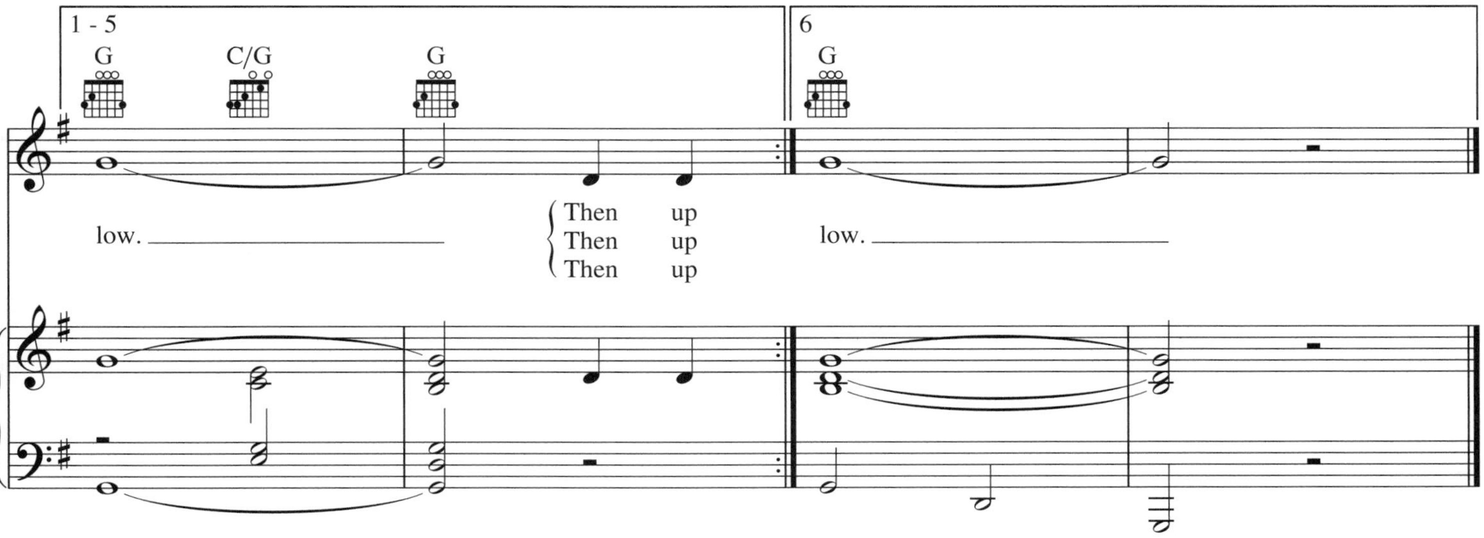
1 - 5
G
C/G
G
6
G
low.
Then up
Then up
Then up
low.

Additional Lyrics

4. Then up spoke the cabin boy of our gallant ship and a brave young lad was he.
   "I have a sweetheart in Salem by the sea and tonight she'll be weeping for me."
   Refrain

5. Then up spoke the cook of our gallant ship and a crazy old butcher was he.
   "I care so much more for my skillets and my pans than I do for the bottom of the sea."
   Refrain

6. Then three times around spun our gallant ship and three times around spun she.
   Three times around spun our gallant ship and she sank to the bottom of the sea.
   Refrain

MINSTREL BOY

Traditional

Steadily
Cm Eb F Bb D7/A Gm Eb/G Ab Eb/G Eb
mf
Ab Bb7 Eb Eb Bb/D Cm Eb/G
N.C.
The min - strel boy to the war is gone. In the
min - strel fell but the foe - man's chain could not
Ab Eb/G Eb Ab Bb7 Eb Eb
N.C.
ranks of death you'll find him. His fa - ther's sword he has
bring his proud soul un - der. The harp he loved nev - er
Bb/D Cm Eb/G Ab Eb/G Eb Ab Bb7 Eb
gird - ed on, and his wild harp slung be - hind him.
spoke a - gain, for he tore its cords a - sun - der and

Copyright © 2003 by HAL LEONARD CORPORATION
International Copyright Secured All Rights Reserved

Cm G7/D Cm/E♭ Cm7♭5 B♭/F F7 B♭ G7 Cm G7/F
"Land of song," said the war - rior bard. "Though all the world be -
said, "No chains shall sul - ly thee, thou soul of love and
Cm/E♭ G/D Cm A♭ E♭ B♭/D Cm E♭/G
trays thee, one sword at least thy rights shall guard, one
brav - er - y! Thy songs were made for the pure and free. They shall
A♭ E♭/G E♭ A♭ B♭7 E♭ E♭/G
faith - ful harp shall praise thee."
nev - er sound in slav - er - y!"
A♭ E♭/G E♭
1 A♭ B♭7 E♭ N.C.
The
2 A♭ B♭7 E♭
molto rit.

THE MOUNTAINS OF MOURNE

Words by PERCY FRENCH
Traditional Irish Melody

Flowing
D
G
mf
G
C
Oh, Mar - y, this Lon - don's a won - der - ful
lieve that when writ - ing a wish you ex -
beau - ti - ful girls here, oh nev - er you
D
G
sight, with peo - ple here work - ing by day and by
pressed as to how the fine la - dies in Lon - don were
mind, with beau - ti - ful shapes na - ture nev - er de -
C
night. They don't plant po - ta - toes nor bar - ley nor
dressed. Well, if you'll be - lieve me, when asked to a
signed. And love - ly com - plex - ions all ros - es and

Copyright © 2003 by HAL LEONARD CORPORATION
International Copyright Secured Used by Permission

D
wheat, but there's gangs of them dig - ging for
ball, they ___ don't wear no top to their
cream, but ___ let me re - mark with re -
G
C
gold in the street. At least when I
dress - es at all. Oh, I've seen them me -
gard to the same, that if that those
G
asked them, that's what I was told, so I
self, and you could not in truth say that
ros - es you ven - ture to sip, the ___
A7
just took a hand at this dig - ging for
if they were bound for a ball or a
col - ors might all come a - way on your

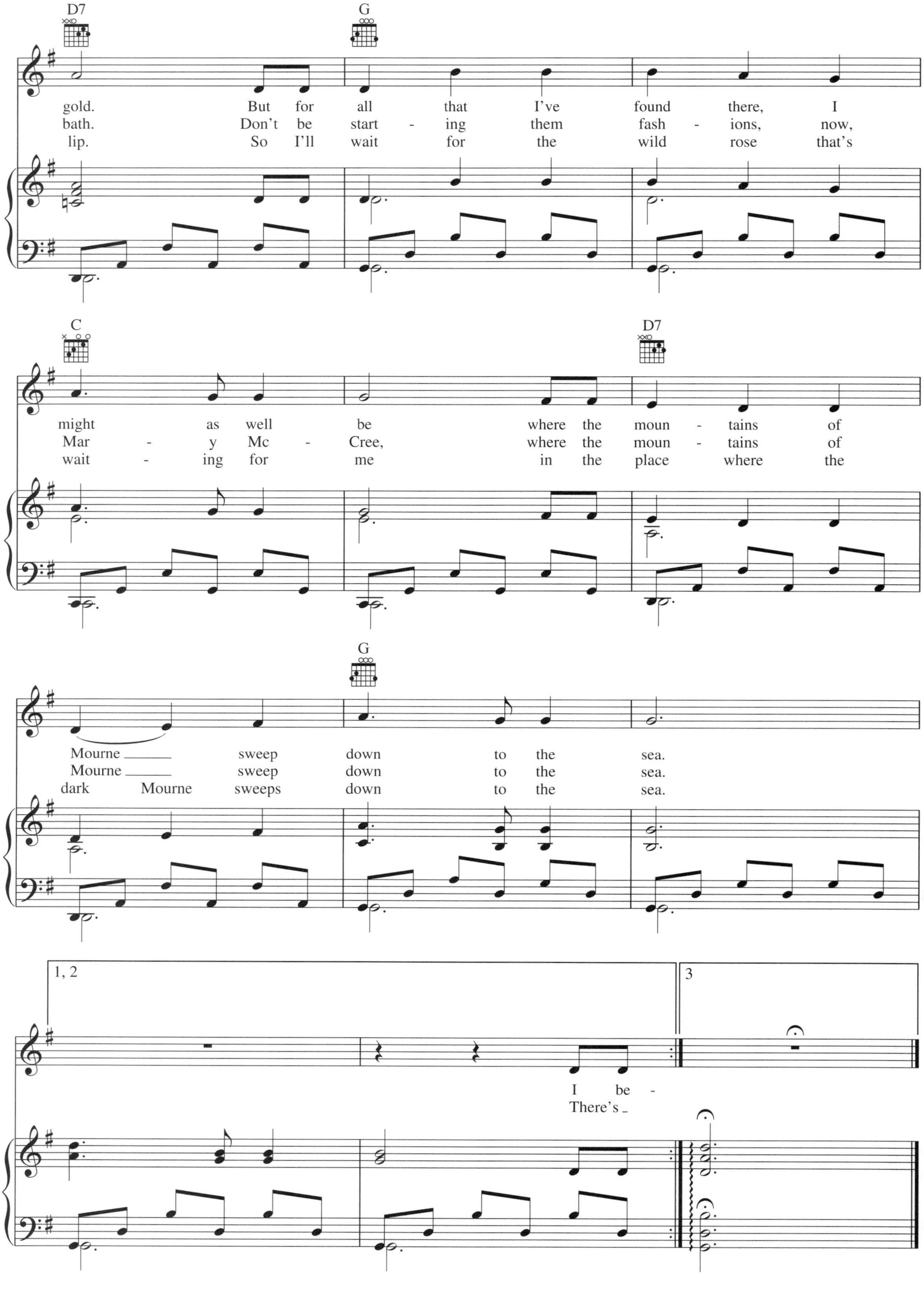
D7
G
gold. But for all that I've found there, I
bath. Don't be start - ing them fash - ions, now,
lip. So I'll wait for the wild rose that's
C
D7
might as well be where the moun - tains of
Mar - y Mc - Cree, where the moun - tains of
wait - ing for me in the place where the
G
Mourne sweep down to the sea.
Mourne sweep down to the sea.
dark Mourne sweeps down to the sea.
1, 2
3
I be -
There's

MY SINGING BIRD

Traditional

Copyright © 2006 by HAL LEONARD CORPORATION
International Copyright Secured All Rights Reserved

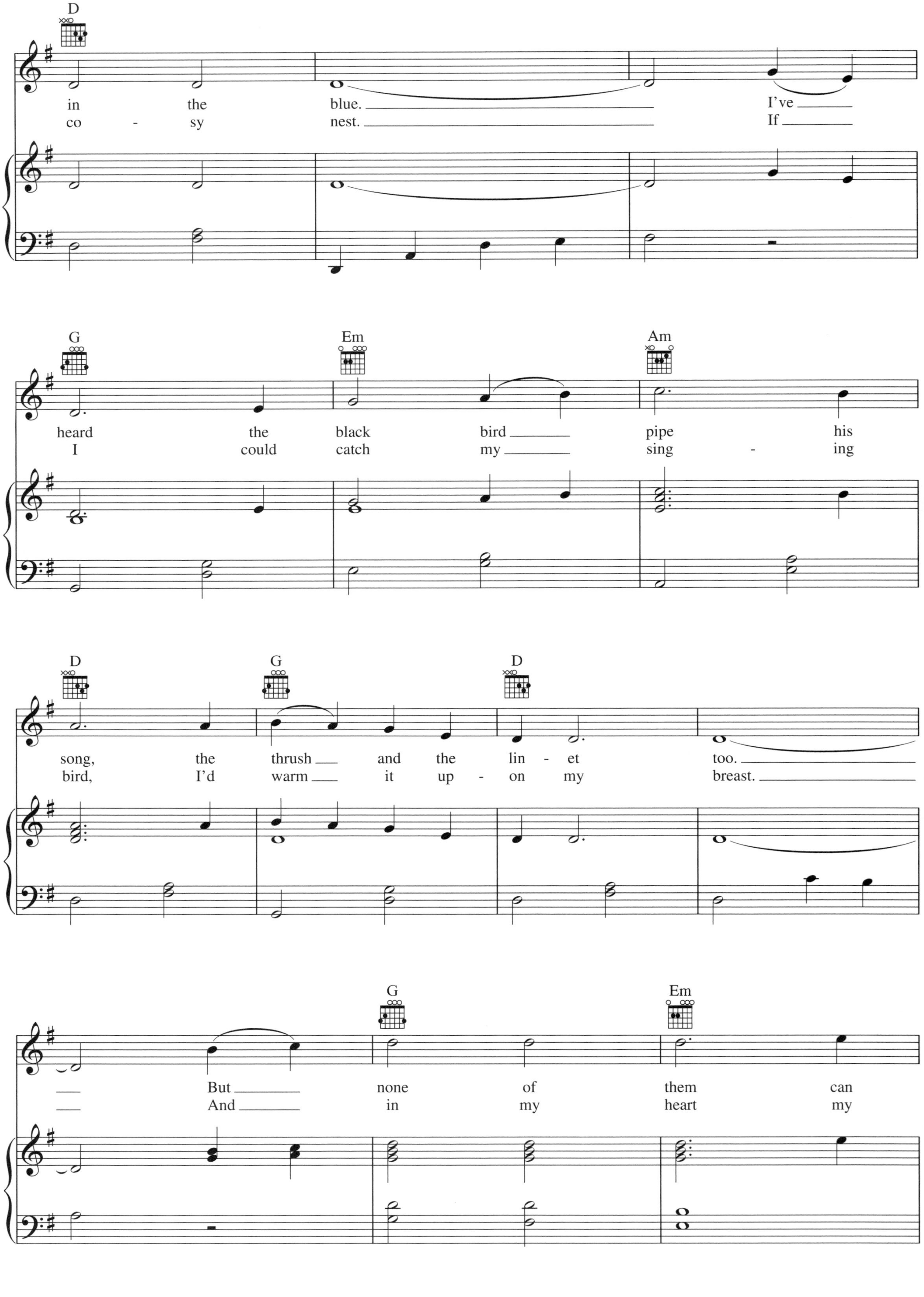
D
in the blue. I've
co - sy nest. If
G Em Am
heard the black bird pipe his
I could catch my sing - ing
D G D
song, the thrush and the lin - et too.
bird, I'd warm it up - on my breast.
G Em
But none of them can
And in my heart my

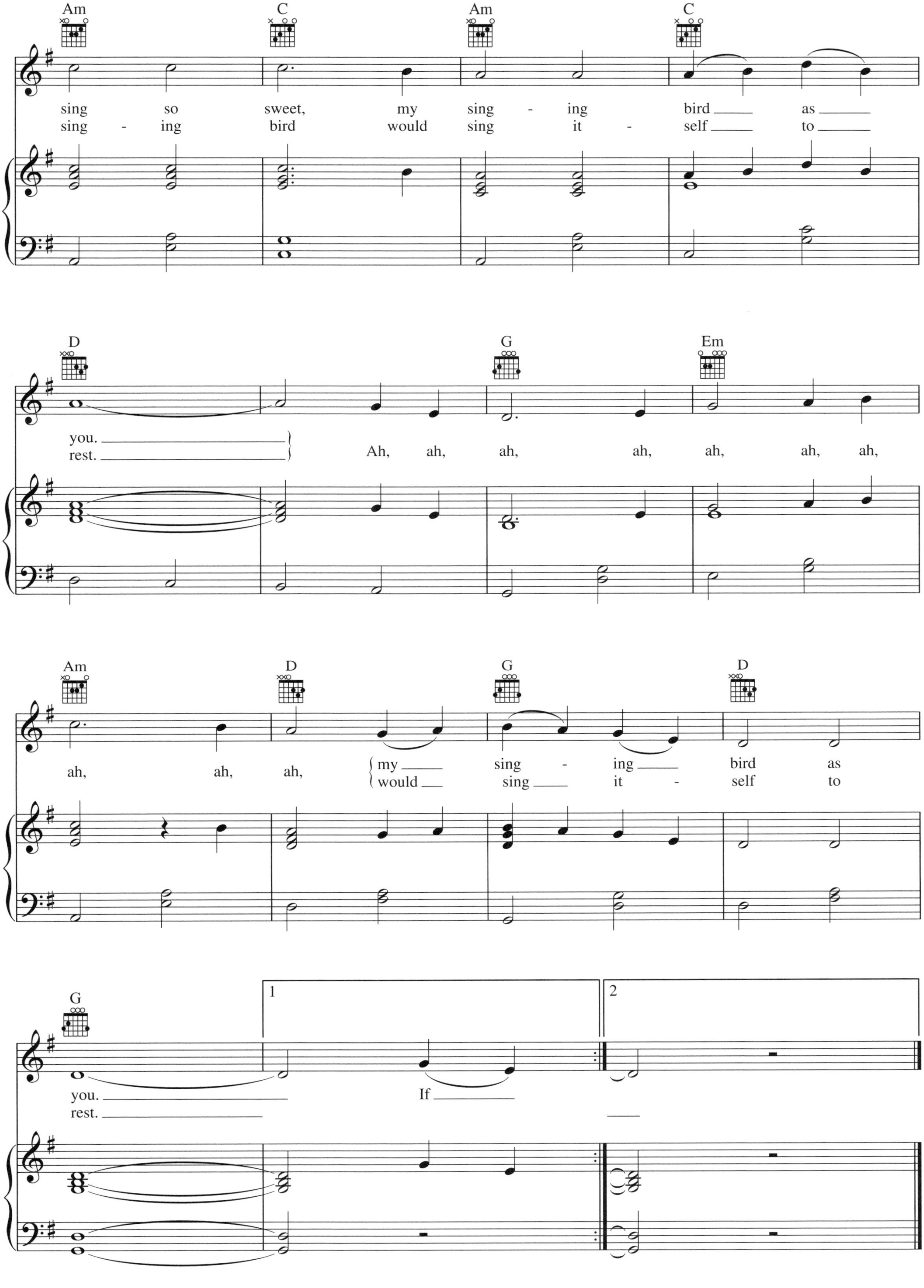
Am C Am C
sing so sweet, my sing - ing bird as to
sing - ing bird would sing it - self to
D G Em
you. rest.
Ah, ah, ah, ah, ah, ah, ah,
Am D G D
ah, ah, ah,
my sing - ing bird as
would sing it - self to
G
1 2
you. If
rest.

MRS. McGRATH

Traditional Irish Folk Song

Lively
Em G Em D G
mf
1. "Oh,
C G D G C
Mrs. Mc - Grath," the ser - geant said, "Would you like to make a sol - dier out of
2. Mrs. Mc - Grath lived on the sea - shore for the space of sev - en long
3. Cap - tain, dear, where have ye been? Have you been sail - ing on the Med - i -
4. up comes Ted with - out an - y legs, And in their place two
5.-9. (See additional lyrics)
G D G C G D G D
your son Ted? With a scar - let coat and a big cocked hat; now Mrs. Mc - Grath, would-n't
years or more, when a great big ship sailed in - to the bay: "Hul - la - loo, bub - a - loo, I think
ter - ra - nean? Have you an - y tid - ings of my son Ted? Is the poor boy liv - ing or
wood - en pegs. She kissed him a doz - en times or two, say - ing, "Ho - ly Mos - es,

Copyright © 2006 by HAL LEONARD CORPORATION
International Copyright Secured All Rights Reserved

G Em G Em D
you like that?"
it is he!"
is he dead?"
'tis - n't you!"
Wid yer too - ri - ay, fol - the - did - dle - day, too - ri - oo - ri -
G Em G Em D
oo - ri - ay. Wid yer too - ri - ay, fol - the - did - dle - ay. Too - ri - oo - ri -
G D
1 - 8
G
9
G
oo - ri - ay.
So
"Oh,
Then

Additional Lyrics

5. "Oh then were ye drunk or were ye blind
That ye left yer two fine legs behind?
Or was it walking upon the sea
Wore yer two fine legs from the knees away?"
Refrain

6. "Oh, I wasn't drunk and I wasn't blind,
But I left me two fine legs behind;
For a cannon ball on the fifth of May
Took me two fine legs from the knees away."
Refrain

7. "Oh, then, Teddy me boy," the widow cried,
"Yer two fine legs were yer mama's pride.
Them stumps of a tree wouldn't do at all,
Why didn't ye run from the big cannon ball?"
Refrain

8. "All foreign wars I do proclaim
Between Don John and the King of Spain.
But by heavens I'll make them rue the time
That they swept the legs from a child of mine."
Refrain

9. "Oh then, if I had ye back again,
I'd never let ye go to fight the King of Spain.
For I'd rather my Ted as he used to be
Than the King of France and his whole Navy."
Refrain

MUIRSHEEN DURKIN

Traditional Irish Folk Song

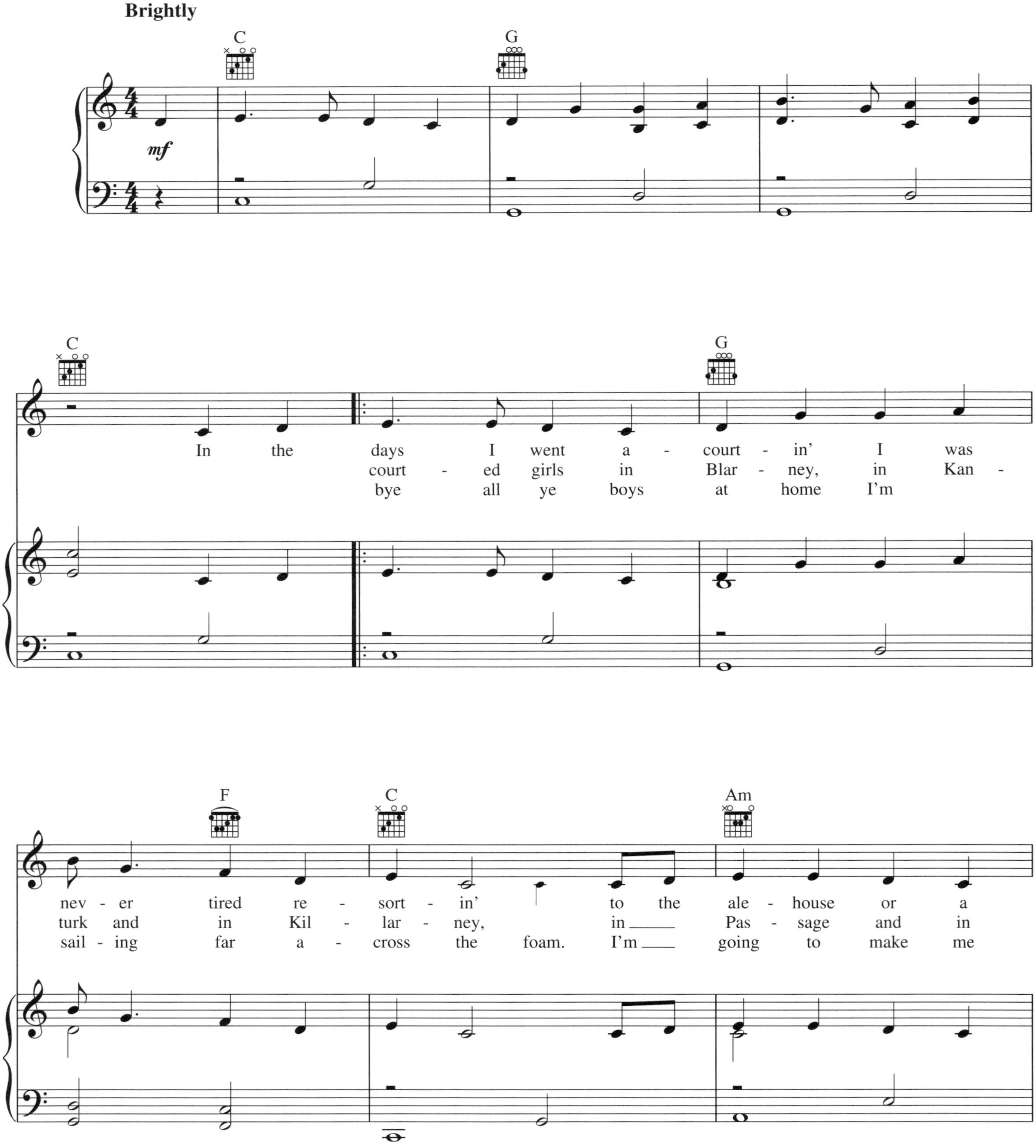
Brightly
C
G
mf
C
G
In the days I went a - court - in' I was
court - ed girls in Blar - ney, in Kan -
bye all ye boys at home I'm
F
C
Am
nev - er tired re - sort - in' to the ale - house or a
turk and in Kil - lar - ney, in Pas - sage and in
sail - ing far a - cross the foam. I'm going to make me

Copyright © 2006 by HAL LEONARD CORPORATION
International Copyright Secured All Rights Reserved

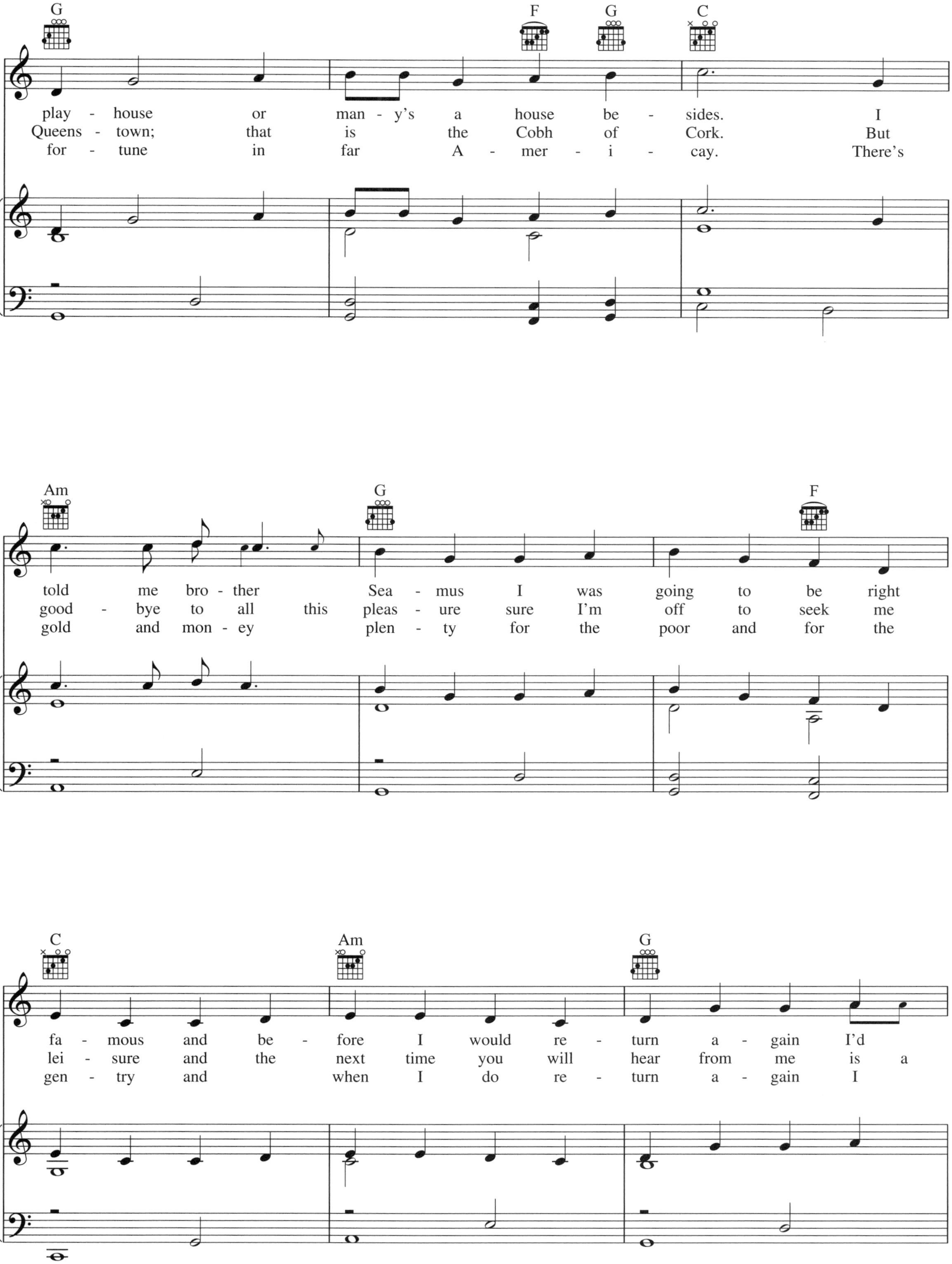
G F G C
play - house or man - y's a house be - sides. I
Queens - town; that is the Cobh of Cork. But
for - tune in far A - mer - i - cay. There's
Am G F
told me bro - ther Sea - mus I was going to be right
good - bye to all this pleas - ure sure I'm off to seek me
gold and mon - ey plen - ty for the poor and for the
C Am G
fa - mous and be - fore I would re - turn a - gain I'd
lei - sure and the next time you will hear from me is a
gen - try and when I do re - turn a - gain I

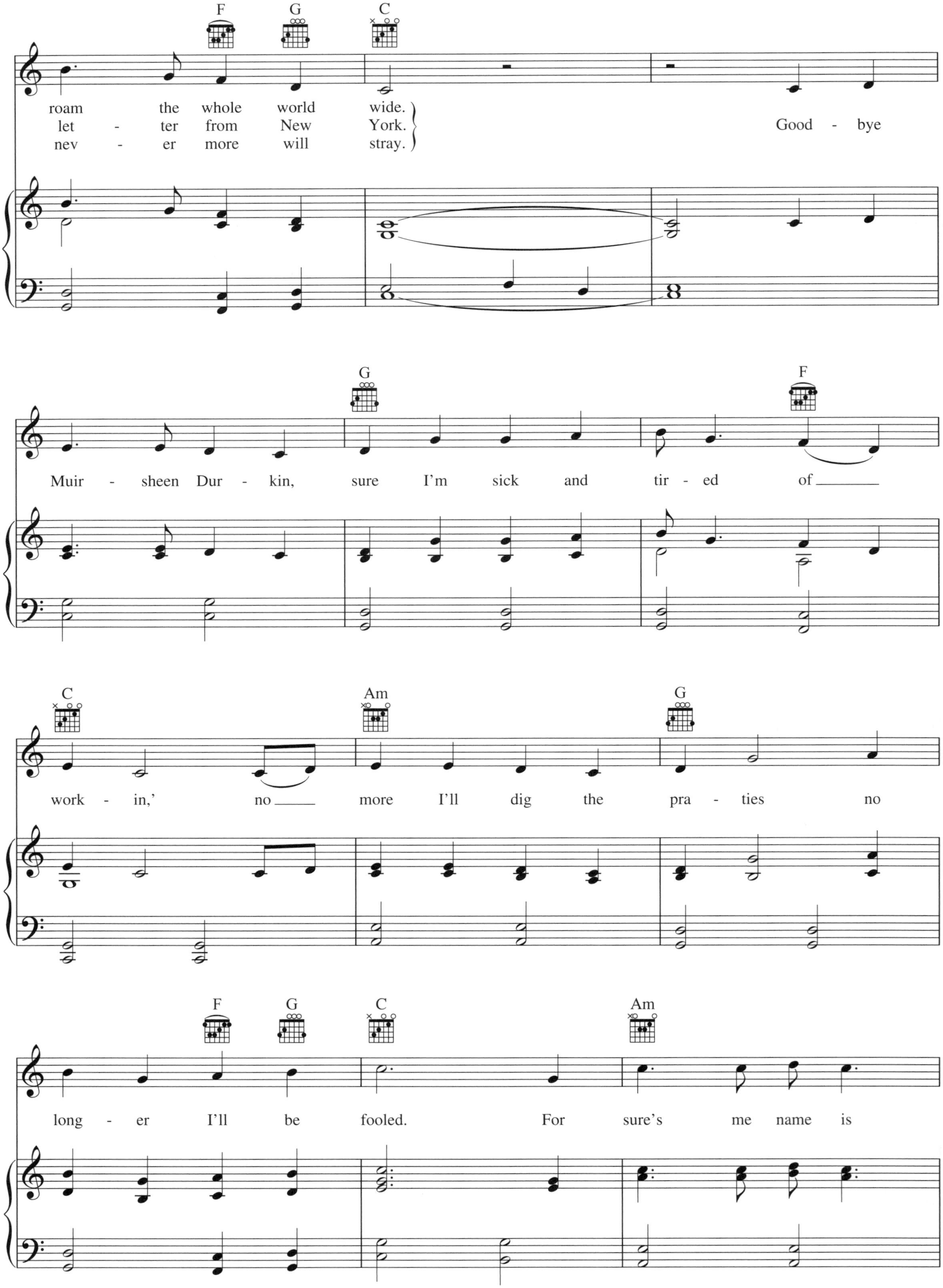
F G C
roam the whole world wide.
let - ter from New York.
nev - er more will stray.
Good - bye
G F
Muir - sheen Dur - kin, sure I'm sick and tir - ed of
C Am G
work - in,' no more I'll dig the pra - ties no
F G C Am
long - er I'll be fooled. For sure's me name is

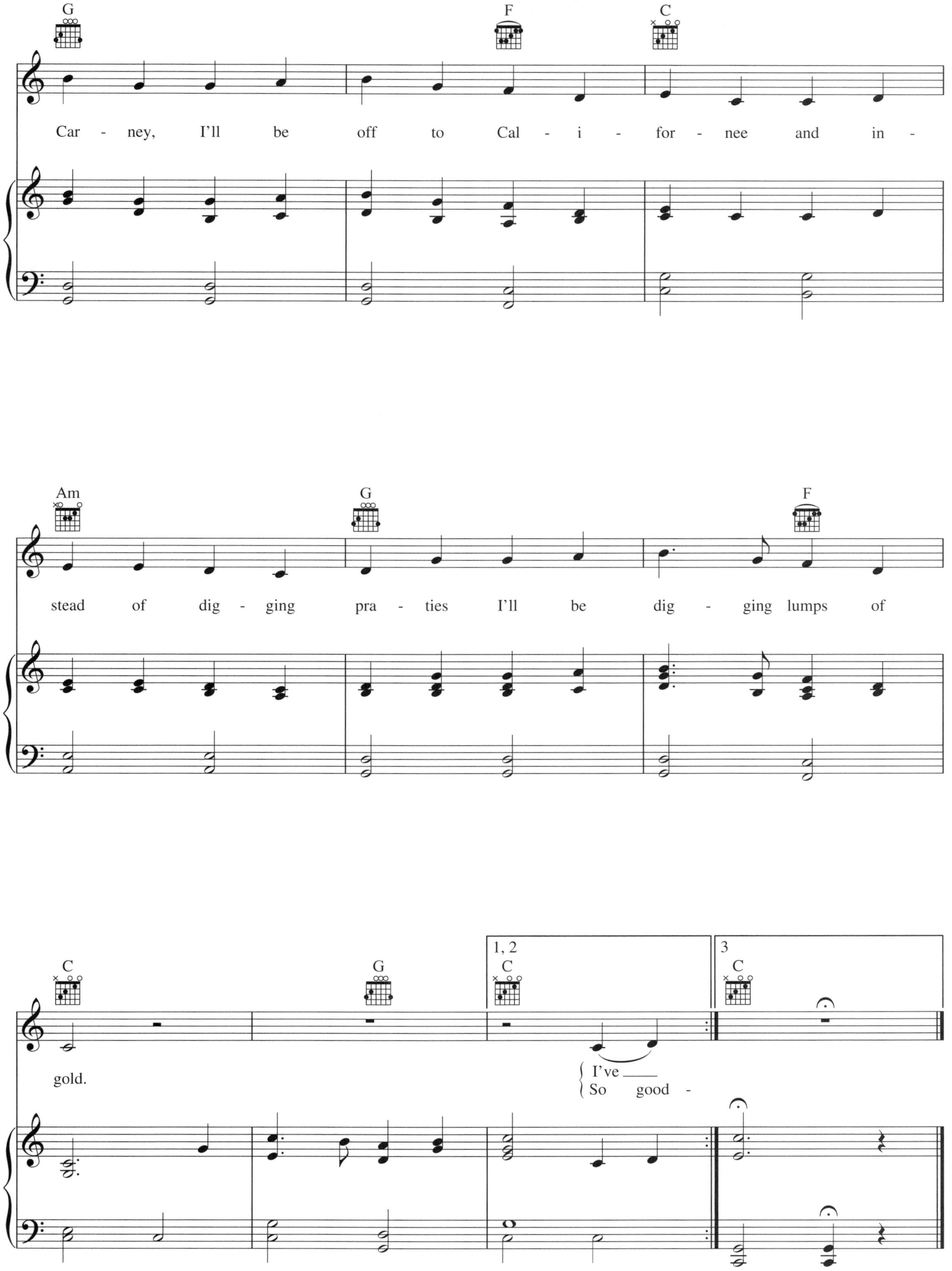
G F C
Car - ney, I'll be off to Cal - i - for - nee and in -
Am G F
stead of dig - ging pra - ties I'll be dig - ging lumps of
C G
gold.
1, 2
C
I've ___
So good -
3
C

MY WILD IRISH ROSE

Words and Music by
CHAUNCEY OLCOTT

Copyright © 2006 by HAL LEONARD CORPORATION
International Copyright Secured All Rights Reserved

Bdim7 F7 B♭ Bdim7
You may search ev - 'ry - where but
F7 B♭ Gm C7
none can com - pare with my wild
F7 Cm7 F7 B♭
I - rish Rose. My wild
E♭m/B♭ B♭
I - rish Rose, the

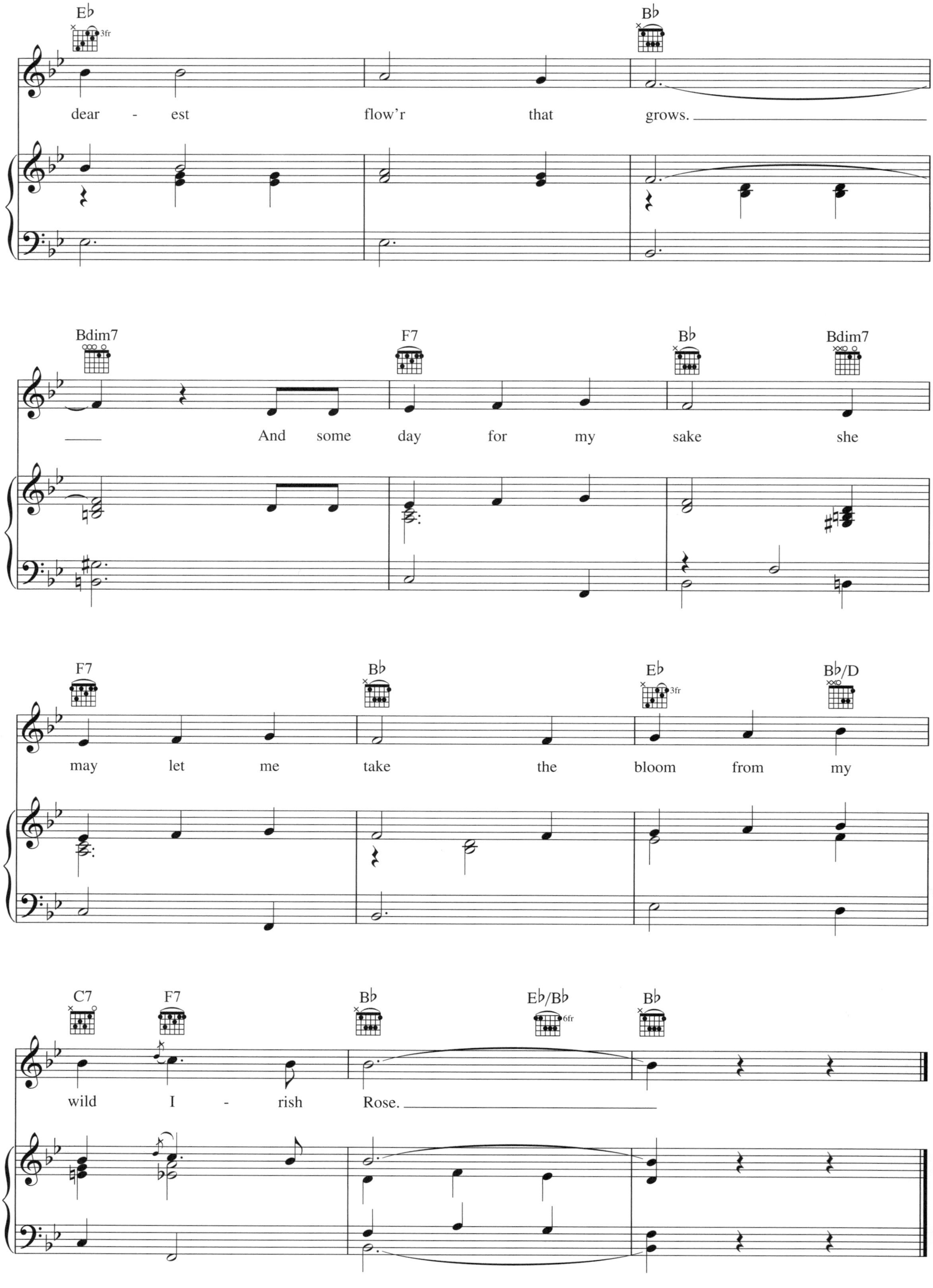
E♭
3fr
B♭
dear - est flow'r that grows.
Bdim7
F7
B♭
Bdim7
And some day for my sake she
F7
B♭
E♭
3fr
B♭/D
may let me take the bloom from my
C7
F7
B♭
E♭/B♭
6fr
B♭
wild I - rish Rose.

A NATION ONCE AGAIN

Words and Music by
THOMAS DAVIS

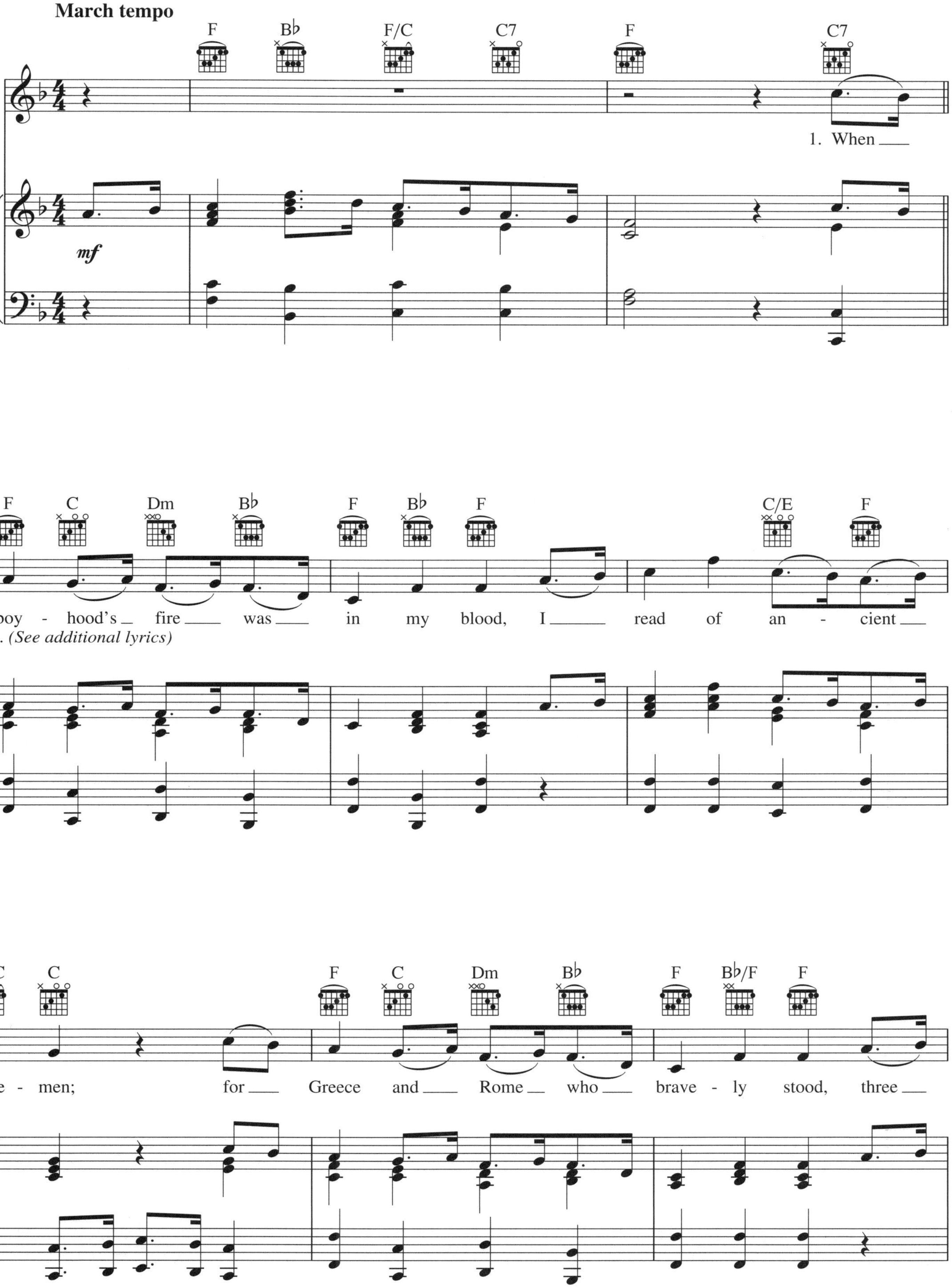
March tempo
F Bb F/C C7 F C7
mf
1. When
F C Dm Bb F Bb F C/E F
boy - hood's fire was in my blood, I read of an - cient
2.-4. (See additional lyrics)
F/C C F C Dm Bb F Bb/F F
free - men; for Greece and Rome who brave - ly stood, three

Copyright © 2003 by HAL LEONARD CORPORATION
International Copyright Secured All Rights Reserved

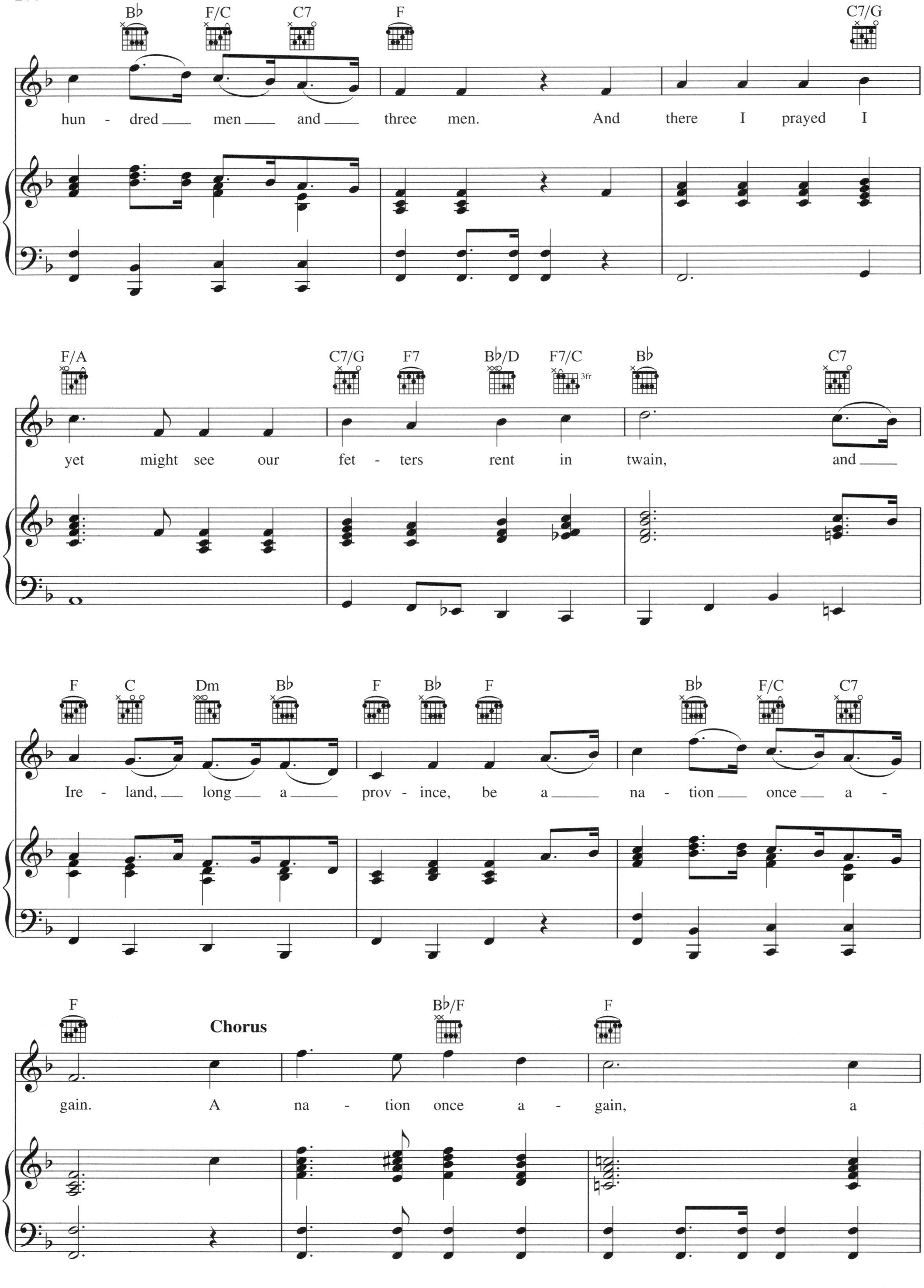
B♭ F/C C7 F C7/G
hun - dred men and three men. And there I prayed I
F/A C7/G F7 B♭/D F7/C B♭ C7
3fr
yet might see our fet - ters rent in twain, and
F C Dm B♭ F B♭ F B♭ F/C C7
Ire - land, long a prov - ince, be a na - tion once a -
F B♭/F F
Chorus
gain. A na - tion once a - gain, a

Bb/F F C7/E F C Dm Bb
na - tion once a - gain. May Ire - land, long a
F Bb F Bb F/C C7
1 - 3 F
4 F
prov - ince, be a na - tion once a - gain. And from gain?

Additional Lyrics

2. And from that time, through wildest woe,
That hope has shown a far light;
Nor could love's brightest summer glow
Outshine that solemn starlight.
It seemed to watch above my head
In forum, field and fane;
Its angel voice sang 'round my bed,
"A nation once again."

3. It whispered too, that "Freedom's Ark"
And service high and holy,
Would be profaned by feelings dark
And passions vain or lowly;
For freedom comes from God's right hand,
And needs a Godly train,
And righteous men must make our land
A nation once again.

4. So as I grew from boy to man,
I bent me at that bidding;
My spirit of each selfish plan
And cruel passion ridding.
For thus I hoped some day to aid.
Oh! Can such hope be vain
When my dear country shall be made
A nation once again?

THE NIGHTINGALE

Traditional Irish Folk Song

Gently
mp
D G D G A7 D Bm G A7 D
As I went a walk - ing one morn - ing in May, I met a young cou - ple who fond - ly did stray. One was a
out of his knap - sack he took a fine fid - dle and he played her such a mer - ry tune with a hi - did - dle - did - dle. And he played her such a
sol - dier, hand-some sol - dier, will you mar - ry me? Oh no, said the sol - dier that nev - er can be. For I have a wife
am off to In - di - a for sev - en long years, drink - ing wine and strong whis - key in - stead of cold beers. And if e - ver I re -

Copyright © 2006 by HAL LEONARD CORPORATION
International Copyright Secured All Rights Reserved

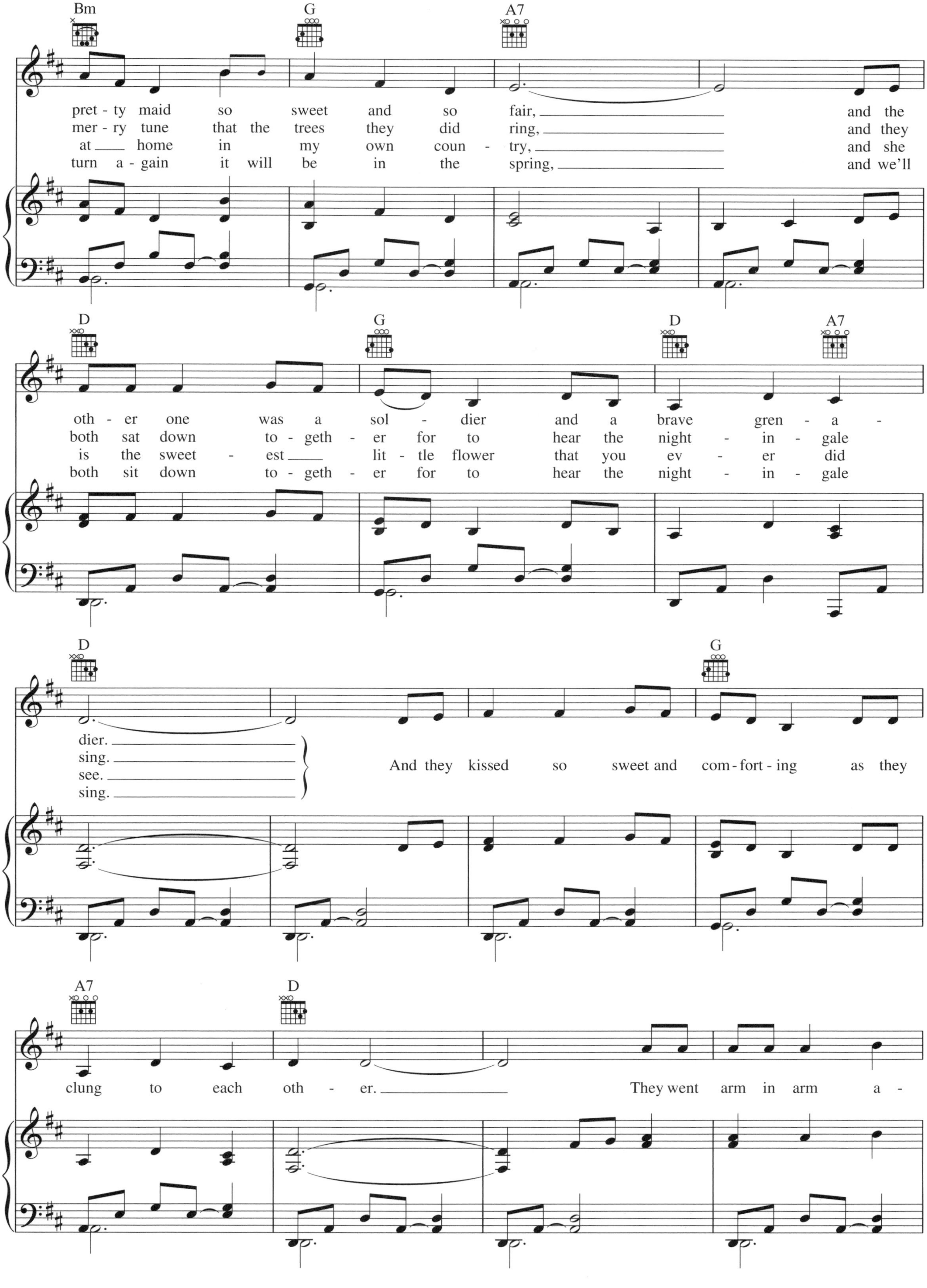
Bm G A7
pret - ty maid so sweet and so fair, and the
mer - ry tune that the trees they did ring, and they
at home in my own coun - try, and she
turn a - gain it will be in the spring, and we'll
D G D A7
oth - er one was a sol - dier and a brave gren - a -
both sat down to - geth - er for to hear the night - in - gale
is the sweet - est lit - tle flower that you ev - er did
both sit down to - geth - er for to hear the night - in - gale
D G
dier.
sing.
see.
sing.
And they kissed so sweet and com - fort - ing as they
A7 D
clung to each oth - er. They went arm in arm a -

Bm G A7
long the road like sis - ter and broth - er. They went
D Bm G A7
arm in arm a - long the road till they came to a stream,
D G D A7
and they both sat down to - geth - er for to hear the night - in - gale
D
sing.
1 - 3
From
Oh,
Now I
4
rit.

PADDY'S GREEN SHAMROCK SHORE

Traditional Irish Folk Song

Gently
C F B♭ F
mf
C
1. Oh fare thee well sweet
2. ship she lies at
3. Lon - don - der - ry we
4.-6. (See additional lyrics)
F B♭ F
Ire - land my own dear na - tive
an - chor now; she's stand - ing by the
did set sail, it be - ing the fourth of
C F C
home. It breaks my heart, to
quay. May for - tune bright shine
May. On a stur - dy ship to

Copyright © 2006 by HAL LEONARD CORPORATION
International Copyright Secured All Rights Reserved

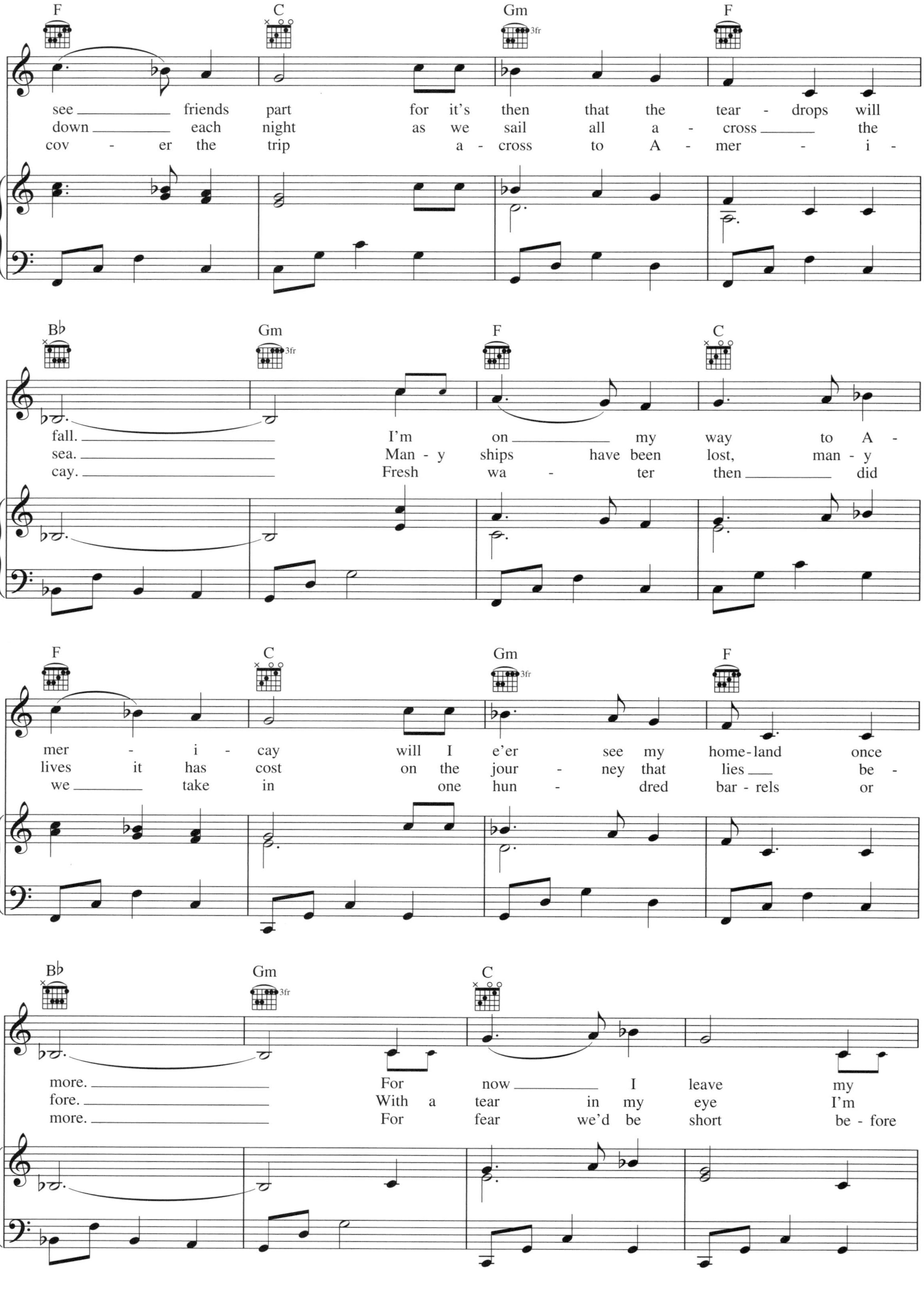
F C Gm F
see friends part for it's then that the tear - drops will
down each night as we sail all a - cross the
cov - er the trip a - cross to A - mer - i -
Bb Gm F C
fall. I'm on my way to A -
sea. Man - y ships have been lost, man - y
cay. Fresh wa - ter then did
F C Gm F
mer - i - cay will I e'er see my home-land once
lives it has cost on the jour - ney that lies be -
we take in one hun - dred bar - rels or
Bb Gm C
more. For now I leave my
fore. With a tear in my eye I'm
more. For fear we'd be short be - fore
3fr

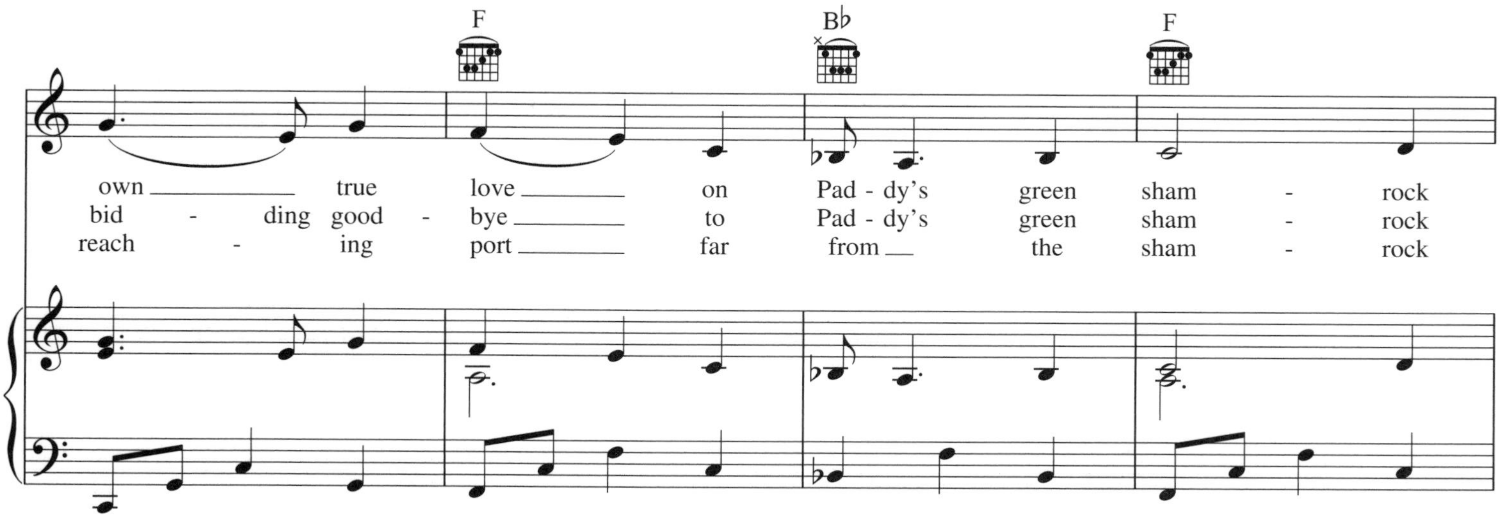
F
B♭
F
own true love on Pad - dy's green sham - rock
bid - ding good - bye to Pad - dy's green sham - rock
reach - ing port far from the sham - rock

C
1 - 5
6
shore. Our
shore. From
shore. Two
rit.

Additional Lyrics

4. Two of our anchors we did weigh before we left the quay
All down the river we were towed till we came to the open sea.
We saw that night the grandest sight we ever saw before,
The sun going down 'tween sea and sky far from Paddy's green shamrock shore.

5. Early next morn, sea-sick and forlorn, not one of us was free
And I myself was confined to bed with no one to pity me.
No father or mother or sister or brother to raise my head when sore,
That made me think of the family I left back on Paddy's green shamrock shore.

6. So are thee well my own true love I think of you night and day.
A place in my mind you surely will find although I'm so far away.
Though I am alone and away from my home I'll think of the good time before,
Until the day I can make my way back to Paddy's green shamrock shore.

O'DONNELL ABOO

Words and Music by
M.J. McCANN

March tempo
G E7/G♯ A7 D G D D
mf
Proud - ly the note of the
Prince - ly O' Neill to our
Wild - ly o'er Des - mond the
Bm A/C♯ D G Em A7 Bm G D
trum - pet is sound - ing, loud - ly the war cries a - rise on the gale.
aid is ad - vanc - ing, with man - y a chief - tain and war - rior clan. A
war wolf is howl - ing, fear - less the ea - gle sweeps o - ver the plain. The
Bm A/C♯ D G E/G♯ A7
Fleet - ly the steed by Lough Swil - ly is bound - ing, to join the thick squad - rons in
thou - sand proud steeds in his van - guard are pranc - ing, 'neath bor - der - ers brave from the
fox in the streets of the cit - y is prowl - ing and all who would scare them are

Copyright © 2003 by HAL LEONARD CORPORATION
International Copyright Secured All Rights Reserved

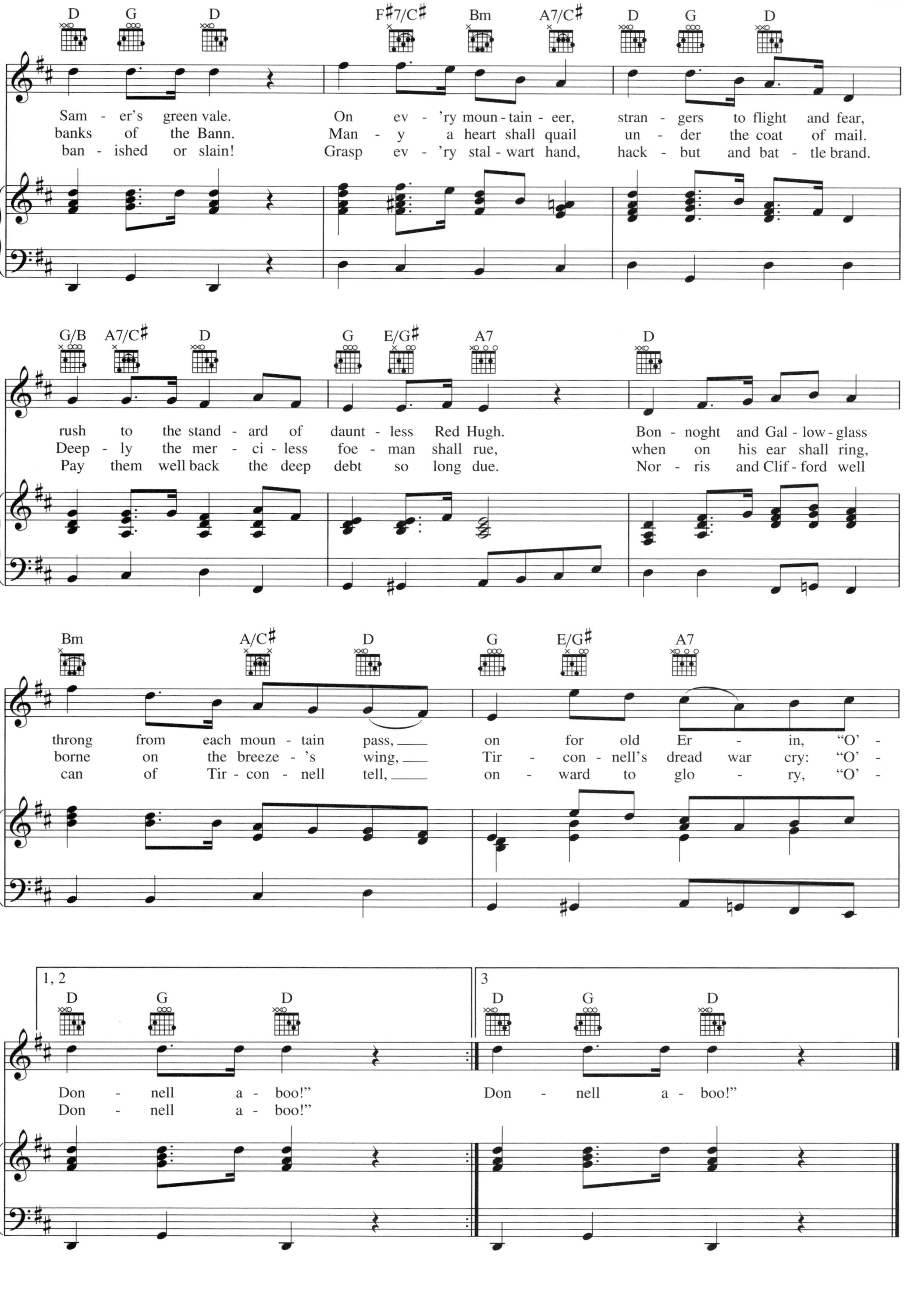
D G D F♯7/C♯ Bm A7/C♯ D G D
Sam - er's green vale. On ev - 'ry moun - tain - eer, stran - gers to flight and fear,
banks of the Bann. Man - y a heart shall quail un - der the coat of mail.
ban - ished or slain! Grasp ev - 'ry stal - wart hand, hack - but and bat - tle brand.
G/B A7/C♯ D G E/G♯ A7 D
rush to the stand - ard of daunt - less Red Hugh. Bon - noght and Gal - low - glass
Deep - ly the mer - ci - less foe - man shall rue, when on his ear shall ring,
Pay them well back the deep debt so long due. Nor - ris and Clif - ford well
Bm A/C♯ D G E/G♯ A7
throng from each moun - tain pass, on for old Er - in, "O' -
borne on the breeze - 's wing, Tir - con - nell's dread war cry: "O' -
can of Tir - con - nell tell, on - ward to glo - ry, "O' -
1, 2 D G D 3 D G D
Don - nell a - boo!" Don - nell a - boo!"
Don - nell a - boo!"

OFT IN THE STILLY NIGHT

Irish Folk Song

With a lilt
A D/A A E7 A
mf
D/A A E A
Oft in the stil - ly night, ere slum - ber's chain has bound me,
When I re - mem - ber all the friends, so linked to - geth - er,
D/A A E7 A
fond mem - 'ry brings the light of oth - er days a - round me. The
I've seen a - round me fall like leaves in win - try weath - er, I
Asus A E7 A
smiles, the tears of boy - hood's years, the words of love then spo - ken, the
feel like one who treads a - lone some ban - quet hall de - sert - ed, whose

Copyright © 2003 by HAL LEONARD CORPORATION
International Copyright Secured All Rights Reserved

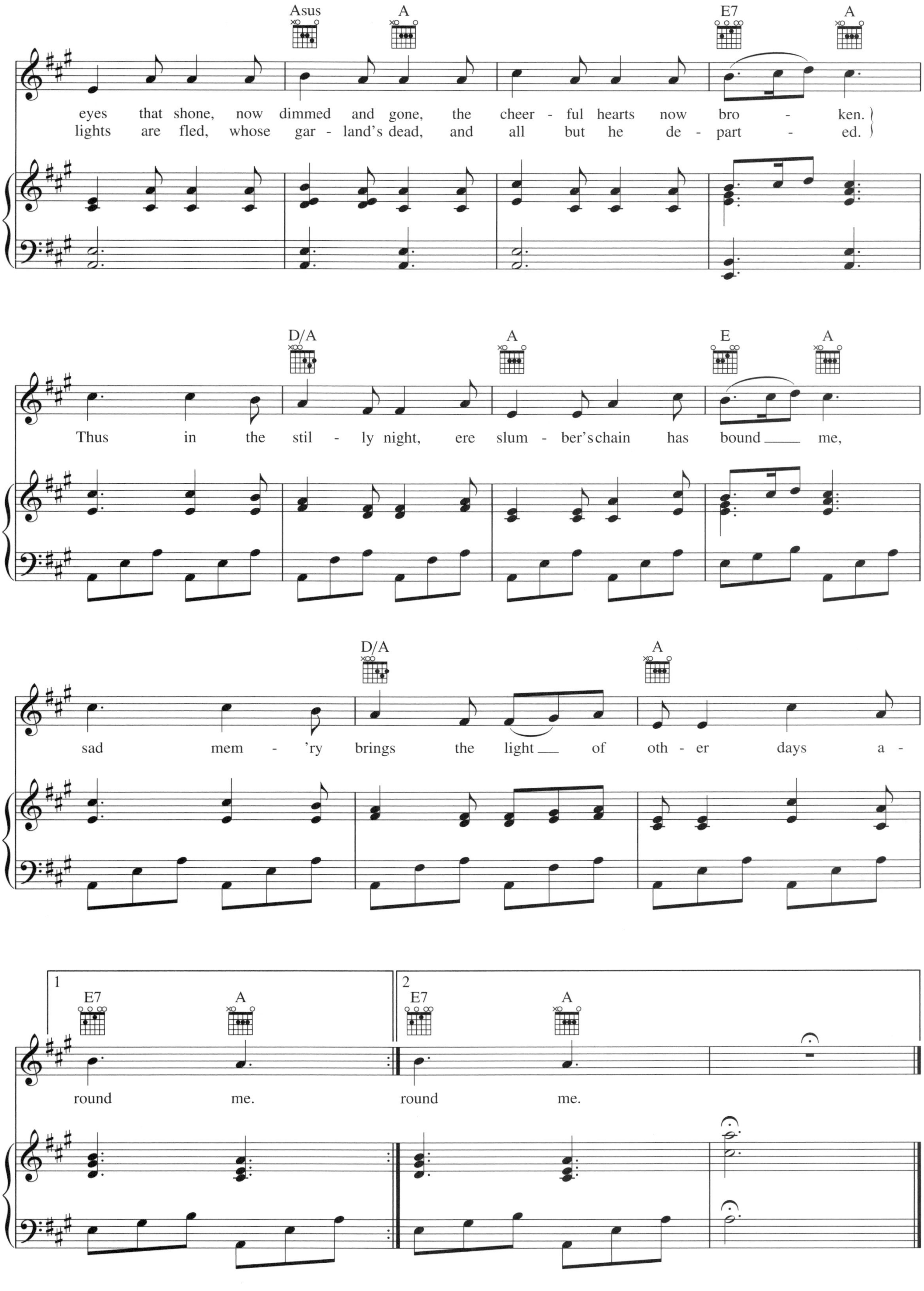
Asus
A
E7
A
eyes that shone, now dimmed and gone, the cheer - ful hearts now bro - ken.
lights are fled, whose gar - land's dead, and all but he de - part - ed.
D/A
A
E
A
Thus in the stil - ly night, ere slum - ber's chain has bound me,
D/A
A
sad mem - 'ry brings the light of oth - er days a -
1
E7
A
round me.
2
E7
A
round me.

OLD MAID IN THE GARRET

Traditional Irish Folk Song

Moderately
G C G D
mf
G/B G
1. I have of - ten heard it said by my fa - ther and my
2. there's my sis - ter Jean; she's not hand - some nor good -
3. cook and I can sew, I can keep the house right
4.,5. (See additional lyrics)
G/B D C
moth - er that go - ing to a wed - ding was the
look - ing, scarce - ly six - teen and a
ti - dy, rise up in the morn - ing and
G D G
mak - ings of an - oth - er. Well if this be
fel - la she was court - ing. Now she's twen - ty -
get the break - fast read - y. There's noth - ing in this

Copyright © 2006 by HAL LEONARD CORPORATION
International Copyright Secured All Rights Reserved

C G Bm
so then I'll go with - out a bid - ding. Oh it's kind Prov - i -
four with a son and a daugh - ter here am I for - ty -
wide world would make me half so cheer - y as a wee fat
G C G
Refrain
dence, won't you send me to a wed - ding!
five and I've nev - er had an of - fer.
man who would call me his own dear - ie.
For it's oh dear
G/B G C G
me, how will it be if I die an old
D
1 - 4
G
5
G
maid in the gar - ret!
Oh now
I can
Oh come
ret!

Additional Lyrics

4. Oh come landsman or come townsman, come tinker or come tailor,
Come fiddler, come dancer, come ploughman or come sailor.
Come rich man, come poor man, come fool or come witty,
Come any man at all who would marry me for pity.
Refrain

5. Oh well I'm away to home for there's nobody heeding,
There's nobody heeding to poor old Annie's pleading.
For I'm away home to my own wee-bit garret
If I can't get a man then I'll surely get a parrot!
Refrain

THE OLD ORANGE FLUTE

Traditional Irish Folk Song

Lively
D F♯m G D A7
mf
D A D
1. In the county Tyrone near the town of Dun-gan-non, where
2. Bob, the de-ceiv-er, he took us all in, he
3. chap-el on Sun-day to a-tone for past deeds, said
4.,5. (See additional lyrics)
Bm A7 D F♯m
man-y the ruc-tions me-self had a han'-in, Bob Wil-liam-son lived, a
mar-ried a Pa-pist named Brid-get Mc-Ginn, turned Pap-ish him-self, and for-
Pa-ters and A-ves and count-ed his beads, till af-ter some time at the
G D A7 D
weav-er by trade, and all of us thought him a stout Or-ange blade. On the
sook the old cause, that gave us our free-dom, re-li-gion, and laws. Now the
priests own de-sire he went with the old flute to play in the choir. He

Copyright © 2006 by HAL LEONARD CORPORATION
International Copyright Secured All Rights Reserved

G
D
twelfth of Ju - ly as it yearly - ly did come, Bob played with his flute to the
boys of the place make some com - ment up - on it and Bob had to fly to the
went with the old flute for to play for the mass, but the in - stru - ment shiv - ered and
A7
D
F♯m
G
D
sound of a drum. You may talk of your harp, your pi - an - o, or lute, but there's
prov - ince of Con - naught. He fled with his wife and his fix - ings to boot, and a -
sighed, oh, a - las. And try though he would, though it make a great noise, the
A7
1 - 4
D
5
A7
D
none can com - pare with the old or - ange flute. Now, Prot - es - tant Boys."
long with the lat - ter his old or - ange flute. At the
flute would play on - ly "The Prot - es - tant Boys." Bob

Additional Lyrics

4. Bob jumped and he started and got in a flutter
And threw the old flute in the blessed holy water.
He thought that this charm would bring some other sound;
When he tried it again it played "Croppies Lie Down."
Now for all he could whistle and finger and blow,
To play Papish music he found it no go.
"Kick the Pope" and "Boil Water" it freely would sound,
But one Papish squeak in it couldn't be found.

5. At the council of priests that was held the next day
They decided to banish the old flute away.
They couldn't knock heresy out of its head,
So they bought Bob a new one to play in the stead.
Now the old flute was doomed and its fate was pathetic,
'Twas fastened and burned at the stake as heretic.
As the flames soared around it they heard a strange noise;
'Twas the old flute still whistling "The Protestant Boys."

THE OLD WOMAN FROM WEXFORD

Traditional Irish Folk Song

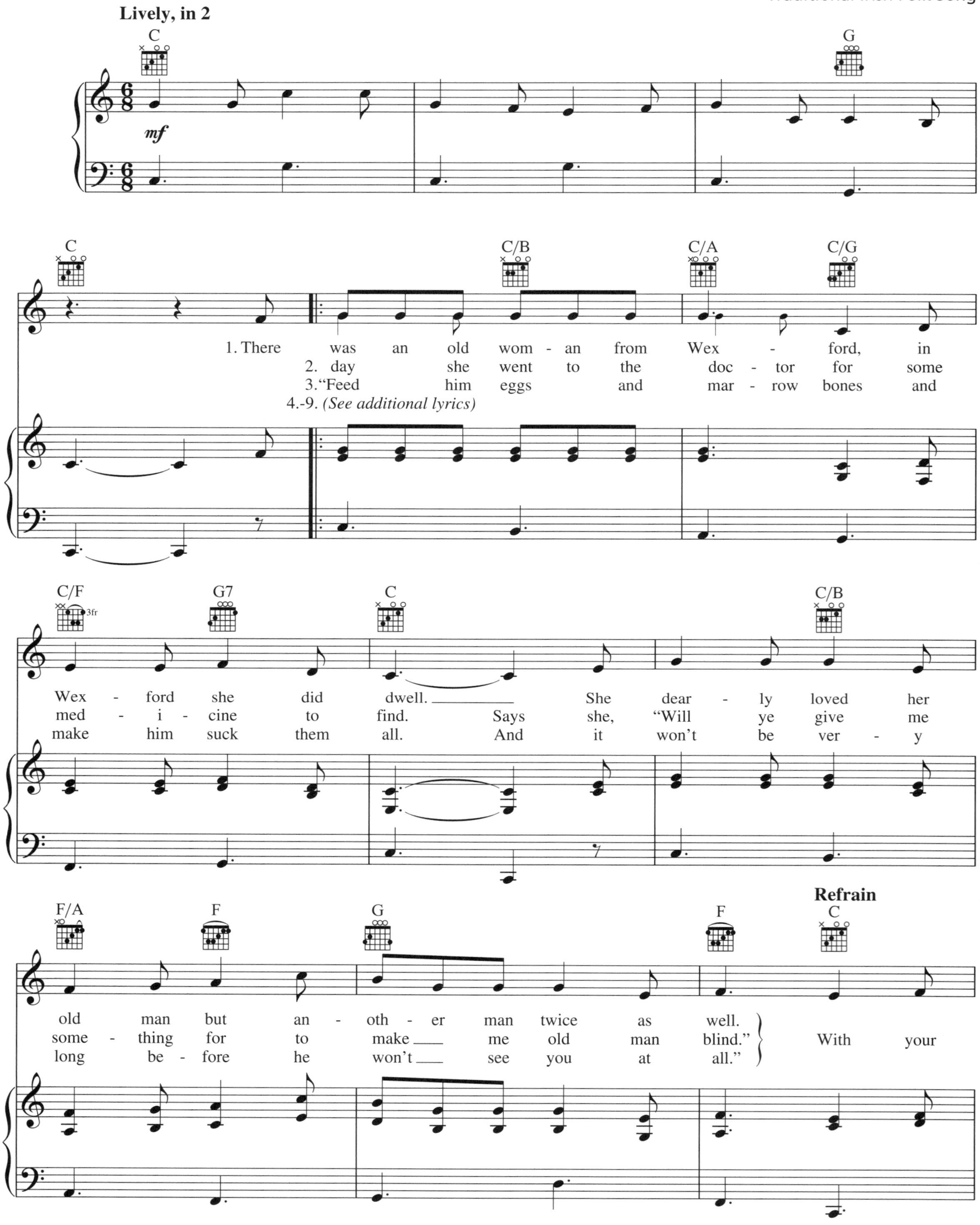
Lively, in 2
C
G
mf
C
C/B
C/A
C/G
1. There was an old wom - an from Wex - ford, in
2. day she went to the doc - tor for some
3. "Feed him eggs and mar - row bones and
4.-9. (See additional lyrics)
C/F
G7
C
C/B
3fr
Wex - ford she did dwell. She dear - ly loved her
med - i - cine to find. Says she, "Will ye give me
make him suck them all. And it won't be ver - y
F/A
F
G
F
Refrain
C
old man but an - oth - er man twice as well.
some - thing for to make me old man blind."
long be - fore he won't see you at all."
With your

Copyright © 2006 by HAL LEONARD CORPORATION
International Copyright Secured All Rights Reserved

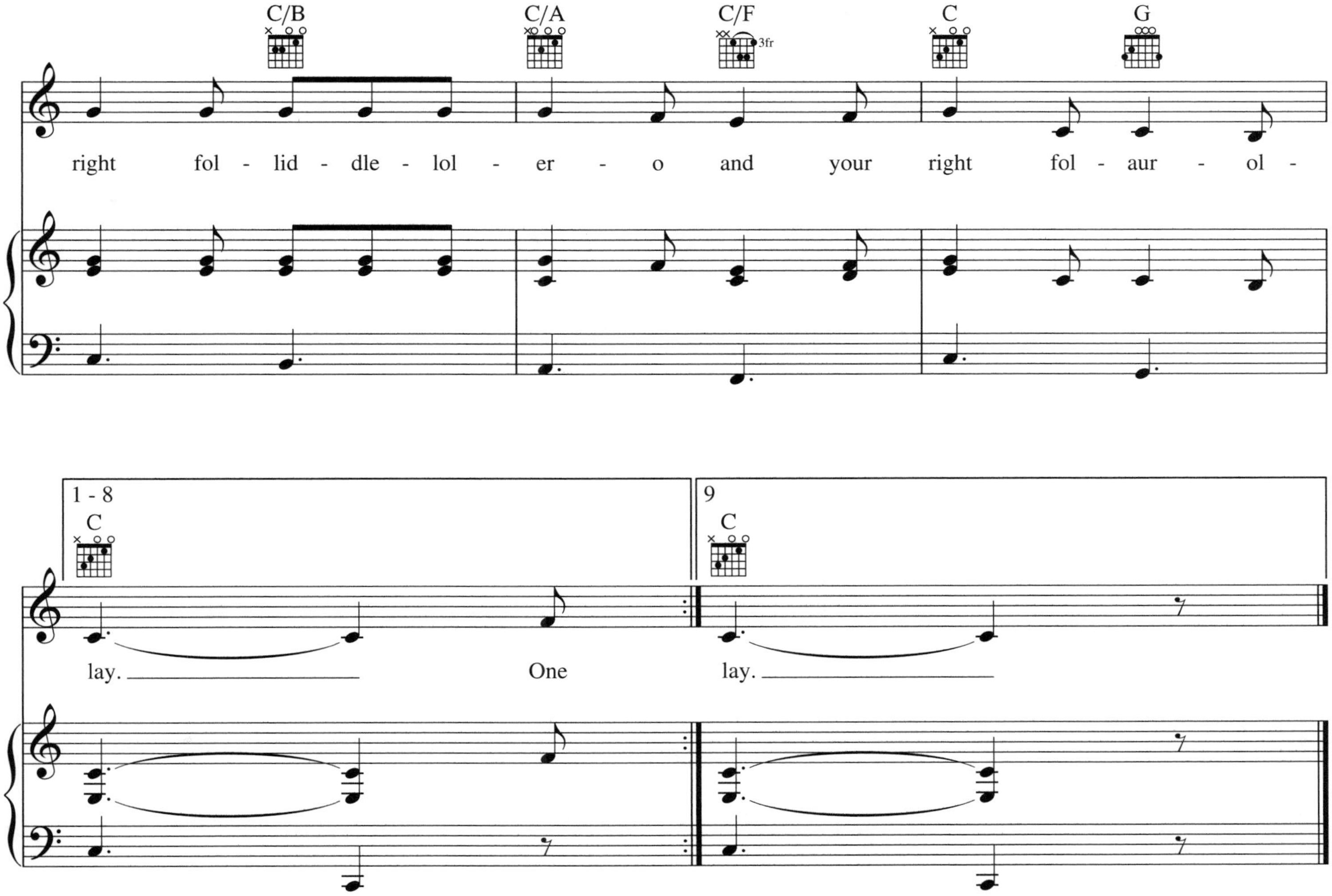
C/B
C/A
C/F
3fr
C
G
right fol - lid - dle - lol - er - o and your right fol - aur - ol -
1 - 8
C
9
C
lay. One lay.

Additional Lyrics

4. The doctor wrote a letter and he signed it with his hand
   And he sent it to the old man so that he would understand.
   Refrain

5. She fed him eggs and marrow bones and made him suck them all
   And it wasn't very long before he couldn't see the wall.
   Refrain

6. Said he, "I'd like to drown myself but that would be a sin."
   Said she, "I'll come along with you and help to push you in."
   Refrain

7. The woman she stepped back a bit to rush and push him in,
   But the old man quickly stepped aside and she went tumbling in.
   Refrain

8. How loudly she did holler oh, how loudly she did call,
   "Yerra hold your whist old woman sure I can't see you at all."
   Refrain

9. Now eggs and eggs and marrowbones may make your old man blind.
   But if you want to drown him you must creep up from behind.
   Refrain

PADDY WORKS ON THE RAILWAY

Traditional

Brightly
F C/E B♭/D C F C
mf
F Dm C
1. In eight - een hun - dred and for - ty - one, my
2. eight - een hun - dred and for - ty - two, I
3. eight - een hun - dred and for - ty - three, I
4.-8. (See additional lyrics)
B♭ F/A G C F Dm
cor - du - roy breech - es I put on. My cor - du - roy breech - es
did - n't know what I should do, I did - n't know what
took a trip a - cross the sea, I took a trip a -
F C/E F C F C
Refrain
I put on to work up - on the rail - way.
I should do to work up - on the rail - way.
cross the sea to work up - on the rail - way.
The

Copyright © 2006 by HAL LEONARD CORPORATION
International Copyright Secured All Rights Reserved

B♭ C F C/E B♭/D C F C
rail - way, I'm wea - ry of the rail - way poor Pad - dy works on the
F C
1 - 7
F
8
F
rail - way.
In
In
In

Additional Lyrics

4. In eighteen hundred and forty-four, I landed on Columbia's shore,
   I landed on Columbia's shore, to work upon the railway.
   Refrain

5. In eighteen hundred and forty-five, when Daniel O'Connell was alive,
   When Daniel O'Connell was alive, to work upon the railway.
   Refrain

6. In eighteen hundred and forty-six, I changed my trade to carrying bricks,
   I changed my trade to carrying bricks, to work upon the railway.
   Refrain

7. In eighteen hundred and forty-seven, poor Paddy was thinking of going to heaven,
   Poor Paddy was thinking of going to heaven, to work upon the railway.
   Refrain

8. In eighteen hundred and forty-eight, I learnt to take my whiskey straight,
   I learnt to take my whiskey straight, to work upon the railway.
   Refrain

THE PARTING GLASS

Irish Folk Song

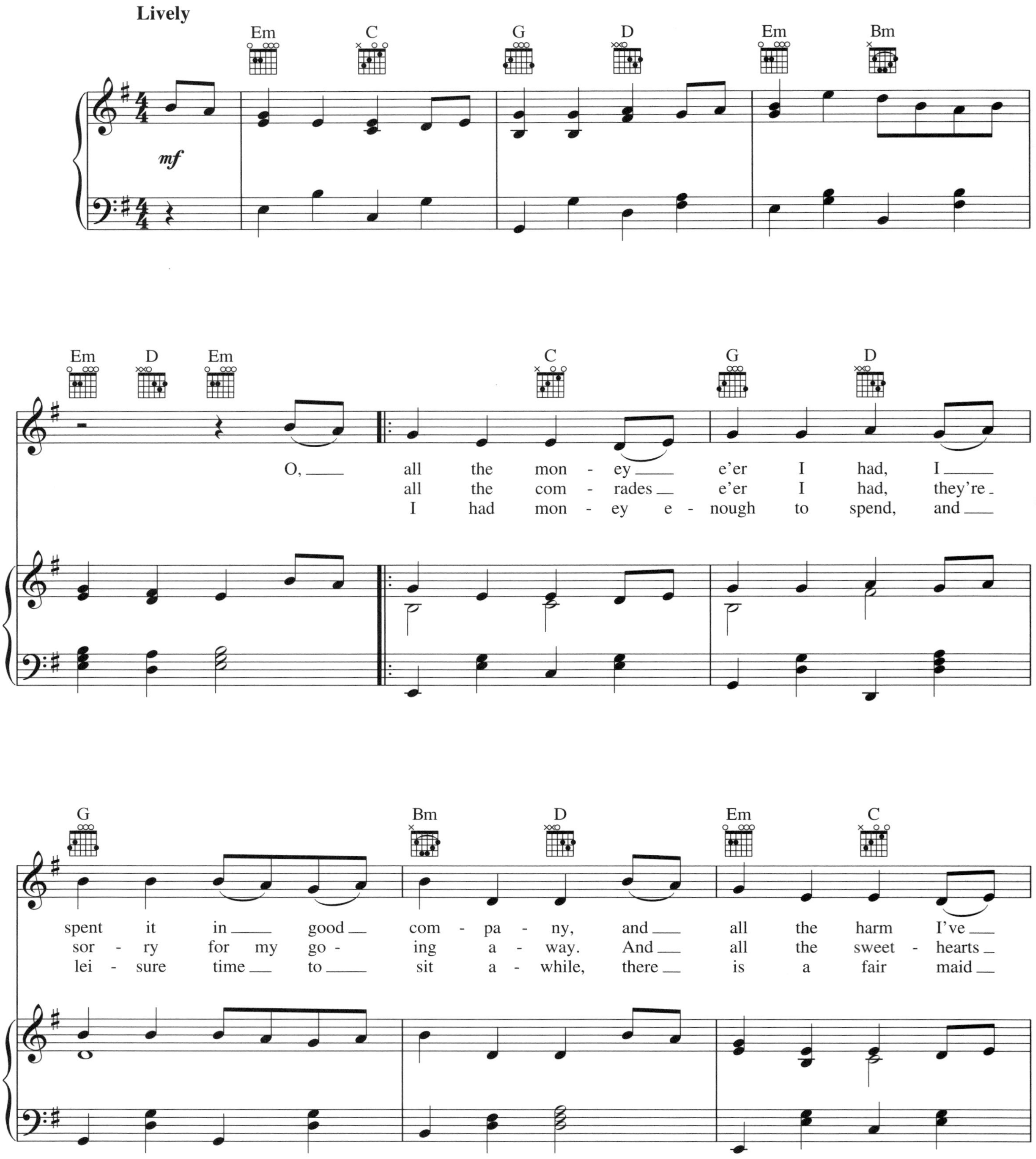
Lively
mf
Em C G D Em Bm
Em D Em C G D
O, all the mon - ey e'er I had, I
all the com - rades e'er I had, they're
I had mon - ey e - nough to spend, and
G Bm D Em C
spent it in good com - pa - ny, and all the harm I've
sor - ry for my go - ing a - way. And all the sweet - hearts
lei - sure time to sit a - while, there is a fair maid

Copyright © 2006 by HAL LEONARD CORPORATION
International Copyright Secured All Rights Reserved

G D G Bm Em
ev - er done a - las, it was to none but me. And
e'er I had, they'd wish me one more day to stay. But
in this town that sore - ly has my heart be - guiled. Her
G Em Bm Am Em
all I've done for want of wit to mem - 'ry now I
since it falls un - to my lot, I gen - tly rise and
ro - sy cheeks and ru - by lips, I own she has my
Bm D Em C G D
can't re - call so fill to me the part - ing glass, good -
soft - ly call, that I should go and you should not. Good -
heart in thrall. Then fill to me the part - ing glass, good -
G Bm
1, 2
Em C Em
3
Em C Em
night and joy be with you all. O, with you all.
night and joy be with you all. If
night and joy be

THE PATRIOT GAME

Traditional Irish Folk Song

Moderately
C F C
mf
G7 C
1. Come
F C
all you young reb - els and
2. name is O' - Han - lon, I'm
3. bare - ly two years since I
4.-8. (See additional lyrics)
G7 C
list while I sing. For
just gone six - teen. My
wan - dered a - way with the

Copyright © 2006 by HAL LEONARD CORPORATION
International Copyright Secured All Rights Reserved

G7 C Am
love of one's land is a
home is in Mon - a - ghan,
lo - cal bat - tal - ion of the
Em G7sus
ter - ri - ble thing. It
there I was weaned. I
bold I - R - A. I
G7 C Am
ban - ish - es fear with the
was taught all my life cruel
read of our he - roes and
Em F
speed of a flame. And
Eng - land to blame. And
want - ed the same, to

C
F
C
makes us all part of the
so I'm a part of the
play up my part in the
G7
C
1 - 7
8
pa - tri - ot game. My
pa - tri - ot game. 'Tis
pa - tri - ot game. They

Additional Lyrics

4. They told me how Connolly was shot in a chair.
His wounds from the battle all bleeding and bare,
His fine body twisted, all battered and lame.
They soon made him part of the patriot game.

5. I joined a battalion from dear Bally Bay,
And gave up my boyhood so happy and gay.
For now as a soldier I'd drill and I'd train,
To play my full part in the patriot game.

6. This Ireland of mine has for long been half free.
Six counties are under John Bull's tyranny.
And still De Valera is greatly to blame
For shirking his part in the patriot game.

7. I don't mind a bit if I shoot down police.
They're lackeys for war never guardians of peace.
But yet at deserters I'm never let aim,
Those rebels who sold out the patriot game.

8. And now as I lie with my body all holes
I think of those traitors who bargained and sold.
I'm sorry my rifle has not done the same
For the quisling who sold out the patriot game.

RED IS THE ROSE

Irish Folk Song

Gently
G
D
A7
D
mp
D
Bm
Come o - ver the hills my bon - ny I - rish lass, come
down by Kil - lar - ney's green wood - lands that we stayed, the
time pass - es on and my dar - ling girl is gone. She's
not for the part - ing tha my sis - ter pains, not
Em
G
D

Copyright © 2006 by HAL LEONARD CORPORATION
International Copyright Secured All Rights Reserved

Bm
o - ver the hills to your
moon and the stars they were
gone and met with an -
for the grief of my
G
A
dar - ling.
shin - ing.
oth - er.
moth - er.
G
You choose the
The moon shone its
I'm full of re -
It's all for the
F♯m
G
rose, love, and I will
beams through her locks of
gret but my heart will
loss of my bon - ny

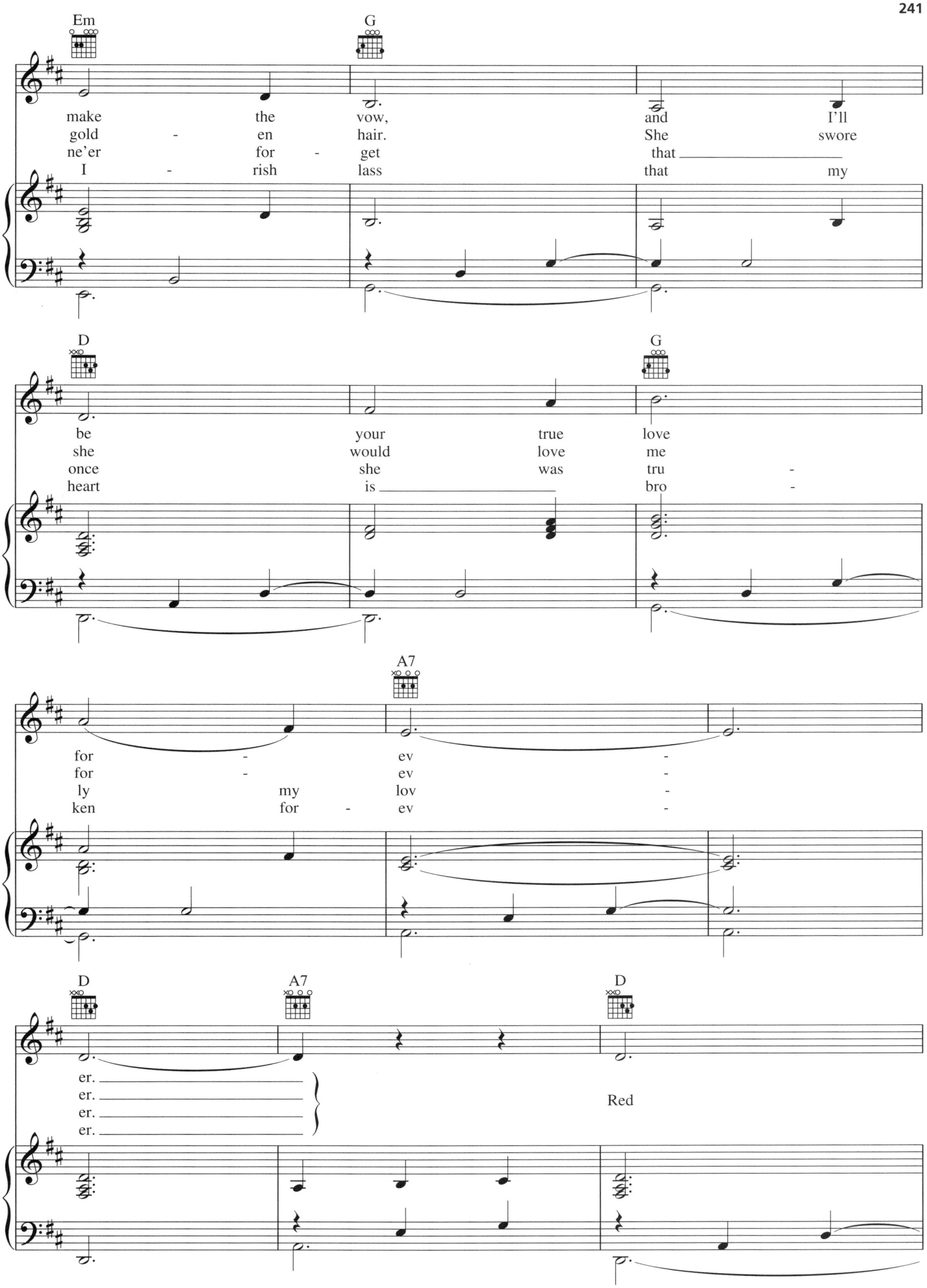
Em
G
make the vow, and I'll
gold - en hair. She swore
ne'er for - get that
I - rish lass that my
D
G
be your true love
she would love me
once she was tru -
heart is bro -
A7
for - ev -
for - ev -
ly my lov -
ken for - ev -
D
A7
D
er.
er.
er.
er.
Red

Bm
Em
is the rose that by yon - der
G
D
gar - den grows.
Fair
Bm
G
is the li - ly of the val -
A
G
- ley.
Clear

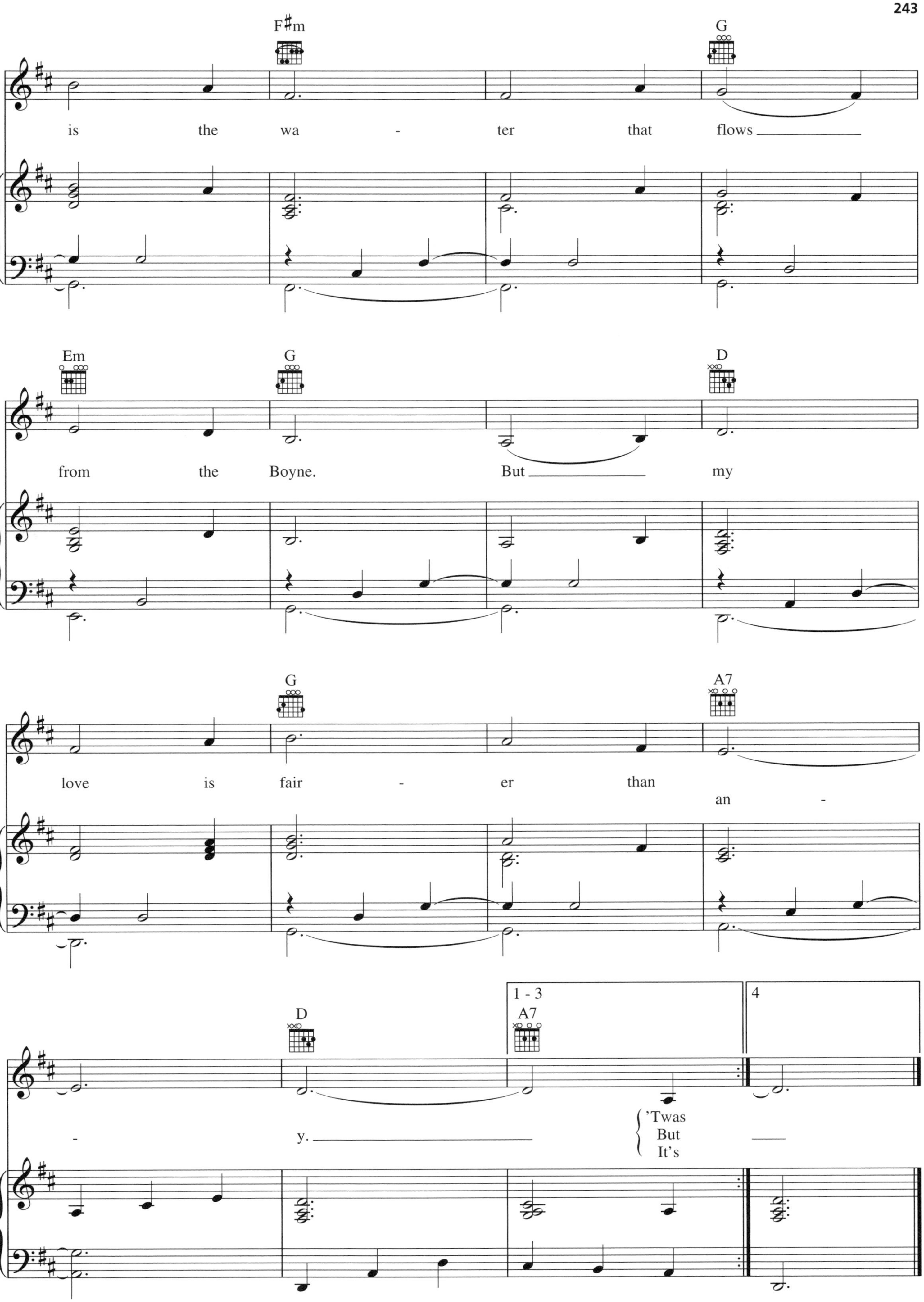
F♯m
G
is the wa - ter that flows
Em
G
D
from the Boyne. But my
G
A7
love is fair - er than an - y.
D
1 - 3
A7
4
'Twas
But
It's

THE QUEEN OF CONNEMARA

Traditional Irish Folk Song

Moderately fast
D A7 D A7
mf
D D G
Oh, my boat can safe - ly float in the teeth of wind and
load - ed down with fish till the wa - ter lips the
light shines out a - far, and it keeps me from dis -
D Bm D E7
weath - er, and out - race the fast - est hook - er be - tween Gal - way and Kin -
gun - wale, not a drop she'll take on board her that would wash a fly a -
may - ing when the skies are ink a - bove us, and the sea runs white with
A D G Em A7
sale. When the black floor of the o - cean and the white foam rush to -
way. From the fleet she'll slip out swift - ly like a grey - hound from her
foam. In a cot in Con - ne - ma - ra there's a wife and wee one

Copyright © 2003 by HAL LEONARD CORPORATION
International Copyright Secured All Rights Reserved

D Bm G A Bm G A
geth - er, high she rides, in her pride, like a sea - gull through the
ken - nel, and she'll land her sil - ver store the first at ould Kin - va - ra
pray - ing to the One who walked the wa - ters once, to send us safe - ly
D F♯m D/F♯ G
gale.
quay.
home.
Oh, she's neat! Oh, she's sweet! She's a beau - ty ev - 'ry
Bm A Bm G
1, 2
D/A A7
line! The Queen of Con - ne - ma - ra is that bound - ing barque of
D
mine.
When she's
There's a
3
D/A A7 D
bound - ing barque of mine!

THE RAGGLE-TAGGLE GYPSY

Traditional

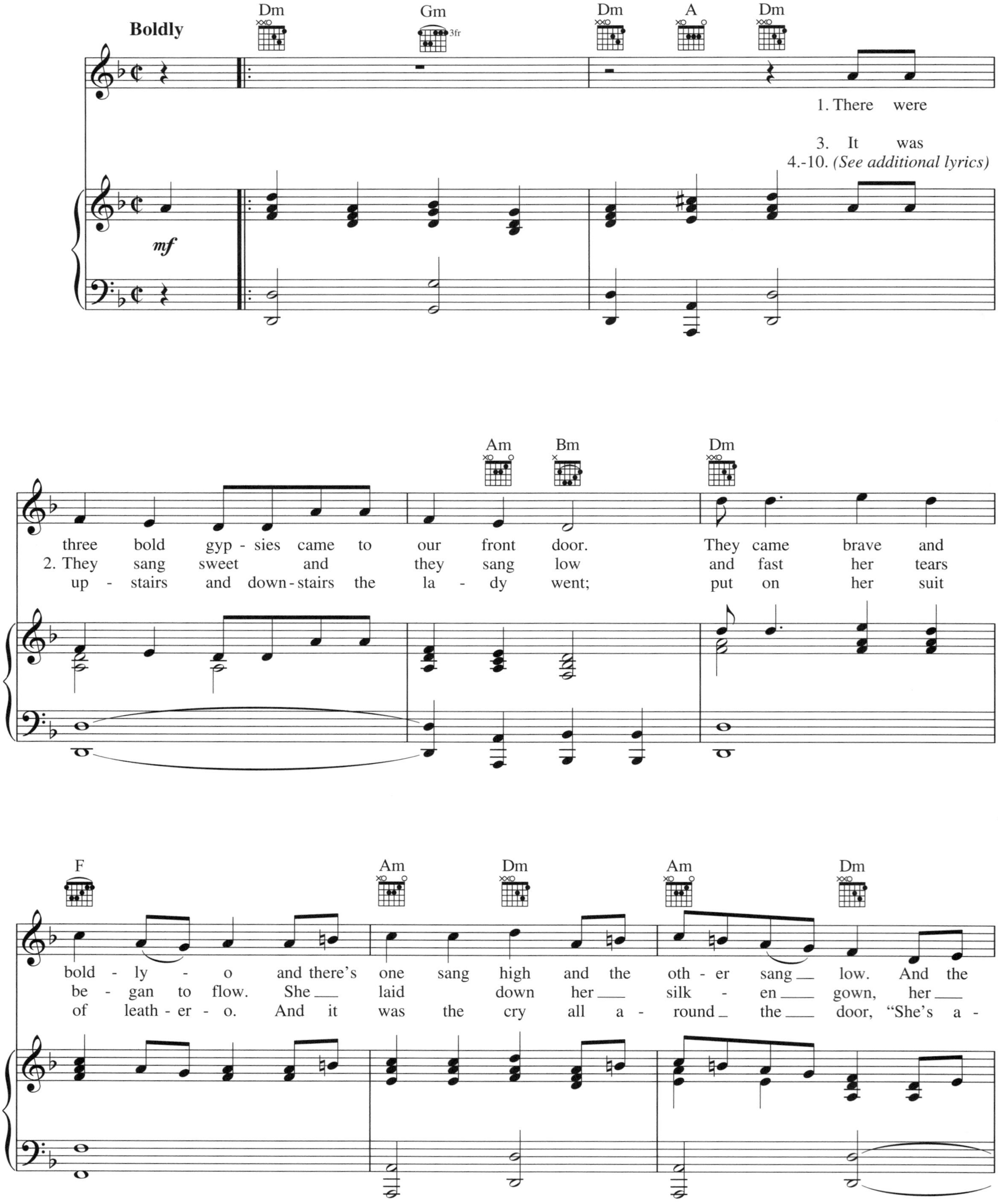
Boldly
Dm Gm 3fr Dm A Dm
mf
1. There were
3. It was
4.-10. (See additional lyrics)
Am Bm Dm
three bold gyp - sies came to our front door. They came brave and
2. They sang sweet and they sang low and fast her tears
up - stairs and down - stairs the la - dy went; put on her suit
F Am Dm Am Dm
bold - ly - o and there's one sang high and the oth - er sang low. And the
be - gan to flow. She laid down her silk - en gown, her
of leath - er - o. And it was the cry all a - round the door, "She's a -

Copyright © 2006 by HAL LEONARD CORPORATION
International Copyright Secured All Rights Reserved

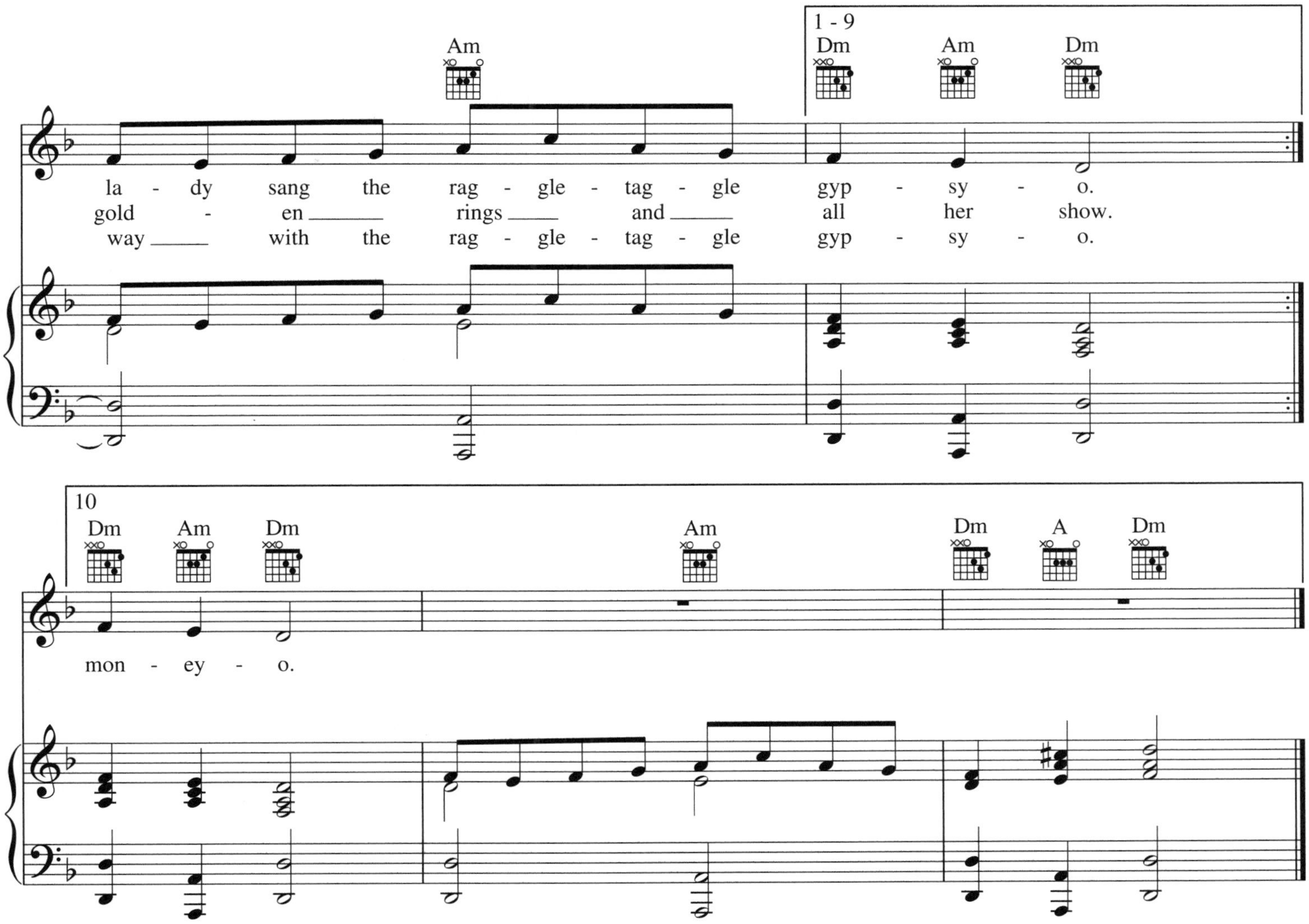
1 - 9
Am
Dm Am Dm
la - dy sang the rag - gle - tag - gle gyp - sy - o.
gold - en rings and all her show.
way with the rag - gle - tag - gle gyp - sy - o.
10
Dm Am Dm Am Dm A Dm
mon - ey - o.

Additional Lyrics

4. It was late that night when the lord came home inquiring for his lady-o.
The servant's voice rang around the house, "She is gone with the raggle-taggle gypsy-o."

5. "Oh then saddle for me, my milk white steed; the black horse is not speedy-o.
And I will ride and I'll seek me bride who's away with the raggle-taggle gypsy-o."

6. Oh then he rode high and he rode low; he rode north and south also,
But when he came to a wide open field it is there that he spotted his lady-o.

7. "Oh then why did you leave your house and your land; why did you leave your money-o
And why did you leave your newly wedded lord to be off with the raggle-taggle gypsy-o."

8. "Yerra what do I care for me house and me land and what do I care for money-o.
And what do I care for my newly-wedded lord; I'm away with the raggle-taggle gypsy-o?"

9. "And what do I care for my goose-feathered bed with blankets drawn so comely-o.
Tonight I'll sleep in the wide open field all along with the raggle-taggle gypsy-o."

10. "Oh for you rode east when I rode west; you rode high and I rode low,
I'd rather have a kiss from the yellow gypsy's lips than all your land and money-o."

THE RISING OF THE MOON

Traditional Irish Folk Song

Moderately
Am C Am G
mf
Am C
Oh, then tell me, Sean O' - Far - rell,
Oh, then tell me, Sean O' - Far - rell,
Out from man - y a mud - wall cab - in
There be - side the sing - ing riv - er
Am G F Em
tell me why you hur - ry so?
where the gath - er - ing is to be?
eyes were watch - ing through the night.
that dark mass of men were seen.

Copyright © 2006 by HAL LEONARD CORPORATION
International Copyright Secured All Rights Reserved

Am
C
Hush, a while, just hush and lis - ten,
In the old spot by the riv - er,
Man - y a man - ly breast was throb - bing
Far a - bove the shin - ing wea - pons
Em
G
Am
and his cheeks were all a - glow.
right well known to you and me.
for the bless - ed warn - ing light.
hung their own im - mor - tal green.
G
Em
I bear or - ders from the Cap - tain,
One word more for sig - nal tok - en
Mur - murs passed a - long the val - ley,
Death to ev - 'ry foe and trai - tor,

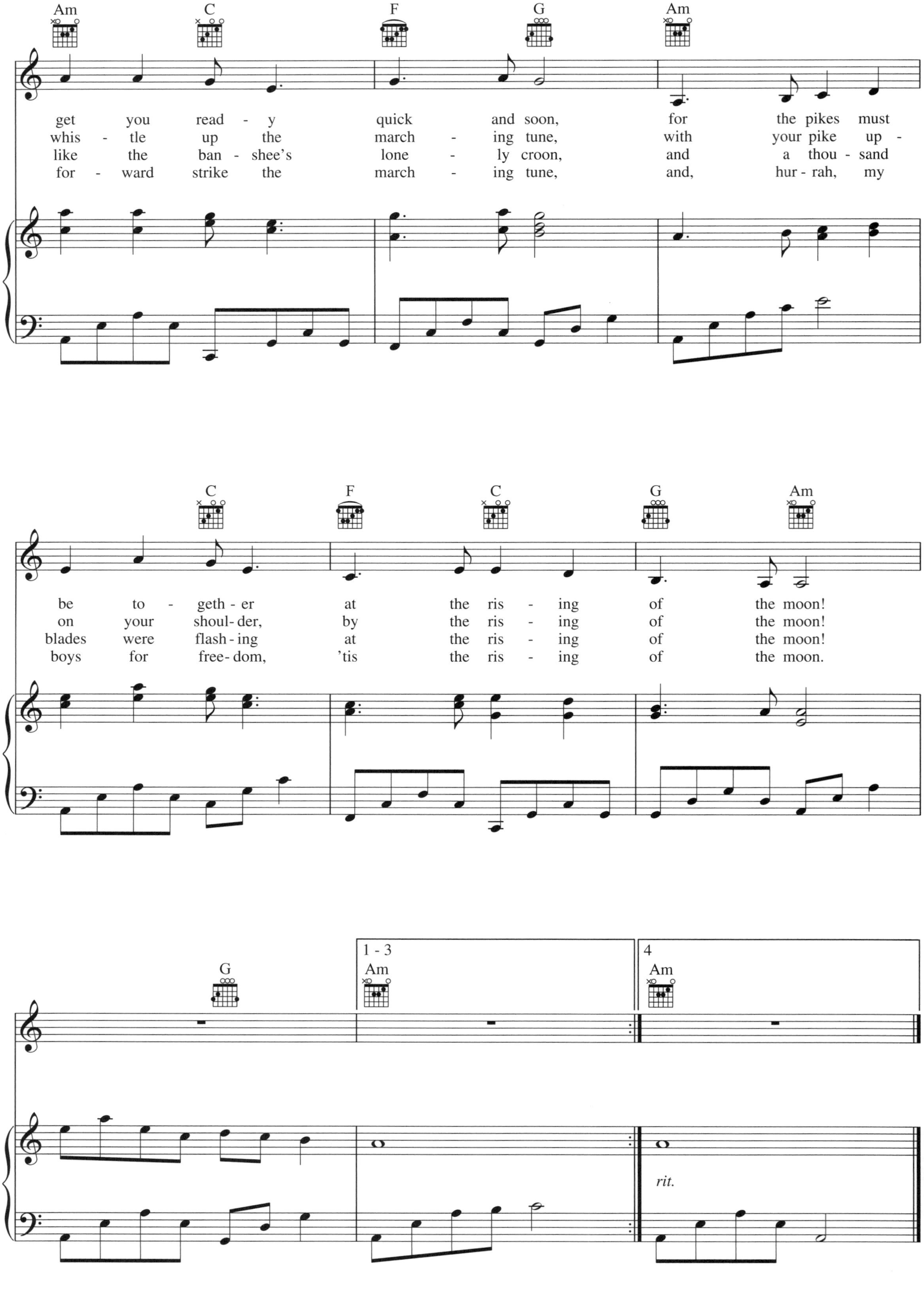
Am C F G Am
get you read - y quick and soon, for the pikes must
whis - tle up the march - ing tune, with your pike up -
like the ban - shee's lone - ly croon, and a thou - sand
for - ward strike the march - ing tune, and, hur - rah, my
C F C G Am
be to - geth - er at the ris - ing of the moon!
on your shoul - der, by the ris - ing of the moon!
blades were flash - ing at the ris - ing of the moon!
boys for free - dom, 'tis the ris - ing of the moon.
G
1 - 3
Am
4
Am
rit.

THE ROCKS OF BAWN

Traditional Irish Folk Song

Moderately
mf
G Am7 D G
G/B G D C
1. Come, all you loy - al he - roes,
2. rise up, love - ly Swee - ney,
3. curse at - tend you, Swee - ney,
4.,5. (See additional lyrics)
G C G
wher - ev - er that you be,
and give your horse some hay,
for you have me near - ly robbed,
Em D G
and don't hire with an - y mas - ter
and give him a good feed of oats
a - sit - tin' by the fire - side

Copyright © 2006 by HAL LEONARD CORPORATION
International Copyright Secured All Rights Reserved

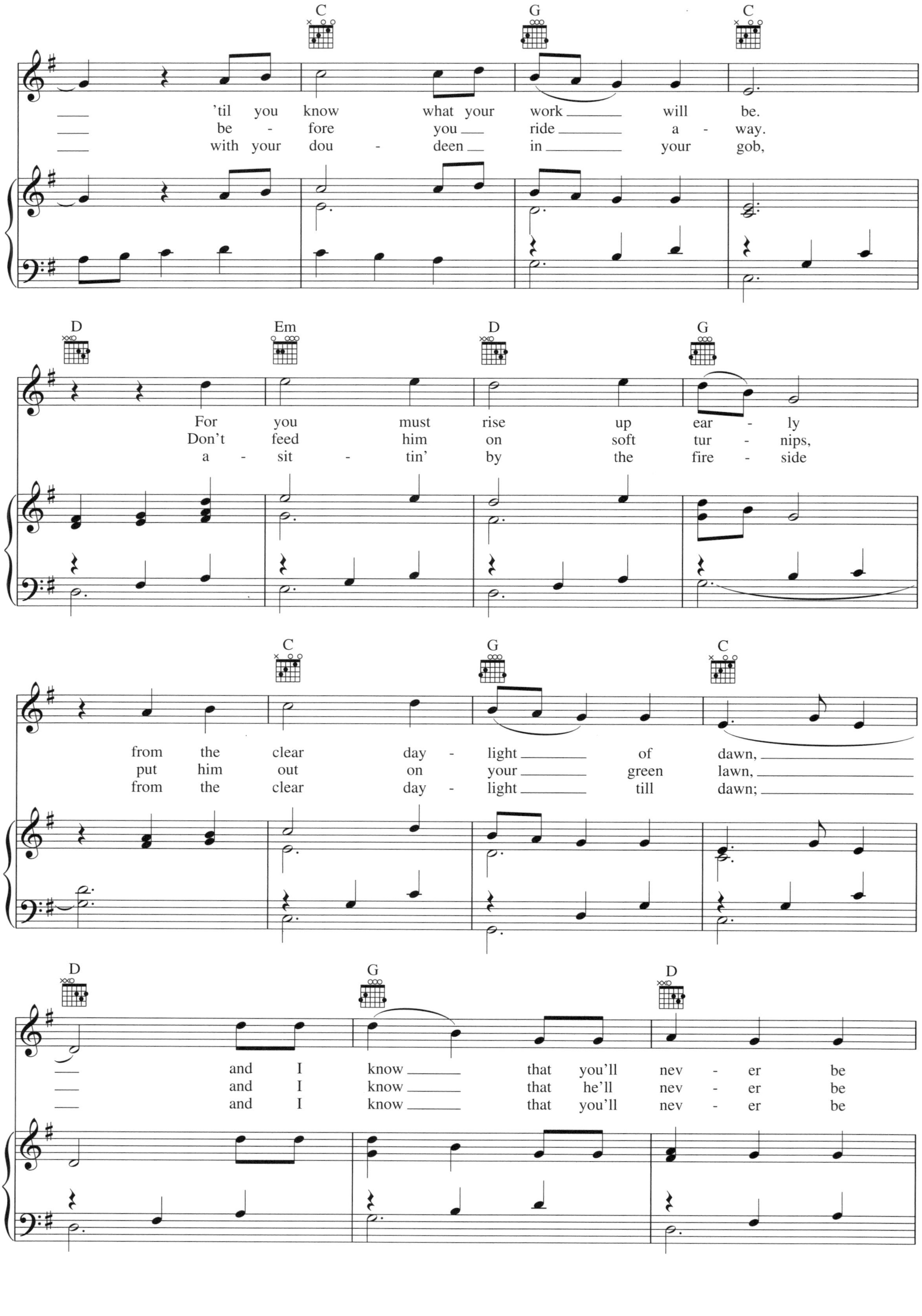
C G C
'til you know what your work will be.
be - fore you ride a - way.
with your dou - deen in your gob,
D Em D G
For you must rise up ear - ly
Don't feed him on soft tur - nips,
a - sit - tin' by the fire - side
C G C
from the clear day - light of dawn,
put him out on your green lawn,
from the clear day - light till dawn;
D G D
and I know that you'll nev - er be
and I know that he'll nev - er be
and I know that you'll nev - er be

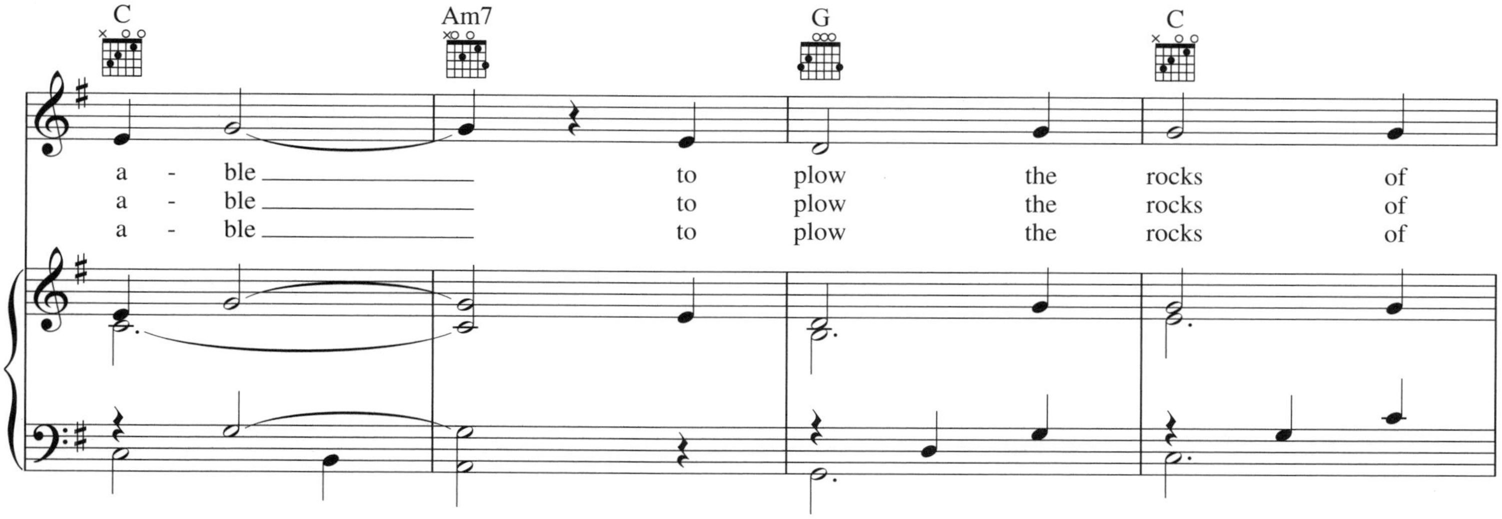
C
Am7
G
C
a - ble to plow the rocks of
a - ble to plow the rocks of
a - ble to plow the rocks of

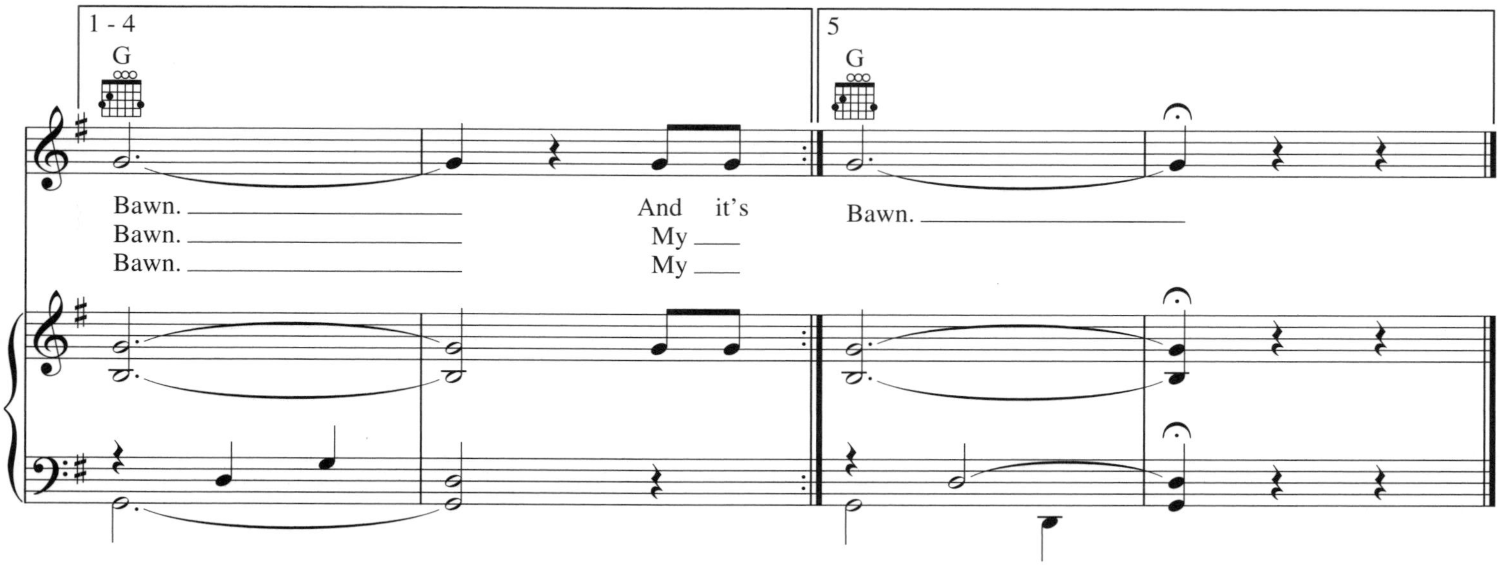
1 - 4
G
5
G
Bawn. And it's
Bawn. My
Bawn. My
Bawn.

Additional Lyrics

4. My shoes they are well worn out, my stockings they are thin,
   And my heart is always trembling for fear that they'll let in.
   And my heart is always trembling from the clear daylight of dawn,
   Afraid I'll never be able to plow the rocks of Bawn.

5. I wish the Queen of England would write to me in time
   And place me in some regiment in all my youth and prime.
   I'd fight for Ireland's glory from the clear daylight of dawn,
   And I never would return again to plow the rocks of Bawn.

THE ROCKY ROAD TO DUBLIN

Traditional Irish Folk Song

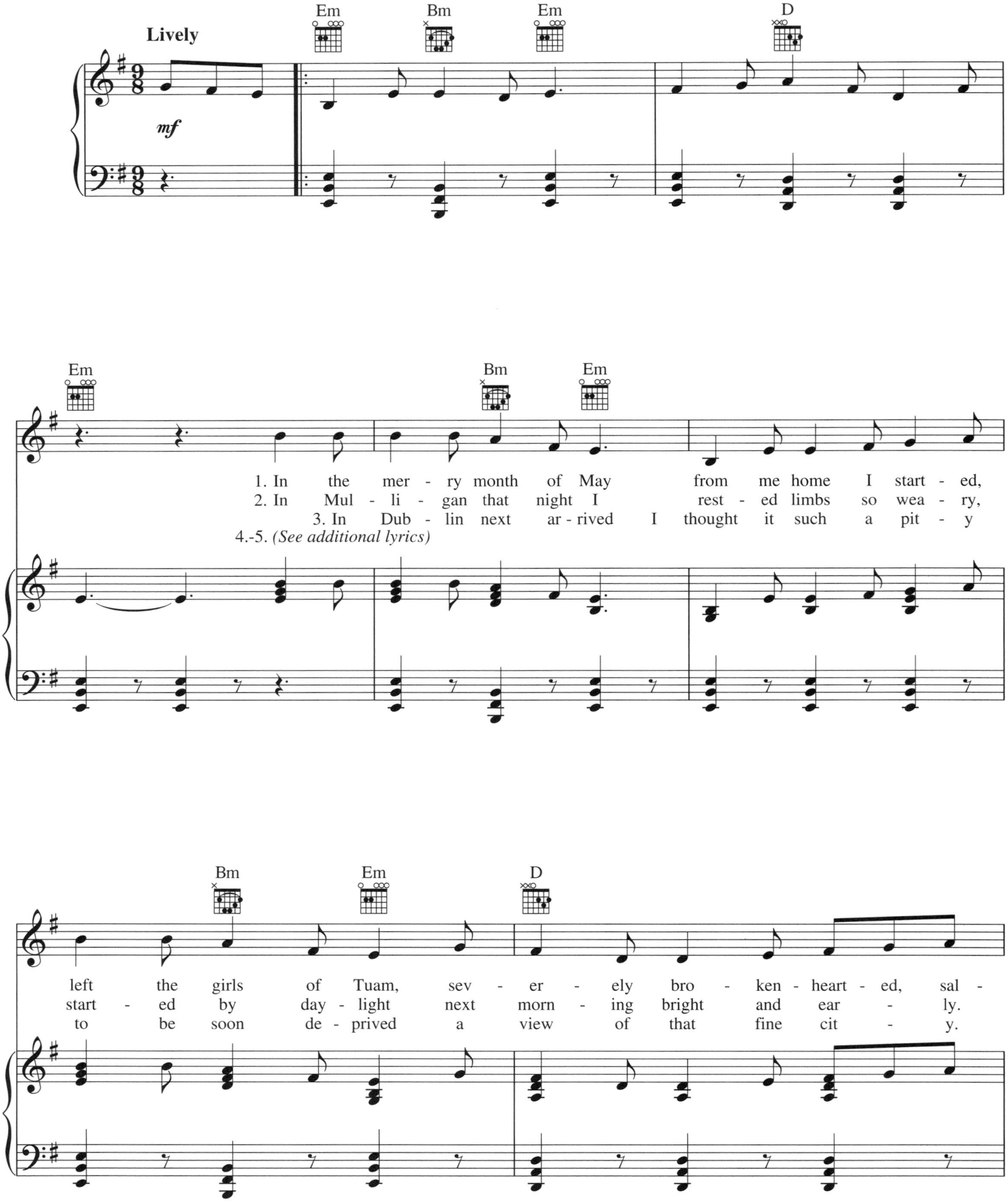
Lively
Em Bm Em D
mf
Em Bm Em
1. In the mer - ry month of May from me home I start - ed,
2. In Mul - li - gan that night I rest - ed limbs so wea - ry,
3. In Dub - lin next ar - rived I thought it such a pit - y
4.-5. (See additional lyrics)
Bm Em D
left the girls of Tuam, sev - er - ely bro - ken - heart - ed, sal -
start - ed by day - light next morn - ing bright and ear - ly.
to be soon de - prived a view of that fine cit - y.

Copyright © 2006 by HAL LEONARD CORPORATION
International Copyright Secured All Rights Reserved

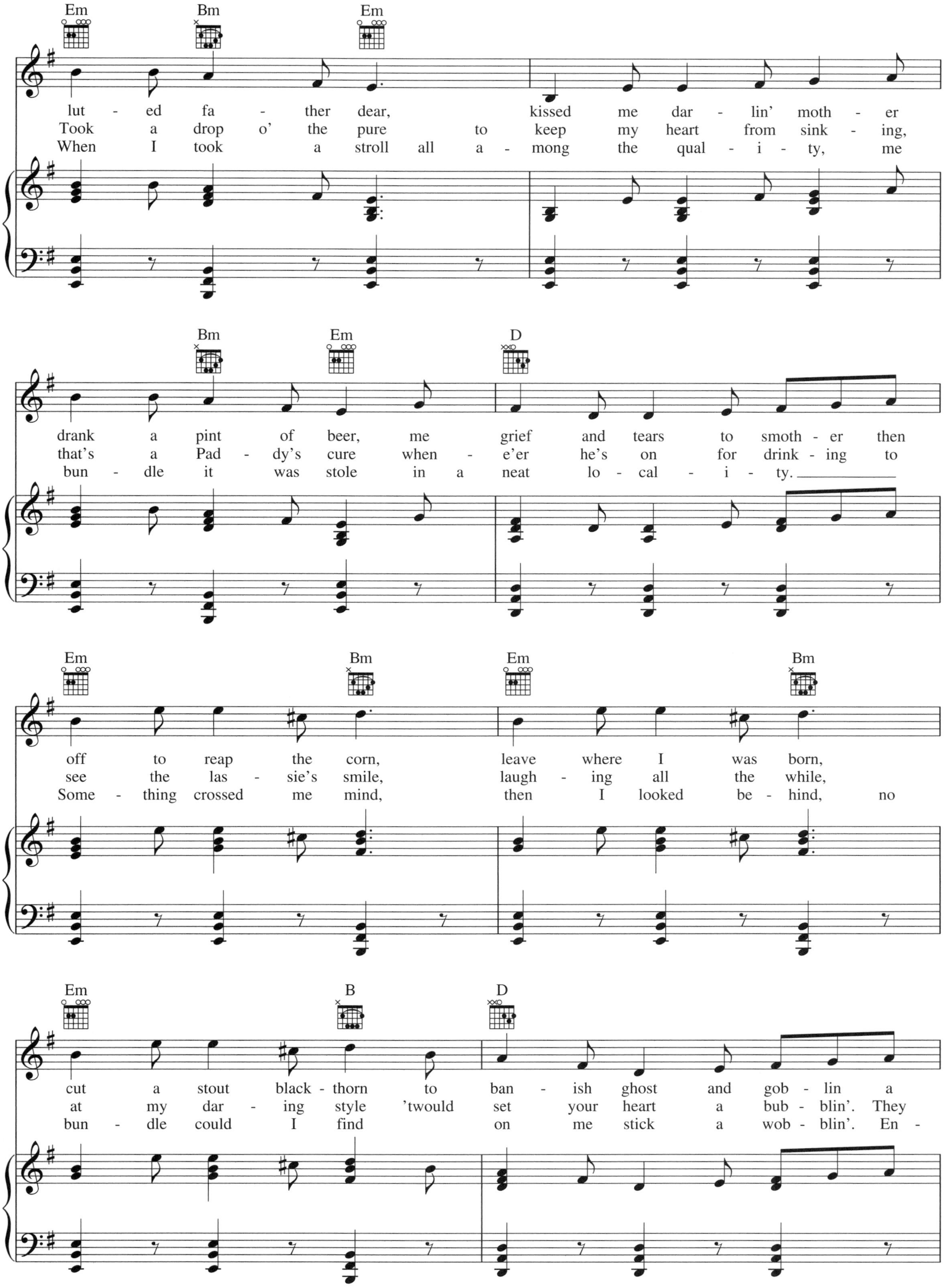
Em Bm Em
lut - ed fa - ther dear, kissed me dar - lin' moth - er
Took a drop o' the pure to keep my heart from sink - ing,
When I took a stroll all a - mong the qual - i - ty, me
Bm Em D
drank a pint of beer, me grief and tears to smoth - er then
that's a Pad - dy's cure when - e'er he's on for drink - ing to
bun - dle it was stole in a neat lo - cal - i - ty.
Em Bm Em Bm
off to reap the corn, leave where I was born,
see the las - sie's smile, laugh - ing all the while,
Some - thing crossed me mind, then I looked be - hind, no
Em B D
cut a stout black - thorn to ban - ish ghost and gob - lin a
at my dar - ing style 'twould set your heart a bub - blin'. They
bun - dle could I find on me stick a wob - blin'. En -

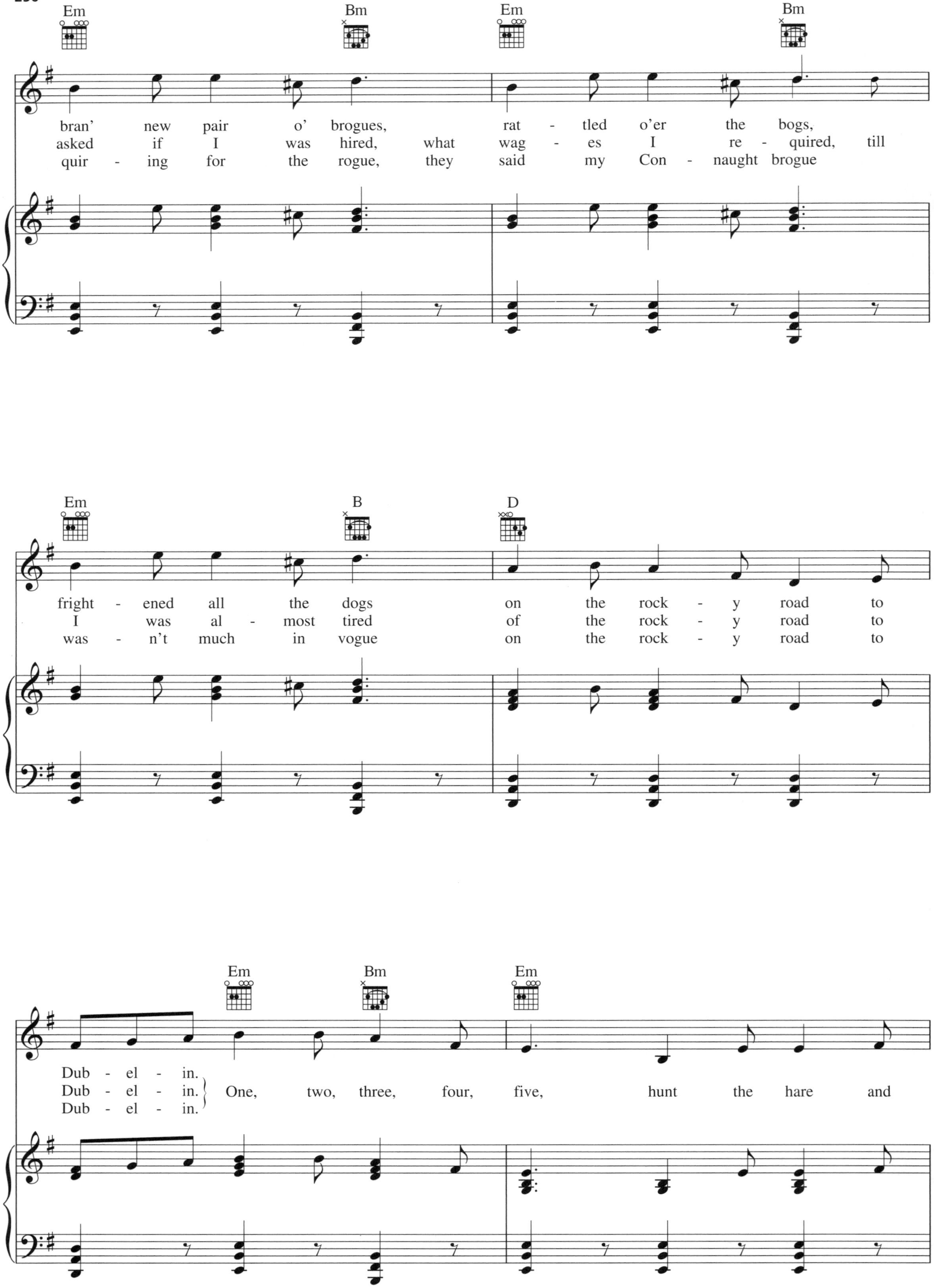
Em Bm Em Bm
bran' new pair o' brogues, rat - tled o'er the bogs,
asked if I was hired, what wag - es I re - quired, till
quir - ing for the rogue, they said my Con - naught brogue
Em B D
fright - ened all the dogs on the rock - y road to
I was al - most tired of the rock - y road to
was - n't much in vogue on the rock - y road to
Em Bm Em
Dub - el - in.
Dub - el - in. One, two, three, four, five, hunt the hare and
Dub - el - in.

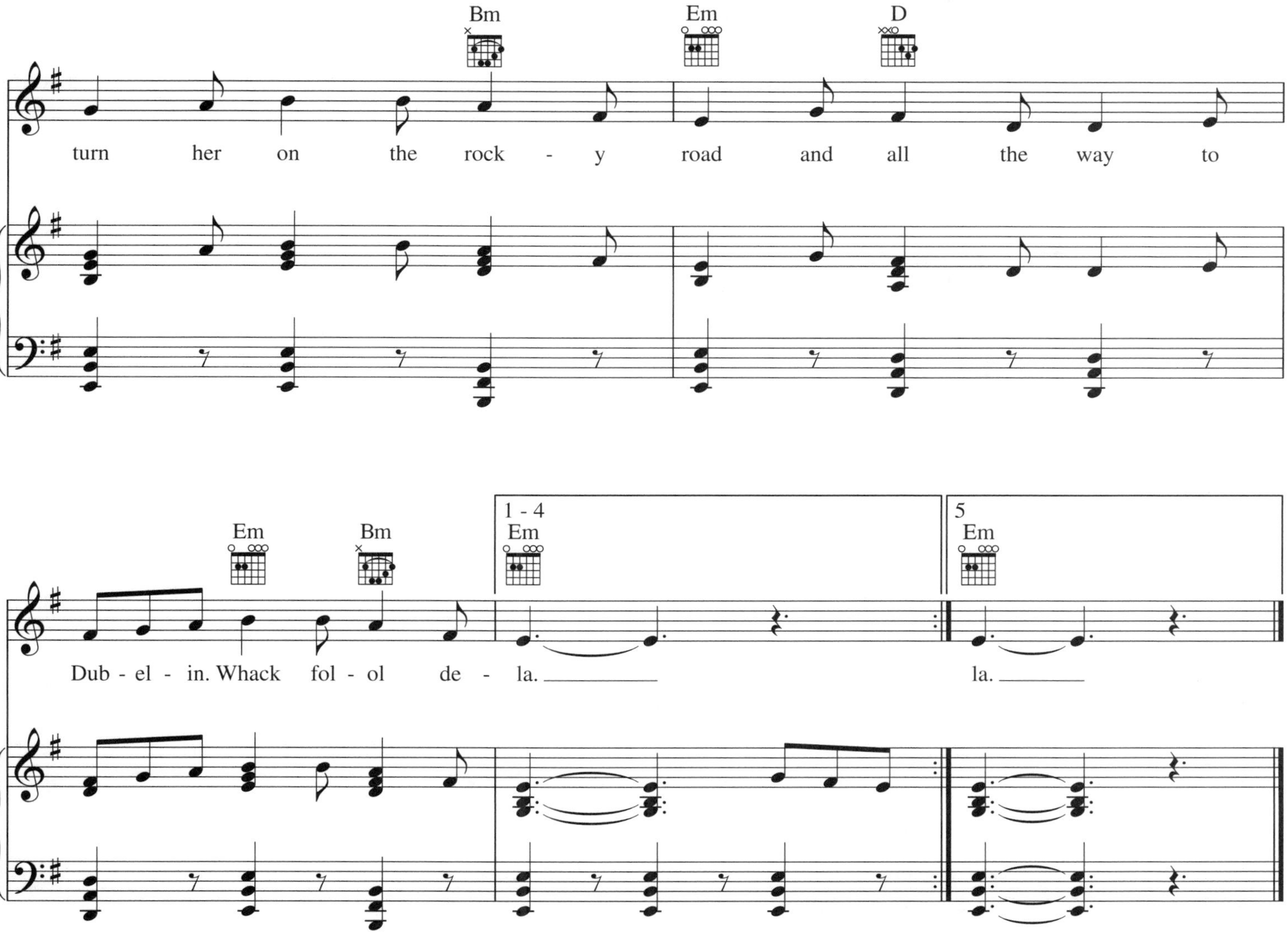
Bm
Em
D
turn her on the rock - y road and all the way to
1 - 4
5
Em
Bm
Em
Em
Dub - el - in. Whack fol - ol de - la.
la.

Additional Lyrics

4. From there I got away, me spirits never failing,
   Landed on the quay as the ship was sailing.
   Captain at me roared, said that no room had he.
   When I jumped aboard, a cabin for Paddy
   Down among the pigs I played some funny rigs
   Danced some hearty jigs, the water 'round me bubblin'
   When off Holyhead I wished meself was dead
   Or better far instead, on the rocky road to Dublin.

5. The boys of Liverpool when we safely landed
   Called meself a fool, I could no longer stand it.
   Blood began to boil, temper I was losing.
   Poor old Erin's Isle they began abusing.
   "Hurrah, me boys," says I, shillelagh I let fly
   Some Galway boys were by and saw I was a-hobblin'.
   Then with loud "Hurray!" they joined in the affray
   And quickly paved the way for the rocky road to Dublin.

RODDY McCORLEY

Traditional Irish Folk Song

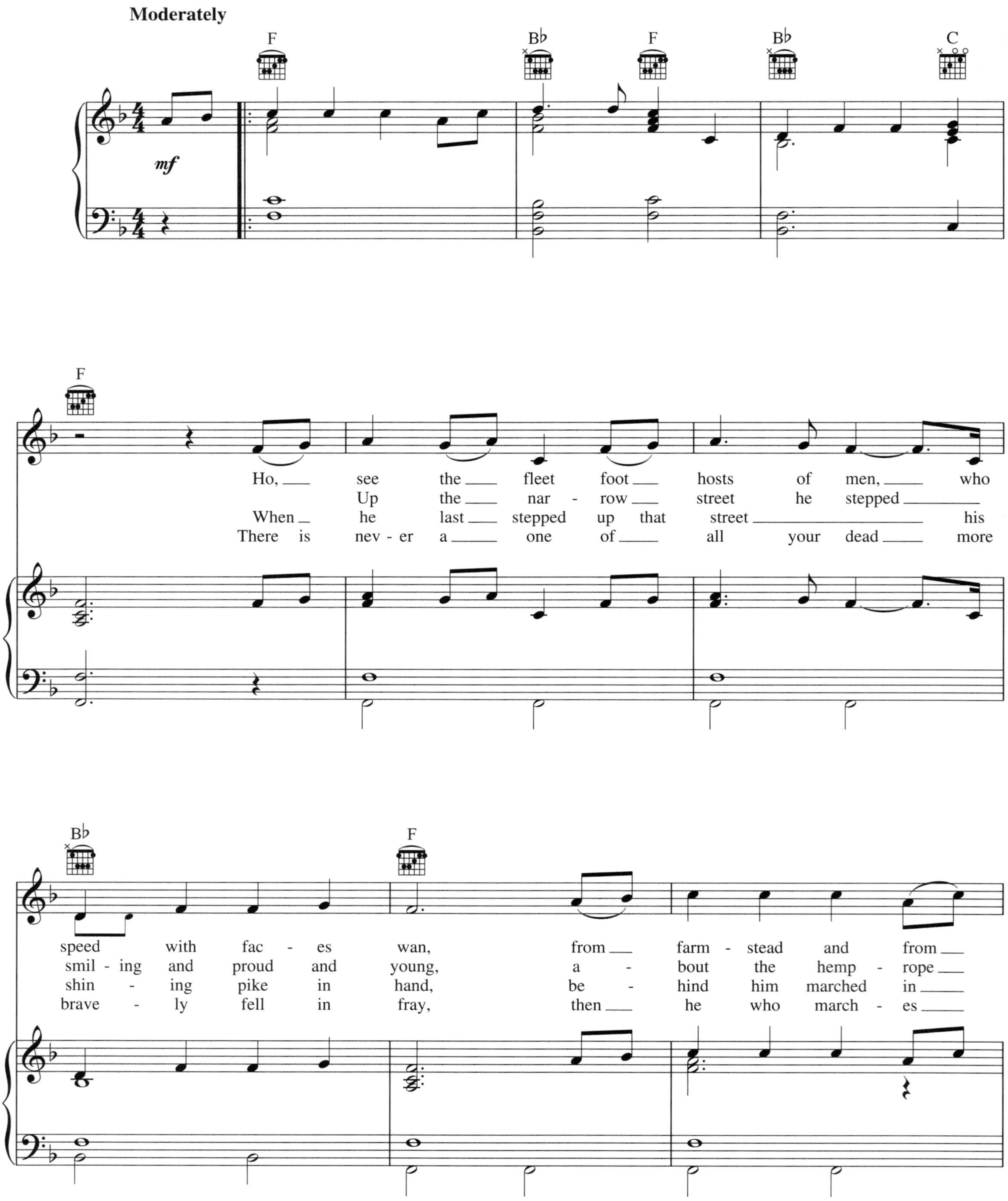
Moderately
F
B♭
F
B♭
C
mf
F
Ho, see the fleet foot hosts of men, who
Up the nar - row street he stepped
When he last stepped up that street his
There is nev - er a one of all your dead more
B♭
F
speed with fac - es wan, from farm - stead and from
smil - ing and proud and young, a - bout the hemp - rope
shin - ing pike in hand, be - hind him marched in
brave - ly fell in fray, then he who march - es

Copyright © 2006 by HAL LEONARD CORPORATION
International Copyright Secured All Rights Reserved

B♭ F B♭ Gm C
fish - er's cot up - on the banks of Bann. They
on his neck the gold - en ring - lets clung. There's
grim ar - ray a stal - wart ear - nest band! For
to his fate on the Bridge of Toome to - day. True
F B♭ F Dm Gm
come with venge - ance in their eyes, too late, too late are
nev - er a tear in his blue eyes both glad and bright are
An - trim town for An - trim town he led them to the
to the last, true to the last, he treads the up - ward
C F
they. For
they. As
fray. And
way. And
young Rod - dy M' - Cor - ley goes to die on the
B♭ C
1 - 3
F
4
F
Bridge of Toome to - day.
day.

THE ROSE OF ALLENDALE

Traditional Irish Folk Song

Simply
C
D
G
C/G
mf
G
The morn was fair, the skies were clear, no breath came o'er the sea when
e'er I wan - dered, east or west, though fate be - gan to lour, a
when my fe - vered lips were parched on Af - ric's burn - ing sands, she
C
G
Am
D

Copyright © 2006 by HAL LEONARD CORPORATION
International Copyright Secured All Rights Reserved

G
C
Mar - y left her high - land
sol - ace still she was to
whis - pered hopes of hap - pi -
G
C
D
home and wan - dered forth with
me in sor - row's lone - ly
ness and tales of dis - tant
G
C/G
G
D
me. Though flow - ers
hour. When tem - pests
lands. My life has
G
C
G
deck'd the moun - tain - side and
lashed our lone - ly barque and
been a wil - der - ness un -

C G D
fra - grance fill'd the vale,
rent her shiv - 'ring sail,
blest by for - tune's gale,
G
by far the sweet - est
one maid - en form with -
had fate not linked my
C G C
flow - er there was the Rose of
stood the storm: 'twas the Rose of
lot to hers, the Rose of
D G C/G G
Al - len - dale.
Al - len - dale.
Al - len - dale.
Was the Rose of

C
Am
Al - len - dale, was the Rose of
D
C
Al - len - dale. by far the
G
C
sweet - est flow - er there was the Rose of
D
G
C/G
1, 2
G
3
G
Al - len - dale.
Wher -
And

THE ROSE OF MOONCOIN

Traditional Irish Folk Song

Gently
D C D G
mf
Oh how
Em C G
sweet 'tis to roam by the Suir's sun - ny stream and to
Mol - ly, dear Mol - ly, it breaks my fond heart to
sailed far a - way o'er the dark roll - ing foam, far a -
here's to the Suir with its val - leys so fair, where
D C G
hear the dove coo 'neath the morn - ing sun - beam. Where the
know that we short - ly for - ev - er must part. I'll
way from the hills of her dear I - rish home. Where the
oft times we wan - dered in the cool morn - ing air. Where the

Copyright © 2006 by HAL LEONARD CORPORATION
International Copyright Secured All Rights Reserved

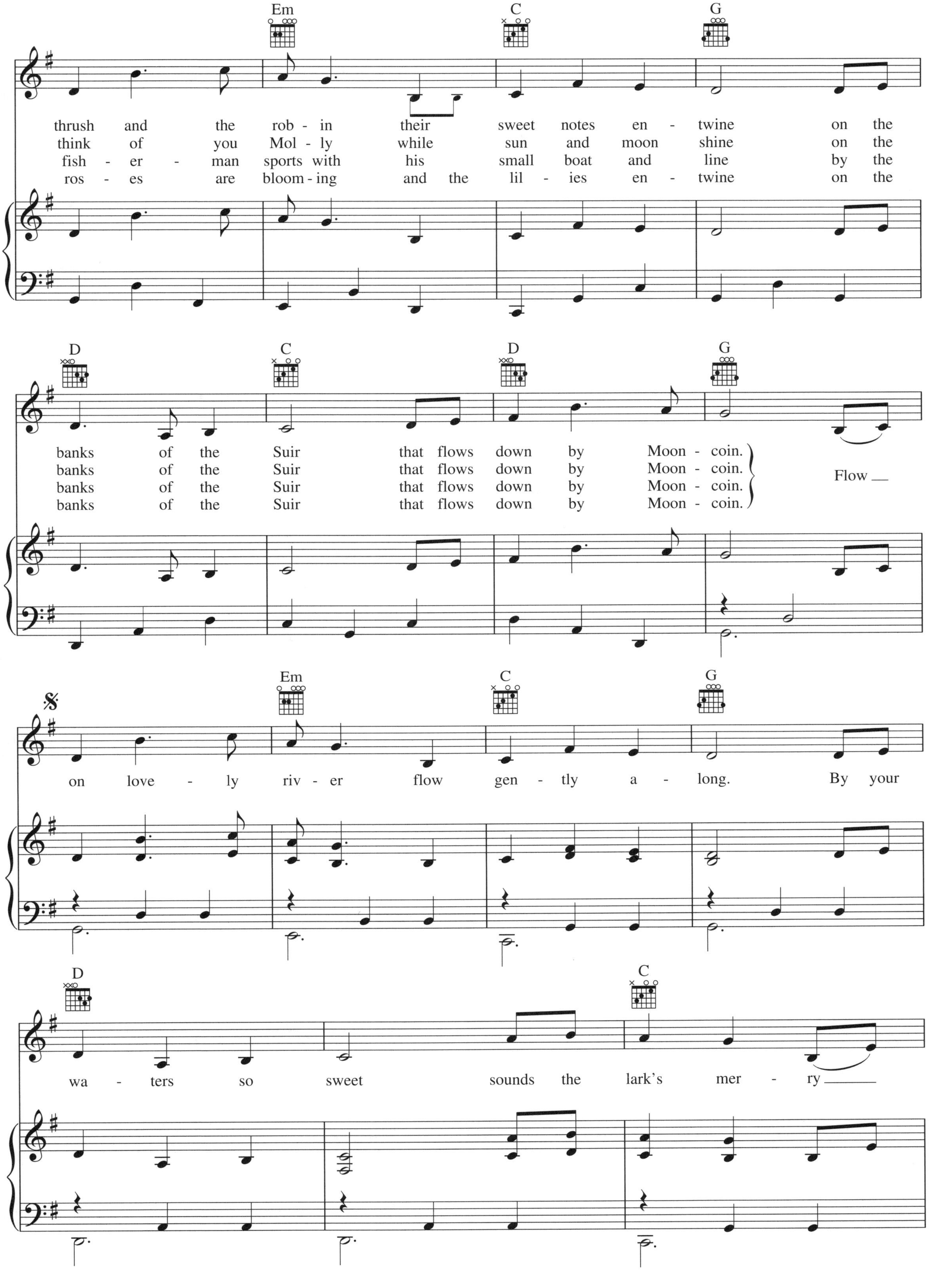
Em C G
thrush and the rob - in their sweet notes en - twine on the
think of you Mol - ly while sun and moon shine on the
fish - er - man sports with his small boat and line by the
ros - es are bloom - ing and the lil - ies en - twine on the
D C D G
banks of the Suir that flows down by Moon - coin.
banks of the Suir that flows down by Moon - coin.
banks of the Suir that flows down by Moon - coin.
banks of the Suir that flows down by Moon - coin.
Flow
Em C G
on love - ly riv - er flow gen - tly a - long. By your
D C
wa - ters so sweet sounds the lark's mer - ry

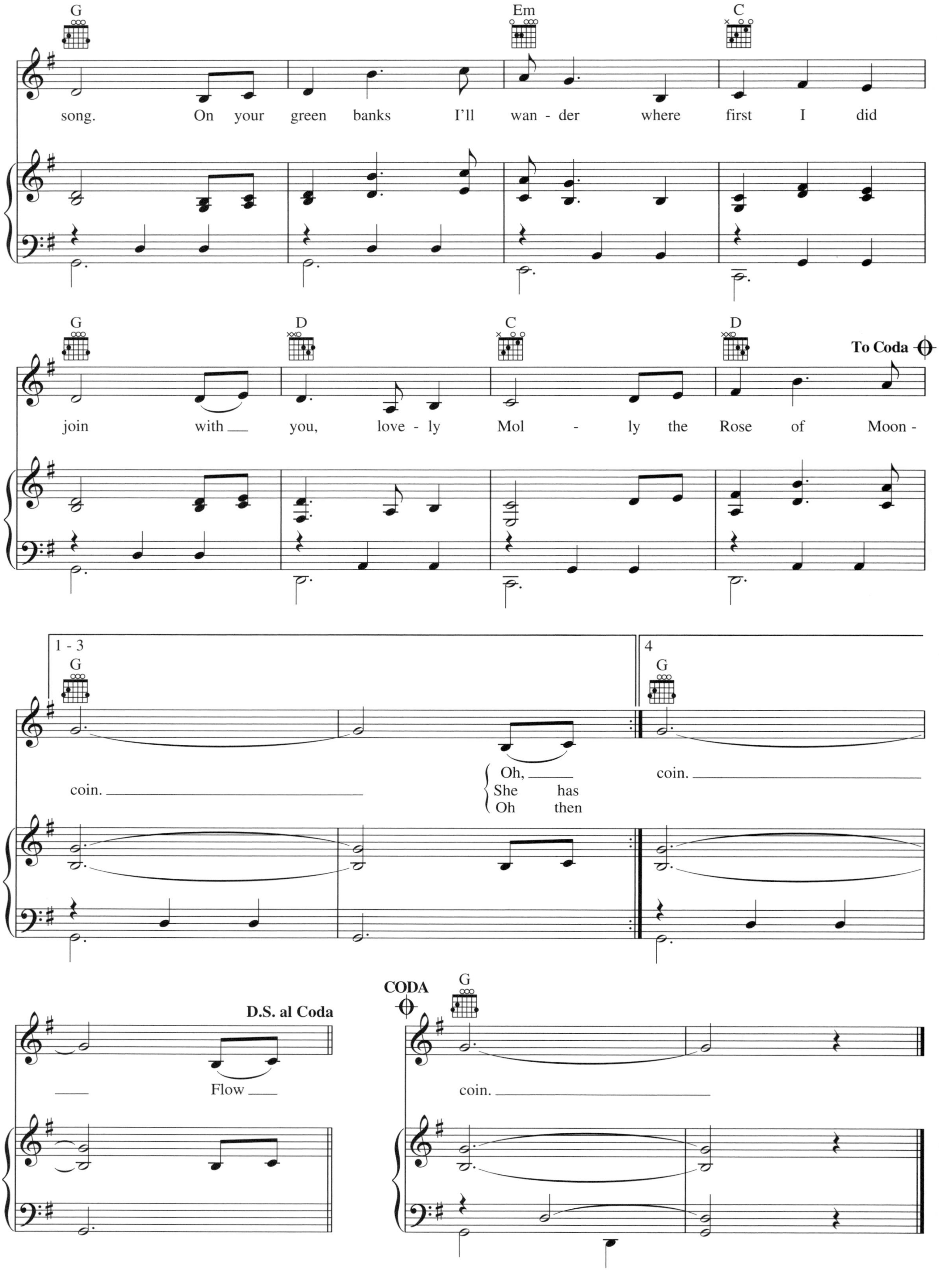
G
Em
C
song. On your green banks I'll wan - der where first I did
G
D
C
D
To Coda
join with you, love - ly Mol - ly the Rose of Moon -
1 - 3
G
4
G
coin.
Oh,
She has
Oh then
coin.
D.S. al Coda
Flow
CODA
G
coin.

THE ROSE OF TRALEE

Words by C. MORDAUNT SPENCER
Music by CHARLES W. GLOVER

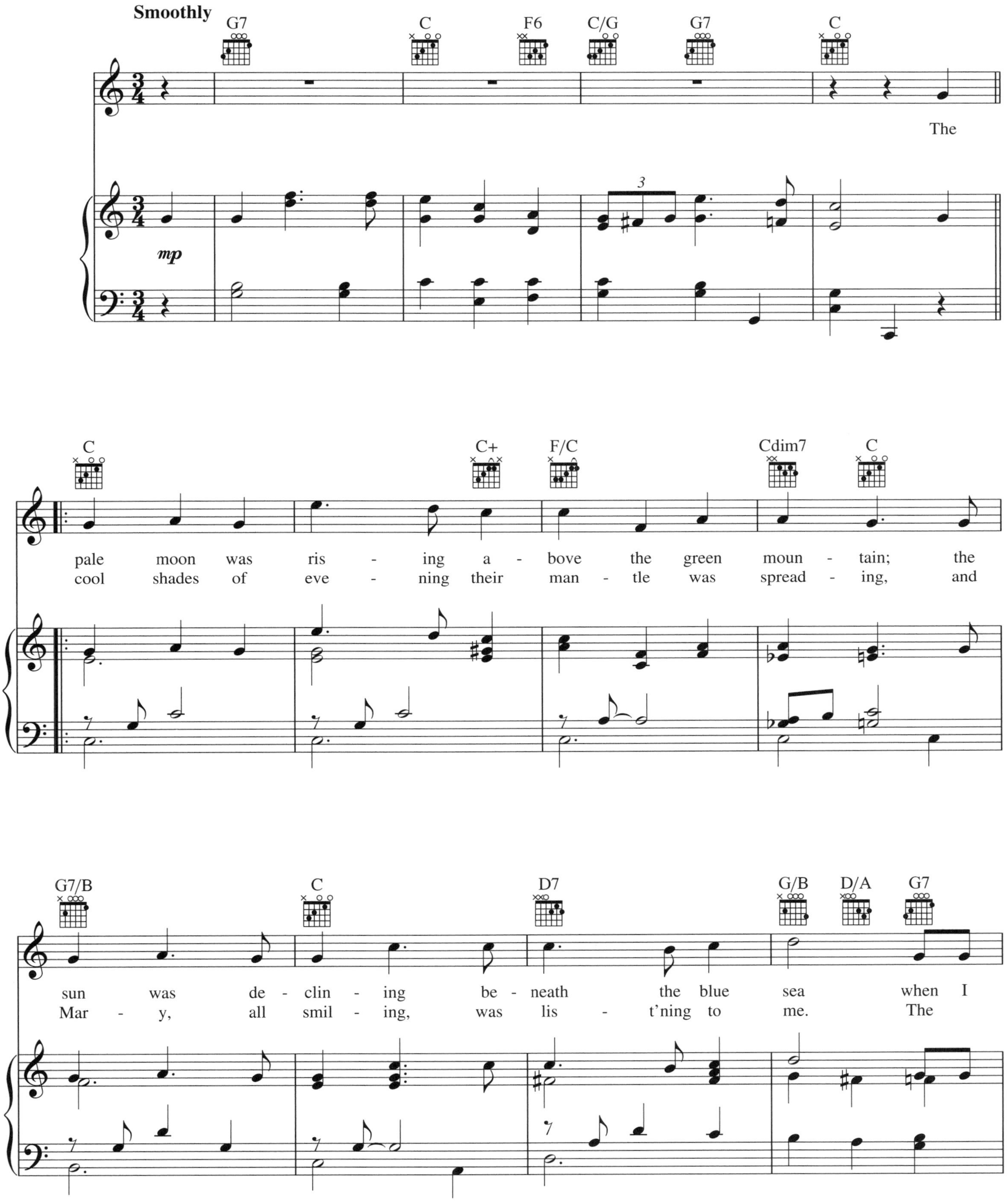
Smoothly
G7
C
F6
C/G
G7
C
The
mp
3
C
C+
F/C
Cdim7
C
pale moon was ris - ing a - bove the green moun - tain; the
cool shades of eve - ning their man - tle was spread - ing, and
G7/B
C
D7
G/B
D/A
G7
sun was de - clin - ing be - neath the blue sea when I
Mar - y, all smil - ing, was lis - t'ning to me. The

Copyright © 1993 by HAL LEONARD CORPORATION
International Copyright Secured All Rights Reserved

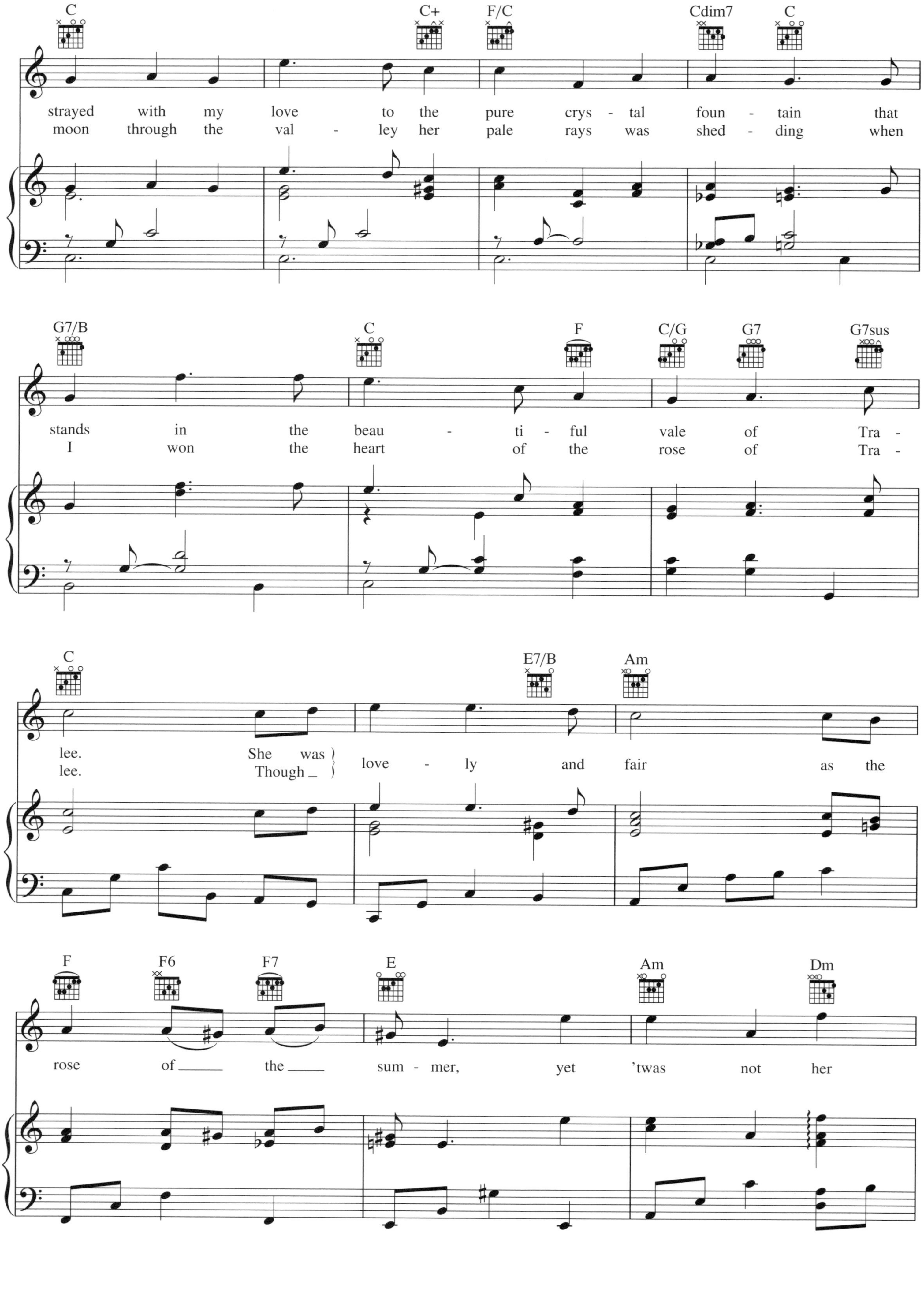
C C+ F/C Cdim7 C
strayed with my love to the pure crys - tal foun - tain that
moon through the val - ley her pale rays was shed - ding when
G7/B C F C/G G7 G7sus
stands in the beau - ti - ful vale of Tra -
I won the heart of the rose of Tra -
C E7/B Am
lee. She was love - ly and fair as the
lee. Though
F F6 F7 E Am Dm
rose of the sum - mer, yet 'twas not her

Am F7 E7 Am Dm7 G7 C
beau - ty a - lone that won me. Oh, no! 'Twas the
rit.
a tempo
C+ F/C Cdim7 C G7/B
truth in her eye ev - er dawn - ing that made me love
C F6 C/G G7 C G7
Mar - y, the rose of Tra - lee.
C F6 C/G G7
1 C
2 C
The
3

ROSIN THE BOW

Traditional

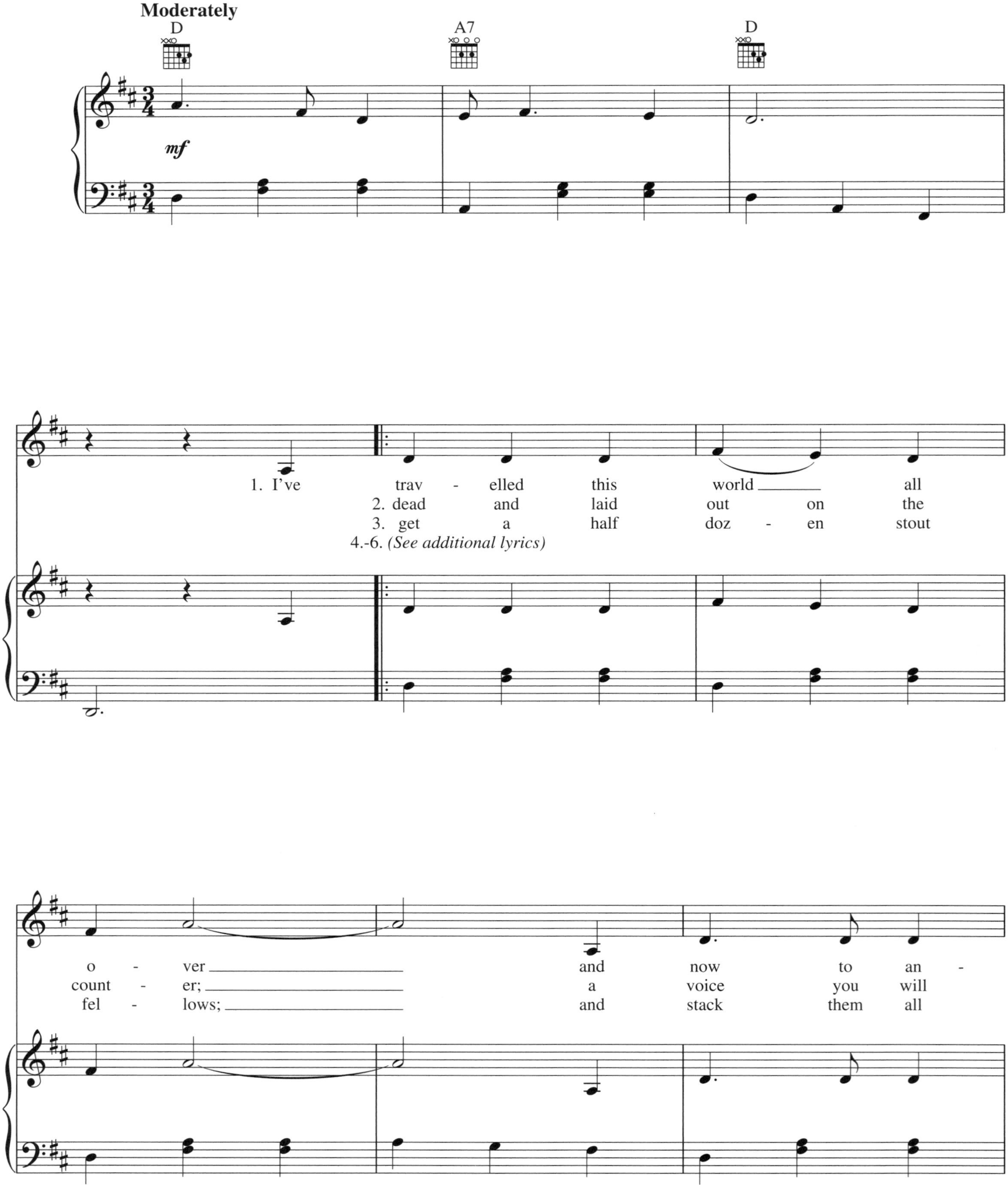
Moderately
D
A7
D
mf
1. I've trav - elled this world all
2. dead and laid out on the
3. get a half doz - en stout
4.-6. (See additional lyrics)
o - ver and now to an -
count - er; a voice you will
fel - lows; and stack them all

Copyright © 2006 by HAL LEONARD CORPORATION
International Copyright Secured All Rights Reserved

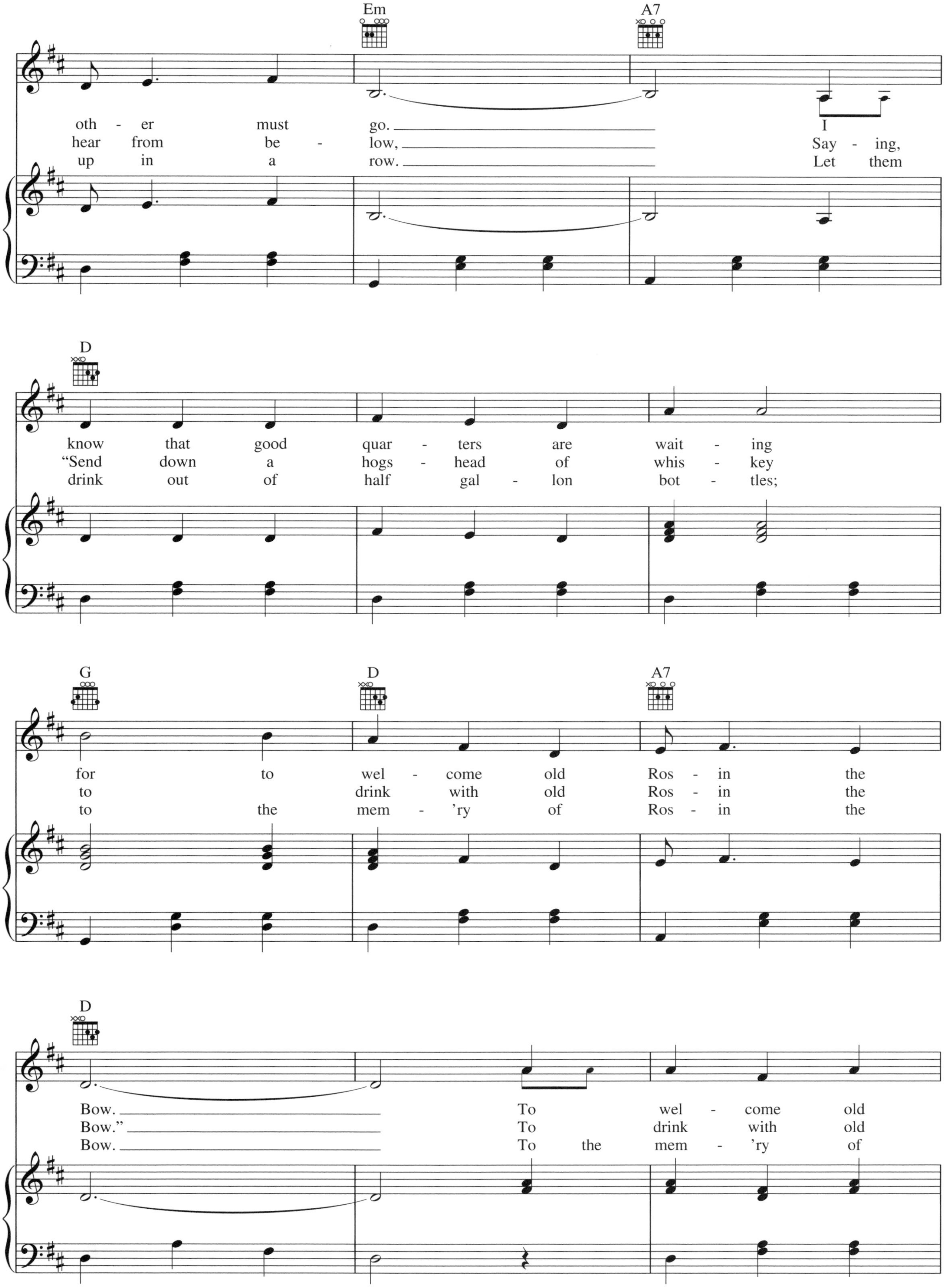
Em
A7
oth - er must go. I
hear from be - low, Say - ing,
up in a row. Let them
D
know that good quar - ters are wait - ing
"Send down a hogs - head of whis - key
drink out of half gal - lon bot - tles;
G
D
A7
for to wel - come old Ros - in the
to drink with old Ros - in the
to the mem - 'ry of Ros - in the
D
Bow. To wel - come old
Bow." To drink with old
Bow. To the mem - 'ry of

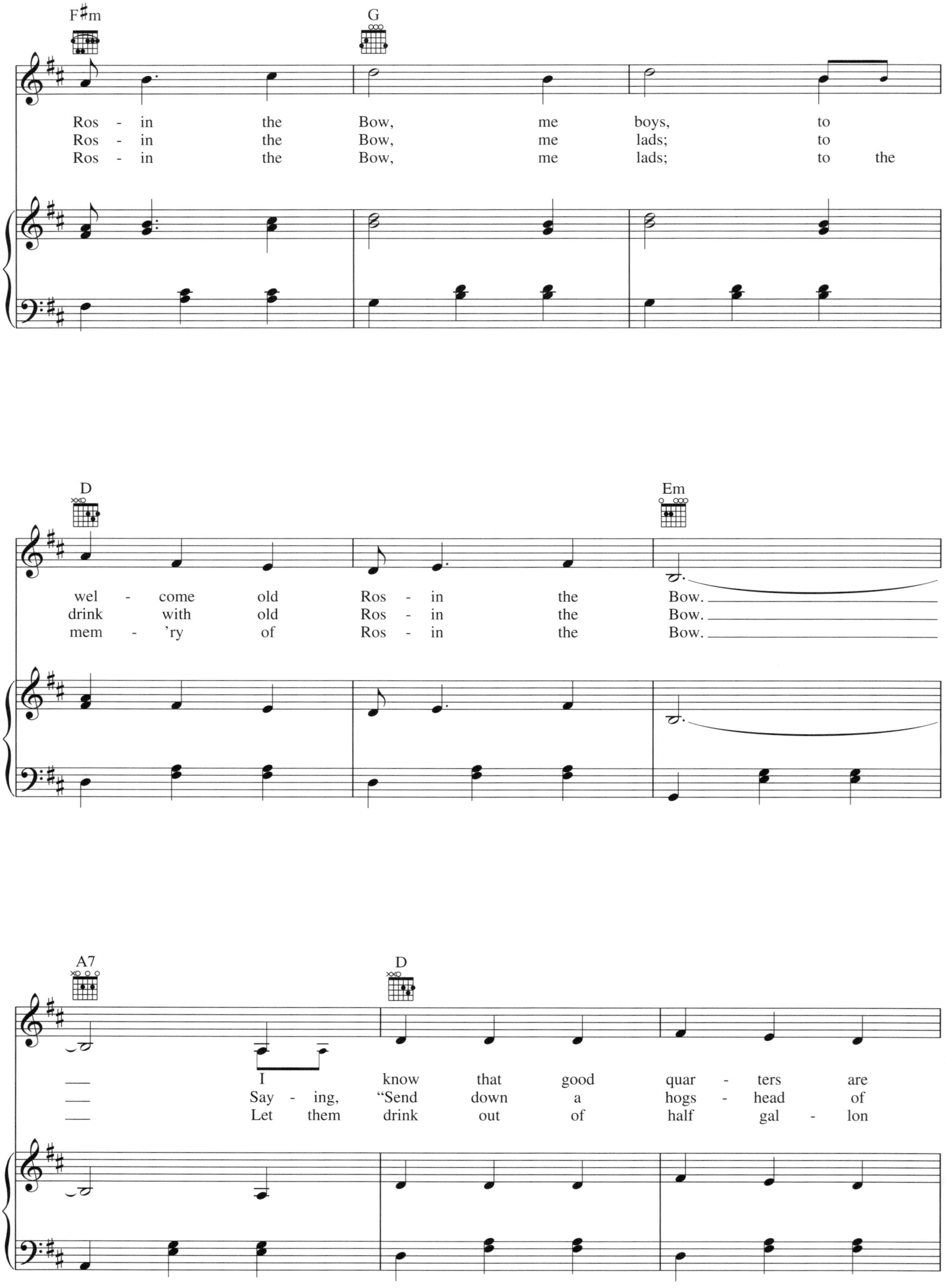
F♯m
G
Ros - in the Bow, me boys, to
Ros - in the Bow, me lads; to
Ros - in the Bow, me lads; to the
D
Em
wel - come old Ros - in the Bow.
drink with old Ros - in the Bow.
mem - 'ry of Ros - in the Bow.
A7
D
I know that good quar - ters are
Say - ing, "Send down a hogs - head of
Let them drink out of half gal - lon

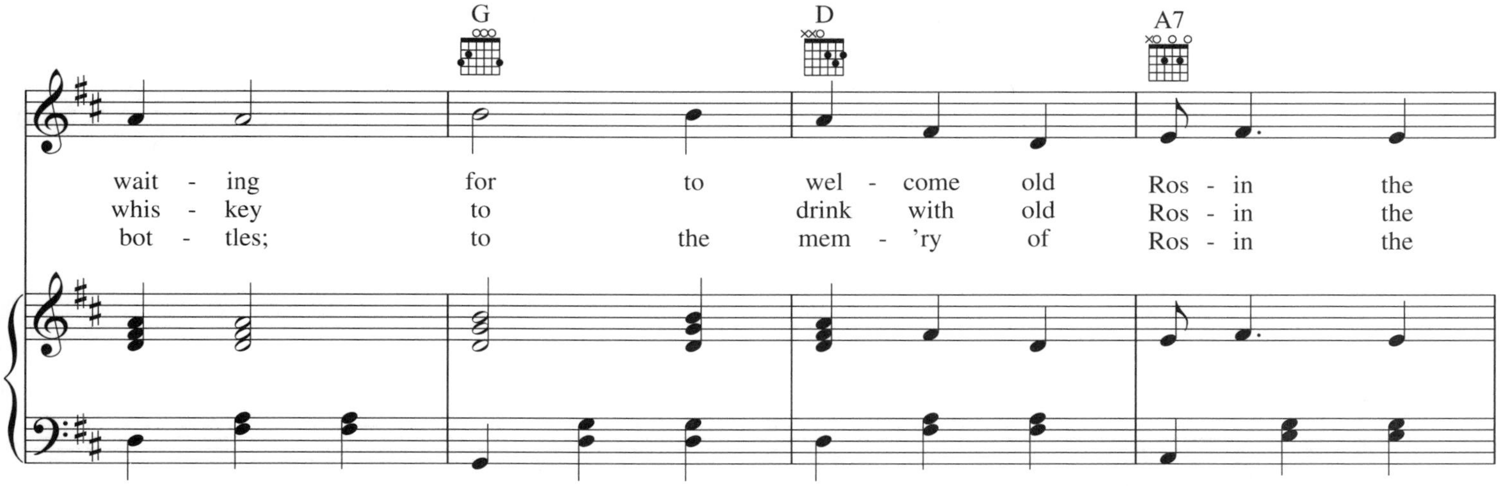
G
D
A7
wait - ing for to wel - come old Ros - in the
whis - key to drink with old Ros - in the
bot - tles; to the mem - 'ry of Ros - in the

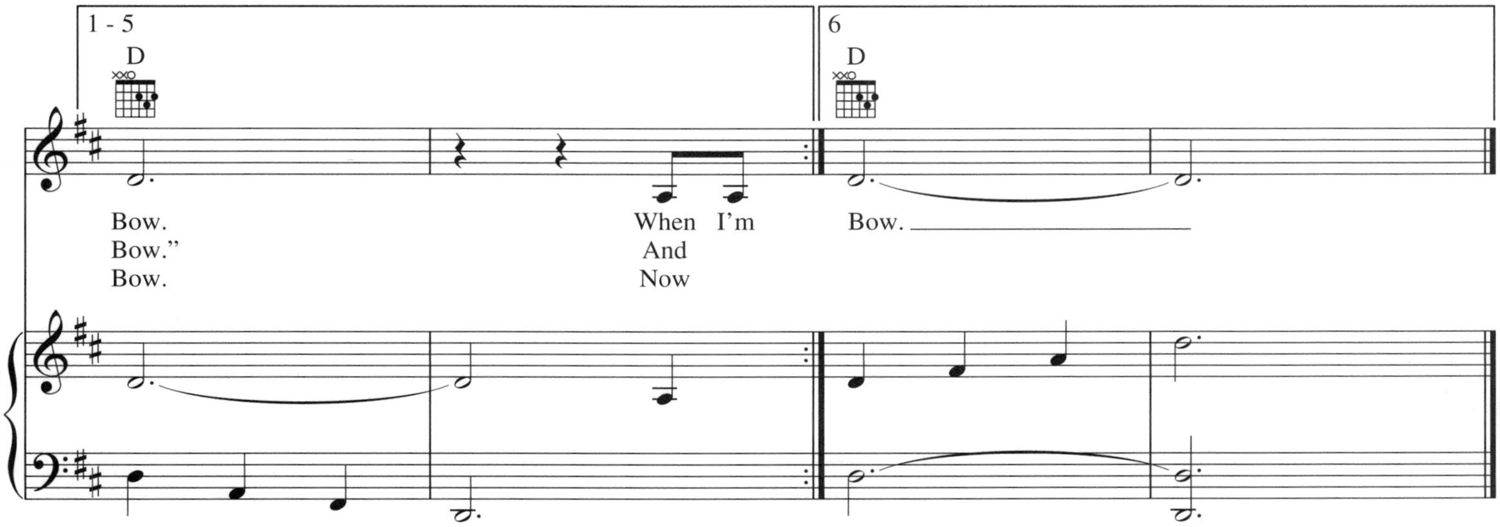
1 - 5
D
6
D
Bow. When I'm Bow.
Bow." And
Bow. Now

Additional Lyrics

4. Now get this half dozen stout fellows; and let them all stagger and go,
   And dig a great hole in the meadow; and in it put Rosin the Bow.
   And in it put Rosin the Bow, me lads; and in it put Rosin the Bow.
   And dig a great hole in the meadow; and in it put Rosin the Bow.

5. Now get ye a couple of bottles; put one at me head and me toe.
   With a diamond ring scratch out upon them; the name of old Rosin the Bow.
   The name of old Rosin the Bow, me lads; the name of old Rosin the Bow.
   With a diamond ring scratch out upon them; the name of old Rosin the Bow.

6. I feel that old Tyrant approaching; that cruel remorseless old foe.
   Let me lift up my glass in his honour; take a drink with old Rosin the Bow.
   Take a drink with old Rosin the Bow, me lads; take a drink with old Rosin the Bow.
   Let me lift up my glass in his honour; take a drink with old Rosin the Bow.

SLIEVENAMON

Traditional Irish Folk Song

Moderately
A7
D
A -
G
D
Bm
lone, all a - lone, by the wave - wash'd
was not the grace of her queen - ly air,
the fes - tive hall, by the star - watched
mf
G
A7
strand all a - lone in a crowd - ed
nor her cheek of the ros - es
shore, my rest - less spir - it

Copyright © 2006 by HAL LEONARD CORPORATION
International Copyright Secured All Rights Reserved

D
G
hall. The hall it is
glow, nor her soft black
cries, "My love, oh my
D
Bm
G
gay and the waves they are grand but my
eyes, not her flow - ing hair, nor was
love, shall I ne'er see you more, and my
A7
D
heart is not here at all. It
it her lil - y white brow. 'Twas
land will you e'er up - rise. By
A7
D
G
A
flies far a - way, by night and by
the soul of truth and of melt - ing
night and by day I ev - er, ev - er

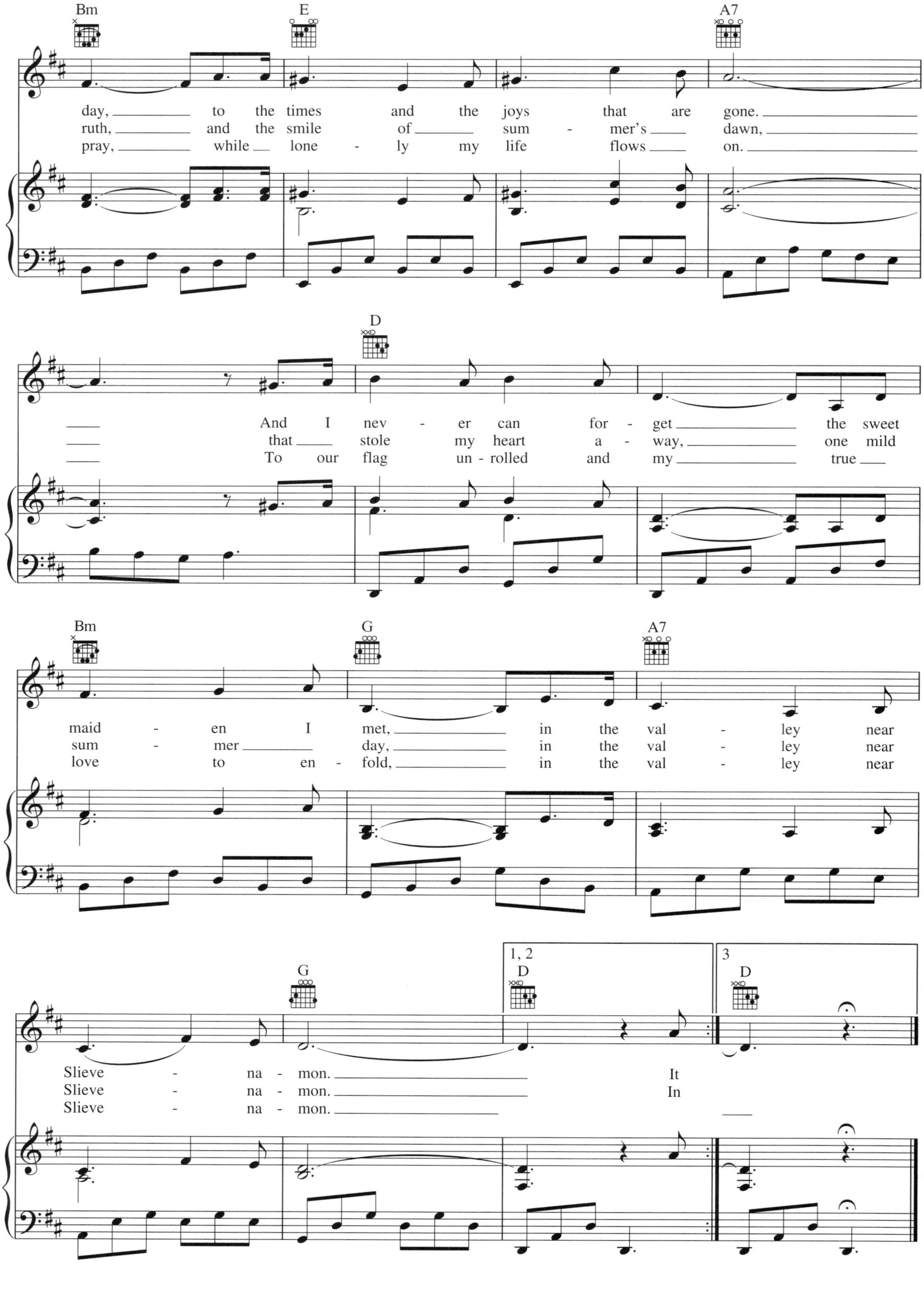
Bm
E
A7
day, to the times and the joys that are gone.
ruth, and the smile of sum - mer's dawn,
pray, while lone - ly my life flows on.
D
And I nev - er can for - get the sweet
that stole my heart a - way, one mild
To our flag un - rolled and my true
Bm
G
A7
maid - en I met, in the val - ley near
sum - mer day, in the val - ley near
love to en - fold, in the val - ley near
G
1, 2
D
3
D
Slieve - na - mon. It
Slieve - na - mon. In
Slieve - na - mon.

SALLY BROWN

Traditional Irish Folk Song

Spirited
G C D G Em
mf
1. Sal - ly Brown she's a
2. Sal - ly Brown she
3. Sev - en long years I
4.-6. (See additional lyrics)
C D G Em D G D Em G D Em Am
bright mu - lat - ter, has a daugh - ter, court - ed Sal - ly,
way hey, roll and go.
She drinks rum and
Sent me sail - in'
Sev - en long years I
Bm Em G D
1 - 5
C D G
6
C D G
chews ter - back - er, 'cross the wa - ter, court - ed Sal - ly,
spent my mon - ey on Sal - ly Brown.
Sal - ly Brown.

Additional Lyrics

4. Sally Brown I'm bound to leave you,
Way hey, roll and go.
Sally Brown, I'll not deceive you,
Spent my money on Sally Brown.

5. Sally she's a "Badian" beauty,
Way hey, roll and go.
Sally she's a "Badian" beauty,
Spent my money on Sally Brown.

6. Sally lives on the old plantation,
Way hey, roll and go.
She belongs to the Wild Goose Nation,
Spent my money on Sally Brown.

Copyright © 2006 by HAL LEONARD CORPORATION
International Copyright Secured All Rights Reserved

SAM HALL

Traditional Irish Folk Song

Brightly
mf
D G D G D A7 D G D
Oh, my name it is Sam Hall, chim - ney sweep, chim - ney sweep. Oh my name it is Sam Hall, chim - ney sweep.
took me to Coote Hill in a cart, in a cart. Oh they took me to Coote Hill in a cart.
preach - er he did come, he did come, he did come. Oh the preach - er he did come, he did come.
lad - der I did grope; that's no joke, that's no joke. Up the lad - der I did grope; that's no joke.
Oh, my
Oh, they
Oh, the
Up the

Copyright © 2006 by HAL LEONARD CORPORATION
International Copyright Secured All Rights Reserved

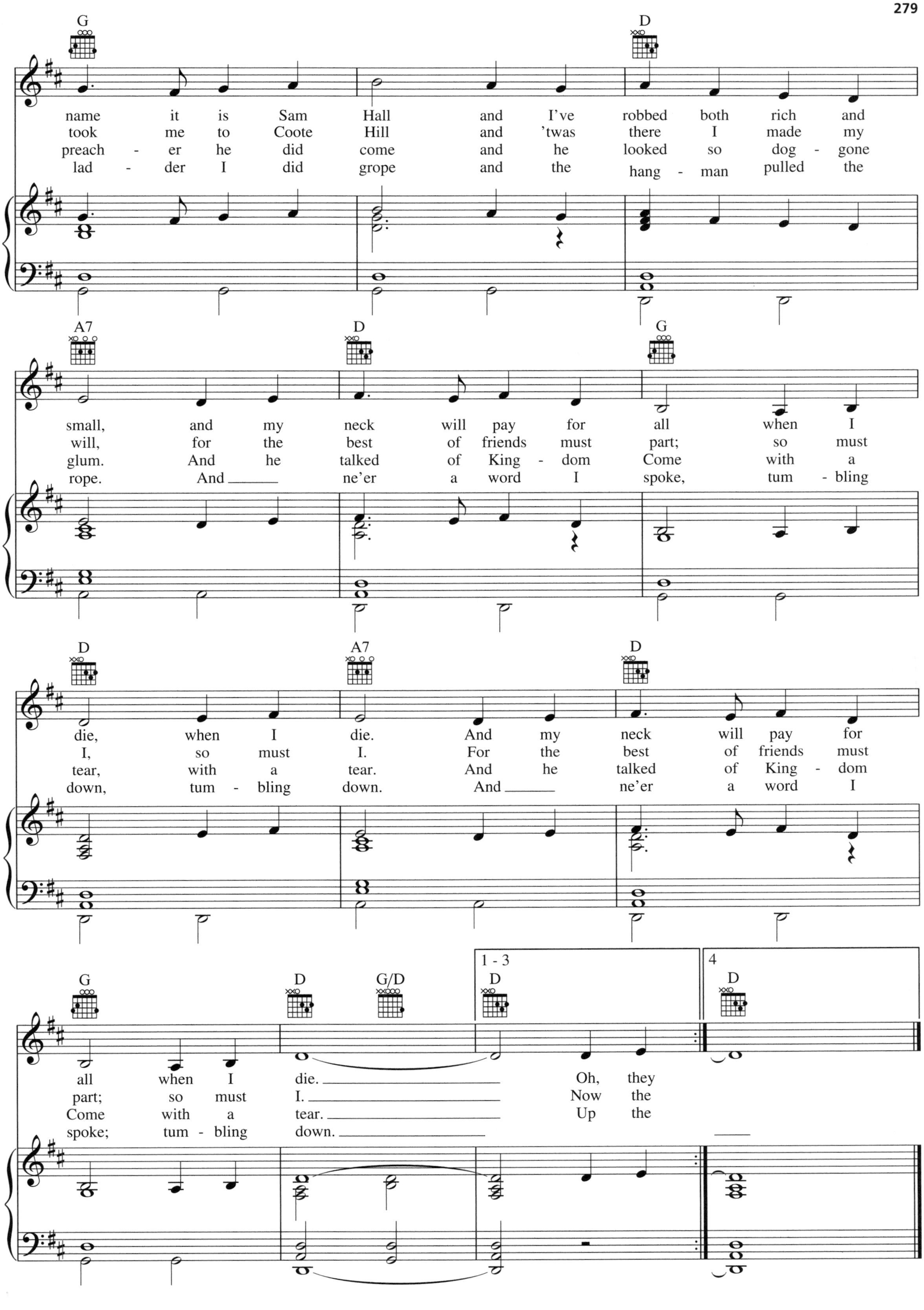
G
D
name it is Sam Hall and I've robbed both rich and
took me to Coote Hill and 'twas there I made my
preach - er he did come and he looked so dog - gone
lad - der I did grope and the hang - man pulled the
A7
D
G
small, and my neck will pay for all when I
will, for the best of friends must part; so must
glum. And he talked of King - dom Come with a
rope. And ne'er a word I spoke, tum - bling
D
A7
D
die, when I die. And my neck will pay for
I, so must I. For the best of friends must
tear, with a tear. And he talked of King - dom
down, tum - bling down. And ne'er a word I
G
D
G/D
1 - 3
D
4
D
all when I die. Oh, they
part; so must I. Now the
Come with a tear. Up the
spoke; tum - bling down.

SKIBBEREEN

Traditional Irish Folk Song

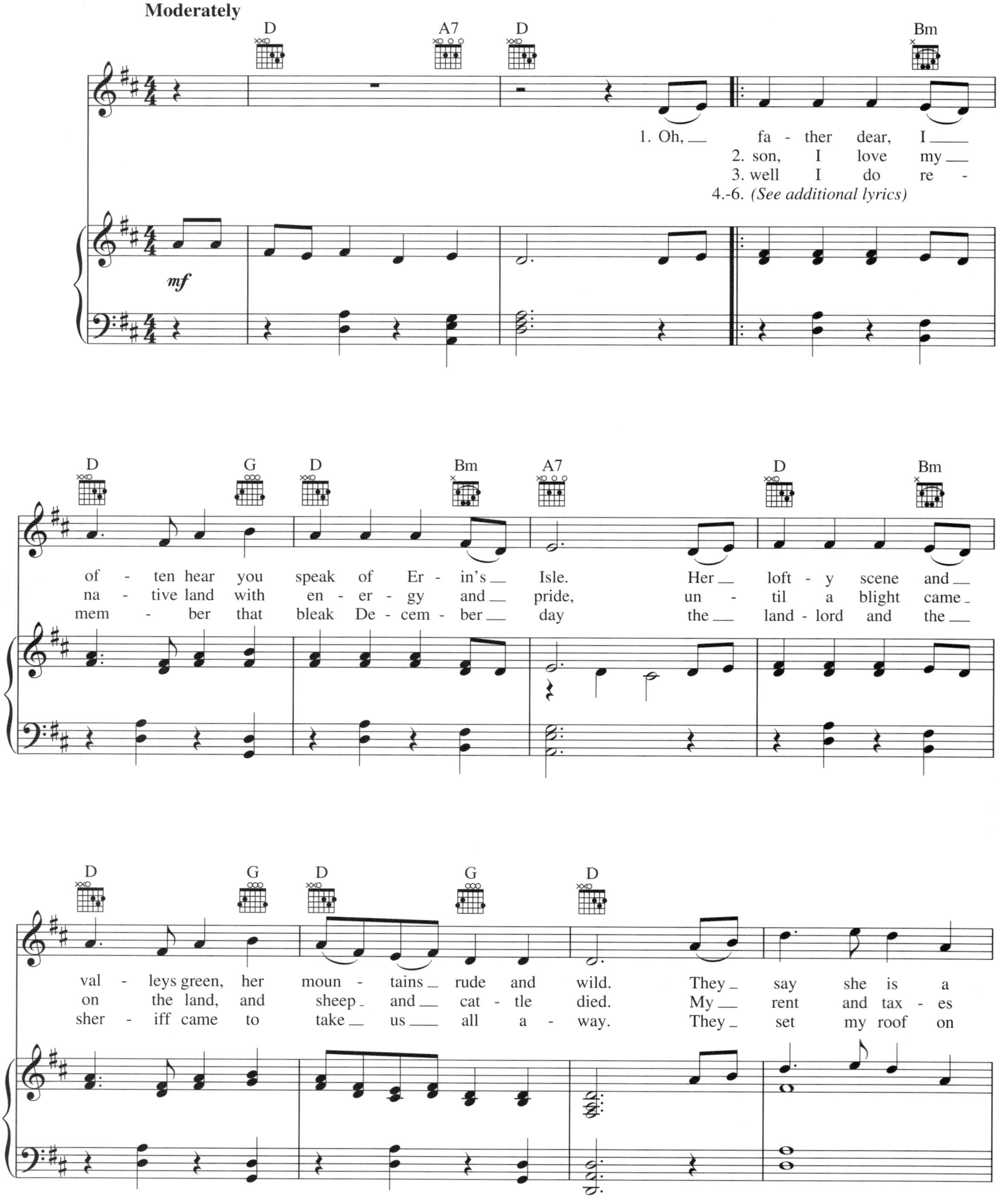
Moderately
D A7 D Bm
mf
1. Oh, fa - ther dear, I
2. son, I love my
3. well I do re -
4.-6. (See additional lyrics)
D G D Bm A7 D Bm
of - ten hear you speak of Er - in's Isle. Her loft - y scene and
na - tive land with en - er - gy and pride, un - til a blight came
mem - ber that bleak De - cem - ber day the land - lord and the
D G D G D
val - leys green, her moun - tains rude and wild. They say she is a
on the land, and sheep and cat - tle died. My rent and tax - es
sher - iff came to take us all a - way. They set my roof on

Copyright © 2006 by HAL LEONARD CORPORATION
International Copyright Secured All Rights Reserved

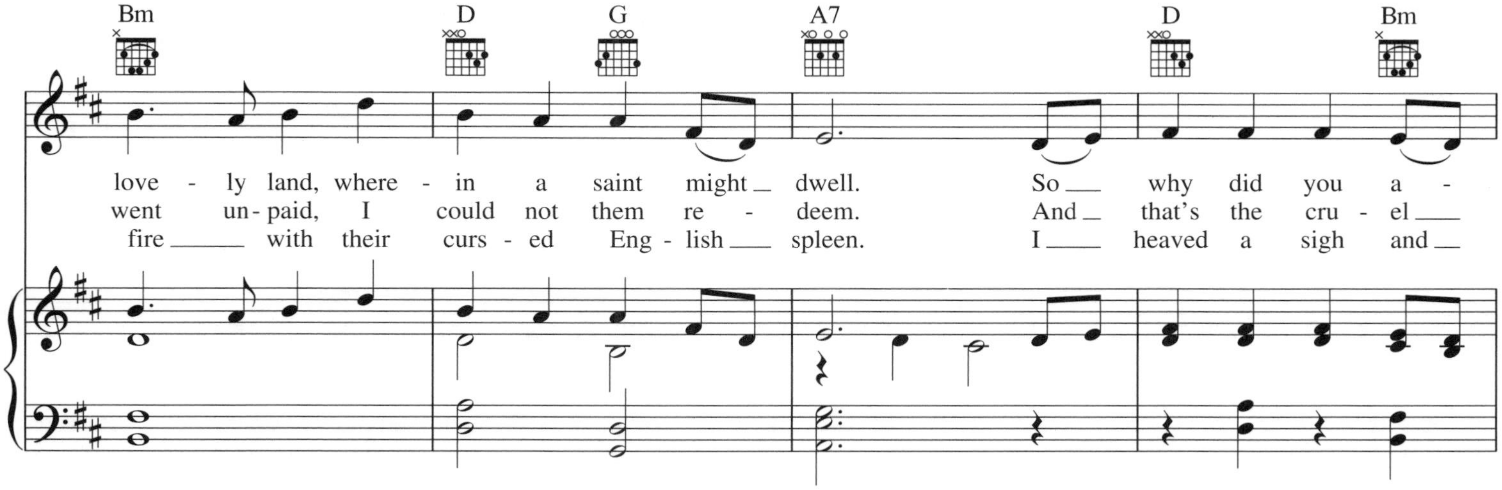
Bm D G A7 D Bm
love - ly land, where - in a saint might dwell. So why did you a -
went un - paid, I could not them re - deem. And that's the cru - el
fire with their curs - ed Eng - lish spleen. I heaved a sigh and

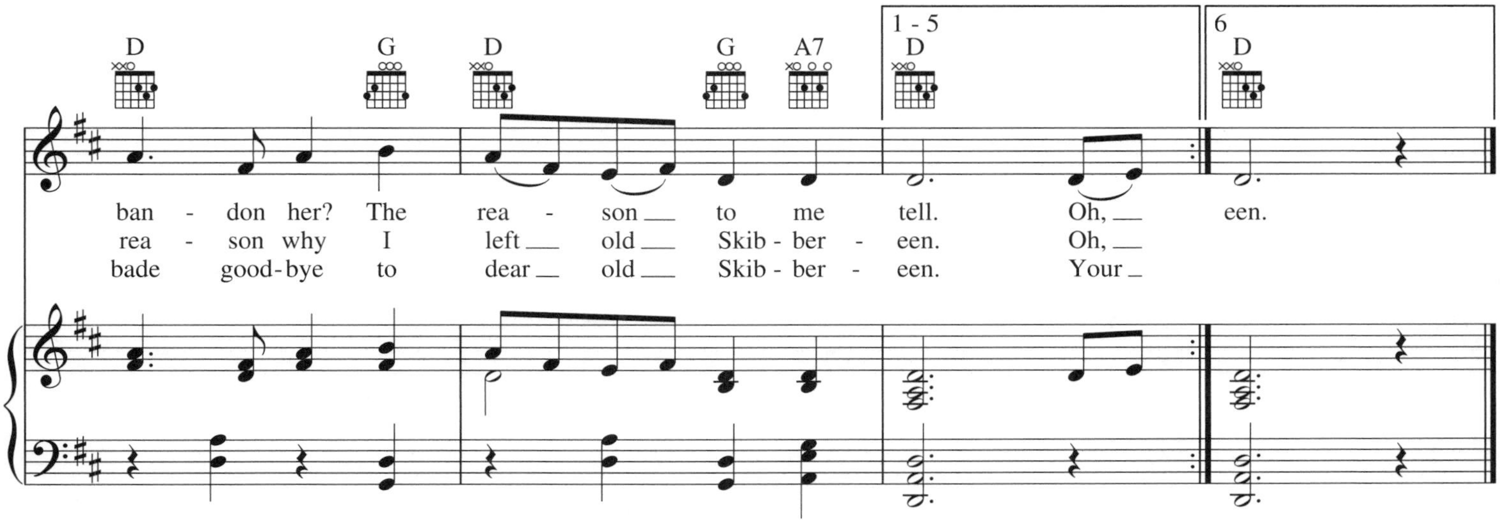
D G D G A7
1 - 5 D
6 D
ban - don her? The rea - son to me tell. Oh, een.
rea - son why I left old Skib - ber - een. Oh,
bade good - bye to dear old Skib - ber - een. Your

Additional Lyrics

4. Your mother too, God rest her soul, fell on the stony ground.
She fainted in her anguish, seeing desolation 'round.
She never rose, but passed away from life to immortal dream.
She found a quiet grave, me boy, in dear old Skibbereen.

5. And you were only two years old and feeble was your frame;
I could not leave you with my friends, for you bore your father's name.
I wrapped you in my cota mor in the dead of night unseen.
I heaved a sigh and said goodbye to dear old Skibbereen.

6. Oh, father dear, the day will come when, in answer to the call,
All Irish men of freedom stern will rally one and all.
I'll be the man to lead the band beneath the flag of green,
And loud and clear we'll raise the cheer: "Revenge for Skibbereen!"

THE SNOWY-BREASTED PEARL

Irish Folk Song

Moderately
C F C Csus C C F/C C
1. There's a col-leen fair as May. For a
2. Oh, thou blooming milk white dove, to whom
1. Tá cail-in deas am chrá le
2. (See additional lyrics)
mf
G C F G C Csus C
year and for a day, I have sought by ev-'ry way her heart to gain. There's no
I've giv-en true love, do not ev-er thus re-prove my con-stan-cy. There are
bliain ag-us le lá, 'S ní fhéad-aim a fáil le bréag-a. Níl
F/C C G C F G
art of tongue or eye fond youths with maid-ens try, but I've tried with cease-less sigh, yet tried in
maid-ens would be mine with wealth in land and kine, if my heart would but in-cline to turn from
ais-te chlis le rá Dá gcan-aid fir le mná nár chai-theam-ar gan tábh-acht

Copyright © 2003 by HAL LEONARD CORPORATION
International Copyright Secured All Rights Reserved

C Csus C G/B C Am G C F/C C
3fr
vain. If to far off France or Spain she'd cross the wa - ter - y main, to
thee. But a kiss with wel - come bland and touch of thy fair hand are
lé - si. Don Fhrainnc nó don Spáinn dá dtéadh mo ghrá, go
Am G/B C F/C C
see her face a - gain the seas I'd brave. And if 'tis heav - en's de - cree that
all that I de - mand, wouldst thou not spurn. For if not mine, dear girl, oh
raghainn - se gach lá dá féach - ain. Is mar an dúinn a - tá i ndán an
G C F G C Csus C
3fr
mine she may not be, may the Son of Mar - y me in mer - cy save!
snow - y - breast - ed pearl, may I nev - er from the fair with life re - turn!
ainn - ir chiúin seo d'fháil, Och! Mac Muir - e na ngrás dár saor - a!

Additional Lyrics

2. *Is a chailín chailcee bhláith,*
Dá dtugas searc is grá,
Ná túir-se gach tráth dhom éara;
'S a liacht ainnir mhín im dheáidh
Le buaibh is maoin 'n-a láimh,
Dá ngabhaimís it áit-se céile.
Póg is míle fáilte
Is barra geal do lámh'
Sé 'n-iarrfainn-se go bráth mar spré leat;
'S maran domh-sa taoi tú i ndán,
A phéarla an bhrollaigh bháin,
Nár thí mise slán ón aonach!

SPANCIL HILL

Traditional Irish Folk Song

Moderately fast
Dm Bb Am Dm Am
mf
C
1. Last night as I lay dream - ing of
2. light - ed with the nov - el - ty, en -
3. be - ing the twen - ty third of June, the
4.-6. (See additional lyrics)
Am Bb Dm
pleas - ant days gone by, me mind bein' bent on
chant - ed with the scene, where in my ear - ly
day be - fore the fair, when Ire - land's sons and
Bb Am F C
ram - bling to Ire - land I did fly. I
boy - hood where of - ten I had been. I
daugh - ters in crowds as - sem - bled there. The

Copyright © 2006 by HAL LEONARD CORPORATION
International Copyright Secured All Rights Reserved

Dm Bb Am Dm F
stepped a - board a vi - sion and fol - lowed with my
thought I heard a mur - mur and I think I hear it
young, the old, the brave and the bold, they came for sport and
C Dm C Am
will. Till next I came to an - chor at the cross near Span - cil
still, it's the lit - tle stream of wa - ter that flows down Span - cil
kill, there were jov - ial con - ver - sa - tions at the cross of Span - cil
1 - 5
Dm
Hill. De -
Hill. It
Hill. I
6
Dm
Hill.

Additional Lyrics

4. I went to see my neighbors, to hear what they might say,
The old ones were all dead and gone, the others turning grey.
I met with tailor Quigley, he's as bold as ever still,
Sure he used to make my britches when I lived in Spancil Hill.

5. I paid a flying visit to my first and only love,
She's white as any lily and gentle as a dove.
She threw her arms around me, saying, "Johnny, I love you still."
She's Mag, the farmer's daughter and the pride of Spancil Hill.

6. I dreamt I stooped and kissed her as in the days of yore.
She said, "Johnny, you're only joking, as many's the time before."
The cock crew in the morning, he crew both loud and shrill,
And I woke in California, many miles from Spancil Hill.

THE SPANISH LADY

Traditional Irish Folk Song

Moderately fast
A D A
mf
E A A D A
As I went down to Dub - lin cit - y, at the hour of
I went back through Dub - lin cit - y, as the sun be -
wan - dered north and I've wan - dered south through Ston - y bat - ter and
E A D A
twelve at night, who should I see but a Span - ish la - dy wash - ing her feet by
gan to set, who should I spy but the Span - ish la - dy catch - ing a moth in a
Pat - rick's close, up and a - round the Glos - ter Dia - mond and back by Nap - per
E A Esus A
can - dle - light. First she washed them, then she dried them o - ver a fire of
gold - en net. When she saw me, then she fled me, lift - ing her pet - ti - coat
Tan - dy's house. Old age has laid her hand on me, cold as a fire of

Copyright © 2003 by HAL LEONARD CORPORATION
International Copyright Secured All Rights Reserved

Esus
A
Esus
am - ber coal. In all my life I ne'er did see a
o - ver her knee. In all my life I ne'er did see a
ash - y coals. In all my life I ne'er did see a
D
A
E
A
maid so sweet a - bout the sole.
maid so shy as the Span - ish la - dy.
maid so sweet as the Span - ish la - dy.
Whack fol the too - ra
D
A
E
A
loo - ra, la - dy. Whack fol the too - ra loo - ra - lay. Whack fol the too - ra
1, 2
3
D
A
E
E
A
loo - ra, la - dy. Whack fol the too - ra loo - ra - lay. As I've loo - ra - lay.

STAR OF COUNTY DOWN

Traditional Irish Folk Song

Moderately
mf
Em A
Em Bm Em Em A
Near to Ban - bridge town in the Coun - ty Down on a
on - ward sped, I ___ scratched my head and I
har - vest fair she'll sure - ly be there, so I'll
Em A Bm Em Em/D C G/B A
morn - ing ___ in Ju - ly, down a bo - reen green came a sweet cai - leen, and she
gazed with a feel - ing ___ quare. There I said, said I to a pas - ser - by, "Who's the
dress in my Sun - day ___ clothes. And I'll try sheep's eyes and de - lud - th'rin lies on the
Em A Em G D/F♯
smiled as she passed me by. Oh, she looked so neat from her two white feet to the
maid with the nut - brown hair?" Oh, he smiled at me, and with pride says he, "That's the
heart of the nut - brown Rose. No ___ pipe I'll smoke, no ___ horse I'll yoke, though my

Copyright © 2003 by HAL LEONARD CORPORATION
International Copyright Secured All Rights Reserved

Em A Bm A Em A
sheen of her nut - brown hair. Such a coax - ing elf, had to shake my - self to make
gem of ___ Ire - land's crown, young Ro - sie Mc - Cann from the banks of Bann; she's the
plough with ___ rust turn ___ brown, till a smil - ing bridge by my own fire - side sits the
Em A Em G D
sure I was real - ly there.
star of the Coun - ty Down.
star of the Coun - ty Down.
Oh, from Ban - try Bay up to Der - ry Quay, and from
Em C Bm C Em A
Gal - way to Dub - lin ___ town, no ___ maid I've seen like the brown cai - leen that I
1, 2
Em A Em
met in the Coun - ty Down.
As she
At the
3
Em A Em
met in the Coun - ty Down.

SWEET CARNLOUGH BAY

Traditional Irish Folk Song

Moderately
D G D C
mf
D
When win - ter was crawl - ing o'er the
said, "My fair las - sie I
turn to the right and go
health to Pat Ham - ill, like -
C
high hills and moun - tains and
sure - ly will tell you the
down by the church - yard, cross
wise the fair las - sie, and to
D G D C
dark were the clouds o'er the deep roll - ing
road and the num - ber of miles it will
o - ver the riv - er and down by the
all you young lads who are lis - t'ning to

Copyright © 2006 by HAL LEONARD CORPORATION
International Copyright Secured All Rights Reserved

D
sea. I spied a wee
be. And if you con -
sea. We'll stop at Pat
me. Ne'er turn your
C
las - sie as the day - light was dawn - ing.
sent I'll con - vey you a wee bit,
Ham - ill's and have a wee drop there,
back on a bon - nie wee las - sie
D
G
She was ask - ing the road to
and I'll show you the road to
just to help us a - long to
when she's ask - ing the road to
D
C
D
1 - 3
4
sweet Carn - lough Bay. I
sweet Carn - lough Bay." "You
sweet Carn - lough Bay." Here's
sweet Carn - lough Bay.

THREE SCORE AND TEN

Traditional Irish Folk Song

Gently
D
Bm
A
D
mf
Bm
G
And it's three score and ten, boys and men were lost from
A
D
G
Em
D
Grims - by Town. From Yar - mouth down to Scar - bor -
Bm
D
G
A
ough man - y hun - dreds more were drowned, their her - ring

Copyright © 2006 by HAL LEONARD CORPORATION
International Copyright Secured All Rights Reserved

D Bm G D
craft, their trawl - ers and their fish - ing nets as well.
F♯m Bm F♯m Bm G A7 D
They longed to fight the bit - ter night and bat - tle with the swell.
To Coda
Bm G
Now me thinks I see a host of gal - lant craft spread - ing
Oc - to - ber night brought such a sight 'twas nev - er
A D G Em D
their sails a - lea. As down the Hum - ber they did
seen be - fore. There were masts and yards of bro - ken

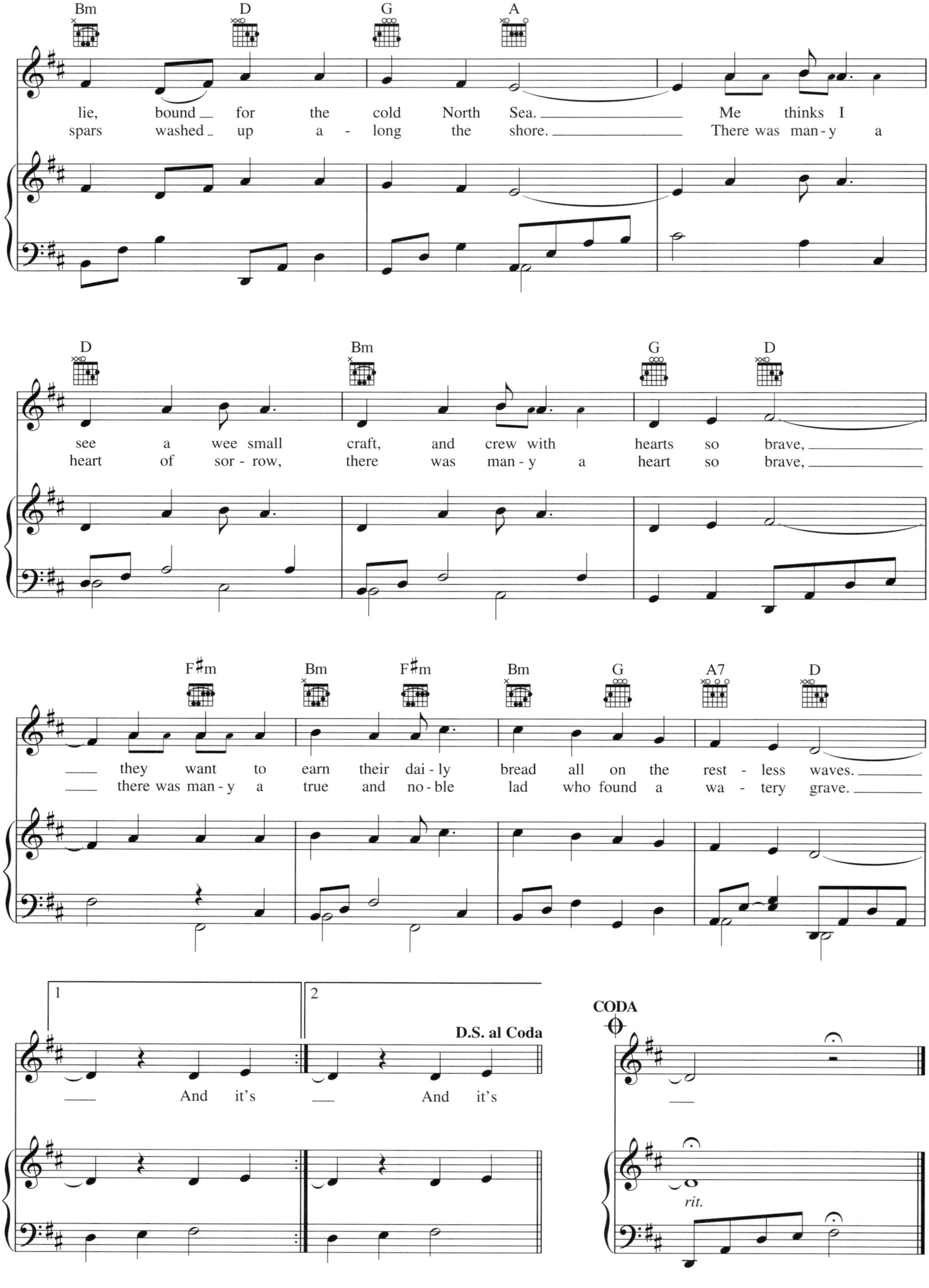
Bm D G A
lie, bound for the cold North Sea. Me thinks I
spars washed up a - long the shore. There was man - y a
D Bm G D
see a wee small craft, and crew with hearts so brave,
heart of sor - row, there was man - y a heart so brave,
F♯m Bm F♯m Bm G A7 D
they want to earn their dai - ly bread all on the rest - less waves.
there was man - y a true and no - ble lad who found a wa - tery grave.
1 2
D.S. al Coda
And it's And it's
CODA
rit.

THE TOWN OF BALLYBAY

Traditional Irish Folk Song

Brightly, in 2
C
G
mf
In the town of Bal-ly-bay there was a las-sie dwell-ing. I knew her ver-y well and this sto-ry's worth the
had a wood-en leg that was hol-low down the mid-dle. She used to tie a string on it and play it like a
said she could-n't dance un-less she had her wellie on, but when she had it on she could dance as well as
lov-ers by the score, ev-'ry Tom and Dick and Har-ry. She was court-ing night and day but still she would-n't

Copyright © 2006 by HAL LEONARD CORPORATION
International Copyright Secured All Rights Reserved

C F G
tell - ing. Her fa - ther kept a still and he
fid - dle. She fid - dled in the hall and she
an - y - one. She would - n't go to bed un -
mar - ry. And then she fell in love with a
F G C
was a good dis - till - er. And when she took to
fid - dled in the al - ley - way. She did - n't give a
less she had her shim - my on. But when she had it
fel - la with a stam - mer, when he tried to run a -
Am F G
drink - ing sure the dev - il would - n't fill her.
damn she had to fid - dle an - y - way.
on she would go as quick as any - one.
way she hit him with a ham - mer.
With me

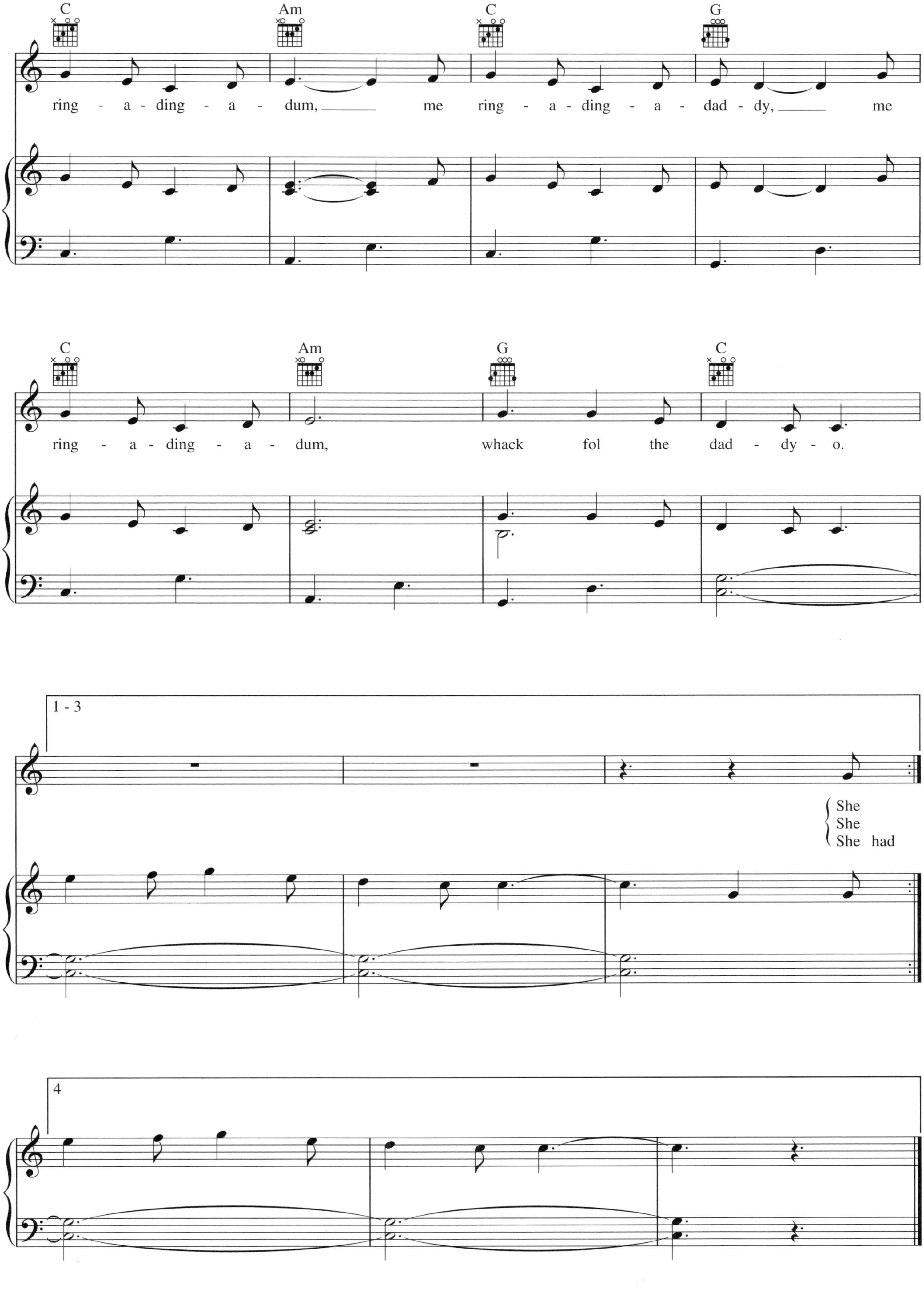
C
Am
C
G
ring - a - ding - a - dum, me ring - a - ding - a - dad - dy, me
C
Am
G
C
ring - a - ding - a - dum, whack fol the dad - dy - o.
1 - 3
She
She
She had
4

TOO-RA-LOO-RA-LOO-RAL
(That's an Irish Lullaby)

Words and Music by
JAMES R. SHANNON

Moderately
B♭ F G7 C7 F
mf
F Dm F/C C7 F
O - ver in Kil - lar - ney, many - y years a - go, me mith - er sang a
Oft, in dreams, I wan - der to that cot a - gain. I feel her arms a
G7 C7 F
song to me in tones so sweet and low. Just a sim - ple lit - tle dit - ty, in her
hug - gin' me as when she held me then. And I hear her voice a hum-min' to me
Dm F/C B♭ F G7
good ould I - rish way, and I'd give the world if she could sing that song to me this
as in days of yore when she used to rock me fast a - sleep out - side the cab - in

Copyright © 1993 by HAL LEONARD CORPORATION
International Copyright Secured All Rights Reserved

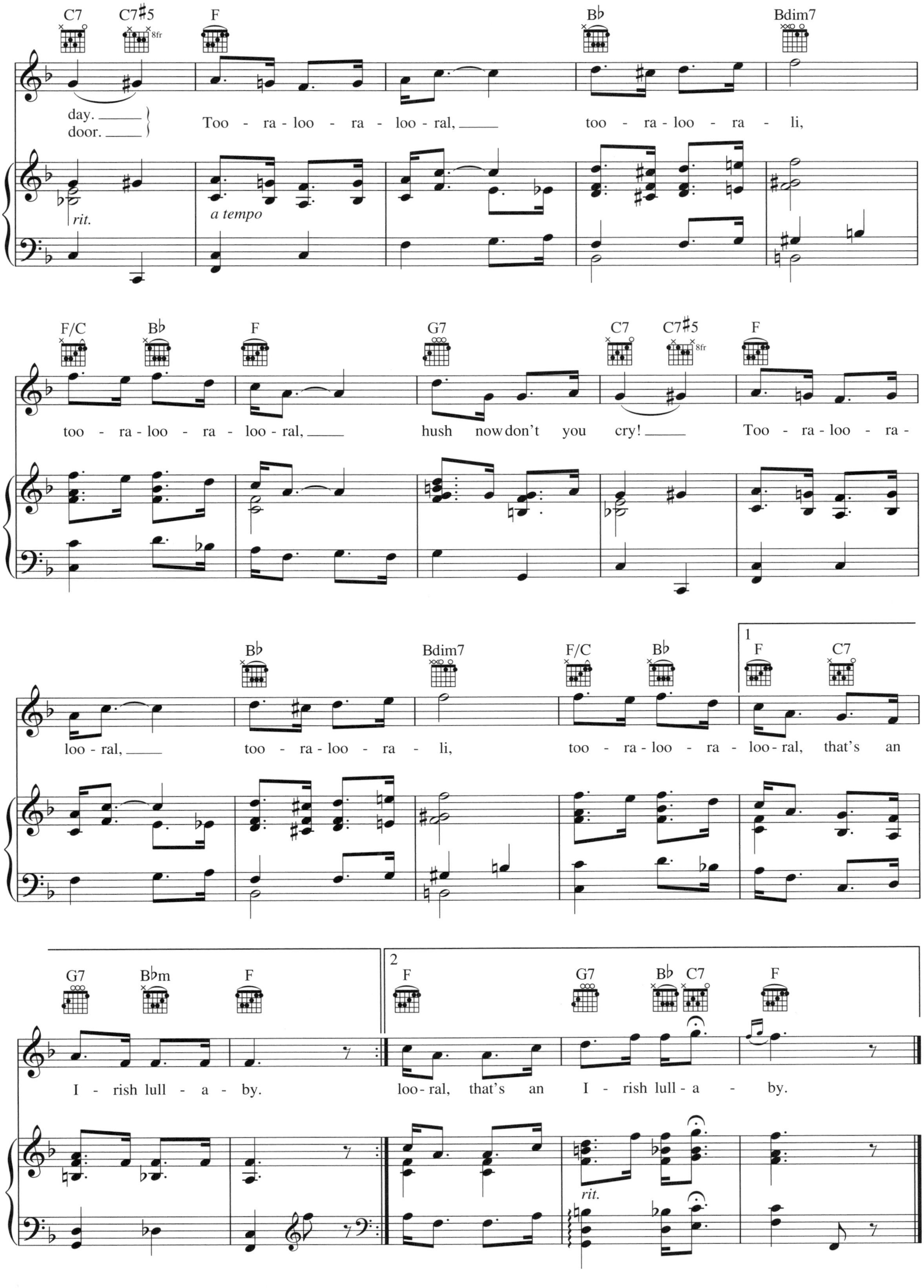
C7 C7♯5 F B♭ Bdim7
8fr
day. door. Too - ra - loo - ra - loo - ral, too - ra - loo - ra - li,
rit.
a tempo
F/C B♭ F G7 C7 C7♯5 F
8fr
too - ra - loo - ra - loo - ral, hush now don't you cry! Too - ra - loo - ra -
B♭ Bdim7 F/C B♭
1
F C7
loo - ral, too - ra - loo - ra - li, too - ra - loo - ra - loo - ral, that's an
G7 B♭m F
2
F G7 B♭ C7 F
I - rish lull - a - by. loo - ral, that's an I - rish lull - a - by.
rit.

THE WEARING OF THE GREEN

18th Century Irish Folk Song

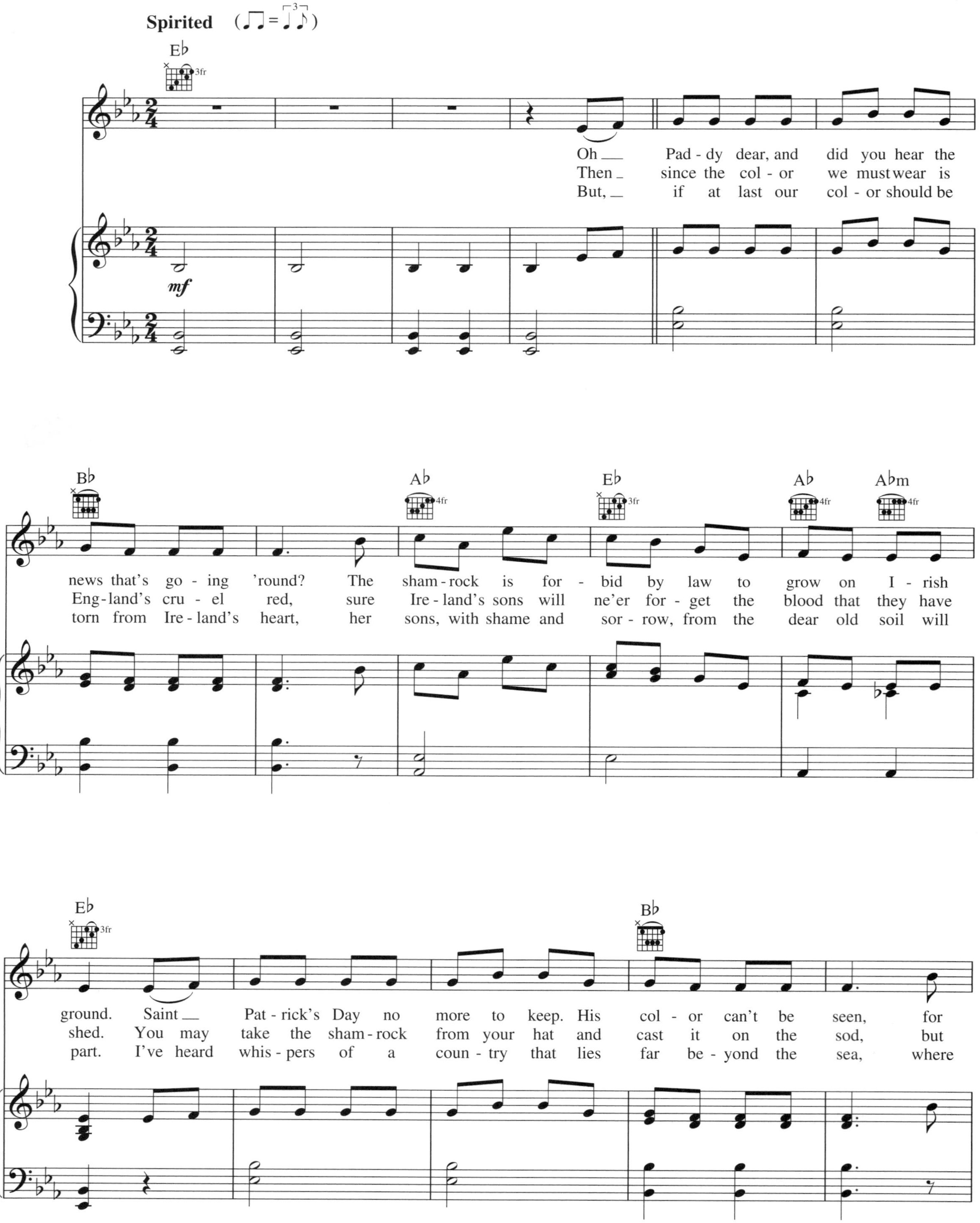
Spirited
E♭
3fr
mf
Oh Pad - dy dear, and did you hear the
Then since the col - or we must wear is
But, if at last our col - or should be
B♭
A♭
4fr
E♭
3fr
A♭
4fr
A♭m
4fr
news that's go - ing 'round? The sham - rock is for - bid by law to grow on I - rish
Eng - land's cru - el red, sure Ire - land's sons will ne'er for - get the blood that they have
torn from Ire - land's heart, her sons, with shame and sor - row, from the dear old soil will
E♭
3fr
B♭
ground. Saint Pat - rick's Day no more to keep. His col - or can't be seen, for
shed. You may take the sham - rock from your hat and cast it on the sod, but
part. I've heard whis - pers of a coun - try that lies far be - yond the sea, where

Copyright © 2003 by HAL LEONARD CORPORATION
International Copyright Secured All Rights Reserved

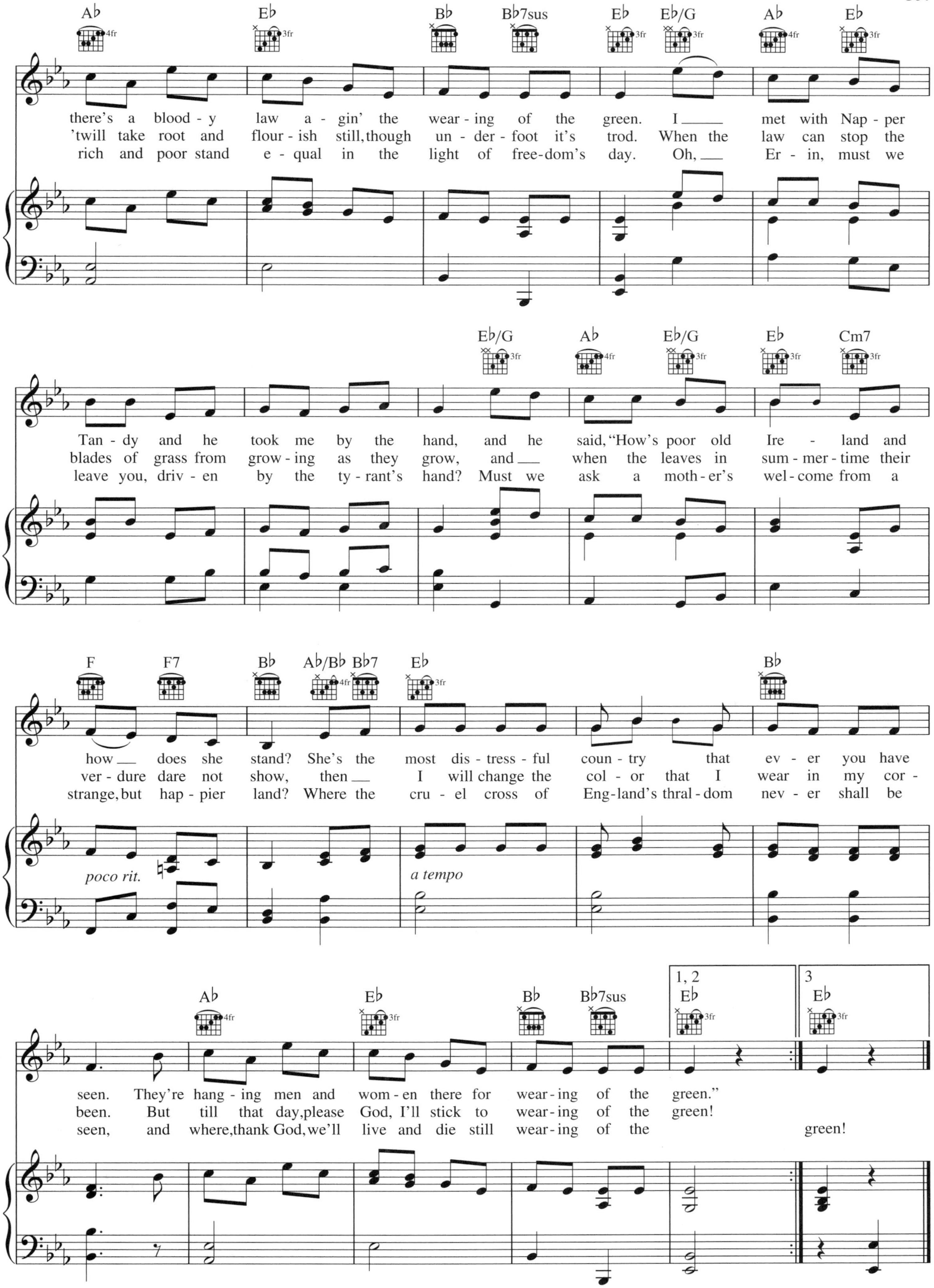
A♭ E♭ B♭ B♭7sus E♭ E♭/G A♭ E♭
there's a blood - y law a - gin' the wear - ing of the green. I met with Nap - per
'twill take root and flour - ish still, though un - der - foot it's trod. When the law can stop the
rich and poor stand e - qual in the light of free - dom's day. Oh, Er - in, must we
E♭/G A♭ E♭/G E♭ Cm7
Tan - dy and he took me by the hand, and he said, "How's poor old Ire - land and
blades of grass from grow - ing as they grow, and when the leaves in sum - mer - time their
leave you, driv - en by the ty - rant's hand? Must we ask a moth - er's wel - come from a
F F7 B♭ A♭/B♭ B♭7 E♭ B♭
how does she stand? She's the most dis - tress - ful coun - try that ev - er you have
ver - dure dare not show, then I will change the col - or that I wear in my cor -
strange, but hap - pier land? Where the cru - el cross of Eng - land's thral - dom nev - er shall be
poco rit.
a tempo
A♭ E♭ B♭ B♭7sus 1, 2 E♭ 3 E♭
seen. They're hang - ing men and wom - en there for wear - ing of the green."
been. But till that day, please God, I'll stick to wear - ing of the green!
seen, and where, thank God, we'll live and die still wear - ing of the green!

WEILE WALIA

Traditional Irish Folk Song

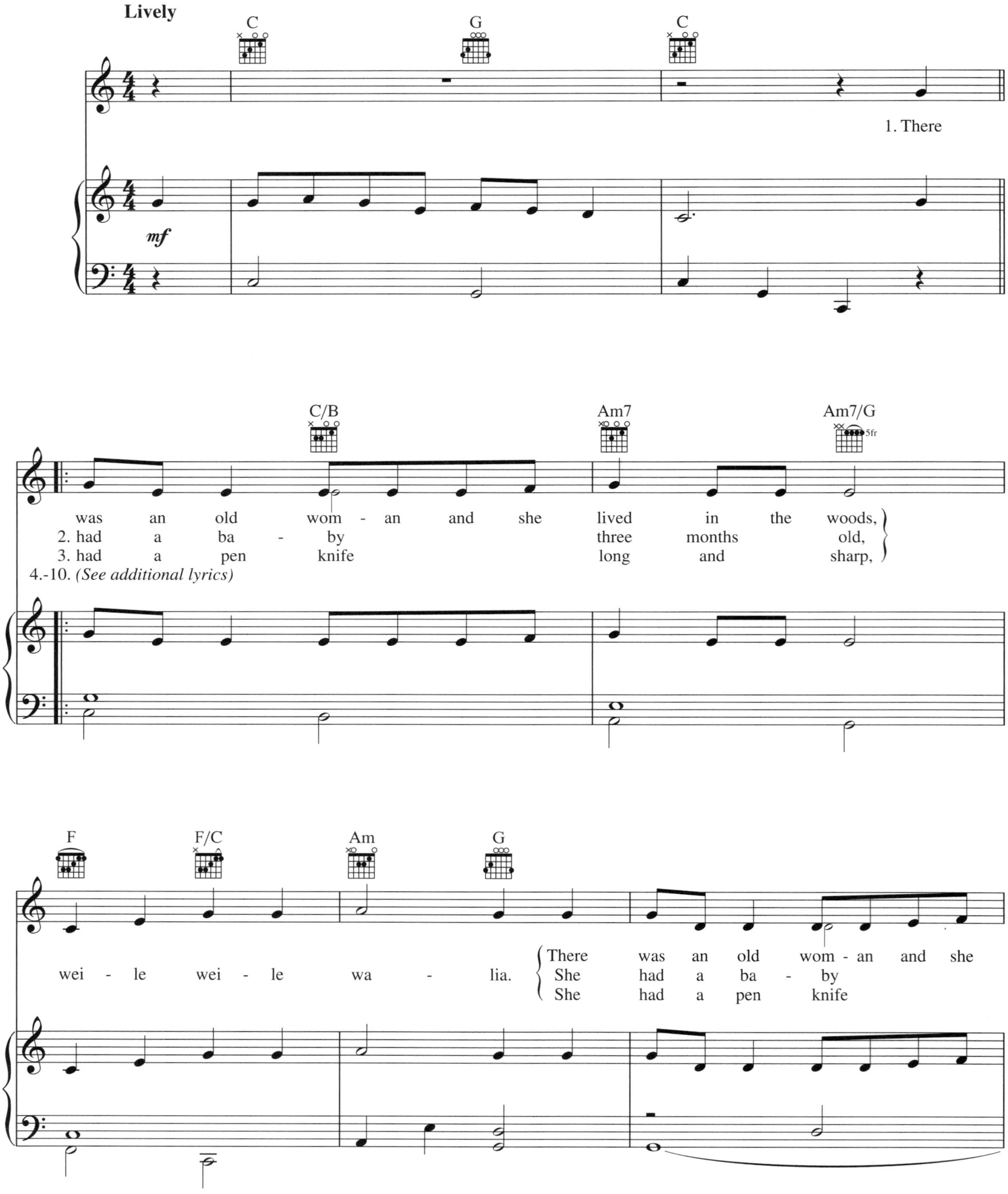
Lively
C
G
C
mf
1. There
C/B
Am7
Am7/G
5fr
was an old wom - an and she lived in the woods,
2. had a ba - by three months old,
3. had a pen knife long and sharp,
4.-10. (See additional lyrics)
F
F/C
Am
G
wei - le wei - le wa - lia.
There was an old wom - an and she
She had a ba - by
She had a pen knife

Copyright © 2006 by HAL LEONARD CORPORATION
International Copyright Secured All Rights Reserved

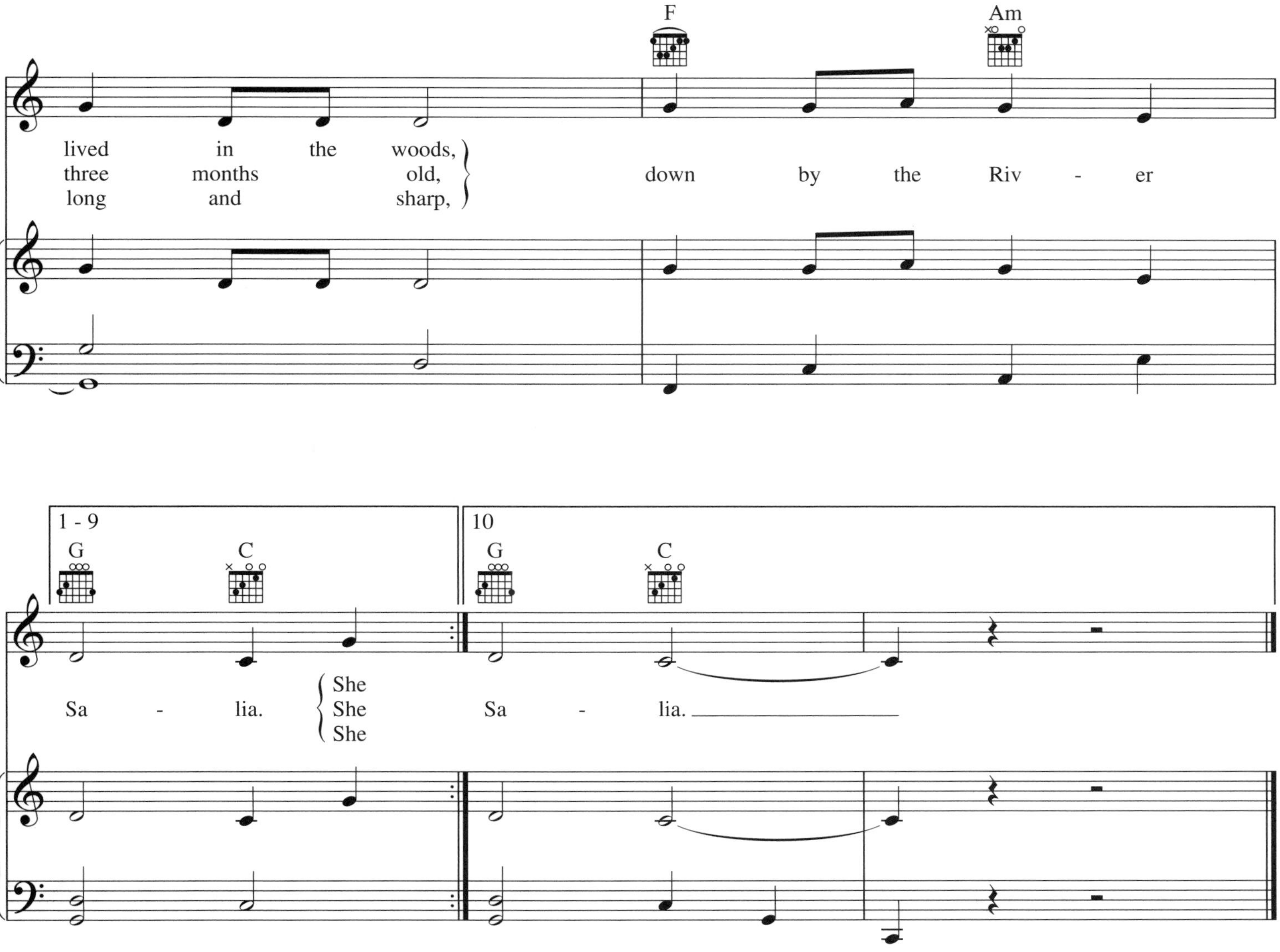
F
Am
lived in the woods,
three months old,
long and sharp,
down by the Riv - er
1 - 9
10
G
C
G
C
Sa - lia.
She
She
She
Sa - lia.

Additional Lyrics

4. She stuck the pen knife in the baby's heart, weile, weile, walia.
   She stuck the pen knife in the baby's heart, down by the River Salia.

5. Three loud knocks came a-knocking on the door, weile, weile, walia.
   Three loud knocks came a-knocking on the door, down by the River Salia.

6. Two policemen and a man, weile, weile, walia.
   Two policemen and a man, down by the River Salia.

7. "Are you the woman that killed the child?" weile, weile, walia.
   "Are you the woman that killed the child?" down by the River Salia.

8. They tied her hands behind her back, weile, weile, walia.
   They tied her hands behind her back, down by the River Salia.

9. The rope was pulled and she got hung, weile, weile, walia.
   The rope was pulled and she got hung, down by the River Salia.

10. And that was the end of the woman in the woods, weile, weile, walia.
    And that was the end of the baby too, down by the River Salia.

THE WEST'S AWAKE

Traditional Irish Folk Song

Heroically
A
F♯m
E
mf
A
F♯m
When all be - side a vig - il keep, the
chain - less wave and love - ly land,
of - ten in O' - Con - nor's van, to
if, when all a vig - il keep, the
E
A
D
west's a - sleep, the west's a - sleep. A - las, and well may
free - dom and na - tion - hood de - mand. Be sure the great God
tri - umph dashed each Con - naught clan, and fleet as deer the
west's a - sleep, the west's a - sleep, a - las, and well may

Copyright © 2006 by HAL LEONARD CORPORATION
International Copyright Secured All Rights Reserved

Bm E D A F♯m
Er - in weep, that Con - naught lies in slum - ber deep. There lake and plain smile
ne - ver planned for slumb - 'ring slaves a home so grand. And long a proud and
Nor - mans ran, through Cur - lew's Pass and Ar - dra - han; and lat - er times saw
Er - in weep, that Con - naught lies in slum - ber deep. But hark, a voice like
D Bm E A Bm
fair and free, 'mid rocks their guard - ian chiv - al - ry. Sing: oh, let man learn
haugh - ty race hon - oured and sen - ti - nelled the place. Sing: oh, not e'en their
deeds as brave, and glo - ry guards Clan - ri - carde's grave. Sing: oh, they died their
thun - der spake, the west's a - wake, the west's a - wake. Sing: oh, hur - rah, let
E A D G 1 - 3 E A 4 E A
lib - er - ty, from crash - ing wind and lash - ing sea. That
son's dis - grace can quite de - stroy their glo - ry's trace. For
land to save at Augh - rim's slopes and Shan - non's wave. And
Eng - land quake, we'll watch 'til death for Er - in's sake.

WHEN IRISH EYES ARE SMILING

Words by CHAUNCEY OLCOTT
and GEORGE GRAFF, JR.
Music by ERNEST R. BALL

Moderately
E♭ Edim B♭/F G7
mf
C7 F7 B♭ B♭
There's a tear in your
smile is a
eye, and I'm won - der - ing why, for it nev - er should be there at
part of the love in your heart, and it makes e - ven sun - shine more
F7/C B♭ F7 B♭
all. With such pow'r in your smile, sure a stone you'd be -
bright. Like the lin - net's sweet song, croon - ing all the day

Copyright © 2003 by HAL LEONARD CORPORATION
International Copyright Secured All Rights Reserved

G7
C7
F
F7
guile, so there's nev - er a tear - drop should fall. When your
long, comes your laugh - ter so ten - der and light. For the
B♭
sweet lilt - ing laugh - ter's like some fair - y song, and your eyes twin - kle
spring - time of life is the sweet - est of all, there is ne'er a real
B♭7
E♭
3fr
C7
bright as can be, you should laugh all the while and all
care or re - gret. And while spring - time is ours through - out
F
C7
F
oth - er times, while, and now smile a smile for me.
all of youth's hours, let us smile each chance we get.

F7 B♭ F7 B♭ B♭7
When I - rish eyes are smil - ing, sure it's
E♭ 3fr B♭
like a morn in spring. In the
E♭ 3fr B♭ G
lilt of I - rish laugh - ter, you can
C7 F F7
hear the an - gels sing. When

B♭
B♭7
E♭
3fr
I - rish hearts are hap - py, all the world seems
bright and gay. And when I - rish
C7/E
B♭/F
G7
C7
eyes are smil - ing, sure they steal your
F7
1
2
heart a - way. For your way.

WHISKEY IN THE JAR

Traditional Irish Folk Song

Moderately fast
D A D
mf
1. As
D D/C# Bm
I was go - in' o - ver the Cork and Ker - ry moun - tains,
2. count - ed out his mon - ey; paid a pret - ty pen - ny.
3. ear - ly in the morn - ing, be - fore I rose to trav - el.
4. (See additional lyrics)
G D D/C# Bm
met with Cap - tain Far - rell and his mon - ey he was count - in'.
Put it in me pock - et and I took it home to Jen - ny.
Up rides a band of foot - men and like - wise rash - er Far - rell.

Copyright © 2003 by HAL LEONARD CORPORATION
International Copyright Secured All Rights Reserved

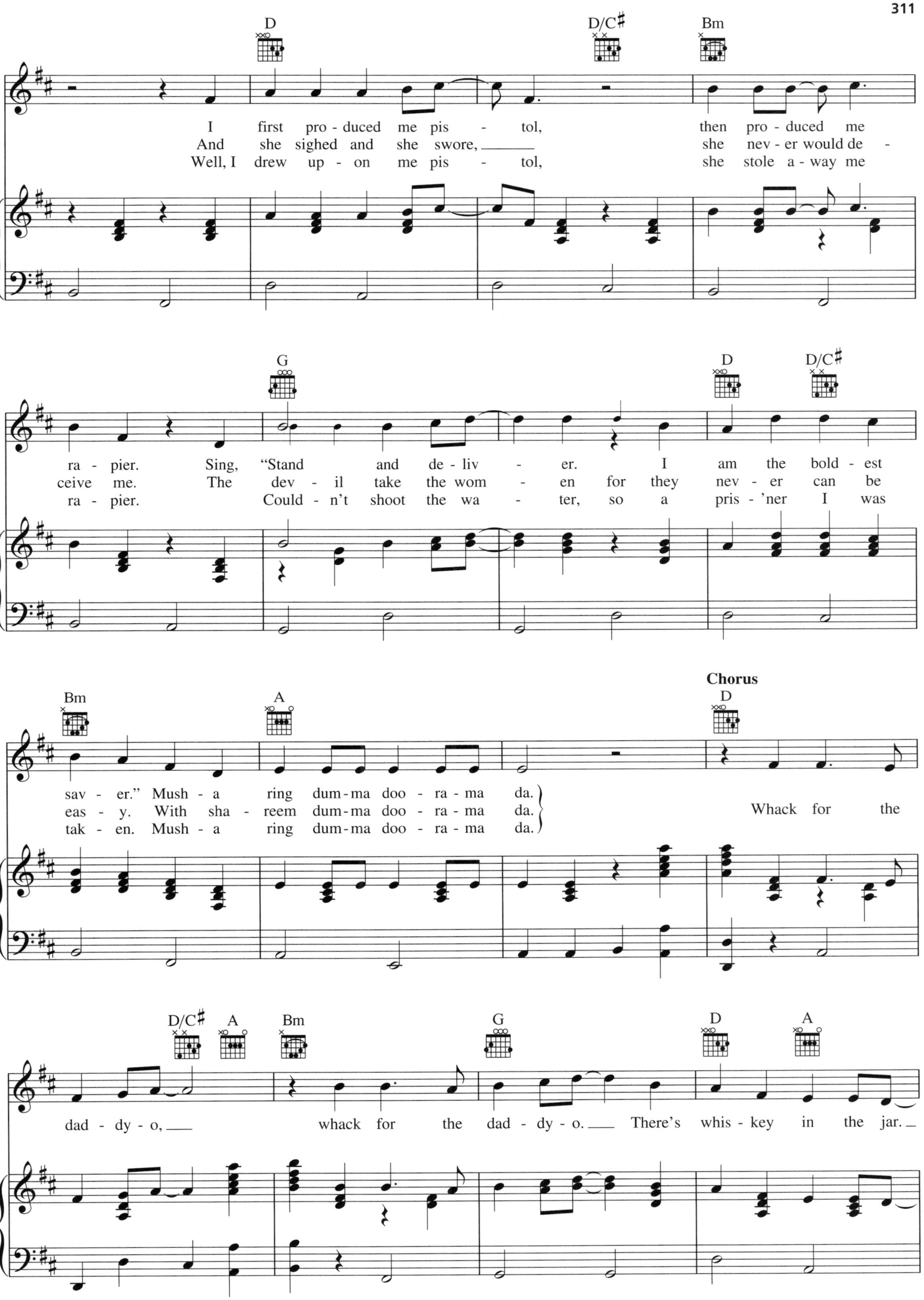
D
D/C♯
Bm
I first pro-duced me pis - tol, then pro-duced me
And she sighed and she swore, she nev-er would de -
Well, I drew up - on me pis - tol, she stole a-way me
G
D
D/C♯
ra - pier. Sing, "Stand and de-liv - er. I am the bold-est
ceive me. The dev - il take the wom - en for they nev - er can be
ra - pier. Could-n't shoot the wa - ter, so a pris-'ner I was
Bm
A
Chorus
D
sav - er." Mush - a ring dum-ma doo - ra - ma da.
eas - y. With sha - reem dum-ma doo - ra - ma da.
tak - en. Mush - a ring dum-ma doo - ra - ma da.
Whack for the
D/C♯
A
Bm
G
D
A
dad - dy - o, whack for the dad - dy - o. There's whis - key in the jar.

1 - 3
4
D
A
I Mush - a ring dum-ma doo - ra - ma
It was
Some
D/C#
Bm
da. Whack for the dad - dy - o, whack for the
G
dad - dy - o. There's whis - key in the jar!

Additional Lyrics

4. Some take delight in the fishin' and the fowlin'.
Others take delight in the carriage gently rollin'.
Ah, but I take delight in the juice of the barley;
Courtin' pretty women in the mountains of Killarney.
Musha ring dumma doo-rama da.
Chorus

THE WILD COLONIAL BOY

Australian Folk Song

Brightly
D G Em
mf
A7 D A7
1. There
G Em
was a wild co - lo - nial boy, Jack
2. ear - ly age of six - teen years, he
3. two long years this dar - ing youth ran
4.-7. (See additional lyrics)
A7 D
Dug - gan was his name. He was
left his na - tive home, and
on his wild ca - reer, with a

Copyright © 2006 by HAL LEONARD CORPORATION
International Copyright Secured All Rights Reserved

A7
born and raised in Ire - land in a
through Aus - tral - ia's sun - ny clime he
heart that knew no dan - ger, their
G
A7
D
place called Cast - le - main.
was in - clined to roam.
jus - tice did not fear.
He
He
He
A7
was his fa - ther's on - ly son, his
robbed the lord - ly squat - ters, their
stuck the Beech - worth coach up, and he
G
A7
D
moth - er's pride and joy,
flocks he would de - stroy,
robbed Judge Mc - E - voy,
and dear - ly
a ter - ror
who trem - bling

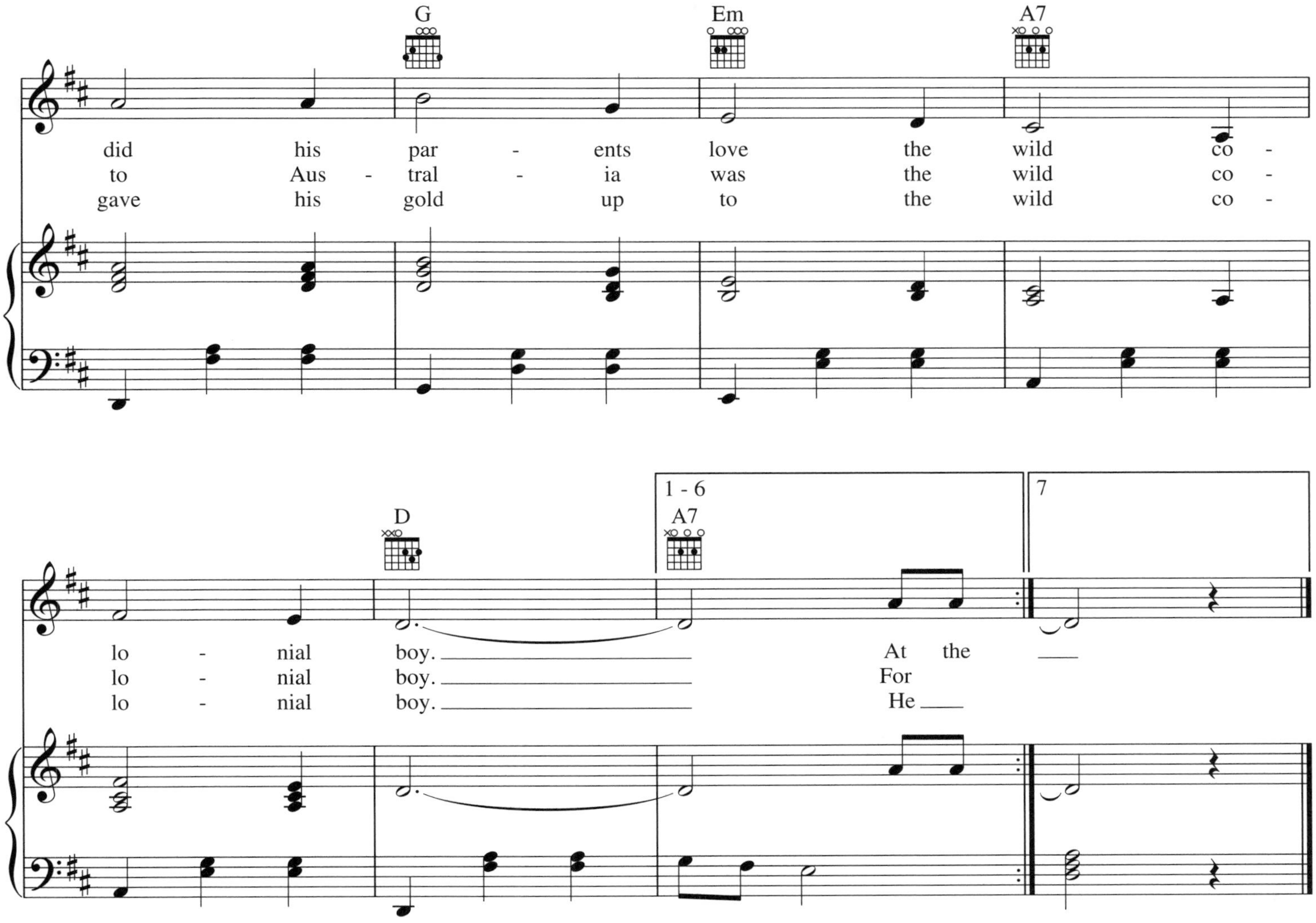
G
Em
A7
did his par - ents love the wild co -
to Aus - tral - ia was the wild co -
gave his gold up to the wild co -
D
1 - 6
A7
7
lo - nial boy. At the
lo - nial boy. For
lo - nial boy. He

Additional Lyrics

4. He bade the judge "Good morning" and he told him to beware,
For he never robbed an honest judge what acted "on the square."
Yet you would rob a mother of her son and only joy,
And breed a race of outlaws like the wild colonial boy.

5. One morning on the prairie Wild Jack Duggan rode along,
While listening to the mockingbirds singing a cheerful song.
Out jumped three troopers fierce and grim, Kelly Davis and FitzRoy,
They all set out to capture him, the wild colonial boy.

6. "Surrender now, Jack Duggan, you can see there's three to one,
Surrender in the Queen's name, sir, you are a plundering son."
Jack drew two pistols from his side and glared upon FitzRoy,
"I'll fight, but not surrender," cried the wild colonial boy.

7. He fired point-blank at Kelly and brought him to the ground.
He fired a shot at Davis, too, who fell dead at the sound.
But a bullet pierced his brave young heart from the pistol of FitzRoy,
And that was how they captured him, the wild colonial boy.

THE ZOOLOGICAL GARDENS

Traditional Irish Folk Song

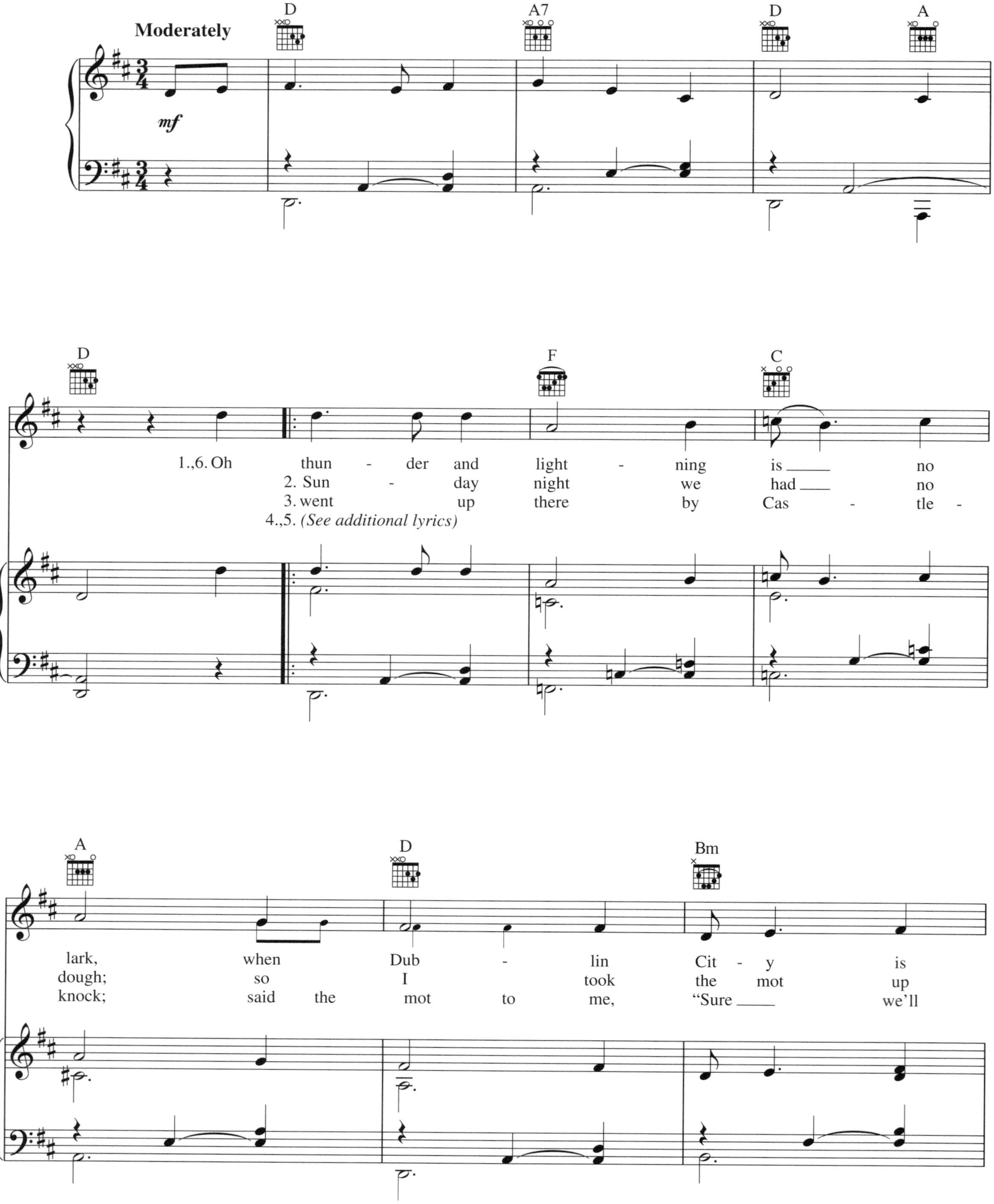
Moderately
mf
D
A7
D
A
D
F
C
1.,6. Oh thun - der and light - ning is ___ no
2. Sun - day night we had ___ no
3. went up there by Cas - tle -
4.,5. (See additional lyrics)
A
D
Bm
lark, when Dub - lin Cit - y is
dough; so I took the mot up
knock; said the mot to me, "Sure ___ we'll

Copyright © 2006 by HAL LEONARD CORPORATION
International Copyright Secured All Rights Reserved

G
A
D
in the dark. If you have an - y
to see the zoo. We saw the
court by the lough." And I knew she was
G
F
G
A
D
mon - ey go up to the Park and view the Zo - o -
li - ons and kan - ga - roos in - side the Zo - o -
one of the rare old stock; in - side the Zo - o -
A7
D
A
1 - 5
D
6
D
log - i - cal Gar - dens. Last dens.
log - i - cal Gar - dens. We
log - i - cal Gar - dens. Said

Additional Lyrics

4. Said the mot to me, "My dear friend Jack;
Would you like a ride on the elephant's back?"
If you don't get outta that I'll give you such a crack;
Inside the Zoological Gardens.

5. We went up there on our honeymoon;
Says she to me, "If you don't come soon
Sure I'll have to jump in with the hairy baboon;
Inside the Zoological Gardens.

6. *(Repeat 1st verse)*

WILD ROVER

Traditional Irish Folk Song

Moderately, with a lilt
G
mf
C
G
D7
G
G
I've been a wild rover for many a year, and I've spent all my money on
into an ale-house I used to frequent, and I told the landlady my
out of my pocket I took sov'reigns bright, and the landlady's eyes opened
back to my parents, confess what I've done, and ask them to pardon their
C
G
D7

Copyright © 2003by HAL LEONARD CORPORATION
International Copyright Secured All Rights Reserved

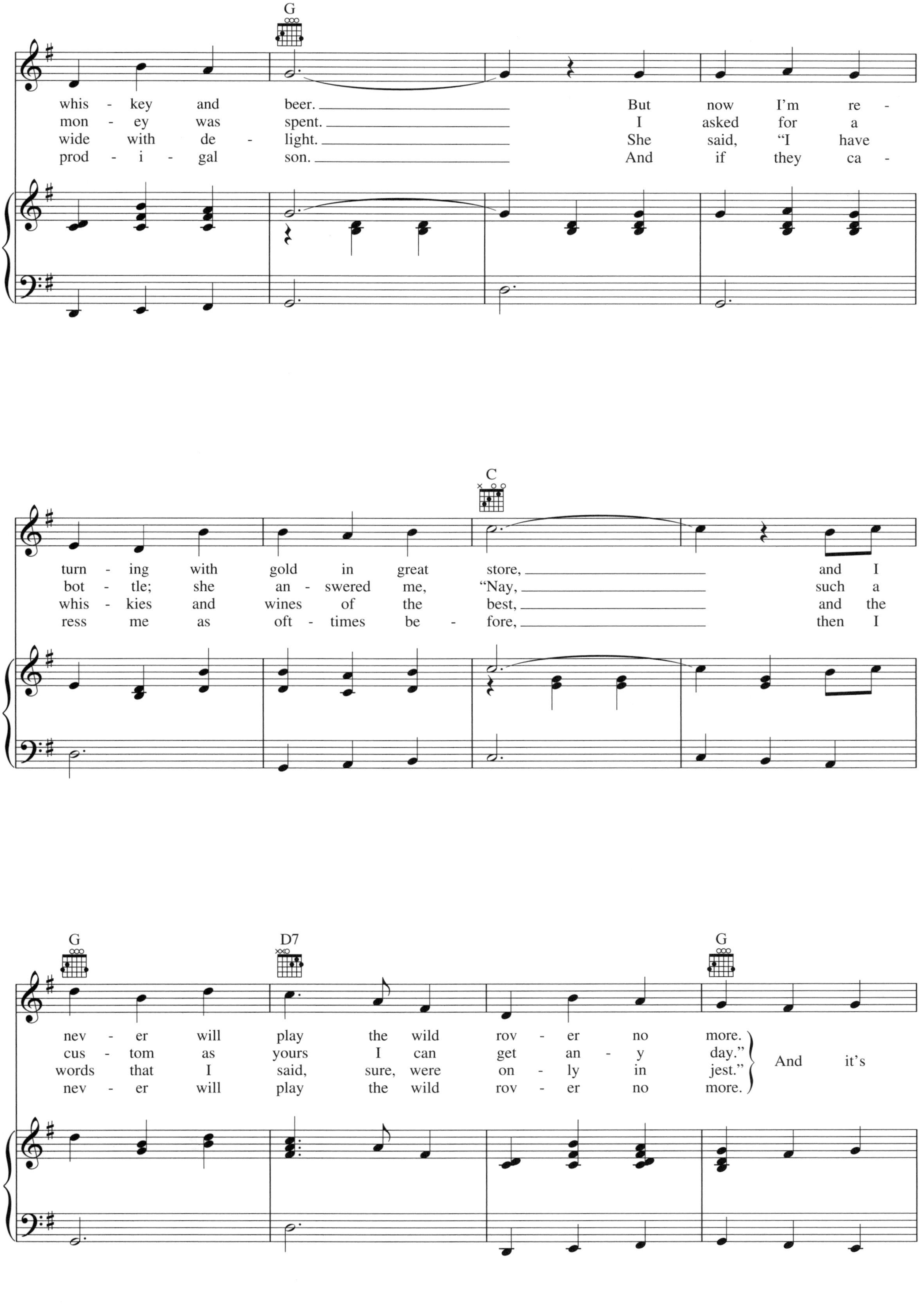
G
whis - key and beer. But now I'm re -
mon - ey was spent. I asked for a
wide with de - light. She said, "I have
prod - i - gal son. And if they ca -
C
turn - ing with gold in great store, and I
bot - tle; she an - swered me, "Nay, such a
whis - kies and wines of the best, and the
ress me as oft - times be - fore, then I
G
D7
G
nev - er will play the wild rov - er no more.
cus - tom as yours I can get an - y day."
words that I said, sure, were on - ly in jest."
nev - er will play the wild rov - er no more.
And it's

D
no, nay, nev - er;
G
C
no, nay, nev - er no more will I
G
C
G
play the wild rov - er, no, nev - er
D7
1 - 3
G
4
G
no more.
I went
Then more.
I'll go
8vb